ENVIRONMENTAL COURTS AND TRIBUNALS

The global phenomenon of specialist environmental courts is showing no sign of abating. This book provides much-needed answers to the questions raised by their development, particularly those concerning legitimacy. Taking the common law as its focus, thc author offers an innovative theoretical foundation for these courts, espousing a bottom-up approach. Despite its conceptual focus, it offers much to practitioners by engaging with this new type of forum. This important book is essential reading for all environmental lawyers.

Environmental Courts and Tribunals

Powers, Integrity and the Search for Legitimacy

Ceri Warnock

The Law Foundation
NEW ZEALAND
SUPPORTING INDEPENDENT LEGAL THINKING.

•HART•
OXFORD • LONDON • NEW YORK • NEW DELHI • SYDNEY

HART PUBLISHING

Bloomsbury Publishing Plc

Kemp House, Chawley Park, Cumnor Hill, Oxford, OX2 9PH, UK

1385 Broadway, New York, NY 10018, USA

HART PUBLISHING, the Hart/Stag logo, BLOOMSBURY and the Diana logo are trademarks of Bloomsbury Publishing Plc

First published in Great Britain 2020

A catalogue record for this book is available from the British Library.

Library of Congress Cataloging-in-Publication data

Names: Warnock, Ceri, author.

Title: Environmental courts and tribunals : powers, integrity and the search for legitimacy / Ceri Warnock.

Description: Oxford, UK ; New York, NY : Hart Publishing, an imprint of Bloomsbury Publishing, [2020] | Includes bibliographical references and index.

Identifiers: LCCN 2020035602 (print) | LCCN 2020035602 (ebook) | ISBN 9781509940066 (hardback) | ISBN 9781509944163 (paperback) | ISBN 9781509940073 (Epub) | ISBN 9781509940080 (epdf)

Subjects: LCSH: Environmental law. | Environmental justice. | Administrative courts. | Environmental impact analysis—Law and legislation.

Classification: LCC K3585 .W369 2020 (print) | LCC K3585 (ebook) | DDC 343.04/60269—dc23

LC record available at https://lccn.loc.gov/2020035602

LC ebook record available at https://lccn.loc.gov/2020035603

ISBN: HB: 978-1-50994-006-6
ePDF: 978-1-50994-008-0
ePub: 978-1-50994-007-3

Typeset by Compuscript Ltd, Shannon

Acknowledgements

LIKE ANY 'SOLE authored' work, this book is the product of a team effort, and after many years of hard work it is wonderful to be able to thank all those who have been so instrumental in its creation. First and foremost, my thanks go to Liz Fisher who has been with me at every tentative step of this research journey. Conversations with Liz encouraged me to reimagine law, excited me as to possibilities and helped enrich my thinking. Academic stars get a lot of attention in our universe, but Liz is undoubtedly a sun … Three wise men also pointed me in the right direction whenever I faltered: Dr Royden Somerville QC in his slightly mischievous way, encouraged me to start walking just to see where I ended up; Principal Judge Laurie Newhook, with his unfailing energy and graciousness, shared his inside knowledge and redirected me when I went off track; and Mark Henaghan – a smart but above all compassionate man, who never speaks of leadership but embodies the very essence of it – brought all the pieces together to make the journey a reality. Special thanks also go to *four* wise women (note, there are more) who have read and commented on various chapters and drafts of this work: Sanja Bogojevic, Janet McLean, Bettina Lange and Alison Young. I am honoured to have had scholars of such standing and intellectual rigour critique my work. Thank you all for your great generosity, interest and insights. Thank you also to Chief Judge Brian Preston – who read and critiqued an early iteration of this work – but my particular gratitude is for Justice Preston's critical contributions to the maturing of environmental law making it fit for a fair and civilised future, an achievement best embodied in the legal wisdom of *Gloucester Resources*. In fact, all the judges and commissioners of the New Zealand Environment Court and New South Wales Land and Environment Court have contributed to this book through their exemplary judicial work. We are indeed lucky to have such skilled and thoughtful adjudicators in Australasia. A special mention goes to Judge Jon Jackson on his retirement and for his intellectual brilliance that has left a rich and stimulating body of work for scholars to draw on. Thanks to many academic colleagues who commented on or supported my endeavours including Ken Palmer and other colleagues at the University of Auckland; Rock and Kitty Pring in Denver; Gita Gill for her great collegiality and shared interests; Āine Ryall; Eloise Scotford; Chris Hilson and others who attended the Society of Legal Scholars conferences in 2015 and 2016; Kathryn Hollingsworth and Ole Pedersen for hosting a seminar at Newcastle University of my early work into environmental adjudication; and two anonymous reviewers for their thoughtful comments. Thanks also to University of Otago colleagues for their 'tea, sympathy and wise words', in particular Shelley Griffiths, Nicola Wheen, Stuart Anderson and John Dawson.

My family has been unfailingly stoic throughout the whole writing process: my mother, Barbara, helped with her eagle-eyed editing (although we will have to agree to disagree about Oxford commas); my sister, Claire, and my husband, Toby, acted as wise sounding boards and guarded against the worst excesses of academic jargon; and my children, Murphy and Gabriel have been ever cheerful. Thank you all for understanding the 'stolen time'.

Finally, this research commenced when I was privileged enough to be selected as the New Zealand Law Foundation (NZLF) 'International Research Fellow – Te Manatū a Ture o Aotearoa Te Karahipi Rangahau Ā Taiao' – based at the University of Oxford. My immense gratitude goes to the NZLF and to Lynda Hagen and Dianne Gallagher in particular for their patience and encouragement through what at times seemed like a never-ending endeavour. Without the Foundation's essential support this book would never have materialised. The NZLF has played a pivotal role in supporting New Zealand legal research over the last four decades, helping scholars to imagine law as it can and should be, and on the eve of its recess I hope it is not presumptuous to thank the Foundation on behalf of the entire New Zealand legal academy. We look forward to your return.

Contents

Acknowledgements .... *v*

1. **Introduction** **1**
   I. The Rise in Specialist Environmental Adjudication 2
   II. An Interactional Theory for Environmental Adjudication 4
   III. The Method of Developing a Theory for Environmental Adjudication 7
   IV. Certain Caveats 21

2. **Specialist Environment Courts: Mapping the Landscape** **24**
   I. Specialist Environment Courts: A Typology 26
   II. Specialist Environment Courts as Dynamic Adjudicatory Forms 30
   III. Introducing the Case Studies: The Environment Court of New Zealand and the Land and Environment Court of New South Wales 37
   IV. Underlying Tensions 59

3. **The Struggle to Make Legal Sense of Specialist Environment Courts** **61**
   I. Normative Legitimacy and Analytical Frames 62
   II. The 'Administrative Justice-Adjudicative Pluralism' Frame 65
   III. The 'Generic Instrumentalism' Frame 73
   IV. The 'Separation of Powers' Frame 76
   V. Developing a Frame that We Can Agree On? 90

4. **Developing the Theory: Adjudicative Integrity** **92**
   I. The Malleability of Adjudication 94
   II. Normative Justifiability and Adjudicative Integrity 111

5. **Developing the Theory: Contextual Foundations** **126**
   I. The Inherent Features of Environmental Problems 128
   II. Interaction and Change 130
   III. Uncertainty 152
   IV. Drawing the Threads Together 155

6. The Interactional Theory in Practice 158
I. Acknowledging the Challenges in Environmental Adjudication..... 160
II. Responding to Uncertainty 165
III. Responding to the Collective Action Nature of Environmental Problems 187
IV. Testing the Theory 195

7. Conclusion 197
I. Findings 197
II. Developing the Theory 199
III. Filling in the Frame 201
IV. Employing the Theory 203
V. Future Directions 204
VI. Conclusion 205

Index *207*

1

Introduction

AT ITS HEART, this is a book about legal integrity. Specifically, it considers the role that integrity plays in legitimising adjudicative institutions and it explores this issue within the context of environmental adjudication for good reason. The exponential growth in specialist environmental adjudication is a remarkable modern phenomenon. Around the world, states have created bodies with novel constitutions and powers in order to reconcile the need for a certain nimbleness – a flexibility and creativity in environmental dispute-resolution – with the values that we expect from adjudication: political neutrality, legal coherence, equality of treatment and calculability. Environment courts and tribunals are now a distinct feature of the legal landscape. Collectively, their decisions impact the environmental, socio-cultural and economic wellbeing of nations, and scholars praise them for their ability to foster environmental legal literacy and to facilitate access to environmental justice. But fault lines are emerging. The unusual legal nature and relative power of these adjudicative institutions impacts wider structures of governance and raises difficult issues of legitimacy. At a national level, they are open to criticism and susceptible to the ebb and flow of varying ideologies, with their powers, functions, duties – existence even – waxing and waning within political tides. And as the analysis in this book shows, environment courts and tribunals are *especially* vulnerable to attack because there is no underlying theory that justifies and shores up the normative legitimacy of specialist environmental adjudication.

The aim of this book is to address that lacuna. Its purpose is to develop a theory[1] for specialist environmental adjudication that is of universal applicability and that sets the parameters for debate about environment courts and tribunals; a theory that is both enabling and constraining, and so useful to policymakers (in creating or reforming these bodies), the judiciary (in their reasoning) and litigants (in managing cases). In this introductory chapter, I sketch a brief overview of the theory that I propose, which I term an 'interactional theory for normative legitimacy'. I outline the methodology employed to develop and test that theory, and illustrate how the use of the interactional theory will help foster effective

[1] Note, I use the term 'theory' in the sense of simply 'going to the bottom of a subject' (see OW Holmes, 'The Path of the Law' (1897) 10 *Harvard Law Review* 457, 477) or as engaging in a search for 'conceptual unity' (see C Harlow, 'Changing the Mindset: The Place of Theory in English Administrative Law' (1994) 14 *OJLS* 419, 420).

environmental dispute-resolution while ensuring adjudicative integrity. To some readers, the theory that I sketch in this chapter may prove provocative, leading to more questions than answers, but I would encourage readers to suspend their judgement until they have reached the end of the book.

I. THE RISE IN SPECIALIST ENVIRONMENTAL ADJUDICATION

Since the turn of the millennium, there has been a huge proliferation in specialist environmental courts and tribunals around the world. There are now over 1,200 such bodies in over 44 nations.[2] In other jurisdictions, debates centre on the need for creating new institutions, alternative adjudicative processes or training judges to oversee the enforcement of environmental law.[3] And in nations with relatively embryonic institutions, the focus of discussion is upon expanding their jurisdiction, the role they might reasonably be expected to play in crafting solutions to environmental problems,[4] and the continuing ability of the ordinary courts to supervise these bodies.[5]

In line with this phenomenon, references to specialist environmental adjudication in the scholarly literature have increased exponentially.[6] This body of literature notes that specialist environment courts and tribunals are unusual and highly complex legal institutions, and representative of modern, dynamic forms of dispute resolution. Many are chaired by independent and tenured judges[7] or legally qualified decision-makers and considered part of the judicial branch of

[2] G Pring and C Pring, *Environmental Courts and Tribunals: A Guide for Policy Makers* (UNEP, 2016) 1.

[3] Nations that have debated but not yet established working environmental courts or tribunals at the date of writing include Abu Dhabi, Argentina and Israel amongst others (see ibid, 89–91). In nations like Indonesia, the judiciary have surmounted the political controversy of introducing a specialist court by creating a certification scheme for judges who have been trained to hear environmental cases (see Christina Libre and Alejandra Rabasa, 'ELI Supports Judiciary of Indonesia in Sound Adjudication of Environmental Cases' (*Environmental Law Institute*, 9 May 2018).

[4] In the UK context, see eg, the work of Richard Macrory proposing that an environment court be established and charting the developments of the First-tier Tribunal: R Macrory and M Woods, *Modernising Environmental Justice: Regulation and the Role of an Environment Tribunal* (UCL, 2003); R Macrory, *Consistency and Effectiveness: Strengthening the New Environment Tribunal* (Centre for Law and the Environment, UCL, 2011); R Macrory, 'The Role of the First Tier Environment Tribunal' (2012) 17 *Judicial Review* 54; R Macrory, 'The Long and Winding Road – Towards an Environmental Court in England and Wales' (2013) 25 *JEL* 371.

[5] Note the critique of the proposed Office for Environmental Protection in the UK, designed to replace European Commission powers in ensuring environmental compliance post-Brexit, and the role that judicial bodies might reasonably play in overseeing its powers, in Maria Lee, 'The next generation of environmental law: Environmental accountability and beyond in the draft Environment (Principles and Governance) Bill' UCL European Institute: Brexit Insights, available at: www.ucl.ac.uk/european-institute/news/2019/mar/next-generation-environmental-law; C Reid, 'The Future of Environmental Governance' (2019) 21 *Environmental Law Review* 219.

[6] See ch 2 (nn 41–96).

[7] eg, National Green Tribunal of India.

government,[8] or are clearly classified as courts within their nations' institutional arrangements (some of the oldest and best-known specialist bodies are courts[9] and held out as exemplars for others to follow).[10] Yet they often have powers that we might not expect to find in judicial bodies. They may mix adjudicative forms and functions with powers more traditionally found in the executive branch, having the authority to prospectively review the merits of proposed activities, permitting the use, despoliation or alternatively, providing for the conservation of natural resources.[11] In this way, they have a role in governing environmental issues. Some have quasi-legislative roles, having the power to amend regulations, policies and plans on the merits.[12] Regardless of their multifunctional nature, many play an important role in developing environmental *law* and in some circumstances, human rights law in their nations.[13] Specialist environment courts (ECs) might therefore be seen as the ultimate 'modern courts'[14] – attempting to determine public benefits while managing impacts on individual rights – and as mentioned, these bodies are charged with adjudicating disputes that collectively have significant importance for the economic, socio-cultural and environmental wellbeing of nations.[15] As this book explains, one could perceive ECs as new sites of disaggregated power and governance in the constitutional matrix.

However, the combination of novel legal form and relative power make ECs vulnerable. Specialist environment courts and tribunals have been seen as politically controversial, fostering an environmental ethic that gets in the way of economic development.[16] They have been criticised for enabling 'judicial

[8] eg, tribunals in England are considered part of the judicial branch (see Franks Committee, *Report of the Committee on Administrative Tribunals and Enquiries* (Cmnd 218, 1957).

[9] eg, Environment Court of New Zealand; New South Wales Land and Environment Court; Land and Environment Courts in Sweden; Environment and Land Court of Kenya; Vermont Superior Court Environmental Division.

[10] M Grant, *Environmental Court Project: Final Report* (DETR, 2000); G Pring and C Pring, *Greening Justice: Creating and Improving Environmental Courts and Tribunals* (World Resources Institute, 2009); Pring and Pring, *Environmental Courts and Tribunals* (n 2).

[11] Pring and Pring, *Greening Justice* (n 10); Pring and Pring, *Environmental Courts and Tribunals* (n 2).

[12] eg, the Environment Court of New Zealand (NZEnvC). The land and environment courts in Sweden also exercise judicial oversight of plans (see A Bengtsson, 'Specialised courts for environmental matters – the Swedish solution' (2017) 29 *Environmental Law & Management* 115).

[13] S Okong'o, 'Environmental adjudication in Kenya: a reflection on the early years of the Environment and Land Court of Kenya' (2017) 29 *Environmental Law & Management* 103.

[14] J Resnik, 'Reinventing Courts as Democratic Institutions' (2014) 143 *Daedalus* 9, 9–10; G Pring and C Pring, 'Twenty-first century environmental dispute resolution – is there an "ECT" in your future?' (2015) 33 *Journal of Energy & Natural Resources Law* 10.

[15] eg, the New Zealand Parliament acknowledged that the TCPA Appeal Board (forerunner to the NZEnvC) was concerned with matters having 'far reaching effects' greatly exceeding the 'run-of-the-mill business that occupied the Supreme Court day by day', New Zealand Parliamentary Debates, 375 NZPD 3589.

[16] R Asenjo, 'Environmental Adjudication in Chile' (International Symposium for Environment Judges, IUCN AEL, Oslo, 21 June 2016). Witness also the response in some media outlets to the New South Wales Land and Environment Courts (NSWLEC) decision in *Gloucester Resources Ltd v Minister for Planning* [2019] NSWLEC 7 (eg, Henry Ergas, 'Absurd Rocky Hill Decision Tarnishes the Rule of Law' *The Australian* (22 February 2019); and response of the Judicial Conference of Australia, 'Media Release by the President – Response to serious allegations against a judge', 27 February 2019).

overreach'[17] and accused of challenging both traditional notions of court-based adjudication and related separation of powers concepts.[18] In some jurisdictions, an anxiety about the appropriate powers and constitutional place of ECs manifests in policy debates,[19] public inquiries[20] and through continual legislative amendments,[21] and the struggle to make legal sense of them plays out in extrajudicial writing[22] and even case law.[23] While there is a surprisingly large literature on ECs, the existing academic scholarship fails to take these concerns and criticisms seriously. By and large the scholarship is promotional, extolling the virtues of specialism in environmental adjudication and encouraging the creation of ECs. These bodies are overwhelmingly seen as a 'good thing'. In the main, the scholarship does not acknowledge that they are highly vulnerable institutions, susceptible to changing political climates.[24] Nor does it attempt to develop a theoretical anchor that helps make legal sense of specialist environmental adjudication. However, without some form of conceptual buttressing that explains and justifies their unusual nature, ECs face continuing criticism and challenges[25] that may undermine their efficacy, development and possibly their continued existence.[26]

II. AN INTERACTIONAL THEORY FOR ENVIRONMENTAL ADJUDICATION

The main purpose of this book is to develop a theory capable of justifying specialist environmental adjudication. It makes sense to sketch out my theory in a relatively pithy way at this point before gradually expanding upon the

[17] GN Gill, 'Mapping the Power Struggles of the National Green Tribunal of India: The Rise and Fall?' [2018] Asian Journal of Law and Society 1, 3.

[18] For further discussion in relation to the NZEnvC and NSWLEC see ch 2.

[19] Ministry for the Environment, *Report of the Minister for the Environment's Technical Advisory Group* (Wellington, 2009) 10; Ministry for the Environment, *Improving our Resource Management System: A Discussion Document* (Wellington, 2013) 13.

[20] eg, JS Cripps et al, *Report of the Land and Environment Court Working Party* (Government of New South Wales, September 2001).

[21] eg, the continual legislative vacillations, expanding or reducing the jurisdiction and functions of the NZEnvC, discussed in ch 2.

[22] S Elias, 'Righting Environmental Justice' [2014] *Resource Management Theory & Practice* 47; see conflicting judicial views concerning the NSWLEC in ch 2 of this book.

[23] eg, in the New Zealand context *Environmental Defence Society Incorporated v Marlborough District Council* [2014] NZSC 38 discussed in ch 2; *RJ Davidson Family Trust v Marlborough District Council* [2017] NZHC 52, [2018] NZCA 316.

[24] With some notable exceptions, eg, see Gill (n 17).

[25] Ministry for the Environment, *Report of the Minister for the Environment's Technical Advisory Group* (n 19) 10; Ministry for the Environment, *Improving our Resource Management System* (n 19) 13.

[26] Kenneth A Palmer, 'Environment Court Reform – More than the Court under Threat?' (Resource Management Law Association, 25 June 2013), available at: rmla.org.nz/obiter/view/id/27. ECs that have been disestablished include courts in Austria, Finland, Hungary, the Netherlands and South Africa (Pring and Pring, *Environmental Courts and Tribunals* (n 2) 94–95 although the reasons are not clear.

explanation in this introduction and the following chapters. The theory is as follows: to attract comprehensive support, adjudication must foster normative legitimacy. In very simple terms, normative legitimacy is created by the shared beliefs of the relevant community, and a shared belief of near universal support is that integrity in adjudication matters. To have integrity, I argue, adjudicators must be able to respond to the legal and factual context that they are working within. Clearly, the concepts that I am using here – normative legitimacy and legal integrity – are complex and contestable and I explain what I mean by these terms in the following paragraphs and more fully in chapters three and four. But in essence, the theory is that in order to foster normative legitimacy, environmental adjudication must have legal integrity and legal integrity will be promoted if the adjudicatory body responds to rather than ignores the inherent nature of the problems it is charged with resolving.

I have termed the theory that I develop an 'interactional theory for legitimacy' because responsive environmental adjudication necessitates contextual interaction. Interaction connotes a dynamic process, requiring an awareness of context, communication that facilitates reciprocal feedback (or a two-way flow of information) and adaptation. Responsive environmental adjudication requires four factors to be considered as integral parts of the whole. First, identifying the distinct characteristics of environmental problems. Second, acknowledging the impact those characteristics have on law and dispute resolution, and the challenges they create for adjudication. Third, developing environmental law doctrine, procedure and remedies that respond to those challenges. Fourth, accepting that particular adjudicative forms and functions facilitate this process – ie, courts with particular constitutions, powers and expertise will be better able to respond to the nature of environmental problems. Taken together, these factors explain the interactional aspect of the theory building.[27] It is the relationship or links between the parts that matters in my theory building and that underpin the legal integrity of the response: these components cannot be considered in isolation, rather the theory argues that a holistic, sequencing approach – with one component leading on to and influencing the next – justifies the specialist nature of environmental adjudication.

Accordingly, we can make sense of specialist environmental adjudication if we develop a deep understanding of the nature of environmental problems and then identify, understand and accept the impact those unassailable features have on adjudication. To illustrate the application of the theory in this context, I consider two inherent features of environmental problems, 'interaction and change', and a core characteristic, 'uncertainty' (although there are undoubtedly more), and I explain how these structural features create both top-down and bottom-up forces, impacting how we adjudicate over environmental disputes.

[27] Note, others have termed similar context-driven approaches a 'pragmatic-principled approach'; see, eg, C Hübner Mendes, *Constitutional Courts and Deliberative Democracy* (Oxford University Press, 2013) 108.

In a top-down sense, the inherent nature of environmental problems impacts the way that law is written. In turn this affects the interpretative role of ECs and their application of the law to the facts. Second, the inherent nature of environmental problems impacts the way that ECs conduct the 'fact-finding' exercise. New legal frameworks have to be developed for resolving factual disputes in environmental adjudication that in turn create wider doctrine in the form of environmental law principles that guide decision-making and remedies. Both factors are relevant in helping to characterise the role of ECs, that is specialist environment courts have an important *governance* role in the system of environmental justice.

The theory that I propose justifies and helps construct a more detailed conceptual frame that government, policymakers, the judiciary (where the existing law is interstitial, uncertain, or they are empowered to exercise discretion), lawyers and participants in environmental adjudication may refer back to. While the *meta-theory* is of universal application, the *resulting frame* will have contours formed by particular legal cultures. Pausing for a moment, it may help to explain the idea of conceptual frames at this point. We often employ conceptual frames or metaphors both to make sense of complex phenomenon and to help constitute or set institutional constraints. By way of example, the 'separation of powers' may be considered to be a conceptual metaphor, used to both explain and constrain the branches of government in certain jurisdictions. Conceptual frames have a role to play in fostering normative legitimacy because institutions that operate within generally agreed frames are more acceptable to the subject community. In this book, I suggest that the conceptual frames being used to make sense of ECs at present are inadequate and that we need to construct a new frame. The theory that I propose will allow environmental adjudication to develop within a frame premised upon the immutable nature of environmental problems rather than political ideology, instrumentalism or particular versions of constitutionalism. Importantly, the theory enables a neutral, detailed frame to be developed, allowing us to talk productively together about environmental adjudication rather than creating division. The frame is neutral because it does not dictate particular substantive results, for example, it does not necessarily prioritise environmental conservation or environmental exploitation.[28] My argument is that we can build a frame capable of common acceptance if we employ the interactional theory that I develop.

The methodological approach that I follow in developing the theory can be broken down into a three-stage process: conducting a process of 'pre-theory building'; then 'theory building'; and finally, 'testing the theory'. I explain each of these stages in greater detail below. Before I do so, I want to emphasise two points. First, developing the theory has necessitated engaging with a vast

[28] Although see the discussion in relation to *Gloucester Resources Ltd v Minister for Planning* (n 16) in chs 5 and 6.

amount of different material including primary and secondary legal materials from different jurisdictions and scholarly commentary drawn from diverse areas of scholarship (covering, for example, environmental, constitutional and administrative law; political science and philosophy; law and biology; law and economics; organisational theory and governance studies). At times, the material will take legally trained readers into areas that they feel less familiar with but this cross-disciplinarity is an essential part of the theory building. Second – and linked to the first point – developing the theory presents structural problems, namely what information should be presented first? As explained above, the theory building follows a sequencing approach – ie, identifying the inherent nature of environmental problem, the challenges this creates for adjudication in general, and considering how responsive adjudicatory forms might emerge – but without first introducing specialist environment courts and tribunals and the criticisms they have attracted, presenting the bare theory would seem meaningless. Accordingly, there is some circularity in the structure of this book and I would ask readers for their tolerance in this regard.

III. THE METHOD OF DEVELOPING A THEORY FOR ENVIRONMENTAL ADJUDICATION

A. Pre-theory

The first stage of my methodology constitutes 'pre-theory'.[29] Simply put, this part examines the present scenario and it identifies criticisms and problems that have emerged that require addressing. I accept that 'pre-theory' is an ungainly term but it accurately captures the process taking place. It is a necessary precursor to theory building as it 'organises information'[30] and it is particularly useful where common practice exists without any theoretical underpinnings. For example, Lawrence uses a process he describes as 'pre-theory building' as the first stage in developing a theory for Environmental Impact Assessments.[31] Environmental Impact Assessments are employed in many jurisdictions; they take multiple forms, are put to various ends, and there are varying perspectives on their fundamental essence. Lawrence uses pre-theory to organise this information and identify common preoccupations, allowing for an inductive process to take place, so extracting core principles upon which to build. In this book, the pre-theory follows a particular sequence.

Chapter two maps specialist environmental adjudication taking place around the world at present. The chapter begins by establishing a typology for

[29] D Lawrence, 'The Need for EIA Theory Building' (1997) 17 *Environmental Impact Assessment Review* 79, 83 citing J Wyant et al, 'A planning and decision-making framework for ecological restoration' (1995) 19 *Environmental Management* 789.

[30] Lawrence, ibid, 83.

[31] ibid.

ECs, notes the unusual mix between form and function and provides illustrations of ECs' dynamic nature. By traversing the international research on ECs, the chapter notes that the literature is predominantly promotional, commending ECs contribution to environmental legal literacy and access to environmental justice. The second part of the chapter looks in closer detail at the legal nature of two particular ECs: the Environment Court of New Zealand (NZEnvC) and the New South Wales Land and Environment Court (NSWLEC), courts used as case studies throughout the book to help develop and test the theory. These jurisdictions have been chosen because the NZEnvC and the NSWLEC are two of the oldest environment courts in the world,[32] they are well referenced in the international literature and often held out as role models for the development of new ECs.[33] However, there is a disjunct between the international and national discourse. Over time the national discussion has moved from a promotional one to much a harsher debate and as a result, those courts have sustained criticisms from various sectors of society. The chapter reports on those criticisms and in doing so provides a foundation for chapter three.

Chapter three analyses the criticisms of the NZEnvC and NSWLEC in greater depth. Critics are particularly concerned about the courts' wide discretionary powers and creative, problem-solving approach to environmental adjudication; supporters praise them for the same reasons. It would be easy to attribute such criticisms to different ideological stances about environmental preservation, but this chapter shows that something more legally challenging is occurring. It explains that contributors to debates about these courts are arguing about the *legitimacy* of these institutions, that is, they argue that certain features or practices of the courts are legitimate or illegitimate.[34] At first sight, categorising the criticism in this way might appear odd. After all, both courts have been deliberately set up by the government and empowered through legislation. In a positivist sense, they are clearly *legally legitimate*. But chapter three explains that debate about the courts has arisen because participants are attempting to capture, constitute and constrain their legal nature by constructing different theories of *normative legitimacy*. That is, they employ different frames of normative legitimacy – or 'shared beliefs and understandings'[35] – within which to critique the courts.

Suffice to say, legitimacy is a highly complex idea: the concept has spawned entire schools of scholarship in the social sciences and there are multiple,

[32] The NZEnvC's heritage can be traced back to 1926: the Town-planning Board was created in 1926 to manage disputes relating to the newly enacted Town-planning Act 1926 (see, s 6). It is possible to trace the evolution of the institution from this Board to the 1953 Town and Country Appeal Board and the 1977 Planning Tribunal, to the NZEnvC in 1997. The NSWLEC was established in 1979 pursuant to the Land and Environment Court Act 1979 (NSW).

[33] Grant, *Environmental Court Project: Final Report* (n 10); Pring and Pring, *Greening Justice* (n 10).

[34] For criticisms see ch 2.

[35] D Beetham, *The Legitimation of Power*, 2nd edn (Political Analysis, 2013) 17.

contested versions of institutional legitimacy.[36] It is not the purpose of this book to enter that debate, rather chapter three explains what I mean by the term and the criteria I am going to employ, and that is the framework developed by Beetham[37] (and reflected in the legal scholarship in the work of Fallon[38] and Van Hoecke).[39] Lawyers might question why I draw on the work of Beetham, a political scientist, to help analyse adjudicative legitimacy. But when we consider the criticisms of these courts, we see that concerns are a mix of political and legal considerations and trying to separate out the two, addressing one concern but not the other, misunderstands what is going on in the discourse. Although it is trite to state that adjudication is a legal process concerned with social ordering, doing so reminds us that siloing the political and the legal is not helpful in this context. Beetham's meta-frame identifies core components of the legitimacy of power and understanding these components helps make sense of the debates taking place in New Zealand and New South Wales because we can pinpoint which aspects of legitimacy commentators are really focused on.

It is helpful to briefly summarise Beetham's framework on legitimacy at this juncture because it plays such an important part in crafting my overall methodology. In *The Legitimation of Power*, Beetham notes that legitimacy is a multidimensional concept and he suggests that power can be said to be legitimate to the extent that it meets three core conjunctive criteria. First, power must be 'acquired and exercised in accordance with prevailing rules', ie, it must have 'legal validity' as Beetham categorises this aspect.[40] Second, those rules must be well grounded in beliefs shared by both dominant and subordinate groups in the power matrix – so termed normative justifiability –[41] ie, power is normative if the 'public regards it as justified, appropriate, or otherwise deserving of support for reasons beyond fear of sanctions or mere hope for personal reward'[42] or habit.[43] As Beetham explains, certain essential factors are necessary for fostering normative legitimacy: there must be some constraints to the power – 'legitimate power is limited power'[44] – and there must be integrity in the exercise of power.[45] Third, the actions of the subordinate must acknowledge and serve

[36] eg, see R Cotterrell, *Law's Community: Legal Theory in Sociological Perspective* (Clarendon Press, 1997); RH Fallon, 'Legitimacy and the Constitution' (2004–05) 118 *Harvard Law Review* 1787; CA Thomas, 'The Uses and Abuses of Legitimacy in International Law' (2014) 34 *OJLS* 729.

[37] Beetham (n 35).

[38] Fallon, 'Legitimacy and the Constitution' (n 36).

[39] M Van Hoecke, *Law as Communication* (Hart Publishing, 2002).

[40] See also M Weber, 'The Three Types of Legitimate Rule' (1958) 4 *Berkeley Publications in Society and Institutions* 1 (this type of legitimacy is described as 'positivist' or 'rational-legal' legitimacy).

[41] Beetham (n 35) ch 3. See also Fallon, 'Legitimacy and the Constitution' (n 36) 1796 (categorising this feature as 'moral' legitimacy).

[42] Fallon, 'Legitimacy and the Constitution' (n 36) 1795.

[43] SM Lipset, *Political Man: The Social Bases of Politics* (Mercury, 1963) ch 3.

[44] Beetham (n 35) 35.

[45] ibid, xiii, 90, 257 (also termed 'due process' by Beetham). For others in agreement see, eg, L Duguit, *Law in the Modern State* (Frida Laski and Harold Laski trs, Allen and Unwin, 1921) 142–43 (administration no longer retains a necessary connection with sovereign will to support

to confirm the power-holders' authority.[46] Beetham predicted that normative justifiability might form 'the core of legitimacy', most likely to prove contentious, with 'legality serving as a pre-condition and aspects of recognition as a mode of reinforcement'.[47] This prediction is borne out in the debates concerning the NZEnvC and the NSWLEC: the precondition of legality (bestowed by Parliament through legislation) exists and must be accepted,[48] and the reinforcing aspects of consensual acceptance are also present, but normative legitimacy is proving contentious.

In chapter three, I discuss the various frames that are being used to address the normative legitimacy of ECs in the New Zealand and Australian contexts. Given the relative similarities between the legal cultures of each state (for example, both adhere to a Westminster model of government, constitutional principles such as the rule of law and separation of powers are important, and government is expected to be accountable to the public), three main conceptual frames are being used in both nations. The first frame is one that views those courts as part of the flexible and responsive administrative justice landscape and as evidence of adjudicatory pluralism. The second is premised upon generic instrumentalism and predominantly concerns efficiency (variously defined and based on ideological preferences).[49] The final frame addresses a certain understanding of constitutional legitimacy, utilising a functional conception of the separation of powers. Constitutionalism can accommodate many different types of adjudication but the particular constitutional frames being used in the debate over ECs tend to exclude this possibility. In chapter three, I explore how the use of these particular frames obscures our understanding of environmental adjudication and can be counterproductive to effective adjudication in this context.

legitimacy, rather we should be looking to its purpose); Van Hoecke (n 39) 63 (if power is exercised in certain ways then it becomes socially acceptable); Hübner Mendes (n 27) 225 ('a court will be more or less legitimate for what it does, not the power that it has formally received … [and] it is more or less legitimate depending upon how well it is able to discharge its deliberative duties'); J Raz, *The Authority of the Law* (Clarendon Press, 1979) 106–08 ('norm-applying institutions should, therefore, be identified by the way they fulfill their functions rather than by their functions themselves' and that courts and tribunals are institutions in which 'norm-making and norm applying are combined in a special way'); T Bustamante, 'The Ongoing Search for Legitimacy: Can a "Pragmatic yet Principled" Deliberative Model Justify the Authority of Constitutional Courts?' (2015) 78 *MLR* 372, 393 ('It rightfully acknowledges that the legitimacy of such courts depends entirely upon their deliberative performance').

[46] Beetham (n 35) 18. Note that this third feature is sometimes termed 'sociological legitimacy', see Fallon, 'Legitimacy and the Constitution' (n 36) 1796; Van Hoecke (n 39) 24 (describing 'sociological institutionalisation' as the 'acceptance of the legal system by the people to whom it is meant to apply'); sociological legitimacy may be based on beliefs concerning obligations, or simply habit, and tends to be evaluated empirically.

[47] Beetham (n 35) 293.

[48] *cf* constitutional debates in USA scenario: RH Fallon, 'Of Legislative Courts, Administrative Agencies, and Article III' (1987–88) (101) *Harvard Law Review* 916.

[49] eg, I explain in ch 3 how the Fifth National Government of New Zealand (2008–17) conflated 'efficiency' with the speed of resource management decision-making and achieved this end by limiting public participation.

I am aware that I am introducing abstract ideas here and an illustration may assist. In relation to the 'separation of powers frame', critics of the NZEnvC and NSWLEC argue that the separation of powers is a constitutional principle acting to legitimise and set natural constraints on the powers and functions of public institutions in those jurisdictions; these ECs flout the separation of powers because they have merged administrative and/or adjudicative and/or quasi-legislative functions, and they appear to be determining values and principles; ergo they are normatively illegitimate.[50] The difficulty with *this* frame, as I argue throughout the book, is that it relies upon sharp demarcations that cannot exist with environmental problem-solving: demarcations between law and policy; the legal and political spheres; and facts, values, opinions and principles. I provide a sketch of the architecture of environmental statute law in the case-study jurisdictions to illustrate this point (albeit the description may be applicable to many more jurisdictions). In essence, the complex regulatory web that has emerged as a response to the inherent nature of environmental problems requires new legal reasoning and the creation of new institutional forms. These forms may not fit neatly within a functionalist separation of powers concept but that is not to say that they are constitutionally illegitimate.[51]

However, chapter three suggests that *all* the conceptual frames being employed to analyse environmental adjudication appear ill-suited to the task and none of the frames, either alone or in conjunction with the others, prove adequate for capturing, constituting and appropriately constraining the legal nature of the courts while preserving their ability to adjudicate environmental disputes. Importantly, the use of different or ill-fitting frames can create real problems, resulting in inconsistent approaches and/or revisionary forces that are misguided. Analysing these inadequate frames in detail proves useful because it helps inform theory building. This exercise sets the parameters of the present debate, identifies the preconceptions and preoccupations of the critics, and tells us what any appropriate theory would need to address. Studying the use of these frames emphasises that the very nature of environmental problems needs to be scrutinised and consideration given as to how the form, functions and powers of any adjudicatory body might best respond to that nature, and it explains the need for discretion and flexibility in environmental adjudication. Analysing different frames also reminds us that efficiency in environmental adjudication

[50] eg, Ministry for the Environment, *Report of the Minister for the Environment's Technical Advisory Group* (n 19); S Rivers-McCombs, 'Planning in Wonderland: The RMA, Local Democracy and the Rule of Law' (2011) 9 *New Zealand Journal of Public and International Law* 43; Ministry for the Environment, *Improving our Resource Management System* (n 19).

[51] Jeremy Waldron suggests 'articulated government through successive phases of governance, each of which maintains its own integrity' is more important than relying on a functionalist separation of powers (see J Waldron, *Political Political Theory* (Harvard University Press, 2016) 70–71) a principle he regards as dying 'a sclerotic death' (see J Waldron, 'Separation of Powers in Thought and Practice' (2013) 54 *Boston College Law Review* 433, 467; while not necessarily advocating for this development, see Waldron, *Political Political Theory*, 22).

matters but that efficiency can be achieved in many ways and we should not accept an impoverished and ideological-driven approach.

Finally, this exercise warns us that in order to foster normative legitimacy, environmental adjudication has to be referable back to some constraints both in practice and conceptually.[52] Clearly, practical methods can act to constrain institutions. Constraints may be explicit and include external checks (such as appeal routes and the ability for Parliament to impose rules etc) and internal checks (such as deliberative processes that employ legal reasoning and ensure transparency). But I argue that conceptual frames are also important in setting constraints. They are models that help us to make sense of the world. In the adjudicatory context, models help us to make sense of adjudicatory practices and new developments can be influenced by and tested against relevant models. If we are to have a productive and informed debate about environmental adjudication, having a common conceptual frame that enables us to talk together is invaluable. If the forms of environmental adjudication are to change and responsive doctrine and procedure is to develop, the normative legitimacy of those developments will be fostered if they accord with a frame that reflects shared assumptions and beliefs. Or, put differently, if responsive, flexible institutions with discretionary powers are to be appropriately constrained, an appropriate frame will help set the parameters for policymakers, judicial decision-makers and the public who use those ECs. That is what my theory attempts to do – to provide the basis for developing a frame that reflects the necessary reality of environmental adjudication; a frame that perhaps we have a better chance of agreeing upon, so allowing us to view these institutions through the same filter.

B. Building the Theory

Building the theory follows three stages. At the outset, I explore the general idea that adjudicative forms and practices are malleable and can morph to context. I then address what makes adjudicative institutions legitimate in a normative sense. Finally, I establish core contextual foundations upon which to build the interactional theory for environmental adjudication. I briefly expand upon each of these stages below but it is worth noting at the outset that chapters four and five situate the research firmly in the wider literature on adjudication, political science and philosophy, and the physical sciences, so helping to militate against the idea that my theory is particularly controversial or radical. Of course, ECs will be considered more or less *constitutionally* legitimate depending upon the jurisdictional context. The particular criticisms of the NZEnvC and the NSWLEC (that have also been levelled at other courts such as the Swedish environmental courts[53] and the National Green Tribunal of India)[54] might not

[52] Beetham (n 35) 35.
[53] Bengtsson (n 12) 116.
[54] Gill (n 17).

eventuate in other nations and some ECs are subject to different pressures (such as the Kenyan[55] or Chinese courts);[56] others appear to attract little criticism at all. Nevertheless, even in those jurisdictions where ECs seem uncontroversial, theory building is a critical exercise because it establishes a frame for normative legitimacy that transcends any possible ideologically based divisions that might emerge in the future.

It is also important to note that, although I use the NZEnvC and NSWLEC as case studies in the theory-building process, I am *not* trying to find a legal transplant – that is, I am not searching for a model that works in certain jurisdictions that could be transplanted to others. Rather I am saying that there are certain structural features of environmental problems that environmental adjudication must respond to, regardless of the jurisdiction in which this occurs. Of course, how that adjudication ultimately manifests is going to depend on legal culture and it will develop in different ways. One of my reasons for selecting two different courts in two different jurisdictions as case studies is to demonstrate this point (and even though the NZEnvC and NSWLEC are relatively similar institutions and operate in similar legal cultures, we still see differences in approach). But the interactional theory provides an essential anchoring: adjudication *has to respond to these features* in some way in order to promote normative legitimacy. Employing the theory enables detailed frames to be built – frames that make sense within particular legal cultures.

Chapter four is more abstract than the other chapters but (perhaps perversely) it provides the essential grounding for the theory. It begins by attempting to counteract narrow thinking about adjudication that would derail the theory-building process and delegitimise ECs. It explores the idea that adjudication is a heavily contested and contestable concept and practice. In practice, adjudication takes place at a multitude of different points – geographical, temporal, within and between social groups and peoples, and it occurs in different institutional forms and employs different problem-solving mechanisms.[57] Nevertheless, chapter four explains that certain core features *are* apparent when we consider what makes a body an adjudicative body. Four core features are particularly apt to the discussion about environmental adjudication: (1) providing a site for the confrontation of arguments; (2) resolving disputes; (3) establishing an acceptable truth; and (4) playing a role in shaping the future. All four features contribute to my interactional theory and help set the parameters for debate about ECs.

[55] Okong'o (n 13).

[56] Zhang Minchun and Zhang Bao, 'Specialised Environmental Courts in China: Status Quo, Challenges and Responses' (2012) 30 *Journal of Energy & Natural Resources Law* 361.

[57] eg, in thinking about 'classic' courts consider the International Court of Justice; European Court of Justice; national generic courts; specialist international courts such as the International Tribunal for the Law of the Sea or World Trade Organization Appellate Body; and specialist national courts (eg, that include in the New Zealand context, the Employment Court, Māori Land Court, Māori Appellate Court, Family Court, Environment Court, Accident Compensation Appeal Authority) etc.

The discussion in this chapter shows that expansive approaches to adjudication, that perceive adjudication as norm-generating, premised on deliberative practices, forward-looking and part of wider governance – all characteristics of ECs – are not outliers; rather they are well traversed and justified intellectually.

The second part of chapter four continues the theory building and draws directly on Beetham's analysis of normative legitimacy. As I explained above, normative legitimacy is founded on shared beliefs and a belief capable of near universal support is that integrity in adjudication matters. Fundamentally, if adjudicative institutions respond to the legal and factual context they are working within they will have more, not less, integrity. I draw on legal and political philosophy to explore the meaning and importance of legal integrity (with Dworkin being the most famous proponent)[58] and use commonalities in the literature to bolster my argument. At its essence, integrity requires thoughts and deeds to cohere with bedrock values – something solid – some core of intelligibility. Within the adjudicative context, scholars often highlight the importance of self-validation in ensuring integrity. Without authority derived from democratic mandate, a court must, as Loughlin suggests, achieve legitimacy by 'the integrity of its own procedures',[59] and the manner in which an institution exercises its functions – its integrity in exercising those functions[60] – contributes to its 'worthiness to be 'recognised',[61] rendering it worthy of trust.[62] But I also explain why integrity has work to do on its own two feet in environmental adjudication – it is not simply metonymic with procedural due process, substantive justice or political fairness (as some critics of integrity as a legal principle have claimed).[63] Rather, the interactional theory that I propose is integrity in action – it is the relationship or integration between the four component parts that matters, and the immutable nature of environmental problems provides the bedrock, anchoring the consequential developments, actions and responses, so fostering an intelligible coherence.

In this part, I also address the question of integrity and responsiveness from a historical angle, noting that environmental adjudication (as we now term it) has always taken on an unusual form, and I consider the swanimotes or ancient forest courts of England and Wales that predate the Magna Carta and still exist today in a surprisingly unchanged form.[64] These ancient dispute-resolution

[58] R Dworkin, *Law's Empire* (Harvard University Press, 1987) chs 6 and 7 in particular.

[59] M Loughlin, *Foundations of Public Law* (Oxford University Press, 2010) 454.

[60] Beetham (n 35) 90, 257; also described by Beetham as 'due process', xiii.

[61] J Habermas, *Communication and the Evolution of Society* (Heinemann, 1979) 178–79.

[62] S Raynor and R Cantor, 'How Fair is Safe Enough? The Cultural Approach to Societal Technology Choice' (1987) 7 *Risk Analysis* 3, 4–5.

[63] D Reaume, 'Is Integrity a Virtue? Dworkin's Theory of Legal Obligation' (1989) 39 *University of Toronto Law Journal* 380; L Alexander and K Kress, 'Against Legal Principles' (1997) 82 *Iowa Law Review* 739.

[64] G Jones, 'Swanimotes, Woodmotes, and Courts of "Free Miners"' in J Langton and G Jones (eds), *Forests and Chases of England and Wales c1500–c1850* (St John's College Research Centre, 2005); P Large, 'From swanimote to disafforestation: Feckenham Forest in the early seventeeth

bodies were not imposed on communities, rather they grew up from within them. They developed over time, facilitating a harmonious interaction between the community, the social ordering (in the form of customs or law), dispute resolution, and the environment that all relied upon. Interestingly for our purposes, these bodies demonstrate that a clear bifurcation between the political state and legalistic courts has seldom been a feature in the resolution of environmental conflicts. Rather, institutional arrangements are closer to that of disaggregated power, with disputes managed by bodies that often have administrative, local regulatory and adjudicative roles. The procedures adopted by the swanimotes also appear to respond carefully to the nature of the dispute.[65] This heritage is important and this embedded tradition creates a displaceable presumption for the normative legitimacy of these bodies, based on their longevity:[66] they have existed for over a millennium.[67] This example is taken from a particular legal culture but nevertheless, thinking about the swanimotes provides a link to the argument developed in chapters five and six that the legal nature of environmental adjudicatory bodies should not be a matter of mere ideological policy choice, rather it is rooted and grows from the nature of the disputes they are charged with resolving.

Chapter five returns specifically to the interactional theory for environmental adjudication. It develops the core stage of the theory building by identifying the inherent features of environmental problems that adjudication must be able to respond to if it is to have integrity. Challenges for adjudication are created by the *natural* state of things – the reality of ecology that fundamentally we cannot change, or rather cannot change with any ease or speed. This nature impacts regulation and statutory interpretation (as chapter three explores) but it also

century' in R Hoyle (ed), *The Estates of the English Crown 1550–1640* (Cambridge University Press, 1992); WS Holdsworth, *A History of English Law Volume 1*, 7th edn (Methuen, 1956); Forest Charter 1217, cl 8 (the companion document to and later reincorporated into the Magna Carta in the Confirmation of Charters 1297).

[65] New Forest Acts of 1838, 1877, 1949; Regulations Of The Verderers Of The New Forest Relating To The Courts Of Swainmote For The Dispatch Of Administrative And Judicial Business As Provided For In Section 24 Of The New Forest Act 1877 As Amended.

[66] *Contra* Weber, longevity alone might not amount to a *res ipsa loquiter* legitimacy argument, see AV Dicey, *Introduction to the Study of the Law of the Constitution*, 3rd edn (Macmillan, 1889) vii–viii; and Holmes (n 1) 469. Note also there may be too much of a difference between the small, localised communities characterised by the need for ongoing relationships amongst disputants that were serviced by the swanimotes and the dispute resolution mechanisms that best address modern environmental conflicts (for general discussion see RL Abel, 'Western Courts in Non-Western Settings: Patterns of Court Use in Colonial and Neo-Colonial Africa' in SB Burman and BE Harrell-Bond (eds), *The Imposition of Law* (Academic Press, 1979)). Nevertheless, longevity may create a displaceable presumption of normative legitimacy. A question (that cannot be answered here) is whether this endurance is simply unthinking tradition or because of necessity? If the latter, it supports the idea developed in this book that the legal nature of adjudicative bodies is not mere policy choice.

[67] Weber described this form of 'believed' legitimacy as established and habitual, and categorised it as traditional legitimacy: the authority of the 'eternal' yesterday, see Weber, 'The Three Types of Legitimate Rule' (n 40); M Weber, *From Max Weber: Essays in Sociology* (HH Gerth and C Wright Mills eds, Oxford University Press, 1946) 78–79.

impacts the fact-finding exercise in environmental adjudication and the application of law to facts in this sphere, leading to the development of new legal frameworks for evaluating evidence.

To make this argument, chapter five looks in some detail at the physical reality of ecology, explaining that the environment consists of multiple elements, constantly combining and reacting together, resulting in changing conditions. This dynamism manifests within and entwines together different realms of society: the natural world, the socio-cultural and economic spheres, so environmental problems manifest as polycentric problems.[68] In turn, the dynamic complexity of environmental problems impacts human understanding: that is, knowledge of environmental problems tends to be incomplete and uncertain. As a result, I argue that 'interaction' and 'change' are two inherent albeit interrelated features of environmental problems, and that 'uncertainty' constitutes a third, characteristic feature.

To illustrate that these inherent and characteristic features are pervasive, regardless of what we as humans do to try and manage or minimise them, chapter five adopts a layered approach. It begins by addressing 'ecological complexity without humans', then considers 'humans as actors of change', adds 'humans as interactionally impacted' and finally, turns to the wider relevance of 'humans' relationship with the environment'. In considering human relationships with the environment, the chapter explains that environmental disputes often appear intractable because the collective action nature of environmental problems brings into play ethical pluralism and contestation. Adjudication is an important outlet for these disputes and I argue that the challenges created by this ethical pluralism exert pressure on the form, content and processes within environmental adjudication. In particular, inherent pluralism means that when we argue about the environment we will employ different reasoning strategies resting on different 'definitions, judgments, assumptions, and contentions'[69] and we will utilise various techniques drawn from different disciplines to justify our stance. Different values impact parties' legal submissions and they will advocate for different approaches to legal reasoning. They also impact on what evidence parties adduce and which mechanisms they argue should be employed to evaluate that evidence (for example, economic rationalists will draw upon various forms of cost–benefit analysis, while deep ecologists will employ ethical reasoning). The challenge for environmental adjudication is to provide a forum that allows disagreements to be aired and resolved by finding common ground, enabling us to talk together.[70] Thus, adopting a layered approach and separating out physical ecology from social systems also helps to illustrate why environmental

[68] L Fuller, 'The Forms and Limits of Adjudication' (1978–79) 92 *Harvard Law Review* 353; *Bulga Milbrodale Progress Association Inc v Minister for Planning and Infrastructure and Warkworth Mining Limited* [2013] NSWLEC 48.

[69] JS Dryzek, *The Politics of the Earth* (Oxford University Press, 1997) Preface.

[70] J Waldron, 'Thoughtfulness and the Rule of Law' (2011) 18 *British Academy Review* 1.

adjudication requires evidence from a myriad of disciplines – science, economics and policy-based experts – and from various sectors in society. And this helps to show why relevant evidence in environmental adjudication may concern past history, present data and opinions as to the future.

Accordingly, chapter five explains that the contextual reality creates challenges for adjudication that traditionally relied upon the application of law to settled facts determined in a discrete context. Environmental problems are undoubtedly complex and to an extent this complexity will be reflected in responsive adjudicatory institutions – their functions, procedures and the doctrine they might develop.[71] But a core theme running through this book is that institutions that operate with integrity while being appropriately constrained can provide a stabilising effect, promoting a coherent and consistent approach to environmental problem-solving.

C. Testing the Theory

Chapter five establishes the essential base – the bottom of the bottom-up process. It describes certain features that are inherent in environmental problems and it explains the challenges these create for adjudication. The penultimate chapter, chapter six, considers the last components of the interactional theory: the development of environmental law doctrine; pragmatic and justified procedural responses; appropriate remedies; and the impact on normative institutional form including the constitutional makeup of any adjudicative body. In doing so, I return to my case studies – the NZEnvC and the NSWLEC – and explore how adjudication in those specialist courts *has* responded to and met the challenges identified. In order to show how the inherent nature of environmental problems creates a force on adjudication, I tease out where developments have occurred when statute law has been incomplete or uncertain, or where ECs have been positively empowered to craft the appropriate legal response. In essence, this chapter employs the interactional theory as a critical foil against which to assess adjudication in ECs but it also starts the process of building the detailed frame for environmental adjudication within those legal cultures.

It is important to clarify that I do not intend to undertake a comprehensive assessment tracing *all* the legal developments that flow from the inherent features of environmental problems, rather I select two developments to follow because the purpose of the exercise is to show the interactional theory at work. The first development links ecosystemic 'interaction', 'change' and 'uncertainty' to the creation of legal doctrine addressing risk assessment and management. I consider the NZEnvC and NSWLEC's use of precautionary approaches to decision-making, procedural developments (for example, concerning the

[71] See E Fisher, *Risk Regulation and Administrative Constitutionalism* (Hart Publishing, 2007) identifying that complex problems may require complex institutional responses.

burdens and standards of evidential proof) and alternative remedies (for example, continuing mandamus and adaptive management). The second example links the collective nature of environmental problems (that encompasses ethical pluralism and interactions between the environment, socio-cultural and economic spheres) with adjudicative approaches to access to environmental justice,[72] and the implications created for standing, costs orders, injunctions, procedure and case management.

In this chapter, I also argue that the nature of environmental disputes and the inherent challenges presented by adjudicating over them, suggest a particular normative form for ECs both in terms of their necessary functions and their constitution. For example, environmental disputes are operating within highly complex legal structures, and may impact wider legal rights and duties, so there is a need for legal expertise and legal reasoning to infuse decision-making by adjudicators who are independent of government. But the pronounced scientific complexity inherent in much environmental adjudication favours a specialist bench. Other considerations come into play and are discussed in the chapter.

D. A Note on Methodology

At the outset, it is important to address the methodological approach that I take in this book. In large part, the methodology sits at the intersection of inductive and deductive reasoning. The interactional theory developed in chapters three, four and five is deductive. But in chapter six, I employ institutional microanalysis premised upon actual practice to support the theory and I want to explain the role of this inductive reasoning. To some legitimacy scholars, employing inductive reasoning in this way is justifiable: 'explaining and justifying the validity of an institutional order' so creating theories 'to legitimize different institutional sectors' is a valid method of developing theory because 'theory is a symbolic construction, distinct from both fact and practice but necessarily linked to reality'.[73] As they explain, inductive reasoning (deriving theory from practice) is a valid theory-building methodology[74] because one cannot ignore what is there.[75] But Cohn warns 'descripto-normative' studies tend to

[72] In the wider sense of the term 'access to justice': see BJ Preston, 'The effectiveness of the law in providing access to environmental justice: an introduction' (11th IUCN Academy of Environmental Law Colloquium, Hamilton, New Zealand, June 2013).

[73] PL Berger and T Luckmann, *The Social Construction of Reality* (Penguin, 1966) 112–13 quoted in CA Thomas, 'The Uses and Abuses of Legitimacy in International Law' (2014) 34 *OJLS* 729 (n 36) 743. See also A Kaplan, *The Conduct of Inquiry* (Chandler, 1964) 295–98, 302. Further, is it ever really possible to ignore the influence on our thinking of reality and have a completely pure appreciation of 'the other'? For reasons why this is impossible (albeit in an interspecies context) see C Foster, *Being a Beast* (Profile, 2016).

[74] Lawrence (n 29) 84.

[75] ibid, 80: 'theory is a symbolic construction, distinct from both fact and practice but necessarily linked to reality' (citing Kaplan (n 73)).

be 'flat'.[76] And Walker writes that this basic methodology of theory building creates dangers of inherent bias because the main focus of enquiry provides a default position and therefore creates a natural predisposition towards that focus.[77] The risk is that the theory becomes explanatory rather than normative and avoids addressing what would be the optimal solution.

In part, these risks are countered by the interactional focus of my theory – by directly addressing the causal interface between the problem and the problem-solving apparatus – that is, identifying the inherent characteristics of environmental problems and establishing that core foundation as the conceptual anchor. Everything else flows from that deductive core. We can test developments against it and so by 'going to the very bottom of things' I hope to do more than build in a 'shallow' way, concerned *only* with describing 'an ordered and structured system'.[78]

Further, the *manner* in which doctrinal and procedural developments in these bodies have occurred is important. These courts are amongst the oldest and most developed ECs in the world and critically, their processes and doctrinal developments have morphed in response to the demands of environmental adjudication. Thus, there has been an accumulation of problem-solving knowledge and expertise, grounded in actual practice, formed over time. This is legal reasoning at the coalface. Environmental adjudication is undoubtedly dynamic and evolving, but the process of evolution in these ECs flows from a reasoned approach, systematically tested against real-life disputes. It has been built iteratively and shaped by legal reasoning.[79] So, I am not taking a static snapshot (as Walker's concern might be) but rather capturing the results to date of reason and persistence.

I would argue therefore that the methodological approach in chapter six acknowledges and embraces the value of a common law-type development and it tests the theory against that process. In a sense, this methodology is deeply ontological[80] – concerned with '*rei naturam intimam*' (the inner nature of things)[81] – and

[76] M Cohn, 'Tension and Legality: Towards a Theory of the Executive Branch' (2016) 29 *Canadian Journal of Law and Jurisprudence* 321, 349. (To avoid unsubstantiated results, Cohn avers, 'a workable depictive model must first be developed to support the normative analysis', at 322).

[77] N Walker, 'EU Constitutionalism and New Governance' in G de Burca and J Scott (eds), *Law and New Governance in the EU and the US* (Hart Publishing, 2006) 30. Walker also expresses concern that an intense focus on institutional design creates an unduly narrow preoccupation, that leads to deeper philosophical questions about values and good governance being ignored.

[78] Harlow (n 1).

[79] Of interest, Thomas Aquinas declared custom superior to the imposition of law for these very reasons, St Thomas Aquinas, *Summa Theologica*, vol note 4, I–II, Q 97, arts 2–3 (1023–24) cited in EL Rubin, 'From Coherence to Effectiveness: A Legal Methodology for the Modern World' in R Van Gestel, H-W Micklitz and EL Rubin (eds), *Rethinking Legal Scholarship: A Transatlantic Dialogue* (Cambridge University Press, 2017) 315 (custom is 'the one human quality that remains a constant as behaviour changes'); and Aristotle believed that 'a man may be a safer ruler than the written law, but not safer than the customary law' (see Waldron, 'Thoughtfulness and the Rule of Law' (n 70) fn 52).

[80] And so, within metaphysics, concerned with the 'ultimate reality': see T Sider, *Writing the Book of the World* (Clarendon Press, 2011) 5.

[81] E de Waal, *The White Road* (Chatto and Windus, 2015) 141.

'no one should fear that the contemplation of characters will lead us away from things themselves; on the contrary it leads us to the interior of things'.[82] Further, by drawing on iterative developments and solutions crafted in specialist adjudication over decades, we move from the singular to a more complex but refined result, reflecting collective communality. The first adjudicative decision on a legal issue is inevitably singular and focused on the interests of the individual parties but, as a body of doctrine develops, small refinements shape it to reflect a multitude of views and perspectives, thus creating a collective response to the problem. Like building a mosaic to reveal the complete picture, doctrine and processes are added to by many participants and a great diversity of thinking – a practice that finds theoretical expression in systems thinking and the idea of 'gradually transforming continuums'.[83] To this extent, the methodology chimes neatly with the subject and there is a pleasing circularity: democratic practices that naturally led to collective environmental concerns became translated into adjudicative *demands*, and particular adjudicative *forms* and *practices* are shaped in turn by inclusivity.

But this methodology creates an additional and interesting perspective: the courts themselves have contributed to a new frame for assessing the normative legitimacy of ECs. Adopting this perspective, at times we can see a clear trend of case law acknowledging the inherent nature of environmental problems, sometimes explicitly so but more often than not implicitly, and responding accordingly. However, in other instances, there appears a disjunct or retreat from this focus, and the approach of the environment courts does not always fit neatly within the theory that I propose[84] but aligns more neatly with legal formalism and a functionalist separation of powers frame (and unsurprisingly, this disjunct is more pronounced at appeal level[85] and these cases can jar and stand out).[86] So actual practice has not always accorded with the interactional approach suggested by the theory. This point helps to counteract, in part, any criticism of my methodology – my theory building is not just expository, masquerading as normative – but it also helps illustrate how the use of different frames might push and pull environmental adjudication in various directions, and why identifying a common frame may help foster consistency and coherence.

[82] In counselling his fellow physicist, Tschirnhaus, on methodology in 17th-century scientific discovery, Leibniz wrote that 'no one should fear that the contemplation of characters will lead us away from things themselves; on the contrary it leads us to the interior of things', ibid, 141. Note this approach has been categorised as theorising 'in shirtsleeves': see L Daston and P Galison, *Objectivity* (Zone Books, 2007) 52.

[83] Cohn (n 76) 325.

[84] eg, the NZEnvC has not always developed an expansive approach to standing even when having the power to do so: see ch 6 for further discussion.

[85] Determined by the ordinary, superior courts.

[86] *Royal Forest and Bird Society of New Zealand Inc v Buller District Council* [2006] NZRMA 193 (HC).

IV. CERTAIN CAVEATS

The concluding chapter returns to each of the points discovered in pre-theory building, that is: the need for ECs to be responsive but constrained, efficient and efficacious and drawing the strands together, explains how the theory may help to address these considerations. It explains how employing the interactional theory helps to develop a frame that reflects a necessary reality – a neutral frame that anchors adjudication in the fundamental and unassailable nature of environmental problems. Such a frame does not have the maladjusted, incomplete, controversial or partisan aspects that haunt some of the other frames in use (as I explore in chapter three). In this sense, it is a frame that perhaps we have a better chance of agreeing upon, so transcending division and allowing us to view these institutions through the same filter. A frame capable of common acceptance will foster efficiency, coherence and consistency.

Reflecting on the theory-building process, three core aspects emerge.[87] The first is that this interactional theory can be used to construct a more detailed frame (or frames, to accommodate different legal cultures) within which we might productively discuss and make sense of specialist environmental adjudication. Second, this frame has normative dimensions – it allows for a principled approach to developing the form, functions, powers and duties of ECs and it can also help craft the development of doctrine. Third, this frame is enabling, helping to bestow authority but it also constrains authority. For all these reasons, the frame is legitimising.

However, certain caveats must be acknowledged. First, the theory building is constrained to a specific regulatory context[88] – environmental adjudication – rather than creating an 'overarching regulatory theory that transcends problem-area and context and that assumes constitutional dimension'.[89] As explained above, it deals with Walker's concerns about creating explanatory rather than normative theory by establishing the clear conceptual anchor, establishing the inherent nature of environmental problems and the ramifications that flow from that core. Nevertheless, the theoretical approach taken that addresses

[87] Walker (n 77) 20 (establishing this three-fold value to model building).

[88] Many scholars have noted the problem of legitimacy created by adjudicatory pluralism ranging from WA Robson, *Justice and Administrative Law*, 2nd edn (Stevens, 1947) 328, to HW Arthurs, 'Rethinking Administrative Law: A Slightly Dicey Business' (1979) 17 *Osgoode Hall Law Journal* 1, 42; and P Cane, *Administrative Tribunals and Adjudication* (Hart Publishing, 2010) 21. But they also acknowledge the difficulties that hinder the creation of meta-theories or universally constructive critiques caused by the sheer diversity in form, functions and purpose of specialist courts and tribunals: see JA Farmer, *Tribunals and Government* (Weidenfeld and Nicolson, 1974) 189; H Genn, 'Tribunals and Informal Justice' (1993) 56 *MLR* 393, 394; RE Wraith and PG Hutchesson, *Administrative Tribunals* (Allen and Unwin, 1973) 15; New Zealand Law Commission, *Tribunals in New Zealand* (NZLC Wellington, 2008) 32. For the difficulties the whole of the administrative state creates for meta-theorising see CR Sunstein and A Vermeule, 'Libertarian Administrative Law' (2015) 82 *University of Chicago Law Review* 393, 471.

[89] S Sturm, 'Gender Equity Regimes and the Architecture of Learning' in G De Burca and J Scott (eds), *Law and New Governance in the EU and the US* (Hart Publishing, 2006) 324.

core interactional components is one that *may* be more universally applied to other forms of specialist adjudication.[90]

Second, I do not profess to create *the* optimal theory for environmental adjudication nor *the* ideal frame for ECs. This would be unrealistic. There are as Komesar notes, only a range of imperfect institutional alternatives:[91] 'no purely rational decisions, ideal institutions, or optimal solutions, but only second bests'.[92] I am seeking to bridge a present divide, not assert a truth (which would be impossible partly because normative legitimacy is a 'variable not a constant' and institutions that are seen as legitimate by some groups may lack legitimacy amongst others).[93] While I argue that my theory promotes principled adjudicative practice and developments, the fundamental aim of the book is to prompt reflection and debate.

Linked to the above point, in developing my theory I maintain that substantive output is not necessarily relevant.[94] There is no wider telos at this first stage of theory building. I am not undertaking any form of empirical work to demonstrate that ECs result in greater environmental protection, for example. Nor do I focus *in isolation* upon the development of substantive legal principles (that may be considered a substantive output) or procedure.[95] As I argue, it is

[90] One possible downside of this highly context-driven theorising is a concern about fragmentation, creating barriers to lay understanding and access by creating an ad hoc assortment of isolated institutions rather than a coherent system of justice; see L Sossin and J Baxter, 'Ontario's Administrative Tribunal Clusters: A Glass Half-Full or Half-Empty for Administrative Justice' (2012) 12 *Oxford Commonwealth Law Journal* 157, 158 noting, '[i]ncreasingly, it seems that the very structures and modes of organization behind the delivery of administrative justice may actually pose barriers for users, even as they separate individual tribunals from the shared knowledge, practices and infrastructure that a more rational and explicitly coordinated administrative justice system would have to offer. The challenge now squarely in front of reformers is to identify suitable approaches to institutional change that will thread these disparate elements into a more coherent whole'. This may be a valid concern although one might wish to see empirical evidence that lay people are disadvantaged by inconsistent approaches across tribunals particularly when many will only ever access one type, so the learning is new and isolated to that body. Responding to context might also mean that processes are more intuitive.

[91] N Komesar, *Imperfect Alternatives: Choosing Institutions in Law, Economics, and Public Policy* (University of Chicago Press, 1994).

[92] E Rubin, 'The New Legal Process, the Synthesis of Discourse and the Microanalysis of Institutions' (1995–96) 109 *Harvard Law Review* 1393, 1421 (citing Komesar, *Imperfect Alternatives* (n 91)).

[93] Fallon, 'Legitimacy and the Constitution' (n 36) 1796. The normative, as Foucault wrote, is inherently value-laden, M Foucault, *Discipline and Punish: The Birth of the Prison* (A Sheridan trans, Vintage, 1979) 184.

[94] L Friedman, *Law and Society: An Introduction* (Prentice Hall, 1977) 139 (arguing only procedural, input-based legitimacy is relevant to determining the legitimacy of a legal institution not outputs); *cf* M Power, *The Audit Society: Rituals of Verification* (Clarendon Press, 1997); Thomas (n 36) 751, fn 116, quoting Buchanan who argues that 'outputs are really concerned with justice – which is an ideal standard – as opposed to legitimacy, which is a threshold concept': A Buchanan and RO Keohane, 'The Legitimacy of Global Governance Institutions' in R Wolfrum and Volker Röben (eds), *Legitimacy in International Law* (Springer, 2008) 34.

[95] Rubin, 'From Coherence to Effectiveness: (n 79) 344, citing Habermas – 'procedure … can never legitimate a legal order'. Perhaps so but this does not mean that it cannot form one part of an integrated whole that contributes toward legitimacy.

the *interactional process* that promotes adjudicative integrity and thus institutional legitimacy. The fact that the institution acknowledges and responds to the composite elements – the nature of problems, impact on law and adjudication, principle and procedure – is what matters.

Finally, some commentators have described the discipline of environmental law as 'incoherent' and 'makeshift', irredeemably so because this reflects the inherent nature of environmental problems themselves.[96] But the argument running through this book is that adjudication can provide a stabilising influence in this context. Environmental problem-solving is located in institutions and institutional practices can provide a necessary stable structure *if* they are appropriately responsive to the nature of the problems they are addressing.[97] Being appropriately responsive will, I argue, foster intelligibility, coherence and normative legitimacy.[98] The interactional theory proposed by this book enables stable frames for environmental adjudication to be developed. If those frames are further articulated and acknowledged, they may provide common ground, enabling us to discuss and debate the appropriate form, functions, duties and powers of particular ECs from a shared set of premises.

[96] O Pedersen, 'Modest Pragmatic Lessons for a Diverse and Incoherent Environmental Law' (2013) 33 *OJLS* 103, 104.

[97] Bell describes a 'nested idea': '[t]he application of legal principles and interpretation of legal rules are nested in institutions, and those institutions adopt particular procedures and maintain particular values', see J Bell, 'The Importance of Institutions' in M Adams and D Heirbaut (eds), *The Method and Culture of Comparative Law* (Hart Publishing, 2014) 217.

[98] Note that the theory I develop is subtly different from simple pragmatism (see, eg, Pedersen (n 96). Those who rely on pragmatism alone have no answer to the challenges to governance and legitimacy created by ECs. Pragmatism does not address the incompleteness of the three frames explored in ch 3. In contrast to pragmatists, I am trying to fix one centrifugal point around which other elements can swirl (rather than have every element unfixed and swirling). What I *am* fundamentally trying to do is kick back against the idea that environmental law is a mess, for good reason, and that it will never change.

2

Specialist Environment Courts: Mapping the Landscape

IN THE LAST decade, there has been a remarkable global growth in specialist bodies adjudicating over environmental disputes.[1] By 2016 there were over 1,200 specialist environment courts (ECs) in over 44 jurisdictions, which was a three-fold increase in seven years.[2] Accordingly, many ECs are at a relatively early stage of development. Some of the oldest ECs are found in Australasia;[3] some of the newest in India[4] and China.[5] Within other jurisdictions, including the UK, the jurisdiction of relatively embryonic ECs is being expanded iteratively.[6] The reasons for this phenomenon are many and varied[7] but in their work for the United Nations, George and Kathryn Pring summarise that

> judges interpreting environmental law at all levels are faced with an increasingly complex legal system, one in which international environmental laws, emerging international environmental principles and new international standards and best practices overlie an already complicated framework of domestic environmental and land use laws. When one adds to the judges' challenges the necessity of evaluating complex and rapidly changing scientific and technical evidence, predicting future impacts and

[1] N Robinson 'Ensuring Access to Justice Through Environmental Courts' (2012) 29 *Pace Environmental Law Review* 363, 381.

[2] G Pring and C Pring, *Environmental Courts and Tribunals: A Guide for Policy Makers* (UNEP, 2016) 1. Further see D Smith, 'Environmental courts and tribunals: changing environmental and natural resources law around the globe' (2018) 36 *Journal of Energy & Natural Resources Law* 137, 138, reporting the number may be as high as 1,500 in 2018.

[3] eg, Queensland Planning and Environment Court was established in 1965; New South Wales Land and Environment Court (NSWLEC) became a superior court of record in 1979; the Environment Court of New Zealand has existed in a similar form since 1953.

[4] GN Gill, 'Environmental Justice in India: The National Green Tribunal and Expert Members' (2016) 5 *Transnational Environmental Law* 175.

[5] AL Wang and J Gao, 'Environmental Courts and the Development of Environmental Public Interest Litigation in China' (2010) 3 *Journal of Court Innovation* 37.

[6] R Macrory, 'The Long and Winding Road – Towards an Environmental Court in England and Wales' (2013) 25 *JEL* 371; R Macrory, 'The Role of the First Tier Environment Tribunal' (2012) 17 *Judicial Review* 54. For an update on the UK's First Tier Environment Tribunal jurisdiction, see HM Courts and Tribunals Service, *General Regulatory Chamber (Environment) rules and rights of appeal (T98A)* (2014), available at: www.gov.uk/government/publications/general-regulatory-chamber-environment-rules-and-rights-of-appeal-t98a.

[7] Including the massive growth in international environmental law (IEL) and consequent development of IEL principles, especially access to justice, in national laws; push by civil society; support by international financial aid organisations; and shortcomings of the generic court service, see Pring and Pring, *Environmental Courts and Tribunals* (n 2) part 1.2.

> balancing the conflicting economic, social and environmental demands of sustainable development, it is no wonder that there is a widespread movement toward the specialized expertise found in [environment courts and tribunals].[8]

However, a number of ECs predate the complex regulatory architecture of modern environmental law, having initially been established to adjudicate over discrete issues. For example, the Swedish EC was established as a water court in the early 1900s[9] and the New Zealand EC only adjudicated over town and country planning disputes until 1991[10] – such limitations being in sharp contrast to the expansive jurisdictional reach they both now have to adjudicate over the sustainable use of natural and physical resources in their nations.[11]

This chapter reports on the EC phenomenon. It begins by mapping the legal landscape and considers specialist environmental adjudication taking place at present. In particular, it notes the unusual admix of form and function in ECs, and provides illustrations of their dynamic and creative nature. The first part of the chapter surveys the academic literature and highlights that the international scholarship on ECs is predominantly promotional, with few scholars critiquing or, as yet, attempting to theorise the phenomenon.[12]

The second part of the chapter considers the legal nature of two ECs in detail: the Environment Court of New Zealand (NZEnvC) and the New South Wales Land and Environment Court (NSWLEC). These bodies act as case studies throughout the book as they are two of the oldest environment courts in the world; are seen as role models for the development of other ECs;[13] are charged with decisions that collectively have significant implications for environmental, socio-cultural and economic wellbeing in their nations; and many of the creative features found in ECs are practised by or present within them.[14] Over time however, their creativity and responsiveness have created tensions and the discussion in both nations has moved from a promotional one to a much harsher

[8] ibid, 9.

[9] A Bengtsson, 'Specialised courts for environmental matters – the Swedish solution' (2017) 29 *Environmental Law & Management* 115, 115.

[10] See text following n 109 below.

[11] Under the Resource Management Act 1991 (NZ) (RMA) and the Swedish Environmental Code 1999.

[12] With the notable exception of Gita Gill's work, see, eg, GN Gill, 'Mapping the Power Struggles of the National Green Tribunal of India: The Rise and Fall?' [2018] *Asian Journal of Law and Society* 1.

[13] G Pring and C Pring, *Greening Justice: Creating and Improving Environmental Courts and Tribunals* (World Resources Institute, 2009) 110; M Grant, *Environmental Court Project: Final Report* (DETR, 2000); DW Kaniaru, 'Environmental Courts and Tribunals: The Case of Kenya' (2012) 29 *Pace Environmental Law Review* 566, 580; D Amirante, 'Environmental Courts in Comparative Perspective: Preliminary Reflections on the National Green Tribunal of India' (2012) 29 *Pace Environmental Law Review* 441, 451.

[14] In the New Zealand context, this was acknowledged by Parliament noting that the Town and Country Planning Act Appeal Board (forerunner of the NZEnvC) was concerned with matters having 'far reaching effects' often involving significant sums of money that greatly exceeded the 'run-of-the-mill business that occupied the Supreme Court day by day', New Zealand Parliamentary Debates, 375 NZPD 3589.

debate. To set up the analysis, I begin by sketching a brief overview of their legal nature, and consider their particular functions, powers and responsibilities. The various concerns and criticisms levelled against these courts are examined at the end of the chapter, laying the groundwork for exploring how commentators use different frames of reference to assess the legitimacy (or illegitimacy) of the courts in the next chapter.

Both chapters two and three contribute to the pre-theory exercise by examining the present scenario, identifying tensions, reporting on actual debates taking place, and looking behind those debates to draw out the *existing* conceptual frames that critics employ to make their arguments. Before starting the process of pre-theory building however it is important to map the EC landscape, and before conducting that cartography-process it is important to establish a typology, explaining what types of institutions I include in my study as an EC.

I. SPECIALIST ENVIRONMENT COURTS: A TYPOLOGY

Around the world, legal disputes concerning the use and development of the environment, or those that have ramifications for environmental wellbeing, are heard in traditional court settings, tribunals, other forms of dispute-resolution bodies, and determined through arbitration and mediation.[15] However, this book is not concerned with all forms of dispute resolution capable of determining environmental disputes but with institutions that have been deliberately designed to undertake specialist environmental adjudication. Empirical researchers charting the rise in these specialist bodies have provided a typology in order to map the field. They describe them as 'judicial or administrative bodies of government empowered to specialize in resolving environmental, natural resources, land use [planning] development, and related disputes'.[16] This specialist nature is important: empiricalists exclude from their purview generalist courts that review executive actions for legality or hear appeals on a point of law, employing generic doctrine and operating within the ordinary boundaries of civil and common law systems of procedure and evidence. They also exclude policymaking bodies situated within the executive that are solely concerned with rule formation as opposed to dispute resolution. But the remaining spectrum ranges from operationally independent courts[17] to 'green chambers' situated within existing courts (that have been given powers to develop responsive adjudicatory procedures, for example, with regard to

[15] Note Lord Carnwath's reminder of the important role that the ordinary courts play in this regard, see R Carnwath, 'Judging the environment – back to basics' (2017) 29 *Environmental Law & Management* 64.

[16] Pring and Pring, *Greening Justice* (n 13) 3.

[17] eg, NSWLEC; NZEnvC; Court of Environment and Agrarian Issues, State of Amazonas, Brazil; land and environment courts in Sweden.

standing, costs and rules of evidence)[18] to dedicated adjudicatory bodies situated within the executive, such as environmental protection authorities.[19]

Specialist environment courts and tribunals constitute a diverse range of bodies: their modes of creation differ;[20] they take varying forms; and they have may have a multiplicity of functions. Accordingly, their *legal nature* varies. In this book, I define legal nature as a three-dimensional concept: it encompasses *what* the institution is (its constitution, powers, duties, functions and procedures); *why* it was created (its purpose and value); and what its *limits* are (the limits to its powers and jurisdiction). Clearly it is important to understand the discrete legal culture and legislative regimes that individual ECs work within to capture fully their legal nature. However, surveys of ECs across jurisdictions show three dominant and important trends.

First, the growth of adjudicatory bodies external to and independent from government departments appears to be increasingly popular internationally.[21] This phenomenon may be linked to conceptions of impartiality. Noting that environmental disputes often involve the impact of executive actions upon individual rights, commentators argue that impartiality will best be facilitated by independence from government[22] or, of equal importance, the public perception of impartiality will be fostered by institutional separation.[23] These independent bodies may be described as 'courts' or 'tribunals' depending on the legal culture and constitutional arrangements in particular jurisdictions (and this factor is discussed further below). But they often take judicial or quasi-judicial forms, are chaired by judges or legally trained members,[24] and they all undertake

[18] eg, Planning and Environment Court, Queensland; Environmental Division of the Vermont Superior Court; environment courts in the Philippines.

[19] eg, The Environmental Appeals Board in the US Environmental Protection Agency; the Exclusive Economic Zone and Continental Shelf (Environmental Effects) Act Board of Inquiry in the New Zealand Environmental Protection Authority.

[20] They may be created by the Constitution (eg, Constitution of Kenya Art 162(2)(b) (2010)); or by special legislation (eg, Land and Environment Court Act 1979 (NSW)); or designated by Supreme Courts (eg, Administrative Order Re: Designation of Special Courts to Hear, Try and Decide Environmental Cases, SC, No 23-2003 (2008) (Phil)).

[21] Pring and Pring, *Greening Justice* (n 13) 21–22. In the UK, the need for tribunals to be independent from the relevant departments of state was one reason for the enactment of the Tribunals, Courts and Enforcement Act 2007 (see A Leggatt, *Tribunals for Users – One System, One Service* (Department for Constitutional Affairs, 2001).

[22] New Zealand Department of Justice, *The Citizen and Power: Administrative Tribunals* (Government Printer, Wellington, 1965) 10; BJ Preston, 'Characteristics of Successful Environmental Courts and Tribunals' (2014) 26 *JEL* 365, 369–72; S Abed de Zavala et al, 'An Institute for Enhancing Effective Environmental Adjudication' (2010) 3 *Journal of Court Innovation* 1, 6–8.

[23] *Gillies (AP) v Secretary of State for Work and Pensions (Scotland)* [2006] 2, [38]; see also V Madner, 'The Austrian Environmental Senate' (2010) 3 *Journal of Court Innovation* 23, 26; P Cane, 'Merits Review and Judicial Review – The ATT as Trojan Horse' (2000) 28 *Federal Law Review* 213, 218; *cf R (Alconbury Developments Ltd) v Secretary of State for the Environment, Transport and the Regions* [2001] UKHL 23 (where the Court accepted the Secretary of State was an impartial tribunal by focusing on the fact he/she was not a party).

[24] That may sit with expert lay members, eg, NSWLEC; NZEnvC; Umweltsenat (Austria); Vaasa Administrative Court (Finland); Mark-och miljödomstolar (Sweden); National Green Tribunal (India); First Tier Environmental Tribunal (UK); environmental courts in Chile; Environmental Appeals Board of British Columbia (Canada).

adjudication[25] in contrast to other forms of dispute resolution such as arbitration, conciliation, mediation and negotiation (albeit they may facilitate these other methods of dispute resolution).

Second, many ECs have a wide jurisdictional remit. For example, they may have original and appellate jurisdiction, and may combine civil powers (deciding *ex post facto* compensatory disputes) with criminal jurisdiction and powers to judicially review administrative action.[26] But an increasing number have the ability to make or review substantive decisions concerning proposed projects on the merits,[27] thus their decisions act to permit or licence activities. Accordingly, some ECs are empowered to use *ex ante* mechanisms, controlling environmental harm and regulating access to and the rate of exploitation of natural resources.[28] A number of well-established ECs have comprehensive functions that include prospective review[29] and newer ECs are being developed with this wide jurisdictional reach,[30] in part because the literature describes this model as constituting best practice in promoting access to justice and resolving environmental disputes efficiently.[31] This book is concerned with these multifunctional adjudicatory bodies and environmental adjudication that encompasses predictive decision-making, and should be read with these points in mind.

Third, ECs undoubtedly have expertise in fact-finding but a strong emerging theme is the contribution of ECs to the development of environmental law, certainly in common law jurisdictions.[32] Specialist environment courts are interpreting and applying statute law, and in doing so their interpretations 'thicken' environmental law. In determining factual disputes, some ECs are crafting the legal constraints within which they operate.[33] Some are playing an instrumental role in advancing environmental law principles.[34] Others are crystallising

[25] A concept and practice discussed in depth in ch 4.

[26] Pring and Pring, *Greening Justice* (n 13) 85.

[27] eg, NSWLEC; NZEnvC; Mark-och miljödomstolar (Sweden); Environment Court of Vermont (USA); Environmental Appeals Board of British Columbia (Canada). They may undertake first-instance trials; alternatively, they may act as appellate bodies that conduct substantive merits review (ie, having the power to remake the original merits decision in various ways) or undertake de novo appeals, see eg, NSWLEC; NZEnvC; Mark-och miljödomstolar (Sweden). For an analysis of the Australian courts' powers in this regard see E Fisher, 'Administrative Law, Pluralism and Legal Construction of Merits Review in Australian Courts and Tribunals' in L Pearson, C Harlow and M Taggart (eds), *Administrative Law in a Changing State: Essays in Honour of Mark Aronson* (Hart Publishing, 2008).

[28] eg, there is the possibility of disputes bypassing initial decision-making by the local authority and being directly referred to the NZEnvC (Resource Management Act 1991 (NZ), s 87D).

[29] eg, NSWLEC; NZEnvC; Mark-och miljödomstolar (Sweden).

[30] eg, Environment and Land Court (Kenya).

[31] Preston, 'Characteristics of Successful Environmental Courts and Tribunals' (n 22) 372–77.

[32] eg, Fisher, 'Administrative Law, Pluralism and Legal Construction of Merits Review in Australian Courts and Tribunals' (n 27) 330. In the New Zealand context, see C Warnock and M Baker-Galloway, *Focus on Resource Management Law* (LexisNexis, 2015) for many examples of the NZEnvC developing legal doctrine.

[33] See discussion in ch 6.

[34] E Scotford, *Environmental Principles and the Evolution of Environmental Law* (Hart Publishing, 2017) ch 5; GN Gill, *Environmental Justice in India: The National Green Tribunal* (Routledge, 2016) ch 4.

environmental rights.[35] Development of the law is perhaps unsurprising with ECs that are superior courts but in some nations, such as New Zealand, ECs are contributing to doctrinal developments even when they are positioned as inferior courts in the court hierarchy.[36] Environment courts appear to be acting as centrifugal forces within environmental management regimes, giving legal meaning to vague environmental objectives and bringing order to the 'messiness' of environmental problem-solving. This idea is introduced below and explained more fully in chapter six. Although I do not examine ECs in civil law countries in any detail in this book, there is a clear scholarly need to examine how those bodies may be developing a body of legal opinion that increases its persuasive and replicable quality.[37]

Before looking in greater detail at ECs, it is worth summarising key ramifications that flow from these three points because even this brief description begins to reveal how legally interesting ECs are. As explained above, many ECs have merged functions – combining prospective review and powers to evaluate and enforce liability for environmental harm. Of necessity, this *ex ante-ex post facto* combination involves the assessment of public benefit and (potential) impact on private rights, and it is this unusual mix of institutional form and function that creates challenges for theorists and legally trained commentators. *Ex ante* powers are usually reserved to the executive members of government because they are perceived to have greater institutional competence in this regard. Bestowing power on ECs to prospectively review and licence activities will mean that they require different dispute-resolution approaches to those traditionally employed by generalist courts. Wider decision-making discretion may be needed. The Prings advocate for 'more creative "problem-solving" processes to balance the social, economic, and environmental impacts of proposed developments and programs'.[38] Yet even when exercising these *ex ante*-type functions, the reasoned decisions of some ECs are undoubtedly contributing to the creation of *law*.[39] Fundamentally, as I explore throughout this book, specialist environment courts appear to be important institutional components of what Black has described as 'polycentric or de-centered regulatory regimes', wherein 'responsibility for addressing collective action problems are dispersed through

[35] S Okong'o, 'Environmental adjudication in Kenya: a reflection on the early years of the Environment and Land Court of Kenya' (2017) 29 *Environmental Law & Management* 103; CB Soyapi, 'Environmental Protection in Kenya's Environment and Land Court' (2019) 31 *JEL* 151; GN Gill, 'Human rights and environmental protection in India: the judicial journey from public interest litigation to the National Green Tribunal' in A Grear and E Grant (eds), *Thought, Law, Rights and Action in the Age of Environmental Crisis* (Edward Elgar, 2015).

[36] C Warnock and O Pedersen, 'Environmental Adjudication: Mapping the Spectrum and Identifying a Fulcrum' [2017] *PL* 643, discussing the critical role that the Environment Court of New Zealand (an inferior court) has played in the development of environmental law doctrine in New Zealand. See also Bengtsson (n 9) 124.

[37] TG Watkin, *An Historical Introduction to Modern Civil Law* (Routledge, 2017) 8–9.

[38] Pring and Pring, *Greening Justice* (n 13) 27.

[39] Warnock and Pedersen (n 36).

multiple actors'.[40] The next part of the chapter considers the novel forms and creative functions that have emerged in ECs, and the way in which ECs have been assessed in the literature in more specific detail.

II. SPECIALIST ENVIRONMENT COURTS AS DYNAMIC ADJUDICATORY FORMS

Despite the relative newness of many ECs, there is a large international literature on the subject. Much is promotional in that it lauds the advantages of ECs. For example, it considers how ECs promote access to justice by facilitating distributive justice (the fair distribution of environmental benefits and harms), procedural justice (how are decisions are made and who has influence), and justice as recognition (who and what is recognised and valued).[41] Specialist environment courts are seen as fostering judicial expertise and environmental literacy,[42] and they can have an important ethical dimension, acting as 'a powerful catalyst of societal movement in the direction of an environmental ethic'.[43] In the Chinese context, Zhang and Zhang suggest that they 'effectively determine not only the legal aspects of disputes but also the non-legal aspects of a dispute' including enhancing environmental awareness.[44] In another study, environment courts in China were found to 'significantly increase corporate environmental investment' through both direct and indirect pressure.[45] In the Philippines, judicial members of ECs are seen by the wider populace to have a particular understanding of 'the philosophy of environmentalism and ecologism'.[46]

Of interest, much writing celebrates the dynamic, innovative nature of ECs. The judiciary is seen as the important partner to other branches of government in creating responses to environmental problems and ECs are viewed as crucial in 'promoting environmental governance, upholding the rule of law and in ensuring a fair balance between environmental, social and developmental

[40] J Black, 'Constructing and contesting legitimacy and accountability in polycentric regulatory regimes' (2008) 2 *Regulation & Governance* 137, 139.

[41] BJ Preston, 'The effectiveness of the law in providing access to environmental justice: an introduction' (11th IUCN Academy of Environmental Law Colloquium, Hamilton New Zealand, June 2013); G Walker, *Environmental Justice: Concepts, Evidence and Politics* (Routledge, 2012).

[42] H Woolf, 'Are the Judiciary Environmentally Myopic?' (1992) 4 *JEL* 1; P McAuslan, 'The Role of Courts and Other Judicial Type Bodies in Environmental Management' (1991) 3 *JEL* 195; BJ Preston, 'Benefits of Judicial Specialization in Environmental Law: The Land and Environment Court of New South Wales as a Case Study' (2011–12) 29 *Pace Environmental Law Review* 396.

[43] S Fulton 'The Rule of Law and Environmental Adjudication' (International Symposium on Environmental Courts and Tribunals, Pace Law School New York, April 2011).

[44] Zhang Minchun and Zhang Bao 'Specialised Environmental Courts in China: Status Quo, Challenges and Responses' (2012) 30 *Journal of Energy & Natural Resources Law* 361, 368.

[45] Qi Zhang, Zhi Yu and Dongmin Kong, 'The real effect of legal institutions: Environmental courts and firm environmental protection expenditure' (2019) 98 *Journal of Environmental Economics and Management* 1, 2.

[46] HG Davide Jr and S Vinson, 'Green Courts Initiative in the Philippines' (2010) 3 *Journal of Court Innovation* 121, 130.

considerations'.[47] The NSWLEC has been described as 'leading' the development of ecologically sustainable development.[48] The National Green Tribunal of India has developed *suo motu* jurisdiction in order to better provide for 'environmental protection and human welfare',[49] the Writ of Kalikasan was developed by the Supreme Court in the Philippines enabling environmental rights cases to be brought directly to court,[50] and the Land and Environment Court of Kenya, whilst of relatively recent origin, is developing a strong human rights-based environmental jurisprudence.[51] Some courts directly contribute to the development of environmental policy[52] or order regulatory authorities to create appropriate environmental standards.[53] For all these reasons, ECs are seen as norm-creating bodies. The creation of statutory regimes premised upon or with the explicit purpose of sustainable development in all its guises[54] – a concept that contains competing values of undefined scope[55] – may also serve to increase the norm-creating role of ECs. The (now retired) presiding judge of the Environmental Court of Appeal in Sweden has described the Swedish environment courts as having a deliberate role in 'weighing' different interests and determining 'the correct balance point' between economic benefits and environmental harm.[56]

Specialist environment courts also have a role in filling in the interstices in environmental regulation and '[w]here environmental laws and values are undeveloped … can add flesh to the skeletal form of those existing laws and values'.[57] A good example is provided by the Planning Principles created by the Land and Environment Court of New South Wales, that constitute a published

[47] Preston, 'Benefits of Judicial Specialization in Environmental Law' (n 42) 397–98; B Preston, 'The role of environmental courts and tribunals in promoting the rule of law and ensuring equal access to justice for all' (2017) 29 *Environmental Law & Management* 72.

[48] B Preston, 'Leadership by the Courts in Achieving Sustainability' (2010) 6 *Resource Management Theory & Practice* 17.

[49] Gill, 'Environmental Justice in India: The National Green Tribunal and Expert Members' (n 4) 198.

[50] J Maninang, 'Writ of Kalikasan and the right to environment' (2019) 4 *University of of Mindanao International Multdisciplinary Research Journal* 95.

[51] Okong'o (n 35); Soyapi (n 35).

[52] The NZEnvC has power to do this and much of its jurisprudence concerns the development of resource management plans for localities, see Warnock and Baker-Galloway (n 32) ch 5 for an overview and see *Manawatu-Wanganui Regional Council One Plan Appeals* [2012] NZEnvC 182 for an example.

[53] GN Gill, 'The National Green Tribunal: Evolving Adjudicatory Dimensions' (2019) 49 *Environmental Policy and Law* 153, 156.

[54] eg, RMA, s 5; Sustainable Planning Act 2009 (Queensland), s 3; and Environmental Protection Act 1994 (Queensland), s 3; Environmental Planning and Assessment Act 1979 (NSW), s 1.3; Milojobalk [Environmental Code] 1999 (Sweden) Pt 1, Ch 1, s 1; Environment and Land Court Act 2011 (Kenya), s 18.

[55] SG Sigurdson, 'Courts and Tribunals Through a Sustainability Lens: Questions and New Expectations' in Shi-Ling Hsu and P Molinari (eds), *Sustainable Development and the Law: People – Environment – Culture* (Canadian Institute for the Administration of Justice, 2008) 40.

[56] U Bjallas 'Experiences of Sweden's Environmental Courts' (2010) 3 *Journal of Court Innovation* 177, 183.

[57] Preston, 'Characteristics of Successful Environmental Courts and Tribunals' (n 22) 391; Leslie A Stein *Principles of Planning Law* (Oxford University Press, 2008) ch 5; L Pearson, 'Policy, Principles and Guidance: Tribunal rule-making' (2012) 3 *Public Law Review* 16, 16.

collection of principles developed in judgments. The Chief Judge describes them as 'rule making by adjudication' that provide 'guidance for other decision-makers, predictability for those who might apply for review, and ... internal consistency in decision-making'.[58] In this way the Court itself provides greater calculability as to how legal disputes will be resolved in specific fact scenarios, in turn narrowing the wide discretion bestowed upon the Court by the legislature. But those rules have been developed within real-life environmental disputes that assess expert evidence and consider legal submissions, thus they reflect the results of iterative legal problem-solving. Specialist environment courts have also played a significant role in developing environmental law principles within their own jurisdictions. For example, many have given greater meaning to sustainable development,[59] employed the 'polluter pays' principle through various mechanisms,[60] and adapted the precautionary principle for use in their own legal cultures.[61] In some instances, ECs have widened the meaning of law, going beyond positivist state law by recognising indigenous customary law in appropriate cases, thereby drawing upon an expanded range of legal principles.[62] Given their expert nature, higher courts may adopt a deferential approach to jurisprudence created by ECs.[63] Although the specialist Environment Court of

[58] Preston, 'Characteristics of Successful Environmental Courts and Tribunals' (n 22) 391; see also T Moore, 'The Relevance of the Court's Planning Principles to the DA Process' (Dealing with DAs in 2009, Sydney, 21 May 2009). Principles concern, eg, compliance and monitoring; the role of non-statutory policies in assessing plans; explaining the role of the precautionary principle; principles of ecological sustainable development and so on. These principles can provide the basis for expert opinion, inform lay participants and guide future decision-making at local and state government level.

[59] eg, Warnock and Baker-Galloway (n 32) ch 3; BJ Preston, 'The Role of the Judiciary in Promoting Sustainable Development: The Experience of Asia and the Pacific' (2005–06) 9 *Asia Pacific Journal of Environmental Law* 109; Gill, *Environmental Justice in India: The National Green Tribunal* (n 34) 137.

[60] Gill, 'The National Green Tribunal: Evolving Adjudicatory Dimensions' (n 53) 154; for how the NZEnvC has approached the polluter pays principle (through attaching conditions to consents, crafting financial compensation and biodiversity offsetting schemes, and in civil and criminal enforcement actions) see generally, Warnock and Baker-Galloway (n 32).

[61] See, eg, *Patrick Kamotho Githinji & Others v Resjos Enterprises Ltd & Others* [2016] *eKLR*: the ELC of Kenya drew upon and developed the meaning of the precautionary principle in the national context, which it also referred to as '*in dubio pro natura*' (see Okong'o (n 35) 108); for a comprehensive assessment of the NSWLEC in this regard see Scotford (n 34) ch 5.

[62] In New Zealand, the NZEnvC has employed tikanga Māori (akin to customary law) in a number of ways: guiding consultation and the ADR process, for example, by undertaking hui at maraes (gatherings at meeting houses); the use of whakataukī (proverbs) and waita (songs) to prove that particular areas of the environment are wāhi tapu (ancestral sacred places) and should be protected from development, and taking into account Māori concepts such as mauri (life force of a river) in legal disputes about water-takes (eg, *Wakatu Inc v Tasman DC* [2012] NZEnvC 75). See also Abed de Zavala et al (n 22) 9–10: the UNGA Permanent Forum on Indigenous Issues make clear that ECs can provide a forum to hear and learn from indigenous peoples and infuse customary law into decision-making.

[63] In the New Zealand context see: *Unison Networks Ltd v Commerce Commission* [2007] NZSC 74 [54]; *Stark v Auckland Regional Council* [1994] 3 NZLR 614, 617 (HC); see also New Zealand Law Commission, *Delivering Justice for All* (NZLC Wellington, 2004) 221 confirming deference is paid to specialist bodies.

New Zealand is an inferior court in the court hierarchy, it plays a significant role in the development of environmental law in New Zealand:[64] the Court is responsible for a vast body of jurisprudence that is seldom displaced on appeal to the higher courts.[65]

Environment courts have also created novel practices, procedures and remedies that directly respond to the challenges of environmental dispute resolution.[66] Examples include adopting a wide approach to *locus standing*[67] and eschewing costs orders against public interest litigants,[68] enabling all those impacted to access justice.[69] Members of ECs travel to litigants and conduct site visits,[70] assist unrepresented litigants by appointing 'submitters' friends',[71] and instruct *amicus curiae*.[72] Many ECs are constituted to combine legal and technical expertise, with judges sitting with expert lay commissioners.[73] Interdisciplinary benches facilitate better understanding of complex scientific evidence and have a greater facility for resolving complex ecological challenges.[74] Alternative approaches to evaluating expert opinion evidence have been developed,[75] traditional burdens of proof displaced,[76] novel forms of remedies (such as environmental compensation and biodiversity offsetting)[77] and risk management (such as adaptive management processes,[78] and the writ of continuing *mandamus*)[79] have been created by ECs. Crafting pragmatic solutions to environmental

[64] For a development of this argument, see Warnock and Pedersen (n 36).

[65] Between 2006 and 2016, the NZEnvC issued 937 substantive judgments; 210 appeals were lodged in the High Court; 53 were allowed or part allowed (5.6%); 12 were further appealed to the Court of Appeal of which two were allowed, three dismissed, five were abandoned and (at the date of communication) two remained outstanding (communication between the author and Ministry of Justice, 31 October 2016).

[66] eg, Davide Jr and Vinson (n 46) 127–29.

[67] Gill, 'Human rights and environmental protection in India' (n 35) 139–40.

[68] S Kós, 'Public participation in environmental adjudication: some further reflections' (2017) 29 *Environmental Law & Management* 60, 61.

[69] Amirante (n 13) 459.

[70] Bengtsson (n 9) 123; Gill, 'The National Green Tribunal: Evolving Adjudicatory Dimensions' (n 53) 155.

[71] New Zealand Environment Court, *Practice Note 2014* (2014), [3.2].

[72] L Newhook, D Kirkpatrick and J Hassan, 'Issues with Access to Justice in the Environment Court of New Zealand' (2017) 29 *Environmental Law & Management* 125, 133; and for an example in the New Zealand context see *Marine Farming Association Inc v Marlborough District Council* [2017] NZEnvC 197.

[73] eg, Milijoministeriet 'Decision-making Processes in Denmark' (1998–2011) para 4.1.3, available at: www2.mst.dk/udgiv/publications/1995/87-7944-324-9/html/4.htm.

[74] Gill, 'Environmental Justice in India: The National Green Tribunal and Expert Members' (n 4).

[75] *Shirley Primary School v Christchurch City Council* [1999] NZRMA 66 (NZEnvC).

[76] ibid; *Gray v Minister of Planning and Others* (2006) 152 LGERA 258 (NSWLEC); *Relator Mon Villa Boas Cueva* AgRg RE No 206748/SP (21 February 2013) (Supremo Tribunal de Justica (Brazil)); *Narmada Bachao Andolan v Union of India* (2000) 10 SCC 664 (Supreme Court of India).

[77] *JF Investments Ltd v Queenstown Lakes District Council* C48/2006 (unrep) (NZEnvC); *Royal Forest and Bird Protection Society v Gisborne District Council* W26/2009 (unrep) (NZEnvC).

[78] *Sustain Our Sounds Inc v New Zealand King Salmon Company Ltd* [2014] NZSC 40.

[79] *Metropolitan Manila Development Authority v Concerned Residents of Manila Bay* GR Nos 171947–48 (SC 18 December 2008) (Philippines).

disputes necessitates considerable expertise on the part of ECs.[80] At times, these creative solutions have been adopted by the wider branches of government, developed into policy, and adapted for other regulatory regimes.[81]

A number of ECs have developed flexible approaches to dispute management, creating 'multidoor' courts that utilise 'different adjudication pathways, Alternative Dispute Resolution (ADR) and other social services' to achieve different pathways to justice.[82] Accordingly, in addition to their adjudicative functions, they have become fora for 'proportional dispute resolution', facilitating conciliation, mediation and negotiation, and many of these bodies are moving from imposing solutions to facilitating compromise within communities. When government bodies are involved in reaching solutions through ADR, this process can play a wider role in policymaking,[83] and thus ECs can provide a site for ground-level policymaking.

In order to pre-empt environmental harm, some ECs are empowered to order injunctions, and may make orders on an *ex parte* basis.[84] When granting injunctive relief, the Kenyan Land and Environment Court and NZEnvC have been reluctant to order 'undertakings as to damages' or 'security for costs' in cases of clear public importance.[85] In an effort to increase compliance, the National Green Tribunal of India has established monitoring committees to oversee the implementation of environmental regulations for air and river pollution and solid waste management.[86] And in terms of environmental offending, various types of responsive enforcement and compliance mechanisms have evolved centred on 'green justice',[87] including restorative justice[88] and mandatory environmental

[80] *cf* the approach of the ordinary courts to judicial review in environmental cases where a decision of illegality might be reached but the public body is usually left to choose how to respond to that finding. In the English context see *R (on the application of Client Earth) No 3 v Secretary of State for Environment, Food and Rural Affairs* [2018] EWHC 315 perhaps reflecting the limit of what a judge in the ordinary administrative courts might be expected to do (thank you to an anonymous reviewer for this observation).

[81] For examples of this occurring in the New Zealand context see ch 6 and also Warnock and Pedersen (n 36) 665.

[82] G Pring and C Pring, 'Increase in Environmental Courts and Tribunals Prompts New Global Institute' (2010) 3 *Journal of Court Innovation* 11, 20; M Rackemann, 'Environmental decision-making, the rule of law and environmental justice' (2011) 7 *Resource Management Theory & Practice* 37, 64–67.

[83] J Dryzek, *The Politics of the Earth*, 2nd edn (Oxford University Press, 2005) 103.

[84] eg, Environment and Land Court Act 2011 (Kenya), s 13(7)(a); Resource Management Act 1991 (NZ), s 320; Environmental Planning and Assessment Act 1979 (NSW), s 9.46.

[85] Okong'o (n 35) 108; cases from New Zealand on the issue include *Walden v Auckland City Council* [1992] 1 NZRMA 101 (PT); *Berhampore Residents Assoc Inc v Wellington City Council* [1992] 1 NZRMA 41 (PT); *Manawatu-Wanganui Regional Council v Fugle* [2011] NZEnvC 315.

[86] Gill, 'The National Green Tribunal: Evolving Adjudicatory Dimensions' (n 53) 158–60.

[87] R Walters and D Solomon Westerhuis, 'Green crime and the role of environment courts' (2013) 59 *Crime, Law and Social Change* 279, 280.

[88] FWM McElrea 'The Role of Restorative Justice in RMA Prosecutions' (2004) 12(3) *Resource Management Journal* 1; B Preston, 'The use of restorative justice for environmental crime' (2011) 35 *Criminal Law Journal* 136.

education.[89] For example, Judge Carim Antonio established a 'night school for environmental law violators' at the Court of the Environment in the Amazonas Region of Brazil.[90] Offenders in New Zealand have been ordered to make reparations to the community by planting trees, funding environmental projects, and making public apologies at local meetings.[91]

Scholars opine that multifunctional ECs, that have a wide subject-matter jurisdiction and 'the ability to adjudicate civil, criminal and administrative issues together' constitute best practice in environmental dispute resolution.[92] Multifunctional bodies have a large array of tools in their problem-solving toolbox and can better respond to the many faceted complexities of environmental disputes. Accordingly, existing bodies with a wide jurisdiction provide role models for the development of new ECs.[93]

Because of their perceived advantages in facilitating access to environmental justice, pressure to create these specialist courts comes at times from the existing judiciary[94] and there are examples of supreme courts actually designating courts as ECs where this is within their jurisdictional remit to do so.[95] Several commentators note that these forms of innovation have occurred in China in the absence of 'central level laws, regulations or policies' even though the 'legal authority for these courts is uncertain and the innovative rules appear to conflict with existing law'.[96]

A. Summarising the Scholarship on Specialist Environment Courts

Given the brief mapping exercise undertaken above, there can be little doubt that many ECs are hugely innovative bodies, creatively responding to the demands of environmental conflict resolution and illustrative of new, dynamic forms of adjudication. One could perceive of these bodies as important sites for

[89] Pring and Pring, 'Increase in Environmental Courts and Tribunals Prompts New Global Institute' (n 82) 19.

[90] Pring and Pring, *Environmental Courts and Tribunals* (n 2) 23.

[91] See, eg, *Auckland City Council v Shaw* [2006] DCR 425 (NZ) (note that offences against the RMA are heard by an Environment Court judge sitting in the District Court). For a similar approach in the NSWLEC see *Chief Executive of the Office of Environment and Heritage v Rinaldo (Nino) Lani* [2012] NSWLEC 115.

[92] Pring and Pring, *Environmental Courts and Tribunals* (n 2) 48; Preston, 'Characteristics of Successful Environmental Courts and Tribunals' (n 22); Pring and Pring, *Greening Justice* (n 13).

[93] Pring and Pring, *Environmental Courts and Tribunals* (n 2); Grant (n 13).

[94] *Andhra Pradesh Pollution Control Board v MV Naidu* (1999) 2 SCC 718 (SCI); *Andhra Pradesh Pollution Control Board II v MV Naidu* (2001) 2 SCC 62 (SCI); and see Gill, 'Human rights and environmental protection in India' (n 35) 136–37.

[95] Davide Jr and Vinson (n 46) 123–24; Zhang, Yu and Kong (n 45) 5.

[96] Wang and Gao (n 5) 44; *cf* Zhang Minchun and Zhang Bao (n 44) 376; Jingjing Liu, 'Environmental Justice with Chinese Characteristics: Recent Developments in Using Environmental Public Interest Litigation to Strengthen Environmental Justice' (2012) 7 *Florida Agricultural & Mechanical University Law Review* 225, 254–58.

environmental governance. Moreover, within the academic literature ECs are overwhelmingly seen as a good thing, playing a critical role in an evolving environmental justice system.

In some jurisdictions, scholars have aligned these innovative bodies with fundamental constitutional, human rights or rule-of-law norms (particularly access to justice), and to that extent justify them by reference to external legitimising frames.[97] Gill has employed the concept of 'epistemic communities' drawn from political science as a legitimising tool for mixed benches[98] and used 'change management theory' to explain the rise and fall in popularity of the National Green Tribunal of India.[99] However, this approach is rare. To date, ECs have seldom been viewed through different analytical frames in the literature and the deeper theoretical legitimacy and resonance of their wide functions are often ignored. Of course, there are many different types of specialised courts and tribunals around the world[100] and a flourishing socio-legal approach to understanding these bodies has emerged.[101] But specialised forms of adjudication have had 'little impact on mainstream public law scholarship',[102] nor been the subject of much legal theorising.[103] Given their impact upon traditional conceptions of the law-state[104] this is surprising. Specialist environmental adjudication creates particularly acute challenges for theorists, policymakers and

[97] Preston, 'Characteristics of Successful Environmental Courts and Tribunals' (n 22) 383; EJ Hollo, P Vihervuori and K Kuusiniemi, 'Environmental Law and Administrative Courts in Finland' (2010) 3 *Journal of Court Innovation* 51, 59; C Warnock, 'Environment and the Law: the normative force of context and constitutional challenges' (2020) 3 *JEL* (forthcoming).

[98] Gill, 'Environmental Justice in India: The National Green Tribunal and Expert Members' (n 4) 181.

[99] Gill, 'Mapping the Power Struggles of the National Green Tribunal of India' (n 12) 4.

[100] Created to adjudicate disputes ranging from employment, immigration, welfare benefits and mental health to competition laws, and to manage antisocial behaviour such as drug or therapeutic courts see, eg, Leggatt (n 21) (UK); New Zealand Law Commission, *Delivering Justice for All* (n 63); Administrative Review Council, *Better Decisions: Commonwealth Merits Review Tribunals* (Australian Government Publishing Service, 1995); R Creyke (ed), *Tribunals in the Common Law World* (The Federation Press, 2008); KYW Holst, 'A Good Score? Examining Twenty Years of Drug Courts in the United States and Abroad' (2010) 45 *Valparaiso University Law Review* 73.

[101] eg, H Genn, 'Tribunals and Informal Justice' (1993) 56 *MLR* 393; M Adler, 'Tribunal Reform: Proportionate Dispute Resolution and the Pursuit of Administrative Justice' (2006) 69 *MLR* 958; N Wikeley, 'Burying Bell: Managing the Judicialisation of Social Security Tribunals' (2000) 63 *MLR* 475; R Thomas, 'Evaluating Tribunal Adjudication: Administrative Justice and Asylum Appeals' (2005) 25 *Legal Studies* 462; J Peay, *Tribunals on Trial: A Study of Decision-making under the Mental Health Act 1983* (Clarendon Press, 1989).

[102] G Richardson and H Genn, 'Tribunals in Transition: Resolution or Adjudication?' [2007] *PL* 116, 118.

[103] Notable exceptions include P Cane, *Administrative Tribunals and Adjudication* (Hart Publishing, 2010); M Elliot and R Thomas, 'Tribunal Justice and Proportionate Dispute Resolution' (2012) 71 *CLJ* 297; and the literature on Article I – Article III Courts in the US, eg, E Pfander, 'Article I Tribunals, Article III Courts and the Judicial Power of the United States' (2004) 118 *Harvard Law Review* 645; TE Baker, 'Federal Court Practice and Procedure: A Third Branch Bibliography' (1999) 30 *Texas Tech Law Review* 909, 1103–14.

[104] HW Arthurs, *Without the Law: Administrative Justice and Legal Pluralism in Nineteenth-Century England* (University of Toronto Press, 1985); RH Fallon, 'Of Legislative Courts, Administrative Agencies, and Article III' (1987–88) 101 *Harvard Law Review* 916.

lawyers because of its very nature,[105] and this analytical omission is problematic because it leads not only to an impoverished scholarly discourse (environmental law research is often criticised as a-theoretical, and some have suggested that it is marginalised from mainstream legal scholarship),[106] but it has also created real, practical difficulties. Drawing on the case studies explains why.

III. INTRODUCING THE CASE STUDIES: THE ENVIRONMENT COURT OF NEW ZEALAND AND THE LAND AND ENVIRONMENT COURT OF NEW SOUTH WALES

Many of the creative features found in ECs and discussed above are practised by or present within the Environment Court of New Zealand (NZEnvC) and the New South Wales Land and Environment Court (NSWLEC), and in that sense they are not atypical environment courts (ECs). In fact, they are seen as role models for the development of ECs around the world.[107] They take the best features of tribunals: specialism and expertise; flexibility and accessibility – and merge them with the best features of courts: independence; stability of personnel; impartiality; insulation from politics; transparency; the application, articulation and publication of legal precedent; and institutional 'mana'[108] – that attracts greater resourcing and quality of legal representation.[109] However, assessments of these courts in their home nations have proven to be much harsher than the general scholarship on ECs might otherwise have suggested. To anchor the discussion in the rest of the book – and to justify the need for better theorising about ECs – I explain the legal nature of the NZEnvC and the NSWLEC in greater detail and describe some of the criticisms and concerns that have been levelled against them: criticisms that flow precisely because we do not have a clear theoretical understanding of ECs.

A. The Legal Nature of the Environment Court of New Zealand

The Environment Court of New Zealand has great longevity. It is possible to trace the Court's heritage back to 1926 when the first Town-Planning Board was established, and to follow its evolution from the 1953 Town and Country Appeal

[105] See chs 3 and 5 for further discussion, and also C Warnock, 'Reconceptualising Specialist Environment Courts and Tribunals' (2017) 37 *Legal Studies* 391; Warnock and Pedersen (n 36).

[106] E Fisher et al, 'Maturity and Methodology: Starting a Debate about Environmental Law' (2009) 21 *JEL* 213.

[107] Pring and Pring, *Greening Justice* (n 13) 110; Grant (n 13); Kaniaru (n 13) 580; Amirante (n 13) 451.

[108] Taken from the Māori 'te reo' language, meaning 'prestige'.

[109] M Asimow, 'Five Models of Administrative Adjudication' (2015) 63 *American Journal of Comparative Law* 3; J King, *Judging Social Rights* (Cambridge University Press, 2012) 89.

Board and the 1977 Planning Tribunal, to the NZEnvC in 1997. While there have been changes to the constitution, functions, duties, powers and jurisdiction of the body over the years,[110] these changes have been mainly incremental apart from a significant change of form in 1953 when the previous ministerial-led Board was replaced by an independent appeal Board, headed by a legally qualified chair supported by professionally qualified members. At that time, Parliament's desire had been to provide a body that could fairly determine the difficult balance between private rights and the public good,[111] independent from central government (though guided by it), and that could travel around the country to be accessible to communities.[112] In 1991, the jurisdictional reach of the Court expanded significantly following major legislative reforms. From that point on, the Court was concerned with disputes concerning all land, air and water in New Zealand as opposed to being confined simply to town and country planning disputes.

In one sense the modern incarnation of the Environment Court is a classic judicial body. It is a court of record (that is, its decisions are recorded and reported)[113] and it is subject to the supervisory jurisdiction of the ordinary courts (appeals on a point of law are made initially to the High Court and then to the Court of Appeal and Supreme Court).[114] The Court can authoritatively determine the facts of the case (the *res judicata* doctrine),[115] interpret both statute law and planning documents (that constitute regulations in the statutory scheme), and apply the law to the facts.[116] It has powers akin to the District Court in terms of commissioning, ordering and managing evidence[117] (although in practice, the evidence and considerations of the Court are usually limited to those brought by the parties), can summons witnesses,[118] and has powers of contempt of court.[119] It tends to follow litigious procedures (although, it can control its own procedures and adopt an inquisitorial approach where appropriate),[120] and

[110] KA Palmer, *Planning and Development Law in New Zealand* (Law Book Company, 1984) 9. Examples of recent statutory vacillations include empowering the NZEnvC to determine challenges to non-notification decisions by local authorities via RMA, s 310 (previously a matter for judicial review before the High Court), suspending, and then removing that power; and introducing new stakeholder plan-making processes but removing appeal rights to the NZEnvC (see C Warnock, 'Differing conceptions of environmental democracy in New Zealand resource management law' (2016) 31 *Australian Environment Review* 253).

[111] *Ideal Laundry Ltd v Petone Borough* [1957] NZLR 1038 (NZSC).

[112] New Zealand Parliamentary Debates, 299 NZPD 689.

[113] RMA, s 297.

[114] RMA, s 299.

[115] There are no merits appeals from the NZEnvC.

[116] C Warnock, 'Reconceptualising the Role of the New Zealand Environment Court' (2014) 26 *JEL* 507.

[117] RMA, s 278.

[118] RMA, s 278.

[119] RMA, s 282.

[120] L Newhook, 'The Constitution, Work, Powers and Practices in Trial and Pre-Trial Work of the Environment Court of New Zealand' (International Forum of Environment Judges, IUCN AEL Colloquium, Oslo, June 2016).

it also enforces the law (albeit has a great deal of flexibility as to the enforcement approach it takes).[121]

But the NZEnvC is a specialist court. It is both a judicial body and a court of expertise, with tenured and independent judges sitting with expert lay commissioners.[122] It is a creature of statute, empowered to determine cases under the Resource Management Act 1991 (RMA), the main environmental statute in New Zealand, and also has jurisdiction under a number of other environmental statutes.[123] The NZEnvC has wide dispute-resolution powers under the various acts that it administers including original jurisdiction[124] and appellate powers (hearing merits appeals *de novo*) in environmental and town planning disputes;[125] hearing legality appeals against compulsory acquisition of land;[126] land valuation;[127] managing ADR processes;[128] civil and criminal enforcement powers;[129] and the ability to make declarations and injunctions.[130]

The main empowering legislation of the Court, the RMA, constitutes a sprawling regulatory regime that encompasses both environmental and town planning disputes. It addresses the use, development and take of land, air, onshore and offshore water; pollution control; biodiversity and nature conservation; adaptation to climate change; and the preservation of cultural heritage, amongst other things. Present reforms also propose bringing the mitigation of climate change into the RMA.[131] In accordance with the statutory objective of the RMA, the Court must promote the 'sustainable management' of natural and physical resources in all its decisions, in order to enable 'people and communities to provide for their social, economic, and cultural well-being'.[132] Natural resources include all land, air and water, and encompass both public and private

[121] RMA, Pt 12.

[122] RMA, s 248.

[123] Including: Biosecurity Act 1993' Crown Minerals Act 1991; Electricity Act 1992; Forests Act 1949; Heritage New Zealand Pouhere Taonga Act 2014; Local Government Act 1974; Public Works Act 1981; Government Roading Powers Act 1989; Exclusive Economic Zone and Continental Shelf (Environmental Effects) Act 2012; Housing Accords and Special Housing Areas Act 2013; Land Transport Management Act 2003.

[124] RMA, s 87D.

[125] RMA, s 290.

[126] Public Works Act 1981 (NZ), s 24.

[127] H Johnson, *Report of the Registrar of the Environment Court for the 12 months ended 30 June 2017* (New Zealand Environment Court, 2017) 7.

[128] RMA, s 268.

[129] RMA, Pt 12.

[130] RMA, ss 309, 320.

[131] Resource Management Amendment Bill 2020. Important management regimes that sit outside the RMA include: the quota management system under the Fisheries Act 1996; the allocation and mining of Crown-owned minerals under the Crown Minerals Act 1991; the management of oceans outside the territorial seas under the Exclusive Economic Zone and Continental Shelf (Environmental Effects) Act 2012; the New Zealand Emissions Trading Scheme under the Climate Change Response Act 2002; the management of concessions on Crown-lands under the Conservation Act 1987, etc.

[132] RMA, s 5(2).

property.[133] How to 'promote sustainable management' of a resource – and the relative weight to be placed upon, for example, economic wellbeing as opposed to environmental protection – will be guided by the legislation and policy framework that the Court must in turn interpret or, as I explain below, may have played a role in crafting, but will also be determined by the relevant context of any given case, including the environmental effects likely to flow.[134] And so, like many ECs, the NZEnvC addresses normative conflicts and allocates risk-burdens.[135] As a result, the superior courts in New Zealand have acknowledged the need for an environmental dispute-resolution body with special expertise and skills.[136]

Under the RMA, the Court also has a role that is more traditionally thought to be for the administration: it is empowered to license specific activities for developing, taking, polluting, or using the environment, that may create adverse environmental effects.[137] In assessing environmental effects, the Court attempts to make predictive decisions about the future as opposed to fact-finding in relation to the past, adopting a precautionary approach where relevant.[138] The Court has considerable flexibility in terms of procedure, methods of interpretation, the decision-making process[139] and remedies.[140] Much of its adjudicative role concerns the assessment of expert opinion evidence as to the likelihood of harm. It tests conflicting scientific opinions within a legal frame, examining the bases for expert opinions through requirements to file evidence that explains and justifies that opinion. It employs expert witness caucusing in some scenarios, cross-examination in others, and gives a reasoned judgment explaining why particular evidence has proven more persuasive in contested disputes.[141]

The Court also has a quasi-regulatory role and is explicitly empowered under the RMA to hear and determine disputes brought to the Court concerning the content of local authority plans and policy documents.[142] It can refine planning documents to ensure that they promote the legislative requirement of

[133] RMA, s 2.

[134] *Environmental Defence Society Incorporated v Marlborough District Council* [2014] NZSC 38, [10–11].

[135] *Shirley Primary School v Christchurch City Council* (n 75).

[136] *Environmental Defence Society Incorporated v Marlborough District Council* (n 134) [150]; *New Zealand Rail Ltd v Marlborough District Council* [1994] NZRMA 70, 86 (HC).

[137] RMA, s 290 and Pt 6: either through its merits appeal function or, in some circumstances, as a first-instance decision-maker.

[138] See ch 6.

[139] With judicial and lay expert commissioners feeding into both the fact-finding and legal analysis process. For criticism of the role of lay commissioners in determining legal aspects of a case, see G Ruka and C Iorns Magallanes, 'Environmental Law or Palm-Tree Justice?' [2009] *NZLJ* 185.

[140] Including civil, criminal and reflexive responses (eg, defendants can undertake restorative justice projects that will be taken into account by the court), see RMA, Pt 12.

[141] Newhook, Kirkpatrick and Hassan, 'Issues with Access to Justice in the Environment Court of New Zealand' (n 72) 125–26; Newhook, 'The Constitution, Work, Powers and Practices in Trial and Pre-Trial Work of the Environment Court of New Zealand' (n 120).

[142] RMA, ss 290, 293.

'sustainable management', and it gives them final approval.[143] Local authority planning instruments have the status of regulations in the legislative scheme and the NZEnvC is the *only* court in New Zealand that can alter regulations on the substantive merits rather than reviewing for legality. One way of conceiving of the Court's plan change function is to regard it as a quality control process for scrutinising delegated legislation against the primary legislation. The Court's role ensures 'fidelity to legislative purpose'[144] and oversees administrative accountability. Crafting the final form of local authority plans is a function that has been consistently reserved to independent dispute-resolution bodies since the inception of the first Town-Planning Board in 1926.[145]

The fact that the Environment Court has merits review powers, rather than being confined to legality review is an important component of the entire regulatory scheme, albeit readers from some jurisdictions will regard this approach as unusual.[146] The New Zealand Law Commission has stated that a right of appeal on contested law and facts is fundamental to the system of justice and rule of law in New Zealand, particularly where administrative decisions impact individual rights.[147] Within resource management, law, policy, discretion and facts can be hard to tease apart, as I discuss in this book.[148] To reiterate, the law often contains proactive tests that look to the future rather than the past – 'should mining be permitted, should biodiversity be preserved?'[149] Rather than determining facts, first-instance decision-makers are very often making predictions based on opinion evidence as to likelihood of effects,[150] and opinions are inevitably a mix of facts, values, methodological choices, biases and heuristics.[151] Further, the legal tests are multifaceted and will often require first-instance

[143] For a judicial explanation as to why the Court has this oversight in relation to local community plans, see *High Country Rosehip Orchards Ltd (and others) v Mackenzie District Council* [2011] NZEnvC 387, [462] (ie, to ensure against short-term political thinking with regard to natural capital, the Court compares its neutral role to that of the Reserve Bank in respect of financial capital under the Reserve Bank of New Zealand Act 1979).

[144] J Jowell, 'The Limits of Law in Urban Planning' (1977) 30 *Current Legal Problems* 63, 78.

[145] Palmer, *Planning and Development Law in New Zealand* (n 110) 9.

[146] A strong tradition in English public law is that courts should not determine the merits of decisions made by public bodies in judicial review. For the difficulties this approach causes in environmental adjudication, see Warnock and Pedersen (n 36).

[147] New Zealand Law Commission, *Delivering Justice for All* (n 63) 4, 220; New Zealand Law Commission, *Tribunals in New Zealand* (Wellington, 2008) 34; New Zealand Law Commission, *Seeking Solutions: Options for change to the New Zealand court system* (Wellington, 2002) 207; Report of the Legislative Advisory Committee on Administrative Tribunals (Report No 3, 1988) cited in New Zealand Law Commission, *The Structure of the Courts* (Wellington, 1989) 285; appeals from tribunals should also be 'general appeals on fact and law' see New Zealand Law Commission, *Tribunal Reform* (Wellington, 2008) 15. In the Australian context see Administrative Review Council, *What decisions should be subject to merits review?* (AGPS, 1999) [2.4].

[148] See also Warnock, 'Reconceptualising Specialist Environment Courts and Tribunals' (n 105).

[149] D Fisher, 'The jurisprudential structure of environmental law' in D Fisher (ed), *Research Handbook on Fundamental Concepts of Environmental Law* (Edward Elgar, 2016) 7.

[150] See, eg, *Shirley Primary School v Christchurch City Council* (n 75).

[151] L Daston and P Galison, *Objectivity* (Zone Books, 2007).

decision-makers to factor in policy guidance that will attract differing legal weight (as I discuss below, in chapter three). In these circumstances, siloing off 'law' from facts, policy and discretion – a necessary feature of traditional judicial review – becomes difficult. And given the deference paid to the discretion of expert decision-makers in technical areas,[152] legality review may not provide an appropriate accountability mechanism. For all these reasons, legality review becomes more challenging; merits review becomes more apposite.[153] The New Zealand Law Commission notes that apart from the ability to 'correct errors affecting individual citizens' there are many public advantages to merits review, including the chance to 'clarify and develop the law', 'improve the quality of primary decision-making … guard against the abuse of powers, and to ensure consistency in the way that powers are exercised' and promote 'executive accountability'.[154] Debates in the New Zealand Parliament noted that the precursor to the NZEnvC, the 1953 Town and Country Appeal Board that also had merits appeal powers, was 'much asked for by town-planning authorities' as 'they like to feel that if there is a mistake another mind can be brought to bear to correct it … they do not want to feel that they are tyrants'.[155]

B. Is the Environment Court a Court or a Tribunal?

One final point of note concerns the constitutional place of the Environment Court of New Zealand. Is it really a court? One might think that a more apt classification for the Court would be 'statutory tribunal': the NZEnvC does not have a general jurisdiction[156] and as the UK Upper Tier Tribunal has stated, statutory '[j]urisdiction is fundamental to the operation of a *statutory tribunal*, because it has no power to act outside its jurisdiction' (emphasis added).[157] But the RMA

[152] In the New Zealand context see *Unison Networks Ltd v Commerce Commission* (n 63) [54]; see also New Zealand Law Commission, *Tribunals in New Zealand* (n 147) 125.

[153] Warnock and Pedersen (n 36); E Fisher, 'Environmental impact assessment: "setting the law ablaze"' in D Fisher (ed), *Research Handbook on Fundamental Concepts of Environmental Law* (Edward Elgar, 2016) 453. For concerns in relation to the current Environment Bill 2019–21 (UK) see Maria Lee, 'The Environment Bill: A framework for progressive environmental law?' (*Brexit and Environment Blog*, 18 October 2019), available at: www.brexitenvironment.co.uk/2019/10/18/framework-progressive-environmental-law; Maria Lee, 'The next generation of environmental law: Environmental accountability and beyond in the draft Environment (Principles and Governance) Bill', UCL European Institute: Brexit Insights, available at: www.ucl.ac.uk/european-institute/news/2019/mar/next-generation-environmental-law.

[154] New Zealand Law Commission, *Tribunals in New Zealand* (n 147) 42, [2.32]; New Zealand Law Commission, *Seeking Solutions: Options for change to the New Zealand court system* (n 147) 207.

[155] New Zealand Parliamentary Debates, 299, 799.

[156] The main constituting statute for inferior courts in New Zealand – the District Courts Act 1947 (NZ) – provides for the constituent features of district courts as 'courts of record, possessing civil [tort, contract] and criminal jurisdiction', including an equitable jurisdiction, ss 3, 34.

[157] *Fish Legal v Information Commissioner* [2015] UKUT 52 (ACC), [18]. Note, adjudicative bodies that contain non-legal expert decision-makers and flexible rules of procedure tend to be classified as tribunals in the British context and tribunals are increasingly favoured for resolving environmental disputes.

refers to the NZEnvC (as it did to the Planning Tribunal before it) as a 'court of record'.[158] Further, the Ministry of Justice includes the Environment Court within the Specialist Courts Unit[159] and the New Zealand Law Commission included the NZEnvC along with other specialist courts in reviews of the *court* system[160] and excluded it from reviews of statutory tribunals.[161] However, there is no clarity on this point constitutionally in New Zealand, and the delineation between courts and tribunals in the UK is similarly opaque. Unlike, for example, the Australian or American constitutions,[162] New Zealand's collection of constitutional documents does not identify which bodies are courts and which are not. The higher courts in New Zealand have had to grapple with what constitutes a 'judicial function' in a number of cases.[163] The Court of Appeal set down a general guide to assist deliberations (for example, one should consider whether the members of the relevant body are appointed by the state; whether the body fulfils a public function and has enforcement powers; whether proceedings before the body are described in statute as ' judicial proceedings') but essentially the issue has to be dealt with on a case-by-case basis and the relevant context taken into account.[164] The NZEnvC certainly has some of the features found in ordinary courts. It meets the criteria established by the Court of Appeal mentioned above, but as explained previously it also has many unusual features that you would not expect to find in a court, for example, the role of lay commissioners in decision-making,[165] its ability to alter policy and planning documents on the merits,[166] its flexible approach to evidence,[167] its ability to impose conditions precedent[168] or to remain seized of a matter in order to monitor the environmental effects post-consent[169] and so on.

[158] RMA, s 247. Although, there is no special magic about the term 'court of record' – it means that proceedings before the Court are recorded and subject to the supervisory jurisdiction of the higher courts, as are many other administrative and adjudicative bodies, tribunals and specialist courts in New Zealand, see New Zealand Law Commission, *Tribunals in New Zealand: An Issues Paper* (NZLC IP6, Wellington, 2007) ch 8.

[159] Johnson (n 127) 5.

[160] New Zealand Law Commission, *Delivering Justice for All* (n 63) although the Law Commission has not directly addressed the issue of the NZEnvC's legal nature.

[161] New Zealand Law Commission, *Tribunal Reform* (n 147).

[162] Constitution of the Commonwealth of Australia, Chapter III; Constitution of the United States of America, Art III (although note Cane, *Administrative Tribunals and Adjudication* (n 103) 5 (not completely clear-cut in the US).

[163] eg, *Waikato Bay of Plenty District Law Society v Harris* [2006] 3 NZLR 755 (CA); *Daimler AG v Sany Group Co Ltd* [2014] NZCA 421; see also A Beck, 'What is a Court?' [2014] *NZLJ* 337.

[164] *Waikato Bay of Plenty District Law Society v Harris* (n 163). When the higher courts were tasked with characterising planning appeal hearings before the Town and Country Planning Appeal Board, they described them as 'quasi-judicial' see, eg, *Denton and Others v Auckland City and Another* [1969] NZLR 256 (SC), 259; see also *New Zealand Dairy Board v Okitu Co-operative Dairy Co Ltd* [1953] NZLR 366 (CA) (quasi-judicial nature ascertained from empowering statute; decision impacting upon individual rights points to need for quasi-judicial proceedings).

[165] RMA, s 253.

[166] RMA, s 293.

[167] Commission of Inquiry Act 1908 (NZ), s 4B(1); RMA, s 276(2).

[168] *Director-General of Conservation v Marlborough District Council* [2004] 3 NZLR 127 (HC).

[169] *Sustain Our Sounds Inc v New Zealand King Salmon Company Ltd* (n 78).

Within New Zealand, as in the UK, the differences between courts and tribunals are often hard to articulate clearly. Writing in 1974, Farmer noted that 'no one has provided a satisfactory definition of what is an ordinary court'.[170] Likewise, in the UK context Genn notes that the term tribunal is not a 'term of art'[171] and 'it is, in fact, impossible to provide a definition'.[172] In the UK, the Tribunals, Courts and Enforcement Act 2007 established the two-tier tribunal system to consolidate and streamline tribunal justice, but not every institution that might be considered a tribunal is included (the Planning Inspectorate is excluded, for example). Although the New Zealand Law Commission created a workable definition of tribunals in its 2008 study (in order to draw a line around the bodies that were to be included in the study and those to be excluded), it acknowledged the relative arbitrariness of this definition.[173] Abel-Smith and Stevens suggest that any differences that do exist between courts and tribunals 'are not in any sense fundamental but at most are differences in degree'[174] – they are all undertaking adjudication.[175] And noting the difficulties, Shapiro suggests that it would be wise to accept

> the vast variety of actual social institutions and behaviours loosely related to that concept without worrying about where 'true courtness' ends and something else begins. For in reality there are few if any societies in which courts are so clearly delineated as to create absolute boundaries between them and other aspects of the political system.[176]

Today it is possible to perceive of a spectrum of adjudicative bodies in New Zealand (and other jurisdictions such as the UK and New South Wales) falling between dispute-resolution bodies housed in the administrative departments of state at one end and the ordinary courts at the other, with a melee of variations in between. But where any particular body is seen to fall on the spectrum is often more a matter of historical happenstance or retrospective constitutional 'housekeeping' than clearly articulated reason. In the UK, tribunals fall within the judicial branch of government but as Richardson and Genn note:

> There is nothing inevitable about this judicial model. Tribunals do not have to lie within the judicial arm of government with all the necessity for demonstrable independence that that involves. In Australia they are seen as part of the executive.[177]

[170] JA Farmer, *Tribunals and Government* (Weidenfeld and Nicolson, 1974) 189.

[171] C Stebbings, *Legal Foundations of Tribunals in Nineteenth Century England* (Cambridge University Press, 2006) 3.

[172] Genn, 'Tribunals and Informal Justice' (n 101) 394.

[173] New Zealand Law Commission, *Tribunals in New Zealand* (n 147) 38–41.

[174] B Abel-Smith and RB Stevens, *In Search of Justice: Society and the Legal System* (Allen Lane, 1968) 224. See also Farmer, *Tribunals and Government* (n 170) 184–89; P Craig, *Administrative Law* (Sweet & Maxwell, 1983) 170.

[175] eg, Franks Committee, *Report of the Committee on Administrative Tribunals and Enquiries* (Cmnd 218, 1957), finding that tribunals in the UK are part of the machinery of adjudication rather than administration.

[176] M Shapiro, *Courts: A Comparative and Political Analysis* (University of Chicago Press, 1981) 1.

[177] Richardson and Genn (n 102) 116.

To a large extent, debates about the appropriate name and status of the NZEnvC reflect these blurred constitutional boundaries. Over the last half-century parliamentary debates on the institution have consistently acknowledged its importance – given that it was concerned with matters having 'far-reaching effects' often involving significant sums of money that greatly exceeded the 'run-of-the-mill business that occupied the Supreme Court day by day' – and an underlying and frequently expressed concern was that its title should reflect its status.[178] Some argued that the body should be elevated to superior court status.[179] In 1997, the Planning Tribunal was renamed the Environment Court, which was an identical body to the Tribunal in all ways save for the name.[180] The more legalistic aspects of the institution were not related to it being renamed a court; they were already firmly in place. By way of example, it was confirmed that the Board could receive evidence on oath by 1966,[181] the body had had committal powers since 1977[182] and the chairs became tenured judges during the Planning Tribunal era.[183] Parliamentary debates from the 1950s acknowledged that while the Board had to deal with 'highly technical' matters[184] and 'its members would also certainly require a general knowledge of administration', the Board would also have 'a good deal of legal work to do'.[185] By the 1970s, the Board had developed a significant body of 'planning principles that were guides to authorities and for use in other disputes'[186] and this process of creating guiding principles and then jurisprudence never ceased.[187] Unaccompanied by any other substantial changes,[188] the renaming to 'Environment Court' in 1997 had an apparent casualness about it. As the Minister for the Environment explained to Parliament,

> the [Planning and Development] committee, having received a wide range of names in submissions, felt that, on balance, this name was the most accurate description of its role and status. So there we have an end to the matter.[189]

One fellow parliamentarian commented, 'I have to say that the word "tribunal", with its overtones of the Roman Empire, has never actually seemed to me to

[178] New Zealand Parliamentary Debates, 416 NZPD 5223.

[179] R Somerville, *Submissions on: Striking the Balance – Appeal Processes – The Specialist Environment Court* (A Review of the New Zealand Court System, New Zealand Law Commission, Wellington, 2002).

[180] RMA, s 247.

[181] New Zealand Parliamentary Debates, 347 NZPD 1587; Commissions of Inquiry Act 1908 (NZ).

[182] Town and Country Planning Act 1977 (NZ), s 142.

[183] ibid, s 131A.

[184] New Zealand Parliamentary Debates, 299 NZPD 742.

[185] New Zealand Parliamentary Debates, 299 NZPD 742.

[186] G Rosenberg, 'Planning Principles in the Light of Appeal Board Decisions' [1966] *NZLJ* 467, 467.

[187] JA Farmer, 'Town Planning Policy and the Law – A Trip in Wonderland with the Chief Justice' [1970] *NZLJ* 542, 542; Warnock and Baker-Galloway (n 32) 73–118.

[188] Resource Management Amendment Act 1996, s 6 (now RMA, s 247).

[189] New Zealand Parliamentary Debates, 557 NZDP 14313.

be particularly user-friendly'.[190] Before moving on to consider criticisms of the Court, it is important to note that these classificatory terms – '(inferior) courts', 'tribunals' and 'specialised courts' – are used in arbitrary ways in New Zealand. Arguably it is better to see them collectively in terms of a 'species of adjudication'[191] focusing on their specific adjudicative nature rather than trying to marshal them into pre-formed categories that correlate with set positions on a spectrum. This point also links to my wider argument – that is, the need to define adjudication in expansive rather than restrictive terms.

C. Criticisms and Concerns about the Environment Court of New Zealand

Perhaps inevitably, given its longevity, the focus has turned from a promotional one to one that scrutinises the Court much more carefully. Criticisms vary. Some argue that decision-making by the Court should be faster and cheaper.[192] In doing so, they align the debate with tribunals-thinking by focusing on administrative efficiencies,[193] and in fact much policy analysis of the Court is premised upon cost–benefit analysis and generic instrumentalism, a matter addressed more fully in chapter three. Others have suggested that the Court's approach to decision-making and certain of its functions and powers are unjustified and illegitimate. I want to explore these latter criticisms in a little more depth at this point because they provide a good introduction to thinking about frames for legitimacy, an exercise undertaken in the next chapter.

A Technical Advisory Group to the Minister for the Environment (the TAG) first raised questions about the legitimacy of the Court's powers in 2009. The specific concerns related to the Court's ability to determine appeals against policies and plans on the merits, and the TAG opined that 'on constitutional grounds alone' there was much to be said for abolishing what they referred to as a 'legislative' function.[194] Specifically, the TAG drew upon the separation of powers in stating:

> There is little precedent for Courts having conferred upon them responsibility for legislative functions, other than in the supervisory jurisdictional role alluded to above [ie judicial review]. The underlying constitutional reasons for this have their origins in the concept of the separation of powers which dates back at least as far as the

[190] New Zealand Parliamentary Debates, 557 NZDP 14315; see also New Zealand Government, *Resource Management Amendment Bill (No 4) as Reported from the Planning and Development Committee: Commentary* (Wellington, 1996) 5. The only explanation given is that the name-change 'is intended to better reflect its intended role and to better convey the scope of work for which the Planning Tribunal currently has jurisdiction', 5.

[191] Cane, *Administrative Tribunals and Adjudication* (n 103) 47–48.

[192] Ministry for the Environment, *Improving our Resource Management System: A Discussion Document* (Wellington, 2013); Law Commission, *Delivering Justice for All* (n 63).

[193] Genn, 'Tribunals and Informal Justice' (n 101).

[194] Ministry for the Environment, *Report of the Minister for the Environment's Technical Advisory Group* (Wellington, February 2009) 10.

> 18th century French political philosopher Montesquieu. Those who make the laws should not enforce them or interpret them. Those who interpret the laws should not themselves be the law-makers.[195]

Other concerns are premised on accountability and representative democracy: the TAG states, while 'appeals on points of law' are an entirely legitimate function for the judiciary, 'appeals on the merits of the policy direction of the plan are, however, a very different proposition' because 'judges are not accountable to the electorate for the decisions they make'.[196]

In a 2013 discussion document on proposed reforms to the RMA, the Minister for the Environment agreed with the view expressed by the TAG, albeit she extrapolated from the discrete criticism a wider concern in relation to the entirety of the Court's functions, stating that: [t]he judiciary should not be placed in the position of having to determine values or policy – this role should be played by publicly accountable, elected representatives'.[197] The background to the Minister's comments was the ongoing discussion concerning the powers of the Court to determine what constituted the 'sustainable management of resources' – a relatively wide and unconstrained statutory objective – in disputes before it,[198] and the discussion document provided the precursor to a highly controversial suggestion from government that the NZEnvC should be abolished as an independent court and its powers assumed by the District Court.[199] The suggestion was quickly withdrawn following a general outcry,[200] but nevertheless the government removed powers from the NZEnvC in relation to the major planning tasks of rebuilding Christchurch after the earthquakes in 2010 and 2011,[201] and redrafting the Auckland Plan after the merging of five city councils and the regional council into the Auckland Council (a unitary authority) in 2010.[202]

In terms of scholarly contributions, Rivers-McCombs deprecated the powers of the NZEnvC on the basis of both institutional competency and constitutional legitimacy.[203] In a carefully crafted argument on constitutional legitimacy, he states:

> With respect to the Environment Court's extensive appellate jurisdiction, the proper test is whether it is appropriate when viewed in light of the values used to draw the

[195] ibid.

[196] ibid.

[197] Ministry for the Environment, *Improving our Resource Management System: A Discussion Document* (n 192) 13.

[198] See, eg, S Elias, 'Righting Environmental Justice' (The Salmon Lecture, Auckland, 25 July 2013).

[199] Kenneth A Palmer, 'Environment Court Reform – More than the Court under Threat?' (Resource Management Law Association, 25 June 2013), available at: rmla.org.nz/obiter/view/id/27; Martin Williams and Simon Berry, 'Reform of the Environment Court – does it make sense?' (Resource Management Law Association, 14 June 2013), available at: www.rmla.org.nz/obiter/view/id/26.

[200] Marie McNicholas, 'Uncertainty Lingers After Court Downgrade Retreat' (*FW Plus*, June 2013), available at: agrihq.co.nz/article/uncertainty-lingers-after-court-downgrade-retreat?p=?p=46%3E.

[201] Canterbury Earthquake Recovery Act 2011 (NZ).

[202] D Nolan et al, 'An Experiment with Expediency: The Unitary Plan Process for Auckland' [2012] *Resource Management Journal* 11.

[203] S Rivers-McCombs, 'Planning in Wonderland: The RMA, Local Democracy and the Rule of Law' (2011) 9 *New Zealand Journal of Public and International Law* 43.

> boundaries between New Zealand's governmental institutions. As the Environment Court is a member of the judicial branch, the limits attached to the role of the ordinary courts would seem particularly relevant.

Rivers-McCombs refers to one case where the Court, using its powers under the RMA, 'rewrote' parts of a local authority plan and concluded that 'the way in which the Environment Court has exercised its jurisdiction threatens the values underlying the rule of law and the separation of powers' (although this decision was upheld by the High Court on a vires point).[204] And in referring to the Court of Appeal's decision in *Watercare Services v Minhinnick*,[205] he states that

> the Court of Appeal was seemingly spot on when it described the Environment Court's task as being to 'weigh all the relevant competing considerations and ultimately make a value judgment on behalf of the community'. However, viewed through a separation of powers lens, this looks more like the job of a democratically elected local government than the Environment Court.[206]

On institutional competency, Rivers-McCombs considers what type of decision might be considered unsuitable for determination by the NZEnvC and he identifies (what he terms) 'political' decisions, where 'there are perceivable differences of opinion in society (or the relevant community) regarding the values which underlie the decision' and where 'the facts are particularly uncertain'.[207] His assessment has echoes of Lon Fuller's analysis in 'The Forms and Limits of Adjudication', that courts may be unsuited to determining polycentric disputes because 'they cannot encompass and take into account the complex repercussions that may result'.[208] Rivers-McCombs' conclusion is that the NZEnvC should not be able to undertake merits review of planning documents.

The Chief Justice of New Zealand, Dame Sian Elias, chose to comment publicly on the debate in the 2013 Salmon Lecture. Her Honour emphasised the wider legal connections that environmental law has with administrative justice which are 'easily overlooked if the subject is viewed as an island' – noting that administrative law serves to check the lawfulness of the exercise of power – and she wonders whether 'the lawyers never really did get' that link.[209] Nevertheless, her Honour expressed some concerns that the legislative framework within which the NZEnvC operated, and the way in which the courts had understood the role of the NZEnvC within that framework, placed few clear limits on its wide discretion. In those circumstances the Chief Justice wondered whether 'the

[204] *Wakatipu Environmental Society Inc v Queenstown Lakes District Council (No 1)* [2000] NZRMA 59 (NZEnvC); *Queenstown Lakes District Council v Lakes District Rural Land Owners Society Ltd* [2002] NZRMA 81 (HC).

[205] *Watercare Services v Minhinnick* [1998] 1 NZLR 294, 305.

[206] Rivers-McCombs (n 203) 71.

[207] ibid, 59 citing K Keith, 'Policy and Law: Politicians and Judges (and Poets)' in BD Gray and RB McClintock (eds), *Courts and Policy: Checking the Balance* (Brookers, 1995) 117.

[208] L Fuller, 'The Forms and Limits of Adjudication' (1978–79) 92 *Harvard Law Review* 353, 394.

[209] Elias (n 198) 2.

use of judicial authority' and 'judicial method' was misplaced. Rather, presciently given the Supreme Court's later decision in the *King Salmon* case[210] (that drew in the wider discretion of the Court in plan change applications),[211] her Honour suggested that in the absence of legislative intervention closer 'appellate consideration' of the structure and workings of the RMA and the NZEnvC's role within it might be appropriate.[212]

I want to highlight the approach that the political and academic critics of the NZEnvC adopt because it provides a good foundation for thinking about conceptual frames and legitimacy, a matter addressed in chapter three. It is important to note that the TAG, the Minister and Rivers-McCombs all follow a similar process in seeking to distinguish between legitimate and illegitimate functions and powers of the Court – a process that appears flawed. As a first step, they address legitimacy within a lacuna. What I mean by this is that they attempt to determine what are illegitimate as opposed to legitimate functions for the Court without having consciously identified the legal nature of the Court. Rather, they make certain assumptions. Most notably they seize on the moniker 'court' and substitute the actual legal nature of the NZEnvC for their knowledge of courts in general, and they give the term 'court' a very specific legal meaning.[213] They assume that the NZEnvC is part of the generalist court system. For example, the Minister for the Environment conflates the involvement of a judicial chairman with the idea that the NZEnvC constitutes 'the judiciary' in general, and then regards the 'judiciary' as synonymous with the ordinary courts. Fundamentally, the metonym 'court' appears to prompt a binary response in the critics: 'courts should do X not Y'.[214]

Second, the critics of the Court do not acknowledge that there are various ways to perceive of legitimacy. They all simply analyse this court (as they see it) through a separation of powers frame, but in doing so privilege a particular conception of the separation of powers based on a pure or literal interpretation.[215] Accordingly, they seem to suggest that within environmental law there is, or should be, a sharp divide between courts and the other branches of government, and between law and policy.[216] Set against modern political arrangements in

[210] *Environmental Defence Society Incorporated v Marlborough District Council* (n 134).

[211] Warnock, 'Reconceptualising the Role of the New Zealand Environment Court' (n 116).

[212] Elias (n 198) 12.

[213] Rivers-McCombs accepts NZEnvC is a specialist court but asserts it's a 'member of the judicial branch' and analyses its legitimacy accordingly; see Rivers-McCombs (n 203) 57.

[214] Thanks to Professor John Burrows for prompting this observation.

[215] Note as Andrew Geddis writes, '[t]he classical formulation of the separation of powers doctrine never comfortably fit the Westminster-style government that New Zealand inherited', A Geddis, 'Parliamentary government in New Zealand: Lines of continuity and moments of change' (2016) 14 *International Journal of Constitutional Law* 99, 101.

[216] HW Arthurs, 'Rethinking Administrative Law: A Slightly Dicey Business' (1979) 17 *Osgoode Hall Law Journal* 1, 24: 'this tendency to oppose law and discretion, and to link judicial decision making with the former and administration with the latter' should not go unchallenged.

New Zealand[217] their unthinking application of a pure separation of powers frame – and what Rubin has termed a reified metaphor with no descriptive validity – appears odd.[218] For example, Rivers-McCombs does not level the same criticisms at local authorities within which there is no clear separation of executive or legislative power (councils promulgate planning instruments and decide applications for consent against them). There is of course a risk, certainly in relation to political commentators with ideological commitments to the free market and a reduced state, that they are not really concerned about constitutionality (and they are using 'dog-whistle' tactics, allowing them 'to capitalize on a certain looseness in the rhetoric').[219] But taking their sincerity at face value, what they must really be concerned with is limiting or constraining power, and they draw on the dispersal of power in the separation of powers concept to provide this limit. Finally, they do not consider any alternative analytical frames, nor do they consider the role of the Court as part of the wider administrative justice system (as the Chief Justice does).

Although the judges of the NZEnvC have not *publicly* debated the legal nature of the Court (in contrast to the judiciary of the NSWLEC – see below) there is no doubt that some anxiety as to the appropriate nature of the Court exists and is apparent in the jurisprudence (as discussed further in chapter six). Examples can be seen in the way that the NZEnvC interpreted their legislative powers to amend plans on the merits narrowly, self-regulating their behaviour.[220] Aligning the Court with more traditional judicial bodies also explains, in part, the narrow approach taken to considerations of economic wellbeing.[221] While the NZEnvC must take into account the 'economic wellbeing' of people and communities in considering sustainable management, it will not receive any evidence of the financial viability or profitability of a development proposal.[222]

[217] New Zealand does not operate a pure or functionalist separation of powers in governmental orderings (eg, ministerial members of the ruling party are part of the executive and legislature, and some have powers to resolve disputes that impact individual rights such as immigration decisions) and there are many bodies with merged quasi-regulatory, administrative and dispute-resolution roles (eg, Electricity Authority, Environmental Protection Authority, Commerce Commission etc).

[218] EL Rubin, *Beyond Camelot: Rethinking Politics and Law for the Modern State* (Princeton University Press, 2005) 47.

[219] J Waldron, *Political Political Theory* (Harvard University Press, 2016) 32. See also N Walker, 'The Idea of Constitutional Pluralism' (2002) 65 *MLR* 317, 319: the 'role of constitutionalism is an ideological resource and the propensity of many to clothe their interests, ideas or aspirations in constitutional garb, not because of a commitment to certain normative standards which may be represented or suggested by constitutionalism but because of the symbolic authority which they hope to draw upon by doing so'.

[220] *Canterbury Regional Council v Apple Fields Ltd* [2003] NZRMA 508 (HC). The Court also determined that plan change applications should be re-notified for public submissions if the Court suggested a change to a plan that had not been proposed by any party to the dispute, despite the statute not requiring this process. Note that s 293 of the RMA was later changed to reflect the approach developed in case law.

[221] *New Zealand Rail Ltd v Marlborough District Council* (n 136); *Friends and Community of Ngawha Inc v Minister of Corrections* [2002] NZRMA 401 (HC).

[222] *New Zealand Rail Ltd v Marlborough District Council* (n 136) 88.

Palmer suggests that 'deference to the financial decisions of public bodies and developers' is a wise approach, as it avoids the Court 'becoming embroiled in executive decisions over capital expenditure and government policy'.[223]

The last part of this chapter turns to consider the NSWLEC, to see if similar concerns and criticisms have emerged in relation to that institution. It begins by sketching the legal nature of the Court before detailing debates that have centred around about the Court's functions, duties and powers.

D. The Legal Nature of the New South Wales Land and Environment Court

The New South Wales Land and Environment Court is similar to the NZEnvC in many respects.[224] It too has a long heritage: the Court evolved from the various institutions that had determined merits appeals in building and other matters following the promulgation of the Local Government Act in 1919.[225] The NSWLEC is also a creature of statute having been created by the Land and Environment Court Act in 1979, and it is empowered to resolve disputes under a plethora of statutes.[226] Like the NZEnvC, it is both a court of record and a specialist court with tenured judges and expert lay commissioners determining disputes.[227]

A significant difference however is that the NSWLEC is a superior court of record, with a status equivalent to the Supreme Court in the New South Wales court hierarchy. It also has a wider jurisdictional remit than the NZEnvC, leading the Chief Judge to describe the Court as a 'one stop shop'.[228] For example, the Court possesses the *inherent jurisdiction* of the High Court to judicially review administrative decisions[229] (although it does not have a general common law jurisdiction and cannot award damages other than those provided by statute) and also has the *statutory* power to judicially review executive action and to determine appeals under a wide array of statutes.[230] These statutes address an expansive range of environmental issues including developmental planning decisions;[231] pollution matters;[232] threatened species

[223] KA Palmer, 'Reflections on the History and Role of the Environment Court in New Zealand' (2010) 27 *Environmental and Planning Law Journal* 69, 71.

[224] S Smith, *A Review of the Land and Environment Court: Briefing Paper No 13/01* (NSW Parliamentary Library Research Service, 2001) 1.

[225] ibid, 1.

[226] Land and Environment Court Act 1979 (NSW), Pt 3.

[227] ibid, Pt 2. Note that the original intention for mixed panels of judges and commissioners in every dispute did not eventuate due to resourcing issues (see P Ryan, 'Court of Hope and False Expectations: Land and Environment Court 21 Years On' (2002) 14 *JEL* 301, 304) however commissioners may sit with and assist judges in an advisory capacity on cases concerning complex scientific and technical matters (Land and Environment Court Act 1979 (NSW), s 37(1)).

[228] Preston, 'Benefits of Judicial Specialization in Environmental Law' (n 42) 604.

[229] *Longwon Pty Ltd v Warringah Shire Council* (1993) 33 NSWLR 13 (CA).

[230] Land and Environment Court Act 1979 (NSW), ss 20(2), (3).

[231] Environmental Planning and Assessment Act 1979 (NSW).

[232] Protection of the Environment Operations Act 1997 (NSW), Pt 9.2.

protection;[233] contractual or land disputes as to minerals claims[234] and ministerial decisions concerning the granting, refusal or cancellation of petroleum titles;[235] aboriginal land claims;[236] compensation for compulsory acquisition[237] and so on. The Court also has a wide range of civil and criminal enforcement powers,[238] including the power to make declarations and injunctions, and it can oversee various ADR processes.

The form that the adjudication takes before the Court – either judicial review, legality appeal, or *de novo* merits review – depends on the issue at hand and the governing regulatory regime. However, approximately two-thirds of its work constitutes merits review appeals.[239] Similar to the rationale in New Zealand, the Australian Administrative Review Council recommends that merits review should be available (absent good reasons) for administrative decisions likely to have an effect on any person, and the Council noted the advantages as including fair treatment for impacted persons; improving the quality and consistency of administrative decisions; and ensuring openness and accountability.[240] The Council believes that 'legislatively unstructured' decisions (where the legislation 'prescribes only general factors that are relevant for consideration' or that may be 'completely silent on relevant factors') are particularly suitable for merits review.[241]

The Court undertakes merits review of certain classes of cases encompassing local and state development decisions; residential development; tree disputes; objections to the valuation of land; compulsory acquisition compensation claims; aboriginal land claims; and miscellaneous appeals under a host of statutes such as the National Parks and Wildlife Act 1974, the Biodiversity Conservation Act 2016, the Water Management Act 2000, and the Environmentally Hazardous Chemical Act 1985.[242] Initial administrative decisions may have been made by local authorities, government ministers, or other members of the executive. In many of those Acts decision-makers are required to consider or apply the 'principles of ecologically sustainable development'.[243] For example, in planning (or

[233] Biodiversity Conservation Act 2016 (NSW).

[234] Land and Environment Court Act 1979 (NSW), s 293.

[235] Petroleum (Onshore) Act 1991 (NSW), s 112B.

[236] Aboriginal Land Rights Act 1983 (NSW).

[237] Land Acquisition (Just Terms Compensation) Act 1991 (NSW); Roads Act 1993 (NSW); Crown Lands Act 1989 (NSW).

[238] Land and Environment Court Act 1979 (NSW), s 20(1), 21 (including appellate powers against convictions in the NSW local courts, ss 21A, 21B); for discussion see Walters and Solomon Westerhuis (n 87).

[239] Z Lipman, 'The NSW Land and Environment Court: Reforms to the Merits Review Process'' (2004) 21 *Environmental and Planning Law Journal* 415. The website for the NSWLEC confirms that approximately 65% of the Court's finalised case load in 2017 were Class 1 merits appeals, see Land and Environment Court 'Class 1: environmental planning and protection appeals, Fast Facts', available at: www.lec.justice.nsw.gov.au/Pages/types_of_disputes/class_1/class_1.aspx.

[240] Administrative Review Council, *What decisions should be subject to merits review?* (n 147) [1.3]–[1.5], [2.1].

[241] ibid, [5.9]–[5.11].

[242] Land and Environment Court Act 1979 (NSW), ss 17–19.

[243] eg, Water Management Act 2000 (NSW), s 3; Biodiversity Conservation Act 2016 (NSW), s 1.3; Protection of the Environmental Operations Act 1997 (NSW), s 3; Pesticides Act 1999 (NSW), s 3; National Parks and Wildlife Act 1974 (NSW), s 2A etc.

development) appeals the objectives of the governing legislation bears similarities to the RMA in New Zealand, requiring all decision-makers to facilitate ecological sustainable development 'by integrating relevant economic, environmental and social considerations in decision-making'.[244] In evaluating development consents, the Court must also consider a list of statutory criteria that includes 'the public interest'.[245] In its merits review role the Court undertakes a rehearing, can admit new evidence, and has all the 'functions and discretions' of the original decision-maker.[246] Proceedings are 'conducted with as little formality and technicality' as the Court permits.[247] The Court is 'not bound by the rules of evidence' and 'may inform itself on any matter in such manner as it thinks appropriate',[248] including drawing on the use of expert evidence.[249] Merits review in effect enables the Court to grant (or to refuse, or to amend) permits, which has traditionally been seen in Australia as a function of the executive branch.[250] Although there is a prohibition in the Australian Constitution against a judicial body exercising administrative functions at federal level,[251] this clear constitutional separation does not apply at state level.[252] Accordingly, there is no prohibition against the NSWLEC exercising both judicial and administrative functions.[253]

From the outset, it would appear that the political intentions in creating the NSWLEC were for a novel form of dispute resolution that would reap efficiencies from co-ordination and specialisation.[254] Upon introducing the Land and Environment Court Bill to the Legislative Council, the (then) Minister for Planning and Environment stated that

> the proposed new court is a somewhat innovative experiment in dispute resolution mechanisms. It attempts to combine judicial and administrative dispute resolving techniques and it will utilize non-legal experts as technical and conciliation assessors. Such a method of operation does not fit harmoniously with the operation of the Supreme Court at present. Nonetheless, I predict that it will not be long before the

[244] Environmental Planning and Assessment Act 1979 (NSW), s 1.3(b) (now s 1.1) (NB: along with a host of other sustainability measures).

[245] ibid, s 4.15.

[246] Land and Environment Court Act 1979 (NSW), s 39(2).

[247] ibid, s 38(1).

[248] ibid, s 38(2).

[249] ibid, s 38(3). For an example see *Telstra Corporation v Hornby Shire Council* [2006] NSWLEC 133. See also B Preston, 'Practice and Procedure in the Land and Environment Court of New South Wales' (Planning, Development and Environmental Law Conference, Sydney, 8–9 February 2007).

[250] See discussion in ch 3.

[251] Commonwealth of Australia Constitution Act 1900; *R v Kirkby; ex p Boilermakers' Society of Australia* (1965) 94 CLR 372 (HCA).

[252] New South Wales Constitution Act 1902; *Trust Company of Australia Ltd (T/A Stockland Property Management) v Skiwing Pty Ltd (T/A Cafe Tiffany's)* [2006] NSWCA 185.

[253] J Cripps et al, *Report of the Land and Environment Court Working Party* (Government of New South Wales, 2001) 45–46.

[254] NSW Parliamentary Debates (1979) No 46, 3349–50

> Supreme Court adopts the novel and innovative structure and method of operation of the Land and Environment Court.[255]

The Court was seen to be an important component in an 'emergent environmental justice system', supported by a whole raft of legislative changes geared towards the 'social and economic welfare of the community and a better environment'.[256] Preston CJ has written (extra-curially) about the great advantages of specialist environment courts such as the NSWLEC, noting that,

> [a]n environment court is better able to address the pressing, pervasive, and pernicious environmental problems that confront society, such as climate change and loss of biodiversity. New institutions and creative attitudes are required to deal with these environmental problems. Specialization enables use of special knowledge and expertise of both the process and the substance of resolution of these problems. Rationalization enlarges the remedies that are available to respond to those problems.[257]

E. Criticisms and Concerns about the New South Wales Land and Environment Court

Over time, the dominant characteristic of the Court does appear to have been one of an innovative, dispute-resolution body.[258] However, there has not always been a unified view between politicians, lawyers and members of the public who use the Court, or even the judiciary as to whether that is an appropriate role for the Court.[259] Rather, a spectrum of views is apparent between those who consider that the Court should be more aligned with the ordinary courts of law, and those who recognise the scope for innovative environmental problem-solving.

Within the wider community, criticisms have been levelled against the NSWLEC that are similar to those made against the NZEnvC – ie, that the Court was or is constitutionally illegitimate; did not have the institutional competence for the role it played; and/or processes should be faster and cheaper. Many believed that the Court should not have merits review jurisdiction at all.[260] From time to time, politicians called for the abolition of the Court, arguing its jurisdiction should be incorporated within the 'ordinary' Supreme Court.[261]

[255] NSW Parliamentary Debates, 21 November 1979, 3345, Second Reading Speech of the Hon Paul Landa MP, Minister for Planning and Environment quoted in Smith, *A Review of the Land and Environment Court: Briefing Paper No 13/01* (n 224) 1.

[256] Ryan (n 227) 301.

[257] BJ Preston, 'Judicial Specialization through Environment Courts: A Case Study of the Land and Environment Court of New South Wales' (2012) 29 *Pace Environmental Law Review* 602, 613–14.

[258] Ryan (n 227) 301; Preston, 'The Role of the Judiciary in Promoting Sustainable Development' (n 59); Preston, 'Characteristics of Successful Environmental Courts and Tribunals' (n 22).

[259] Smith, *A Review of the Land and Environment Court: Briefing Paper No 13/01* (n 224).

[260] eg, Local Government Association, see text accompanying nn 263–68 below.

[261] P Stein, 'Specialist Environment Courts: the Land and Environment Court of New South Wales Australia' (2002) 4 *Environmental Law Review* 5, 7.

In 2001, a Working Party chaired by Justice Cripps, a retired Chief Judge of the NSWLEC, was established by the NSW government to review the Court.[262] The Review invited public submissions. Those critical of the Court were concerned that it should not make or consider matters of policy[263] or determine 'value judgements';[264] was systematically biased towards developers;[265] had made socially and aesthetically controversial decisions;[266] and was out of touch with local concerns.[267] The President of the Local Government Association was reported as saying, '[i]t's appalling that you have one character sitting up there thinking they know the area better than nine or 12 elected representatives of the people'.[268] The prescription, critics thought, was to restrict the Court to matters of law[269] (a view that contrasted starkly with lawyers' earlier concerns that the Court's civil and criminal jurisdiction is 'more properly the province of traditional courts').[270] They believed that court-based decisions should be reserved for procedural judicial review rather than substantive review. Strong themes emerged in the submissions with opponents drawing on ideas concerning adjudicatory formalism, parliamentary supremacy and representative democracy. Critical submissions tended to focus on the inappropriateness of judicial method in this context and ignored the specialised, expert nature of the Court.

Others thought that difficulties in environmental management and planning were caused by the imprecise and uncertain nature of local policies, reflected in planning instruments containing wide discretionary standards, rather than by the nature of the Court itself.[271] Thus, the *form* that environmental law takes complicated the debate. To a large extent these concerns reflect Mashaw's observation (made in another context) that 'the common vagueness and vacuity of statutory directives stretches the thread that binds administrative action to electoral preferences virtually to breaking point',[272] and the question as to who

[262] Cripps et al (n 253).

[263] Sydney City Council submission cited in P Lalich and P Neilson, 'Review of the Land and Environment Courts Jurisdiction' (2001) 7 *Local Government Law Journal* 52.

[264] Smith, *A Review of the Land and Environment Court: Briefing Paper No 13/01* (n 224) 16.

[265] *L&E Court Review* Issue 3, 'Decisions, Decisions: A score card on the decision makers of the Land and Environment' (City of Sydney, 2001), quoted in Smith, *A Review of the Land and Environment Court: Briefing Paper No 13/01* (n 224) 11.

[266] Sydney City Council, *Unwanted Legacies* (Sydney City Council, 2001).

[267] Smith, *A Review of the Land and Environment Court: Briefing Paper No 13/01* (n 224) 7.

[268] 'Call to overhaul the Land and Environment Court' (*The Australian Financial Review*, 8 July 1999), quoted in Smith, *A Review of the Land and Environment Court: Briefing Paper No 13/01* (n 224) 7.

[269] See, eg, J Cooke, 'Design merit appeals and the test of reasonableness' (1996) 13 *Environmental and Planning Law Journal* 431 (design quality should be subject to judicial review only given subjective nature of assessment).

[270] Street CJ, 'Proliferation and Fragmentation of the Australian Court System' (1978) 52 *ALJ* 594–96 cited in Ryan (n 227) 301.

[271] Smith, *A Review of the Land and Environment Court: Briefing Paper No 13/01* (n 224) 12.

[272] J Mashaw, *Reasoned Administration and Democratic Legitimacy: How Administrative Law Supports Democratic Government* (Cambridge University Press, 2018) 7.

should exercise that directive became more acute. Many emphasised that the legislative classes of merits appeal decisions impacted individual rights, including private property rights, and it was necessary for legal rights to be protected by a court.[273]

Supporters of the Court pointed to the enhancement of primary administration afforded by merits review[274] and suggested that it was perverse to assume that a judicious approach (ie, the application of natural justice, testing evidence in an adversarial manner and the duty to give reasons) led to a less just outcome.[275] Some argued that local authorities operated in a politicised climate where election cycles led to short-term thinking that could prove problematic when the law required decisions to balance economic benefits against, for example, the long-term advantages of preserving biodiversity. In contrast, independent courts were suitably impartial.[276] Supporters tended to see the advantages of a flexible, creative, problem-solving body but also stressed the importance of independent court-based resolution. An independent court was necessary, they argued, not just to protect legal rights but also as an important facet in deliberative democracy;[277] it would provide the best hope for facilitating neutral, apolitical decision-making about the environment. Supporters tended to focus on the specialist, expert nature of the Court rather than upon judicial method. Many contributors to the debate thought *less* legal formality and a greater use of the inquisitorial process with increased ADR was important for accurately ascertaining the public interest and solving problems creatively.[278] Fundamentally, however, all groups of submitters to the Review – those opposed to the Court, those supportive, and all in between – were concerned with the legitimacy of institutions and perhaps ultimately, the idea of institutional trust.

At its conclusion, the Cripps Review recommended few substantive changes and the retention of full merits review.[279] The core features and functions of the NSWLEC remained and recommendations were focused primarily on streamlining litigation before the Court (although following the Review, the objective of 'ecologically sustainable development' was explicitly incorporated into statute

[273] eg, submissions by the Environmental Defender Office, see Smith, *A Review of the Land and Environment Court: Briefing Paper No 13/01* (n 224) 11.

[274] Cripps et al (n 253) 90.

[275] Lalich and Neilson (n 263) 51.

[276] ibid.

[277] Reflecting Elster's analogy of court-based adjudication and 'deliberative democracy'. Elster argues that the forum or setting for deliberative democracy, 'as a set of institutional conditions that promotes impartiality' is important, and that deliberative democracy (ie the procedure of debating one another before an audience) is analogous to adversarial proceedings in the courtroom ... the interchanges can serve to weed out falsehoods and inconsistencies and thus enable the [decision maker] to make a good decision', see J Elster (ed), *Deliberative Democracy* (Cambridge University Press, 1998) 8, ch 4.

[278] Cripps et al (n 253) 90, 91, 93; Lalich and Neilson (n 263) 58.

[279] Cripps et al (n 253) ch 6. The core features and functions of the NSWLEC remained; recommendations were focused primarily on streamlining litigation before the Court.

law).[280] In addressing the crux of the debate, the Report reminded those who saw merits decisions made by the Court as illegitimate but those made by the Local Authorities as legitimate that

> [l]ocal councils are corporations created by the Parliament of NSW and assigned the function of administering the planning laws. **A decision by a council on an application for planning permission is essentially an administrative decision. It does not cease to be so by reason of it being made by people who are elected to office.** When considering whether to grant consent to a development application and, if so, subject to what conditions, the discretion of a council is not at large (as is ordinarily the case with respect to legislative decision making). The discretion is constrained by considerations set out in section 79C of the *Environmental Planning and Assessment Act 1979* (emphasis added).[281]

Accordingly, the Cripps Review did not credit the idea, implicit in much opposition to the Court, that 'people are better off delegating judgements and decisions to their elected representatives on the grounds that elected representatives are better informed and have more knowledge at their command'.[282] Merits decisions were not *political* decisions (which can be categorised as 'do what you want, your only constraint is the ballot box'), rather they were constrained by statute law. Nevertheless, the Review did capture the deep tension between alternating points of view, particularly the need for legal certainty and formalism versus more organic resolution and oversight.

This debate as to the Court's appropriate nature is also reflected in judicial thought, and tracing various extrajudicial statements neatly illustrates this point. As Justice Pain reports, some divisions of the Court readily embraced legal innovation.[283] For example, 20 years after the creation of the Court, Justice Stein, opined that

> there is the opportunity, if not the obligation, in the absence of clear legislative guidance, to apply the common law and assist in the development and fleshing out of the principles. Our task is to turn soft law into hard law. This is an opportunity to be bold spirits rather than timorous souls and provide a lead for the common law world. It will make a contribution to the ongoing development of environmental law.[284]

[280] Lipman (n 239).

[281] Cripps et al (n 253) 49; (note, s 79C replaced by s 4.15 Environmental Planning and Assessment Act 1979 (NSW)).

[282] F Vibert, *The Rise of the Unelected: Democracy and the New Separation of the Powers* (Cambridge University Press, 2007) 13.

[283] N Pain and S Wright, 'The Rise of Environmental Law in New South Wales and Federally: Perspectives from the Past and Issues for the Future' (National Environmental Law Association Annual Conference, Broken Hill NSW, 24 October 2003).

[284] P Stein, 'New directions in the prevention and resolution of environmental disputes – specialist environmental courts' (South-East Asian Regional Symposium on the Judiciary and the Law of Sustainable Development, Manila, 6 March 1999) [30]. See also Street CJ, 'The scheme of the [Environmental Protection and Planning Act] … places upon [the NSWLEC] a wide ranging responsibility for the protection of the environment. Commensurate with that wide ranging responsibility is a wide ranging jurisdiction designed to give to that Court exclusive control to determine how, in the public interest and in the interests of the parties and other affected or interested persons, particular dispute situations should be resolved', *F Hannan Pty Ltd v Electricity Commission of New South Wales* [No 3] (1989) 66 LGRA 306 (NSWSC), 310.

His Honour's jurisprudence reflects that view. Famously, in *Leatch v National Parks and Wildlife Service*[285] Stein J found that the precautionary principle was a relevant consideration in refusing a licence 'to take or kill' the endangered Yellow-bellied Glider and Giant Burrowing Frog, even though no mention was made of the principle in the relevant legislation (the case is discussed in detail in chapter six).

In contrast, only a few years later Pearlman CJ expressed her view that: [t]he most obvious function of the Court is ... to apply the law, and so in applying the law there is often little scope to achieve the advancements in environmental law that some people may wish to see.[286] Her Honour's extra-curial comments align with the reasoning she employed in *Greenpeace Australia Ltd v Redbank Power Co Ltd*[287] – a case concerning a merits appeal of a development application for a power plant that used coal tailings. While acknowledging the climate change forcing impact of the application, Pearlman CJ granted consent, finding that there was no legal prohibition against the application and stating that regulating greenhouse emitting projects was for the government not the Court, taking 'into account the competing economic and environmental interests'.[288] Arguments for the application of the (still nascent) precautionary principle were dismissed, with the Court stating 'there are instances of scientific uncertainty on both sides'.[289] Other judges of the NSWLEC have also played down the legally innovative nature of the Court. For example, Sheahan J stated, 'in giving "proper consideration" to the appeal, the judge or commissioner is bound, like the council, by s 79C(1) of the planning legislation ... Those are our statutory instructions, and we cannot take into account any extraneous matters'.[290] The incorporation of ecological sustainable development (ESD) into a number of New South Wales environmental statutes (either as a relevant consideration or as a stated purpose), also prompted judicial debate as to how doctrinally innovative the Court could be.[291] Pearlman CJ opined:

> [T]he successful application of ESD requires the principles themselves to be made more workable and tangible. It is for the legislature to provide more guidance to the Court as to how it wishes this objective to be achieved, and particularly how it relates

[285] *Leatch v National Parks and Wildlife Service* (1993) 81 LGERA 270 (NSWLEC); see also *Carstens v Pittwater Council* [1999] NSWLEC 249.

[286] ML Pearlman, 'Managing Environmental Impacts – The Role of the Land and Environment Court of New South Wales' (New Zealand Planning Congress, Wellington, New Zealand, 9 April 2002), quoted in Pain and Wright (n 283) 9.

[287] *Greenpeace Australia Ltd v Redbank Power Co Ltd* (1994) 86 LGERA 143 (NSWLEC).

[288] ibid, 153.

[289] ibid, 154.

[290] T Sheahan, 'Environmental Law – Present and Future – Lessons Learned and Visions for the Future – the Experience of the Land and Environment Court of New South Wales, Australia' (International Seminar on Environmental Law, Superior Court of Justice Auditorium, Brasilia, 9–11 May 2001).

[291] Pain and Wright (n 283) 13–14.

to other provisions. The Court has a limited role in that it must act according to law. It cannot be expected to fill gaps in policy, or to stretch the law where it does not go.[292]

In sharp contrast, Preston CJ has written of the *leadership* of the Court in filling in the legislative interstices and fleshing out ESD principles.[293] Cases decided by His Honour (and other divisions of the NSWLEC, and indeed other ECs in Australia) have incorporated and developed the precautionary principle, principles of ecological integrity and biodiversity conservation, principles of user-pays and polluter pays, a nascent public trust doctrine,[294] and inter and intra-generational equity.[295]

Even with this brief exploration we can see a tension in extrajudicial opinions, reflected at times in the case law. Some jurists situate the Court firmly within traditional constitutional constraints, while others view the Court as a dynamic adjudicatory form capable of developing new legal doctrine to aid complex decision-making. This inconsistency is politically interesting and legally important. Despite operating within the same institutional structure and under the same legislative regime judicial reasoning differs, reflecting subtly different understanding of the Court's role, resulting in different approaches to decision-making and the development of the law.

IV. UNDERLYING TENSIONS

Clearly, commentators in different jurisdictions will view ECs as being welcomed or problematic depending upon the wider legal culture.[296] However, exploring the debate over the NZEnvC and the NSWLEC begins to reveal a number of core themes. First, many contributors appear to hold pre-formed, homogenised views about adjudication, what it is and how it should be undertaken. Second, there is a clear tension between those who believe that resolving disputes as to whether we should use, develop, discharge into, harvest, conserve or despoil the

292 Pearlman (n 286) 3, although in the same speech Pearlman J conceded 'the Court has been the catalyst for an emerging environmental and planning jurisprudence that is quite unique. The increasing complexity and range of cases which have come before the Court have developed the law and extended its boundaries, but this all within the scope of what the law allows'.

293 Preston, 'Leadership by the Courts in Achieving Sustainability' (n 48).

294 B Preston, 'Judicial Implementation of the Principles of Ecologically Sustainable Development in Australia and Asia' (Law Society of NSW, Regional Presidents Meeting, Sydney, 21 July 2006).

295 See, eg, *Gloucester Resources Ltd v Minister for Planning* [2019] NSWLEC 7, [398] (referenced within a comprehensive decision that addresses the complex regulatory regime and the environmental impacts of the proposed mine).

296 These adjudicatory bodies do not 'sit well' with jurisdictions that have adopted the 'Westminster system' (Law Commission, *Tribunals in New Zealand: An Issues Paper* (n 158) 35). In Sweden opponents to the specialised land and environment courts argued that, 'issuing permits was a task for administrative authorities and not for the courts' (see Bengtsson (n 9) 116). In more general terms see JO Freedman, *Crisis and Legitimacy* (Cambridge University Press, 1978); *cf* P Cane, 'Review of Executive Action' in M Tushnet and P Cane (eds), *The Oxford Handbook of Legal Studies* (Oxford University Press, 2005) 150–51.

environment should be left to political decision-making as opposed to those who believe this function should be determined in an apolitical forum and/or judicialised. In turn, these seemingly binary stances are underpinned by a complex web of thought concerning constitutionalism, the role of and the rule of law (including thick and thin conceptions of the rule of law), and even different understanding about the very meaning of law. Third, the debates concerning both courts demonstrate that the way commentators and even the judges themselves *frame* disputes before the courts, matters. The use of different frames can impact people's views as to the appropriate constitution, functions, powers and procedures of ECs, and can even impact the development of doctrine. While governments may decide to create ECs – establishing particular institutional structures, enacting empowering legislation, and bestowing certain functions upon that body – judicial reasoning within that institution can still differ depending upon the frames of reference employed. The next chapter explores this point further by identifying and analysing the various conceptual frames used in the New Zealand and New South Wales discourse to see if they make sense of capturing, constituting and constraining the legal nature of ECs.

3

The Struggle to Make Legal Sense of Specialist Environment Courts

THIS CHAPTER LOOKS behind the concerns and criticisms expressed about the Environment Court of New Zealand (NZEnvC) and the New South Wales Land and Environment Court (NSWLEC) to consider why people have such divergent views about these bodies. It explains that commentators attempt to make legal sense of the courts – capturing, constituting and constraining the legal nature of environment courts (ECs) – by constructing or adopting different conceptual frames of normative legitimacy. I begin by explaining the idea of framing and normative legitimacy in greater detail, describing how I understand and employ these concepts. I then identify the three *main* conceptual frames that are being employed in the debates concerning the NZEnvC and the NSWLEC (albeit, other frames undoubtedly exist) and explain how the use of frames helps justify different dimensions of legal nature: *what* the institution is, *why* it was created and what its *limits* are. The first frame views the courts as part of the administrative justice landscape and as evidence of adjudicatory pluralism. The second is premised upon generic instrumentalism. The final frame concerns the separation of powers. Analysing these frames in detail enables us to see how they are constructed, what their internal criteria are, and to understand how each one falls short of making legal sense of the NZEnvC and NSWLEC and environmental adjudication more generally.

The chapter concludes that critics analyse the NZEnvC and NSWLEC using conceptual frames that appear ill-suited to the task, and that this approach has threatened their continued existence and/or provided a basis for undermining the functions of the courts. But I also argue that none of the frames prove adequate for capturing, constituting and appropriately constraining the legal nature of the courts, either alone or in conjunction with the others, while preserving their ability to adjudicate environmental disputes. Nevertheless, identifying why and how each frame is being used is a valuable part of pre-theory building because it helps to identify concerns and preoccupations that must be addressed by any new theory for environmental adjudication.

I. NORMATIVE LEGITIMACY AND ANALYTICAL FRAMES

Like many other environment courts, the NZEnvC and NSWLEC were created by statute and have wide powers deliberately granted by Parliament. They are, accordingly, forms of 'state sponsored legal pluralism'[1] and have democratic legitimacy in a positivist or 'rational-legal' way.[2] But critics of the NZEnvC and NSWLEC are looking beyond notions of parliamentary sovereignty in an attempt to refine the legal nature of the courts, arguing that certain powers are legitimate while others are illegitimate. This approach is telling because they are attempting to specify and limit the legal nature of the courts by drawing upon *deeper* concepts of institutional legitimacy. Legitimacy in this context appears therefore to be a complex matter, operating at several levels. Accordingly, the discourse surrounding the NZEnvC and NSWLEC accurately reflects Beetham's conception of legitimacy as a multidimensional concept.[3]

In *The Legitimation of Power*, Beetham suggests that power can be said to be legitimate to the extent that it meets three core conjunctive criteria. First, power must be 'acquired and exercised in accordance with prevailing rules',[4] ie, it must have 'legal validity', as Beetham categorises this aspect; second, those rules are well grounded in normative beliefs shared by both dominant and subordinate groups in the power matrix, so-called 'normative justifiability';[5] and third, actions of the subordinate group acknowledge and serve to confirm the power-holders' authority. Underpinning Beetham's multidimensional framework is the idea of integrity[6] and constraint, ie, 'legitimate power … is limited power'.[7]

Drawing on Beetham's core components enables us to pinpoint the specific focus of the New Zealand and New South Wales debates. The NZEnvC and NSWLEC have so-called 'legal validity': the NZEnvC is constituted and empowered by the Resource Management Act 1991 (RMA);[8] the NSWLEC by the Land and Environment Court Act 1979. Further, although certain individuals may resent and oppose particular decisions of the courts, or restrictions on their

[1] E Fisher, 'Jurisdictional Facts and Hot Facts: Legal Formalism, Legal Pluralism and the Nature of Australian Administrative Law' (2015) 38 *Melbourne University Law Review* 968, 973.

[2] M Weber, 'The Three Types of Legitimate Rule' (1958) 4 *Berkeley Publications in Society and Institutions* 1.

[3] D Beetham, *The Legitimation of Power*, 2nd edn (Political Analysis, 2013). Note I acknowledge that legitimacy is a highly contested concept in both political and legal scholarship (for good overviews see, eg, CA Thomas, 'The Uses and Abuses of Legitimacy in International Law' (2014) 34 *OJLS* 729; J Black, 'Constructing and contesting legitimacy and accountability in polycentric regulatory regimes' (2008) 2 *Regulation & Governance* 137) but do not intend to enter those debates in this monograph.

[4] Beetham (n 3) xii.

[5] Others term this concept 'moral' legitimacy, see, eg, RH Fallon, 'Legitimacy and the Constitution' (2004–05) 118 *Harvard Law Review* 1787.

[6] How power is exercised, ie, the need for due performance, is critical: see Beetham (n 3) xiii.

[7] Beetham (n 3) 35.

[8] Resource Management Act 1991 (NZ) (RMA), Pt 11.

activities per se in the name of environmental protection,[9] in general there is widespread acceptance of the courts' authority.[10] The debates surrounding the NZEnvC and NSWLEC are concerned therefore with the second aspect of Beetham's conception – 'normative justifiability'. As Beetham explains, rules cannot be justified by the mere fact that they are rules: they must be justified with reference to 'considerations which lie beyond them'.[11] Normative justifiability can be taken to mean that the 'public regards [power] as justified, appropriate, or otherwise deserving of support for reasons beyond fear of sanctions or mere hope for personal reward'[12] or unthinking habit.[13] Normative justifiability is grounded on shared beliefs that might not have any formal or tangible existence but nevertheless constitute a type of inter-subjective understanding.[14]

Beetham predicted that normative justifiability might form 'the core of legitimacy', most likely to prove contentious, with 'legality serving as a pre-condition and aspects of recognition as a mode of reinforcement'.[15] This prediction is borne out in the New Zealand and Australian discourse: that is, the precondition of legality (bestowed by their respective parliaments) exists and must be accepted by commentators,[16] but the normative justifiability of the courts' legal nature is proving contentious.

At this point it is also worth considering the use of analytical frames in evaluating normative justifiability in a little more detail because, as Belin counselled,

> [t]he first step to the understanding of men is the bringing to consciousness of the model or models that dominate and penetrate their thought and action … The second task is to analyse the model itself, and this commits the analyst to accepting or modifying or rejecting it, and, in the last case, to providing a more adequate one in its stead.[17]

[9] eg, *Conway v R* [2013] NZCA 438.

[10] Kenneth A Palmer, 'Environment Court Reform – More than the Court under Threat?' (RMLA, 25 June 2013), available at: rmla.org.nz/obiter/view/id/27; Marie McNicholas, 'Uncertainty Lingers After Court Downgrade Retreat' (*FW Plus*, June 2013), available at: agrihq.co.nz/article/uncertainty-lingers-after-court-downgrade-retreat?p=?p=46%3E; P Stein, 'Specialist Environment Courts: the Land and Environment Court of New South Wales Australia' (2002) 4 *Environmental Law Review* 5, 7.

[11] Beetham (n 3) 69.

[12] Fallon, 'Legitimacy and the Constitution' (n 5) 1795.

[13] SM Lipset, *Political Man: The Social Bases of Politics* (Mercury, 1963) 77. Compare 'habit' to 'tradition': the former is 'unthinking', the later embodies 'the accumulated wisdom of successive generations' (Beetham (n 3) 74).

[14] JS Dryzek, 'Paradigms and Discourses' in D Bodansky, J Brunnée and E Hey (eds), *The Oxford Handbook of International Environmental Law* (Oxford University Press, 2007).

[15] Beetham (n 3) 293.

[16] *cf* constitutional debates in USA scenario: RH Fallon, 'Of Legislative Courts, Administrative Agencies, and Article III' (1987–88) 101 *Harvard Law Review* 916.

[17] I Berlin, 'Does political theory still exist?' in P Laslett and WG Runciman (eds), *Philosophy, Politics and Society (2nd series)* (Blackwell, 1962) 19.

Conceptual models are often more powerful than the tangible components of our legal systems: the laws, constitutions and institutions.[18] They can provide (in positive terms) a reference point or (negatively) a distorting perspective of the subject. How the NZEnvC and NSWLEC are perceived and to an extent, all three dimensions of legal nature – the *what*, the *why* and the *limits*[19] – are impacted upon by the discourses that we are engaged in and as the critics demonstrate, the paradigms of governance that we draw upon.[20] Put more simply, we make legal sense of the courts by using frames of reference and these frames create models of legitimacy: that is, 'a worthiness to be recognised'.[21] Inevitably, frames of reference and the models they create are 'simplifications of reality'[22] that enable 'better questioning, exploration, handling and manipulation' of complex areas of social ordering that are otherwise difficult to conceptualise.[23] Framing is 'by its nature also an instrument of exclusion'[24] and models are 'constructed for a purpose or set of purposes'.[25] Accordingly, frames and models are not necessarily the truth: they do not constitute unassailable doctrine, nor are they wholly comprehensive or irreplaceable.[26] These caveats are important. It is not the focus of this chapter to explore them further but the essential point is that to address the normative legitimacy of the courts, we are drawn into sketching frames. If the analysis is to be extended to other ECs (that may, depending upon the relevant legal culture, be subject to different arguments about normative legitimacy) this point is foundational.

Overall, contributors to the debate about the NZEnvC and NSWLEC are drawing upon different collective understandings of the legal world to create frames through which to analyse the courts, and they privilege certain understandings at the expense of others. They identify their frame as the natural order of things, rather than as a privileged conception.[27] Importantly, the use of each frame leads to a different emphasis in terms of normative legitimacy: the three frames used each create different perceptions as to the appropriate legal nature of the courts, and privilege different powers and functions as legitimate,

[18] Dryzek (n 14) 45–47. See also Dryzek's interchangeable use of 'paradigm' and 'frame of reference'; but he sets a distinction between these two concepts and 'discourse' noting '[b]oth paradigms and discourses are constitutive, but they constitute subjects in different ways'.

[19] For further discussion, see ch 2.

[20] Dryzek (n 14) 46; B Jessup and K Rubenstein, 'Introduction: Using discourse theory to untangle public and international environmental law' in B Jessup and K Rubenstein (eds), *Environmental Discourses in Public and International Law* (Cambridge University Press, 2012) 5; Berlin (n 17) 19.

[21] J Habermas, *Communication and the Evolution of Society* (Heinemann, 1979) 178–79.

[22] National Research Council, *Models in Environmental Regulatory Decision Making* (National Academies Press, Washington DC, 2007) 31.

[23] E Fisher, P Pascual and W Wagner, 'Understanding Environmental Models in Their Legal and Regulatory Context' (2010) 22 *JEL* 251, 266.

[24] D Winickoff et al, 'Adjudicating the GM Food Wars: Science, Risk, and Democracy in World Trade Law' (2005) 30 *Yale Journal of International Law* 81, 94.

[25] Fisher, Pascual and Wagner (n 23) 266.

[26] E Goffman, *Frame Analysis: An Essay on the Organization of Experience* (Northeastern, 1974).

[27] Dryzek (n 14) 46.

rejecting others as illegitimate. However, a difficulty with using these frames to analyse the courts is that none can fully explain the legal nature of the NZEnvC and NSWLEC. The next part of the book considers each frame in turn in order to demonstrate that point.

II. THE 'ADMINISTRATIVE JUSTICE-ADJUDICATIVE PLURALISM' FRAME

In chapter two we saw that some commentators viewed the NZEnvC and the NSWLEC as critical components in an environmental justice system that requires the courts to be creative legal problem-solvers. The previous Chief Justice of New Zealand reminds us that environmental law is a branch of administrative law and quoting Sir Robin Cooke, notes environmental justice has to respond to

> the demand for essential fairness of procedure and impartial consideration in an essentially judicial manner – goals often seen as particularly linked with the protection of individual rights; the demand for a substantial degree of democratic participation in processes of decision-making that affect many people or even virtually the whole community; and the demand for harnessing the skills of specialist professions and sciences.[28]

Proponents of the NZEnvC and NSWLEC argued that the courts' specialist legal nature means that they are better attuned to these demands, and while they share characteristics with the generalist courts they should not be conflated with them. Accordingly, the first analytical frame views ECs as part of the administrative justice landscape and as evidence of adjudicatory pluralism. Within this frame, environmental law is considered part of the law of administration[29] and the associated institutional architecture part of the administrative justice landscape. This frame views administrative and environmental justice as a necessary part of a complex state: fluid and flexible;[30] and its decision-making 'inherently discretionary'.[31]

This frame focuses upon and privileges the *specialist* in specialist environmental courts, ie, the particular and expert nature of these bodies.[32] Sometimes seen as a necessary adjunct to parliamentary decision-making in order to expand

[28] S Elias, 'Righting Environmental Justice' (The Salmon Lecture, Auckland, 25 July 2013) 3.

[29] ibid, 2.

[30] F Frankfurter, 'The Task of Administrative Law' (1926) 75 *University of Pennsylvania Law Review* 614, 619.

[31] Lord Cooke of Thorndon, 'The Discretionary Heart of Administrative Law' in C Forsyth and I Hare (eds), *The Golden Metwand and the Crooked Cord: Essays in Honour of Sir William Wade QC* (Oxford University Press, 1998) 220.

[32] Note that I use 'expert' in the sense of an extended contributory expertise as opposed to rarefied scientific expertise (see HM Collins and R Evans, 'The Third Wave of Science Studies: Studies of Expertise and Experience' (2002) 32 *Social Studies of Science* 235; B Wynne, 'Seasick on the Third Wave? Subverting the Hegemony of Propositionalsim: Response to Collins and Evans' (2002) 33 *Social Studies of Science* 401, 402).

its influence,[33] specialist decision-making is seen as advantageous because of 'pressure on parliamentary time, technicality of subject matter, difficulty in foreseeing all contingencies, allowing for constant adaptation and flexibility, permitting experimentation, [and] coping with emergencies'.[34] *Adjudication* is integral to this frame and regarded as a deliberate and deliberative part of administrative governance,[35] with Chayes' conception of public law adjudication providing the internal criteria for the frame. The essential components are that,

> the scope of the lawsuit is not exogenously given but is shaped primarily by the court and parties; the party structure is not rigidly bilateral but sprawling and amorphous; the fact inquiry is not historical and adjudicative but predictive and legislative.[36]

Further, Chayes notes that adjudicative relief is flexible, the administration of the decree may require 'the continuing participation of the court', and may have 'important consequences for many persons including absentees'.[37] Notably, the judge is actively responsible for 'organizing and shaping the litigation to ensure a just and viable outcome'.[38] Chayes says that this conception of adjudication is not particularly revolutionary – it looks like equity, with its specifically crafted and prospective forms of relief, capable of accommodating 'the range of interests involved'.[39]

The 'administrative justice-adjudicative pluralism' frame is a legitimising frame constructed on historical foundations, strengthened by embedded tradition,[40] and evincing a form of legitimacy 'built up over time through processes of struggle and compromise'.[41] This frame reflects the reality of much modern governance in New Zealand and New South Wales (and other jurisdictions). Governance practices that were originally inherited from Britain were developed and became embedded in the national legal culture. In both nations, a whole array of dispute-resolution bodies has been established to resolve legal problems between citizens and the state. We can understand how we have ended up with ECs in these jurisdictions (and potentially others) by examining the

[33] WA Robson, *Justice and Administrative Law*, 2nd edn (Stevens, 1947) 331; Donoughmore Committee, *Committee on Ministers' Powers* (Cmd 4060, 1932) 84; J McLean, *Searching for the State in British Legal Thought: Competing Conceptions of the Public Sphere* (Cambridge University Press, 2012) 46.

[34] M Taggart, 'From "Parliamentary Powers" to Privatization: The Chequered History of Delegated Legislation in the Twentieth Century' (2005) 55 *University of Toronto Law Journal* 575, 608.

[35] *cf* G Frug, 'The Ideology of Bureacracy in American Law' (1983–84) 97 *Harvard Law Review* 1276, 1336, fn 199.

[36] A Chayes, 'The Role of the Judge in Public Law Litigation' (1975) 89 *Harvard Law Review* 1281, 1302.

[37] ibid, 1302.

[38] ibid.

[39] ibid, 1292–94.

[40] M Weber, 'The Three Types of Legitimate Rule', *From Max Weber: Essays in Sociology* (HH Gerth and C Wright Mills eds, Oxford University Press, 1946) 78–79.

[41] Beetham (n 3) 35.

historical evolution in Britain of the legal landscape that was transferred to but then adapted within New Zealand and Australia, and in doing so we address the *why* in our tripartite of legal nature.

A. Adjudication Less Ordinary

For centuries, adjudicatory pluralism was the norm in Britain and this correlated to the fact that the jurisdiction had a long history of decentralised and dispersed (as opposed to delegated) state power.[42] Importantly for the present argument, local dispute-resolution bodies emerged organically, as a necessary response to local concerns and the form they took – their legal nature – was responsive to the forms of conflict that they were concerned with. Many were hybrid bodies that had adjudicative, administrative and regulatory functions.[43] As Maitland commented in the 1880s, in England 'the [administrative and the judicial] have for ages been inextricably blended'[44] and in fact, state-sponsored adjudication 'began as a mode of administration'.[45]

A well-known example of adjudicatory pluralism concerns commercial dispute-resolution bodies. The commercial community always managed, to a large extent, to maintain its own legal system and developed various responsive forms of dispute resolution,[46] in part premised on the need for the dispute-resolution process to avoid blaming and preserve future commercial relationships. However, a lesser-known example concerns the swanimotes – the ancient forest courts of England and Wales that continue to operate to date. Swanimotes managed the 'controlled exploitation' of forest areas; creating local regulations, deciding specific disputes and collecting administrative dues.[47] And swanimotes (discussed further in chapter four) were just one example of the prevalent pluralism manifest in environmental dispute-resolution historically.[48] Interestingly, these bodies demonstrate that the resolution of environmental conflicts has always taken a novel form and a clear bifurcation between policy and adjudication has not been such a dominant feature in this

[42] McLean, *Searching for the State in British Legal Thought* (n 33) 23, 305 and ch 6.

[43] RE Wraith and PG Hutchesson, *Administrative Tribunals* (Allen and Unwin, 1973) 17–22; WS Holdsworth, *A History of English Law Volume 1*, 7th edn (Methuen, 1956) 478; RM Jackson *The Machinery of Justice in England* (Cambridge University Press, 1967) 351.

[44] FW Maitland, 'The Shallows and Silences of Real Life' in HAL Fisher (ed), *The Collected Papers of Frederic William Maitland: Downing Professor of the Laws of England*, vol 1 (Cambridge University Press, 1911) 478.

[45] P Cane, 'Public Law in the Concept of Law' (2013) 33 *OJLS* 649, 660–61.

[46] Wraith and Hutchesson (n 43) 19; HW Arthurs, *Without the Law: Administrative Justice and Legal Pluralism in Nineteenth-Century England* (University of Toronto Press, 1985) 50–53.

[47] P Large, 'From swanimote to disafforestation: Feckenham Forest in the early seventeeth century' in R Hoyle (ed), *The Estates of the English Crown 1550–1640* (Cambridge University Press, 1992).

[48] The medieval stannary (tin-mining) courts were another example, see: R Pennington, *Stannary Law: A History of the Mining Law of Cornwall and Devon* (David & Charles, 1973).

area. Rather, institutional arrangements are closer to that of disaggregated power, with disputes managed by bodies that also have both administrative, regulatory and adjudicative roles.

Although there was perceived to be some drawing back of adjudicatory pluralism in nineteenth-century Britain,[49] this position was reversed by the development of the great socially reforming regulation, beginning with the Factories Act 1833 and growing to encompass Health and Housing Acts and the Town and Country Planning regimes that were the precursors to modern environmental planning legislation.[50] These regimes required novel compliance mechanisms and so administrators developed more flexible forms of adjudication such as 'investigation, report, negotiation and rule-making'[51] in order to address shared collective risks.[52] Reference to the ordinary courts was only one tool in the toolbox and often taken as a last resort, predominantly because of their incapacity to *respond* to socially reforming legislation or to the wider public interest. Where legislation was intended to interfere with common law property rights, to rely upon the ordinary courts was, Jennings argued, inherently flawed.[53] Certainly cases such as *Ryder v Mills*,[54] *Cooper v Wandsworth Board of Works*[55] and *Attorney General v Birmingham Corporation*[56] wherein the protection of private property interests dominated all other considerations and crowded out public wellbeing, supported his contention. As Robson noted, it was 'the failure of the judicature to endow the general public with an enforceable interest in matters where a regard for the social good is of the first moment that led to the development of the administrative tribunals'.[57]

In the early twentieth century, alternative forms of adjudication became phenomena that were consciously theorised by Robson, Jennings, Laski and Willis to name but a few – thus adding a normative legitimacy actively deliberated upon to the 'traditional legitimacy' manifest in these bodies – and this was

[49] Arthurs (n 46) 188: 'centralism was a Victorian artefact', but in the late nineteenth century pluralism increased, at 192; also see C Stebbings, *Legal Foundations of Tribunals in Nineteenth Century England* (Cambridge University Press, 2006).

[50] R Macrory, 'Environmental Courts and Tribunals in England and Wales – A Tentative New Dawn' (2010) 3 *Journal of Court Innovation* 61, 62.

[51] Arthurs (n 46) 117.

[52] CR Sunstein, *The Partial Constitution* (Harvard University Press, 1993) 320.

[53] W Ivor Jennings, 'Courts and Administrative Law – The Experience of English Housing Legislation' (1935–36) 49 *Harvard Law Review* 426, 435–37; see also E Taborsky, 'A Case for Administrative Tribunals' (1943–44) 7 *MLR* 209.

[54] *Ryder v Mills* (1850) 19 LJMC (pt 2) 82 (Exch) (use of children in factories; mill owner brought action against Factories Inspector who had interpreted relevant legislation as limiting children's working hours to 10 hours in any one day; courts allowed mill owner to use relay shifts to get around this limit).

[55] *Cooper v Wandsworth Board of Works* (1863) 143 ER 414 (slum clearances; natural justice afforded to landlords to challenge the clearances on the basis of their property rights).

[56] *Attorney General v Birmingham Corporation* (1858) 4 K&J 528 (rights of individuals to defend their property against nuisance regardless of any countervailing public interest; judge opined the court was not a public safety committee, his concern was solely to enforce the plaintiff's legal rights).

[57] Robson (n 33) 69.

the ethos that domestic tribunals developed within.[58] Returning directly to the core argument, planning and environmental law, where the wider interests of the public may take precedence over 'narrow 19th century preoccupations with property rights',[59] is often seen as a prime example of socially reforming legislation that requires different forms of dispute resolution to accommodate not only the delicate balance between private rights and public wellbeing but also the inevitable merging of law and policy.[60] In fact, everything about the traditional courts suggested that they were the wrong bodies to be dealing with environmental adjudication.[61] The generic courts' approach to evidence was (and is) heavily conscribed,[62] which is unhelpful with an evaluative role that is predictive. And the judicial method of statutory interpretation – attuned as it is 'to the [common law] accents of the forgotten past'[63] – is inappropriate in circumstances better suited to a process more akin to 'legislative fact-finding'.[64] Rather, as the New Zealand Supreme Court has recognised, appropriate interpretation in this context often constitutes 'a practical question involving an exercise of informed judgment. There must be an adequate understanding of contemporary standards and aspirations and the decision must be made in terms of the real world as it actually is today'.[65] Overall, specialist courts and tribunals were perceived to have a greater facility for this informed judgement.[66]

All this suggests, historically at least, a legal landscape characterised by adjudicative pluralism, with courts, tribunals, commissioners, bodies within government departments and various external boards all doing the job of legal dispute-resolution,[67] and in these new adjudicative bodies, 'form is made to

[58] McLean, *Searching for the State in British Legal Thought* (n 33) 16, 113; see also M Loughlin, *Foundations of Public Law* (Oxford University Press, 2010) 442–43; Robson (n 33) 31; RS Summers, 'Pragmatic Instrumentalism in Twentieth Century American Legal Thought – A Synthesis and Critique of our Dominant General Theory about Law and its Use' (1980–81) 66 *Cornell Law Review* 861. For a modern judicial assessment of tribunals see *Rasanen v Rosemount Instruments Ltd* (1994) 17 OR (3d) 267 (CA).

[59] *Falkner v Gisborne District Council* [1995] NZLR 622, 630 (HC).

[60] Robson (n 33) 334; JAG Griffith, 'Tribunals and Inquiries' (1959) 22 *MLR* 125, 129; TRS Allan, 'Doctrine and theory in administrative law: an exclusive quest for the limits of jurisdiction' [2003] *PL* 429, 433.

[61] Arthurs (n 46) 208, noting it is 'hard to justify insistence upon conformity by all types of bodies to the single model of adversarial adjudication typically associated with the courts'. For a modern example of this argument in the environmental context, see P McClellan, 'Environmental Issues – How should we resolve disputes?' [2005] *Resource Management Theory & Practice* 35, 44–48.

[62] E Gellhorn, 'Rules of Evidence and Official Notice in Formal Administrative Hearings' [1971] *Duke Law Journal* 1; KC Davis, 'An Approach to the Problems of Evidence in the Administrative Process' (1942) 55 *Harvard Law Review* 364.

[63] J Willis, *The Parliamentary Powers of English Government Departments* (Harvard University Press, 1933) 51 quoted by Taggart (n 34) 589.

[64] Davis (n 62). Legislative fact-finding concerns data collection to assess wider social or scientific conditions.

[65] *Robson v Hicks Smiths and Sons Ltd* [1965] NZLR 113 (SC), 1124. See also *Stark v Auckland Regional Council* [1994] 3 NZLR 614, 617 (HC).

[66] New Zealand Parliamentary Debates, 299 NZPD 689, 799.

[67] Robson, *Justice and Administrative Law* (n 33) ch 3.

follow function'.[68] It also reflects a fluidity to the separation of powers. This pluralism was not initially the result of any conscious master plan; rather, this bottom-up dispute-resolution reflected necessity and manifested iteratively, with developments responding to the adjudicative context. This idea of adjudicatory *responsiveness* is a critical factor in my argument and I develop it in chapter four.

Returning to the present, the governance practices that originated in Britain were inherited by New Zealand and Australia, and today administrative complexity and adjudicative pluralism is a dominant feature of the state architecture in both these jurisdictions. The NZEnvC is one of many specialist courts and tribunals in New Zealand,[69] working alongside quasi-independent regulatory bodies that merge investigatory, regulatory and adjudicatory functions.[70] Within Australia a similarly complex landscape exists, certainly at state level.[71] For the purposes of the present discussion, this embedded tradition followed by the deliberate evolution of the administrative state and the continuing prevalence of multifunctional adjudicative bodies, provides a form of normative legitimacy. But there are problems with using this frame to analyse the legal nature of the NZEnvC and NSWLEC, certainly in isolation, and this weakness reflects a wider difficulty in accommodating the whole 'adjudicative spectrum'[72] within existing conceptual frames.

B. An Incomplete Frame?

In general, the uncodified British and New Zealand constitutions 'try to keep law and politics apart'[73] and within the Australian *federal* Constitution, judicial and administrative functions are kept separate and allocated to different branches of government.[74] But specialist courts, administrative tribunals and other multifunctional adjudicatory forms 'inhabit a twilight world where the two intermingle; they are in the sense the orphaned child of both'.[75] Specialist environment courts are institutions that stand on 'the frontiers between law and

[68] Arthurs (n 46) 192.

[69] New Zealand Law Commission, *Tribunals in New Zealand* (NZLC Wellington, 2008). Other notable examples include the Māori Land Court and Māori Appellate Court, Employment Court, Family and Youth Court.

[70] eg, the Electricity Authority, Environmental Protection Authority, Commerce Commission and Financial Markets Authority etc.

[71] P Cane, *Administrative Tribunals and Adjudication* (Hart Publishing, 2010); E Fisher, 'Administrative Law, Pluralism and Legal Construction of Merits Review in Australian Courts and Tribunals' in L Pearson, C Harlow and M Taggart (eds), *Administrative Law in a Changing State: Essays in Honour of Mark Aronson* (Hart Publishing, 2008).

[72] Cane, *Administrative Tribunals and Adjudication* (n 71) 47–48.

[73] Wraith and Hutchesson (n 43) 17.

[74] *R v Kirby, ex parte Boilermakers' Society of Australia* (1955–56) 94 CLR 254 (HCA).

[75] Wraith and Hutchesson (n 43) 17.

administration'.[76] Given their wide discretionary powers they may be seen to be too far from 'democratic legitimacy'.[77] Reflecting more general concerns, the previous Chief Justice of New Zealand has stated the need for more effective mapping and theorising of the New Zealand constitution and, in particular, the need 'to take account of the way in which public power is now distributed through bodies that are not part of the executive'.[78] Even the enthusiasm of the original advocates for administrative tribunals became muted when greater thought was given to their constitutional place,[79] although the troublesome position was alleviated somewhat by the extension of judicial review to these bodies, the crystallisation of public law principles,[80] and alternative theoretical perspectives that helped to support their legitimacy (particularly the scholarship on delegated powers).[81] However, the possible application of judicial review (or appeals on a point of law)[82] may do little to answer the critics of the NZEnvC and NSWLEC given the deliberately wide powers granted to these specialist courts,[83] concerns that are heightened by the significant impact that their substantive merits decisions have on national economic, socio-cultural and environmental wellbeing.[84] All these observations suggest an important flaw with using the 'administrative justice-adjudicative pluralism' frame to analyse the NZEnvC and NSWLEC in isolation: the *frame itself* cannot be used to establish limits, restraining the wide discretionary powers of the courts; rather, it is a frame that privileges institutional flexibility in decision-making.

I want to think about the idea of limits in a little more detail at this point to illustrate the shortcomings of the 'administrative justice-adjudicative pluralism' frame. Clearly, establishing limits to power is important and to have legitimacy adjudication must be constrained in some way. Constraints may be both explicit and implicit. *Explicit* constraints include external and internal checks on the institution's power that are practical and content neutral. External checks can

[76] New Zealand Law Commission, *Tribunals in New Zealand: An Issues Paper* (NZLC IP6 Wellington, 2007) 34.

[77] See Loughlin (n 58) 448–49.

[78] S Elias, 'Mapping the Constitutional' [2014] *NZLR* 1, 8.

[79] Robson (n 33) 328.

[80] Loughlin (n 58) 444–45; TRS Allan, 'The Constitutional Foundations of Judicial Review: Conceptual Conundrum or Interpretative Inquiry?' (2002) 61 *CLJ* 87.

[81] See Taggart (n 34).

[82] In the New Zealand context, see RMA, s 299. In the New South Wales context, see Land and Environment Court Act 1979, Pt 5.

[83] Especially given High Court deference to expert institutions: New Zealand Law Commission, *Delivering Justice for All* (NZLC Wellington, 2004) 221; *Stark v Auckland Regional Council* (n 65); see also M Elliot and R Thomas, 'Tribunal Justice and Proportionate Dispute Resolution' (2012) 71 *CLJ* 297.

[84] See general criticism of the 'judicial review model' in Frug (n 35) 1352. The concern about the relative impotency of judicial review in the context of specialised decision-making is one reason why the Kerr Report recommended the establishment of the Administrative Appeals Tribunal in Australia (see Commonwealth Administrative Review Committee, *Commonwealth Administrative Review Committee Report ('Kerr Committee Report')* (Parliament of Australia, Parl Paper No 144, 1971)).

include statutory intervention and external supervision, achieved in an adjudicatory sense by an appeal route (forms of checks and balances evincing, as Cane notes, perhaps not a functionalist separation of powers but interdependency between the branches of government, or a sharing of power).[85] Adjudication *in and of itself* can be a form of practical constraint if it is conducted in a transparent way that promotes accountability. For example, a commitment to decision-making through public reasoned deliberation is a form of constraint.[86] The knowledge that decisions have legal effect (ie, they develop law rather than just resolving discrete disputes between the parties) is also a form of constraint on decision-makers. Explicit constraints are established by the 'prevailing rules' and as Beetham argues, if judicial power is exercised in accordance with those rules it will have *legal validity*.[87]

In contrast, in order to promote *normative justifiability*, adjudication must be constrained *implicitly*. Normative justifiability is based on an understanding or the shared beliefs of the community that justify the explicit rules.[88] Conceptual metaphors or frames that explain and justify particular governmental orderings are examples of shared beliefs (such as the separation of powers). But frames also help to constitute and constrain adjudication, in turn promoting the normative justifiability of particular forms of adjudication.[89] The theory that I develop in this book is a form of implicit constraint. Requiring fidelity between the four component parts of the theory acts as a constraint. And building a more detailed frame from the theory will create greater constraints still. It will also have relevant content that would assist judicial reasoning (in circumstances where the law is incomplete or adjudicators are afforded wide discretion), for parties (in determining what evidence to adduce and how to direct their arguments) and policymakers and the legislature in creating ECs. Accordingly, my theory sets both possibilities *and* parameters for environmental adjudication. All these matters are explained further in the following chapters. But before leaving the discussion on the 'administrative justice-adjudicative pluralism' frame it is important to sum up the analysis so far.

In terms of our tripartite test of legal nature – the *what*, *why* and the *limits* – the 'administrative justice-adjudicative pluralism' frame superbly addresses the first two issues. It is a good frame for explaining both why New Zealand and NSW have environment courts and for capturing their legal nature in part and

[85] Cane, *Administrative Tribunals and Adjudication* (n 71); P Cane, *Controlling Administrative Power: An Historical Comparison* (Cambridge University Press, 2016).

[86] J Cohen, 'Deliberation and Democratic Legitimacy' in J Bohman and W Regh (eds), *Deliberative Democracy: Essays on Reason and Politics* (MIT Press, 1997) 69; see also, eg, H Arendt, *The Human Condition* (University of Chicago Press, 1958); J Resnik, 'Reinventing Courts as Democratic Institutions' (2014) 143 *Daedalus* 9; J Waldron, *Political Political Theory* (Harvard University Press, 2016).

[87] Beetham (n 3) xii.

[88] ibid, 17 (an idea discussed in greater detail in ch 4).

[89] Black, 'Constructing and contesting legitimacy and accountability in polycentric regulatory regimes' (n 3) 145.

in that sense, providing a legitimising frame for the courts. Using this frame, one can chart a disaggregation of power (achieved lately by piecemeal but nevertheless deliberate delegation), a diffusion of power that is arguably necessary in the context of environmental conflict resolution. Environmental courts may be seen to be creating a bridge between the political and formal law, and part of governance in a positive sense, facilitating social policy.[90] Certainly, the NSWLEC was *explicitly* established as an innovative adjudicative experiment.[91] But legal institutions must have limits[92] and the administrative justice frame is a little blurry and out of focus – its lines 'cannot be drawn with a ruler' –[93] reflecting a normative contestability or uncertainty that administrative lawyers know all too well.[94] Certainly, it does not help to delineate conceptual boundaries for the courts – for that we need to look elsewhere (and the challenges for creating greater practical limits through legislative strictures are explored below). But considering this frame does help suggest what a theory for environmental adjudication would have to address, and that includes acknowledging the failings of the ordinary courts in this sphere. In particular, the very nature of environmental adjudication needs to be scrutinised, and consideration given to how the form, functions and powers of any adjudicatory body might best respond to that nature: the *what* and the *why* need to infuse a new frame. If we fail to embrace this interaction we will end up with a theoretical misfit that is so far from reality it does nothing to illuminate our understanding.

III. THE 'GENERIC INSTRUMENTALISM' FRAME

The second analytical frame is premised upon generic instrumentalism: a frame that tends to dominate the current policy discourse in New Zealand and one that played a significant factor in the Cripps Review of the NSWLEC.[95] Although generally dismissed by lawyers, the use of this frame *does* impact upon the legal nature of the Court but its use in the New Zealand context also highlights its weaknesses.

As a general concept, instrumentalism views law as a practical tool for serving specific political goals. Rather than containing a set of general legal axioms, law is seen as simply a means to an end: a means to achieve external

[90] Resnik (n 86) 10.

[91] NSW Parliamentary Debates, 21 November 1979, 3345, Second Reading Speech of the Hon Paul Landa MP, Minister for Planning and Environment quoted in S Smith, *A Review of the Land and Environment Court: Briefing Paper No 13/01* (NSW Parliamentary Library Research Service, 2001) 1.

[92] See J Raz, 'The Institutional Nature of Law' (1975) 38 *MLR* 489, 499.

[93] L Jaffe, *Judicial Control of Administrative Action* (Little and Brown, 1965) 324.

[94] C Harlow and R Rawlings, *Law and Administration*, 3rd edn (Cambridge University Press, 2009) 1; Lord Cooke of Thorndon (n 31).

[95] JS Cripps et al, *Report of the Land and Environment Court Working Party* (Government of New South Wales, 2001).

goals derived predominantly from 'the dictates of democratic processes and the "policy sciences"' and for the instrumentalist, 'uses of law can be justified only by reference to whatever values they fulfill'.[96] *Generic* features of an instrumentalist approach to dispute resolution might address issues concerning access to justice, speed and cost, and malleability.[97]

The predominant focus of the policy agenda in New Zealand has been to 'simplify and streamline' environmental dispute-resolution processes, making them quicker and cheaper. The Fifth National Government (2008–17) produced or commissioned over 19 reports directly linked to this imperative.[98] In fact, the title of the first set of amendments to the Act brought in by that government is the Resource Management (Simplifying and Streamlining) Amendment Act 2009. In the New South Wales context, the Civil Procedure Act 2005 places a statutory duty on the NSWLEC to facilitate the just, quick and cheap resolution of disputes.[99]

However generic instrumentalism, certainly as it is used in the New Zealand policy context, is a highly exclusionary frame. It is concerned with 'ends' and 'output' legitimacy that is quantifiable and 'results-focused'.[100] It does not take in to account, for example, the contribution of the NZEnvC to developing environmental jurisprudence and filling in the gaps of highly interstitial legislation (discussed below and in chapter six). Other difficulties with the use of this frame accurately reflect Tamanaha's description that instrumentalism has no inherent integrity. Rather, it implies the need for 'compromise or contest between group interests within the democratic process' and the '[s]poils go to the winners'.[101] Accordingly, the instrumentalist 'law-as-politics-approach' is inherently susceptible to ideological forces.[102]

We can see how these concerns play out in New Zealand by using one particular example. In an attempt to speed up final decisions, legislative amendments removed the statutory presumption in favour of public notification for resource-consent applications,[103] thus reducing the ability of the public to make submissions that would feed into decision-making.[104] Local authorities have a wide discretion whether to notify applications but if there is no notification the

[96] Summers (n 58) 863.

[97] H Genn, 'Tribunals and Informal Justice' (1993) 56 *MLR* 393, 395 (referring to the advantages of tribunals).

[98] See Ministry for the Environment (NZ) 'Publication Search', available at: www.mfe.govt.nz/publication-search?search_api_views_fulltext=&f[0]=field_section_topic%3A170.

[99] Civil Procedure Act 2005 (NSW), s 56(1), (2).

[100] For explanation of output legitimacy see E Fisher, 'The European Union in the Age of Accountability' (2004) 24 *OJLS* 495, 508.

[101] B Tamanaha, *On the Rule of Law: History, Politics, Theory* (Cambridge University Press, 2004) 79.

[102] ibid, 79–80.

[103] Akin to permitting and/or planning permission.

[104] Resource Management (Simplifying and Streamlining) Amendment Act 2009 (NZ), ss 95A, 87C-I.

effect is to lock the wider public out of decision-making processes altogether. Non-submitters cannot bring or be party to any appeal to the NZEnvC or superior courts.[105] In tandem, court fees have been substantially increased.[106] All these moves run contrary to the common law principle of access to justice and the critical role this principle plays in upholding the rule of law,[107] and they impact upon the legal nature of the Court by limiting its subject-community. Although speed of decision is often conflated with promoting access to justice in general, this is not the case in the New Zealand context. Rather, the frame is – as Tamanaha suggested – being used to advance a particular ideological agenda. Resource consents are applied for in order to develop, pollute or take natural resources, not to preserve or conserve them: developers are Tamanaha's winners, getting faster decisions by having less public input. In an attempt to deflect criticisms based upon generic instrumentalism, the judiciary have found themselves having to defend hearings in the NZEnvC as against other adjudicatory models,[108] explaining the Court's own innovations to cut costs while emphasising the importance of access to justice and fairness, particularly for self-represented litigants.[109]

In summary, the generic instrumentalist frame is useful for focusing *in part* on what we might want the courts to do, but clearly it is not able to account fully for their legitimacy, to set limits or to explain their legal nature. The risk is that a frame premised upon generic instrumentalism allows environmental adjudication to be buffeted and formed by incidental currents, and in the New Zealand context it has drawn the judicial members of the Court into a cost–benefit debate that they should not be required to address. However, the fact that this frame is used at all – and how it has been constructed in New Zealand at least – has important lessons for the development of any future theory: efficiency in environmental adjudication is important. But rather than accepting an impoverished and ideologically driven frame, theoretical responses must consider how

[105] The only recourse against non-notification is judicial review of the non-notification decision before the High Court, but this is extremely difficult to argue (given the fact the statutory presumption in favour of notification was removed in 2009 and the statute gives local authorities who make the decision as to non-notification an incredibly wide discretion) unless there is clear evidence of procedural irregularity. Those wishing to respond to an appeal may attempt to argue they come within RMA s 274 (see ch 6).

[106] eg, the filing fee in the NZEnvC rose from NZ$55 to NZ$500 in 2014 (Resource Management (Forms, Fees, and Procedure) Regulations 2003, cl 35(1).

[107] See the powerful opinion of the UKSC on the role access to justice plays in the rule of law: *R (On the application of UNISON) v Lord Chancellor* [2017] UKSC 51, [65]–[85]; in the New Zealand context see C Warnock, 'Environment and the Law: the normative force of context and constitutional challenges' (2020) 3 *JEL* (forthcoming).

[108] LJ Newhook, 'Current and Recent-Past Practice of the Environment Court Concerning Appeals on Proposed Plans and Policy Statements' [2012] *Resource Management Journal* 13; LJ Newhook, *Comparative costs of different NZ Resource Management hearing models: a discussion paper* (Environment Court of New Zealand, 2015); New Zealand Environment Court, *Annual Review by Members of the Court* (Environment Court, Wellington, 2014).

[109] LJ Newhook, 'Justice without Barriers: Technology for greater access to justice' (Australasian Institute of Judicial Administration, Brisbane, 21–22 May 2015).

best to foster normative legitimacy by embracing wider solutions such as exploring how conceptual clarity, responsive procedures and tailored principles will help facilitate *both* efficiency *and* access to justice.

IV. THE 'SEPARATION OF POWERS' FRAME

Lawyers may be uncomfortable with the two frames explored above (albeit, they use both to explain what it is they do) but the final frame will prove familiar. As a normative meta-theory, the separation of powers provides the main legitimising frame for institutions of government in New Zealand, Australia and many other nations, and it constitutes a powerful idea. The separation of powers can mean different things – an idea explored below – but at its simplest it provides an organising frame, helping to constitute, empower and limit the branches of government (the legislature, executive and judiciary) by managing their relationships to each other.

Within the legal cultures of New Zealand and New South Wales, a separation of powers frame helps to justify why bodies independent of government have been chosen to determine environmental and planning law disputes that invariably impact upon the rights of individuals. Both the New Zealand Law Commission and the Department of Justice consider that an impartial adjudicator should determine disputes involving government actions that impact upon rights.[110] And during the Cripps Review, submitters argued that the independent NSWLEC was an appropriate body to determine disputes that impacted individual rights, including property rights.[111] International commentators also stress the need for ECs to be impartial, which some commentators argue will best be facilitated by independence from government.[112] Although Hale LJ (as she was then) draws a distinction between impartiality and independence, her Ladyship acknowledges that that the two are often conflated:

> Impartiality is not the same as independence, although the two are closely linked. Impartiality is the tribunal's approach to deciding the cases before it. Independence is

[110] New Zealand Department of Justice, *The Citizen and Power: Administrative Tribunals* (Government Printer, Wellington, 1965) 10.

[111] Smith (n 91) 11.

[112] BJ Preston, 'Characteristics of Successful Environmental Courts and Tribunals' (2014) 26 *JEL* 365, 369–72; S Abed de Zavala et al, 'An Institute for Enhancing Effective Environmental Adjudication' (2010) 3 *Journal of Court Innovation* 1, 6 and 8. Note that the European Convention on Human Rights Art 6 guarantees an independent and impartial tribunal addresses 'civil rights and obligations' (see *Ringeisen v Austria* (No 1) App no 2614/65 (A/13), (IHRL 8) (ECHR 1971) 16 July 1971 European Court of Human Rights [ECHR]) and states with constitutional environmental rights-protections must ensure decision-makers' independence from government (see V Madner, 'The Austrian Environmental Senate' (2010) 3 *Journal of Court Innovation* 23, 26); *cf* UK – Minister is ultimate arbiter of planning disputes (*R (Alconbury Developments Ltd) v Secretary of State for the Environment, Transport and the Regions* [2001] UKHL 23) and note controversy about ministerial decision-making in discrete applications in general in UK: L Johnson, 'Back to the drawing board? Article 6 and homelessness review decisions following *Tsfayo v United Kingdom*' [2007] *Journal of Housing Law* 9.

> the structural or institutional framework which secures this impartiality, not only in the minds of the tribunal members but also in the perception of the public.[113]

Certainly, public perception of impartiality is fostered by independence.[114] A constant theme in the New Zealand parliamentary debates on planning and environmental legislation has been that an independent adjudicative body is the right body to manage the delicate balance between individual rights and the use and development of natural resources.[115] Previous government ministers contended that independent adjudication would be fairer, and public participation and the right to object and be heard would be infinitely greater if decisions were taken by an independent body.[116]

Nevertheless, the separation of powers frame is employed most readily by *critics* of the courts, in order to attack the normative legitimacy of the courts. Critics draw upon a particular conception of the separation of powers to construct their arguments, namely a pure or literal version (often referencing Montesquieu directly). The separation of powers frame also influences judicial opinion. In part, the NSWLEC judiciary appear divided between those who align the Court's role more closely with a functionalist separation of powers conception and those who acknowledge the role of the 'administrative justice-adjudicative pluralism' frame.

The next part of the chapter reflects upon why the separation of powers frame dominates the discussion about the courts and what critics of the courts understand its internal criteria to be. In particular, the challenges created for law by the nature of environmental problems are considered more closely in order to explain why a separation of powers frame struggles to accommodate environmental adjudication.

A. A 'Pure' Approach to the Separation of Powers

In conceiving of the separation of powers in the 1748 *Spirit of Laws* Montesquieu's concern was the 'avoidance of tyranny'.[117] His observation was that the English constitution avoided excessive concentrations of power in one

[113] *Gillies (AP) v Secretary of State for Work and Pensions (Scotland)* [2006] UKHL 2, [38].

[114] New Zealand Law Commission, *Tribunals in New Zealand: An Issues Paper* (n 76) 24 (because it fosters 'public confidence and [creates] greater acceptance of the policy in new statutory regimes').

[115] New Zealand Parliamentary Debates, 347 NZPD 2866, 2871; 442 NZPD 4063.

[116] RJ Bollard, 'Editorial' (2005) 6 *Resource Management Bulletin* 61, 61. This focus on independence helps explain the iterative moves in NZ towards cementing judicial tenure within specialist environmental adjudication. Under the 1977 Town and Country Planning Act, Planning Tribunal judges initially had a warrant for five years. Under the RMA, judges hold office indefinitely provided that they retain concurrent status as a District Court Judge or Maori Land Court Judge, see RMA 1991, s 250(2).

[117] Charles de Secondat Baron de Montesquieu, *The Spirit of Laws*, vol XI (Thomas Nugent trans, Batoche Books, 2001) 173–74.

person, group or agency – and thus avoided dictatorship – by ensuring that 'the three great departments of power' were 'separate and distinct'.[118] But it is important to appreciate the subtleties of the concept because there are different ways to perceive of the separation of powers – a fact that complicates the present debate. Marshall identifies within the phrase a cluster of overlapping and at times contradictory ideas including 'the differentiation of the concepts 'legislative', 'executive', and 'judicial' … the isolation, immunity, or independence of one branch of government from the actions or interference of another … [and by contrast, suggesting a necessary inter-relationship] the checking or balancing of one branch of government by the action of another'.[119] And he notes that '[r]eferences to the separation of powers may be references to any one or to any combination of these ideas'.[120] However, contributors to the NZEnvC and NSWLEC debates appear to be using the separation of powers in a *pure* sense: as Cane observed, 'only with a pure form of separation of powers are specialist adjudicative bodies seen as problematic'.[121] Essentially, a pure theory privileges a *qualitative* separation of the different functions of government.[122] Only the legislature can regulate, only the judiciary can adjudicate, and only the executive can administer the law. The conceptual frame is seen as hard and shiny and its internal criteria are underpinned by the idea that

> there are three intrinsically distinct functions of government; the legislative, the executive, and the judicial: these distinct functions ought to be exercised respectively by three separately manned departments of government; … [and] the legislative may not delegate its powers.[123]

Critics of the NZEnvC[124] adopt a pure approach and they need to do so in order to make the separation of powers work as a frame, to draw clear limits of legitimacy for the Court – to argue, for example, that the Court should not have a role in determining disputes over policy and planning documents thus crafting the final regulatory regimes for localities. In the New South Wales context, submitters to the Cripps Review believed that the judicial branch should not have powers of merits review that in effect placed the Court in the role of permitting activities.[125] Critics of both courts maintain that the courts' merged functions are illegitimate because they are making decisions that draw upon, evaluate and

[118] J Madison, 'Number XLVII' in EH Scott (ed), *The Federalist and other Constitutional Papers* (Albert, Scott & Co, 1898) 266.

[119] G Marshall, *Constitutional Theory* (Clarendon Press, 1980) 100.

[120] ibid.

[121] Cane, *Administrative Tribunals and Adjudication* (n 71) 32.

[122] J Waldron, 'Separation of Powers in Thought and Practice' (2013) 54 *Boston College Law Review* 433, 433–34.

[123] Marshall (n 119) 100.

[124] eg, S Rivers-McCombs, 'Planning in Wonderland: The RMA, Local Democracy and the Rule of Law' (2011) 9 *New Zealand Journal of Public and International Law* 43; Ministry for the Environment, *Report of the Minister for the Environment's Technical Advisory Group* (Wellington, 2009).

[125] See ch 2.

in turn impact socio-cultural, economic and environmental policy issues, a role that has traditionally been allocated to the executive arm of government and that – they argue – is best suited to the institutional capacity of that branch.[126] They ignore the specialist, expert nature of the courts, and the role that specialism plays in court processes, reasoning and decision-making. They also ignore the participatory, transparent and deliberative processes common to ECs.

But closer attention shows that there are certain dangers in privileging a frame based on a pure conception of the separation of powers, not least the fact that it has often been maligned as 'an antique and rickety' frame:[127] it is contestable and contested, theoretically and in practice, historically and at present.[128] I do not intend to add to the debate or argue that a metaphor based on a pure form is always unhelpful – that is not the purpose of this chapter – but I do suggest that the rigidity of the frame that is being used to analyse the legal nature of the ECs appears ill-equipped for the task at hand. My fundamental argument is that there is too much blurring of the traditional delineations that a pure approach to the separation of powers relies upon – ie, between law, policy, discretion and fact – in environmental law and environmental adjudication to construct stable frames for legitimacy using this conception. Environmental adjudication may not be *sui generis* in this regard (certainly, a *pure* model of the separation of powers does not operate in many other areas of modern social ordering either)[129] but this legal-form admixture is an inherent and immutable feature of environmental dispute-resolution. To make this argument, the next part of this chapter provides a sketch of the architecture of environmental statute law in the case study jurisdictions (and in fact, many other jurisdictions) to show the blurring of boundaries created by the inherent nature of environmental problems.

B. The Architecture of Modern Environmental Regulation

The inherent features of environmental problems present challenges for problem-solving through law. By way of brief explanation: ecosystems are dynamic and

[126] J Jowell, 'Of vires and vacuums: the constitutional context of judicial review' [1999] *PL* 448.

[127] Robson (n 33) 14. Robson's discrete metaphor is vehicular: 'an antique and rickety chariot ... for the conveyance of fallacious ideas'. See also W Ivor Jennings, *The Law and the Constitution*, 5th edn (University of London Press, 1969) 7–28 and Appendix I; Marshall (n 119) ch 5; EL Rubin, *Beyond Camelot: Rethinking Politics and Law for the Modern State* (Princeton University Press, 2005).

[128] EG Earl Halsbury and Viscount Halisham, *Halsbury's Laws of England*, vol 6, 2nd edn (Butterworth, 1931) 385; AV Dicey, *Introduction to the Study of the Law of the Constitution*, 3rd edn (Macmillan, 1889) 309, 322; Madison (n 118) 268; Maitland (n 44) 478; Henry Lord Viscount St John Bolingbroke, *The Works of the Late Right Honourable Henry St John Lord Viscount Bolingbroke*, vol 2 (O Goldsmith ed, J Johnson, 1809) 190–91; P Craig, 'Public law, political theory and legal theory' [2000] *PL* 211, 218–19; L Claus, 'Montesquieu's Mistakes and the True Meaning of Separation' (2005) 25 *OJLS* 419; Cane, *Administrative Tribunals and Adjudication* (n 71) 28; Rubin (n 127).

[129] Cane, Administrative Tribunals and Adjudication (n 71) and see ch 2.

scientific uncertainty is prevalent, which means that the factual backdrop for environmental problem-solving is neither fixed nor comprehensively known; problems are polycentric, impacting the environmental, socio-cultural and economic realms, which means that normative conflicts abound.[130] As Fisher notes, environmental problems do not lend themselves to simple solutions:

> Environmental problems are inherently messy and thus not easily managed by engineered solutions. The non-linear processes of ecosystems, the unpredictability of human behaviour and the problems of scientific uncertainty all make the process of assessing environmental harm an intricate and often intractable business.[131]

All these features are discussed in detail in chapter five as part of the theory-building process, but for present purposes it is important to note that this contextual messiness – dynamism, uncertainty and contestability – has a normative force on the appropriate regulatory response. In turn, this regulatory response creates ramifications for the possibility of maintaining sharp divisions between law, policy, discretion and facts, and between the different branches of government.

Problem-solving in this context seldom yields to rules-based solutions worked out in the abstract in advance because, there may be uncertainty and gaps in knowledge;[132] scenarios change rapidly; the scope of activities and their relative impacts on specific environments and peoples (including future generations) can vary enormously; localised solutions may be preferred; localised knowledge may be essential; and there may be a societal desire to facilitate compromise and to allow those being regulated and impacted upon to participate in the formation of norms.[133] Government may lack the requisite knowledge and therefore be unable to exercise evaluative judgement in the abstract, creating predetermined rules-based regimes. Politicians may be unable to signal what the 'answer' to a discrete dispute is before it manifests, undermining representative democracy arguments for placing ministers in the position of resolving disputes.[134] In this context, creating primary legislation that sets down clear and certain rules can

[130] eg, *Falkner v Gisborne District Council* (n 59) (coastal defences versus private property); *Royal Forest and Bird Society of New Zealand Inc v Buller District Council* [2006] NZRMA 193 (HC) (endangered fauna versus coal); *Bleakley v Environmental Risk Management Authority* [2001] 3 NZLR 213 (HC) (Māori cultural beliefs versus genetic modification).

[131] E Fisher, 'Unpacking the Toolbox: Or Why the Public/Private Divide Is Important in EC Environmental Law' in JB Auby and M Freedland (eds), *The Public Law/Private Law Divide: une entente assez cordiale* (LGDJ Diffuseur, 2004) 231.

[132] eg, P Gluckman 'The Place of Science in Environmental Policy and Law' (The Salmon Lecture, Wellington, 2 September 2015); B Wynne, 'Uncertainty and environmental learning: reconceiving science and policy in the preventative paradigm' (1992) 1 *Global Environmental Change* 111.

[133] C Warnock, 'Reconceptualising Specialist Environment Courts and Tribunals' (2017) 37 *Legal Studies* 413.

[134] Although seemingly not in UK planning law where the Minister plays an important policy and decision-making role in relation to discrete disputes (albeit he/she delegates this latter role to the Planning Inspectorate). See also C Warnock, 'Differing conceptions of environmental democracy in New Zealand resource management law' (2016) 31 *Australian Environment Review* 253.

be tricky and, as Gunningham notes, 'the more complex the environmental problem, the more obvious become the limitations (and the inefficiencies) of direct regulation in addressing it',[135] certainly in isolation.

This contextual force has impacted legal responses in jurisdictions around the world. Scholarship has traced the changing architecture of environmental law, regulation and governance in 'Anglo-Saxon' nations over the last 50 years, charting the inadequacies of traditional legislative approaches.[136] Alternative responses to 'command control-type' regulation have evolved, categorised variously as 'smart regulation',[137] 'new environmental governance',[138] and 'integrationist and multi-modal' models.[139] Gunningham opines that new environmental governance is now a dominant model in many 'Anglo-Saxon' nations.[140] New environmental governance embraces regulatory pluralism, collaboration between multiple actors,[141] and includes 'an ability to handle diversity, facilitating experimentation, promoting learning, and allowing flexibility and revisability'.[142] Although government may no longer be responsible for the entire regulatory response in new environmental governance, it still has an important 'steering' role to play, using legislation to establish higher-order objectives and creating downstream management frameworks.[143] Fisher describes how many environmental statutes

[135] N Gunningham, 'Environmental Law, Regulation and Governance: Shifting Architectures' (2009) 21 *JEL* 179, 184.

[136] eg, ibid; JB Ruhl, 'Climate Change Adaptation and the Structural Transformation of Environmental Law' (2010) 40 *Environmental Law* 363; D Trubek and L Trubek, 'New Governance & Legal Regulation: Complementarity, Rivalry, and Transformation' (2006) 13 *Columbia Journal of European Law* 539; R Percival, 'Regulatory Evolution and the Future of Environmental Policy' [1997] *University of Chicago Legal Forum* 159; D Farber, 'Continuity and Transformation in Environmental Regulation' (2019) 10 *Arizona Journal of Environmental Law & Policy* 1; D Esty, 'Red Lights to Green Lights: From 20th Century Environmental Regulation to 21st Century Sustainability' (2017) 47 *Environmental Law* 1; J Steele and T Jewell, 'Law in Environmental Decision-Making' in T Jewell and J Steele (eds), *Law in Environmental Decision-Making: National, European, and International Perspectives* (Clarendon Press, 1998).

[137] N Gunningham, P Grabosky and D Sinclair, *Smart Regulation: Designing Environmental Policy* (Oxford University Press, 1998).

[138] Gunningham, 'Environmental Law, Regulation and Governance' (n 135) 204; Trubek and Trubek (n 136); G De Burca and J Scott (eds), *Law and New Governance in the EU and the US* (Hart Publishing, 2006) particularly the introduction, chs 8 and 11; M Lee, *EU Environmental Law, Governance and Decision-Making* (Hart Publishing, 2014) ch 4.

[139] C Arnold, 'Fourth-generation environmental law: Integrationist and multimodal' (2011) 35 *William & Mary Environmental Law and Policy Review* 771.

[140] Gunningham, 'Environmental Law, Regulation and Governance' (n 135) including New Zealand, 203; C Holley and N Gunningham, 'Natural Resources, New Governance and Legal Regulation: When Does Collaboration Work?' (2011) 24 *New Zealand Universities Law Review* 309.

[141] Gunningham, 'Environmental Law, Regulation and Governance' (n 135) 203 referencing Trubek and Trubek (n 136) 542.

[142] Trubek and Trubek (n 136) 451; for a critique of new governance albeit in a different context, see J Black, 'Paradoxes and Failures: "New Governance" Techniques and the Financial Crisis' (2012) 75 *MLR* 1037.

[143] Gunningham, 'Environmental Law, Regulation and Governance' (n 135) 210, quoting D Osborne and T Gaebler, *Reinventing Government: How the Entrepreneurial Spirit is Transforming the Public Sector* (Addison-Wesley, 1992).

now constitute 'power maps',[144] setting legislative objectives, delegating roles and responsibilities to various bodies including specialist adjudicatory bodies, and providing them with flexible powers to craft solutions in respect of environmental conflicts.[145] The important point to take from this restructuring is that complex, multi-scalar, and polycentric environmental problems require different legal solutions from those that may suffice in other areas of social ordering. Critically, a common feature of this new legal architecture is that it serves to the blur the boundaries between law and policy, between law and facts, and between functionally separate institutions. It removes the sharp divisions that critics of the NZEnvC and the NSWLEC rely upon in using a separation of powers frame. If we consider first the structure and then the content of modern environmental statutes, we see clearly the normative force this reality has had on the law.[146]

Structurally, statutes within many jurisdictions (and particularly in our case study nations, New Zealand and Australia) have morphed to become guidance frameworks containing high-level norms and objectives. These statutory frameworks facilitate the use of more flexible regulatory tools, and must be filled in where possible by more dynamic forms of delegated legislation and non-binding 'soft-law'. For example, in the New Zealand resource management context, a whole suite of secondary instruments exists to give effect to legislative direction: policy; plans; regulations; national and international technical standards (on, for example, electro-magnetic frequency); and guidelines (such as the Statement on National Priorities for Biodiversity).[147] Some may provide flexible, qualitative standards (in relation to matters such as biodiversity conservation and land use change for instance); others may contain clear mandates and precise directions (such as end-of-pipe pollution regulations). But even where quantifiable targets are included, how to meet those targets may be left unspecified, or standards may be capable of being changed upon the application of impacted persons.[148] These instruments are created in myriad ways by different groups, with forms of knowledge and expertise drawn from different disciplines, and all these instruments attract different legal weight.[149] They may not always attract 'finished parliamentary draftsmanship' as statutes do,[150] but nevertheless provide an important part of the legal framework within which decisions

[144] E Fisher, 'Towards Environmental Constitutionalism: A Different Vision of the Resource Management Act 1991?' (2015) 11 *Resource Management Theory & Practice* 63.

[145] The Resource Management Act 1991 (NZ) and the Environmental Planning and Assessment Act 1979 (NSW) are classic examples.

[146] D Fisher, 'The jurisprudential structure of environmental law' in D Fisher (ed), *Research Handbook on Fundamental Concepts of Environmental Law* (Edward Elgar, 2016).

[147] Ministry for the Environment, *Statement of National Priorities for Biodiversity 2007* (MfE, Wellington).

[148] Including National Environmental Standards; rules in Regional and District plans; and see *Auckland Regional Council v North Shore City Council* [1995] 3 NZLR 18 (NZCA).

[149] E Scotford and J Robinson, 'UK Environmental Legislation and Its Administration in 2013 – Achievements, Challenges and Prospects' (2013) 25 *JEL* 383.

[150] *Sandstad v Cheyne Developments Ltd* (1986) 11 NZTPA 250, 256 (NZCA). See also I Williams, 'Interpreting Resource Management Plans' [2004] *NZLJ* 324.

must be assessed, disputes resolved and legal rights and responsibilities decided. In turn, this regulatory layering creates a permeable interface between law and policy. Scotford and Robinson have observed that in the UK context the 'close legal interaction between environmental legislation and policy shows that there is no clean constitutional separation of environmental policy from the scope of environmental law'; there is no clear definition of policy in environmental law and it may be 'legislatively constructed and constrained', created by a myriad of different bodies and pervasive.[151]

This regulatory and institutional restructuring impacts the possibility of maintaining a sharp law–policy divide in other ways. In particular, the close interaction between law and policy in environmental law creates challenges for traditional legal reasoning. In *Environmental Defence Society Incorporated v Marlborough District Council* (*King Salmon*) the correct legal approach to understanding a higher order policy directive divided the New Zealand Supreme Court.[152] The majority employed close statutory interpretation to extract a clear direction from the New Zealand Coastal Policy Statement. The Policy stated that adverse effects in outstanding natural areas should be avoided. The majority found that the use of 'avoid' set up an absolute prohibition, literally meaning environmentally harmful activities were 'not allowed'[153] (and to that effect acted as a regulatory rule). The minority opined that 'avoid' was contextually contingent, so acting as a qualitative standard: it meant taking into account the qualities of the receiving environment as set against the wider socio-economic value of the development, and minimising adverse effects by imposing conditions.[154] Interestingly, all the justices agreed that the statutory purpose of the relevant Act, ie, 'the promotion of sustainable management', which is explained in complex terms in the statute,[155] was more akin to policy guidance and should not be subject to close statutory interpretation in order to extract a precise meaning.[156] As *King Salmon* makes clear, environmental law can up-end traditional hierarchies: policy may be susceptible to classic statutory interpretation and can have greater legal force in practice than statutory text;[157] statutory text may be treated as policy guidance.[158] This restructuring – forced by the inherent nature of environmental problems – is causing the

[151] Scotford and Robinson (n 149) 397–99.

[152] *Environmental Defence Society Incorporated v Marlborough District Council* [2014] NZSC 38; contained in the New Zealand Coastal Policy Statement 2010, and see [96].

[153] ibid, [93]. The majority also drew upon the wider statutory context to support this approach to interpretation.

[154] ibid, [194]–[198].

[155] RMA, s 5.

[156] *Environmental Defence Society Incorporated v Marlborough District Council* (n 152) [24].

[157] And this justifies in part the quality-control oversight of the NZEnvC in scrutinising these plans. For an example see *Manawatu-Wanganui Regional Council One Plan Appeals* [2012] NZEnvC 182.

[158] *Environmental Defence Society Incorporated v Marlborough District Council* (n 152), [24]–[25].

traditional hierarchies that a functionalist separation of powers relies upon to dissolve.[159]

Further, given the inherent dynamism, uncertainty and contestability in environmental problem-solving, policy instruments that attract legal weight cannot be set in stone. In many regulatory complex areas, but especially in environmental law, 'solutions must be attempted, but they often cannot be anything but tentative working hypotheses subject to continual reconsideration'[160] and to expect comprehensive perfection from environmental management plans and the professionals who draft them is to ask too much. Rather, policy and planning instruments are living constitutions for the environment that have to be tested in and against real-life scenarios and amended accordingly.[161] These instruments, and any amendments to them, must accord with legislative direction. And given many directly affect individual rights (they may impact people's rights to access a healthy environment, potable water, clean air and unpolluted land, and seriously curtail property rights)[162] there is a need for a neutral mechanism to check these instruments for legality, ensuring they fall within the four corners of the empowering statute while not transgressing legal rights without clear statutory power to do so. The choice of institution to perform this task is not a simple one. Siloing off 'law' from facts, policy and discretion becomes difficult. Institutions need to be constituted and have functions that facilitate the interface between public policy and legal rights. Governments in democracies may see the value of an independent, impartial and apolitical body performing this role, in accordance with the rule of law.[163] Specialist environment courts may be particularly well suited to determining disputes over environmental planning instruments, and using Chayes' conception this would permit

> ad hoc applications of broad national policy in situations of limited scope. The solutions can be tailored to the needs of the particular situation and flexibly administered

[159] C Warnock and O Pedersen, 'Environmental Adjudication: Mapping the Spectrum and Identifying a Fulcrum' [2017] *PL* 643; Warnock, 'Environment and the Law' (n 107).

[160] JA Farmer, *Tribunals and Government* (Weidenfeld and Nicolson, 1974) 198.

[161] See, eg, the role that the NZEnvC played in the development of the Tasman District Council coastal management plan in *Golden Bay Marine Farmers v Tasman District Council* W42/2001 (unrep) (NZEnvC); *Golden Bay Marine Farmers v Tasman District Council (Second Interim Report)* W19/2003 (NZEnvC); *Golden Bay Marine Farmers v Tasman District Council (Final Report)* W89/2004 (unrep) (NZEnvC); and the Manawatu-Wanganui 'One Plan' in *Day v Manawatu-Wanganui Regional Council* [2012] NZEnvC 182.

[162] For a hard facts case where the local plan impacted individual property rights see *Falkner v Gisborne District Council* (n 59).

[163] New Zealand Law Commission, *Tribunals in New Zealand* (n 69) 23 noting 'The Department [of Justice] considered that a tribunal was appropriate in situations where an individual was entitled to have an impartial adjudication of his dispute with authority' citing New Zealand Department of Justice, *The Citizen and Power* (n 110) 29; see also B Latour, *The Making of Law: An Ethnography of the Conseil D'Etat* (M Brilman and A Pottage trans, Polity, 2010) (impartial bodies created the rules to regulate the state precisely because it would be perverse if the oppressor (ie, the state) created the rules and adjudicated over its own behaviour in its affairs with individual citizens); see also M Dorf, 'Legal Indeterminancy and Institutional Design' (2003) 78 *New York University Law Review* 875, 945: 'courts are perceived as *neutral parties* that lack a direct stake in the outcome of litigation'.

> or modified as experience develops with the regime established in the particular case.[164]

The inherent nature of environmental problems has impacted the internal *content* of statutes too, in turn blurring the boundaries between law, policy and facts. In both statutes and delegated legislation, principles abound.[165] Terms that Stone described as containing 'multiple concealed references'[166] are rife, and sustainability and precaution with their inherent tensions are the leitmotifs.[167] Sustainability is commonly employed as an *objective* in statute law[168] (as the discussion of the *King Salmon* case above illustrates) yet Dryzek comments that sustainable development is 'a discourse, not a concept, and still less a scientific concept'[169] because it contains competing ecological, socio-cultural and economic considerations of wide and undefined scope.[170] As I mentioned above, the Supreme Court of New Zealand acknowledged this reality by describing the 'sustainable management' purpose of the RMA as 'a guiding principle which is intended to be applied by those performing functions under the RMA rather than a specifically worded purpose intended more as an aid to interpretation'.[171] In order to determine what constitutes sustainability, decision-makers may be faced with a list of statutory criteria or policy directives that can, in certain factual scenarios, conflict.[172] As the Chief Judge of the NSWLEC opined in *Bulga-Milbrodale* (a merits review of the Minister's decision to consent to a coal mine) employing syllogistic reasoning would not help in that case because 'the range of interests affected, the complexity of the issues and the interdependence of these issues, means that decision-making involves a polycentric problem'.[173] Rather, the relevant legal test of 'ecological sustainable development' requires

[164] Chayes (n 36) 1307.

[165] J Fogarty, 'Giving Effect to Values in Statutes' in J Finn and S Todd (eds), *Law, Liberty, Legislation: Essays in Honour of John Burrows QC* (Lexisnexis, 2008) and in the RMA context, this can be true of the primary Act *and* delegated legislation, including planning instruments.

[166] Multiple concealed references are the 'lurking place of a motley crowd of distinct conceptions operating in the cases in mutual conflict and reciprocating chaos': J Stone, *Legal System's and Lawyers' Reasoning* (Stanford University Press, 1964) 246.

[167] P Martin et al (eds), *The Search for Environmental Justice* (Edward Elgar, 2015) 2.

[168] eg, Resource Management Act 1991 (NZ); Environmental Planning and Assessment Act (NSW); Hallbar utveckling med miljobalken, 1999 (Swedish Environmental Code, 1999); Environment Act 1995 and Planning and Compulsory Purchase Act 2004 (UK).

[169] Dryzek (n 14) 56.

[170] J McLean, 'New Zealand's Resource Management Act 1991: Process with Purpose?' (1992) 7 *Otago Law Review* 538; I Williams, 'The Resource Management Act 1991: Well Meant But Hardly Done' (2000) 9 *Otago Law Review* 673; MC Cordonier Segger and A Khalfan, *Sustainable Development Law: Principles, Practices and Prospects* (Oxford University Press, 2004); AD Tarlock, 'Ideas without Institutions: The Paradox of Sustainable Development' (2001) 9 *India Journal of Global Legal Studies* 35.

[171] *Environmental Defence Society Incorporated v Marlborough District Council* (n 152) [24].

[172] eg, NZ adjudicators must (in many RMA disputes) take into account the 'matters of national importance' set out in s 6 of the RMA, but these can conflict: see, eg, *Dart River Safaris Ltd v Kemp* [2000] NZRMA 440 (NZHC) (conflict between public access to waterways (s 6(d)) and preservation of natural character of rivers and lakes (s 6(a)).

[173] *Bulga Milbrodale Progress Association Inc v Minister for Planning and Infrastructure and Warkworth Mining Limited* [2013] NSWLEC 48, [31].

an 'intuitive synthesis' of qualitative environmental, social and economic impacts,[174] and 'the resolution of one issue will have repercussions on the other issues; the other issues may change in nature and scope depending on how the first issue is resolved'. Deciding upon a sustainable outcome in any given case will require the input of (past and present) facts, (lay) values and (expert) opinions as to future effects, and Fogarty J of the New Zealand High Court has explained that the outcome of a case inevitably favours one or other statutory criteria over others.[175] As Allan notes, in regulatory scenarios where Parliament confers jurisdiction 'not to determine rights and duties already given, but to determine some facet of the public interest or administer a scheme, where executive "discretion" (or choice) is an integral component of each decision',[176] 'a fundamental distinction between administrative policy and legal right' just does not exist.[177] It certainly makes for an unstable premise in environmental law where it is often impossible to determine where policy ends and law begins, or indeed where law ends and facts begin.[178]

This latter point – the merging of law and fact – becomes particularly acute with the common use of standards in environmental law. The inherent nature of environmental problems forces environmental law to employ statutory terminology that is both descriptive and evaluative. For example, decision-makers are required to undertake qualitative assessments (such as determining the 'wholesomeness' of drinking water);[179] compare environments (protect 'outstanding' landscapes);[180] or determine other relativistic concepts (such as 'inappropriate development',[181] 'natural' environments,[182] or to decide if substances are

[174] ibid, [41].

[175] Fogarty (n 165).

[176] TRS Allan, Law, *Liberty and Justice: The Legal Foundations of British Constitutionalism* (Clarendon Press, 1994) 57.

[177] ibid, 53; see also Robson (n 33) 333–36.

[178] P Cane, 'Merits Review and Judicial Review – The ATT as Trojan Horse' (2000) 28 *Federal Law Review* 213, 220.

[179] eg, Health Act 1956 (NZ), s 69G requires suppliers to take 'all reasonable steps' to ensure that water is 'wholesome' and meets the 'aesthetic determinand' guidelines, which are in themselves qualitative including 'smell, colour and taste' leading to contestability as to whether those qualitative standards have been met.

[180] RMA, s 6(b), and see *Arrigato Investments Ltd v Auckland Regional Council* [2002] NZEnvC; *Wakatipu Environmental Society Inc v Queenstown Lakes District Council (No 1)* [2000] NZRMA 59 (NZEnvC); *cf West Coast Regional Council v Friends of Shearer Swamp Inc* [2012] NZRMA 45 (NZHC).

[181] RMA, s 6(b), and see *New Zealand Rail Ltd v Marlborough District Council* [1994] NZRMA 70 (HC); *Genesis Power v Franklin DC* [2005] NZRMA 541 (NZEnvC); *Environmental Defence Society Incorporated v Marlborough District Council* (n 152).

[182] RMA, s 6(a), (b) and see difficulties created by use of this statutory term in a succession of cases attempting to determine whether the Port Hills area of Christchurch, New Zealand was a 'natural environment': *Flanagan v Christchurch City Council* [2002] NZRMA 279 (NZEnvC); *Rutherford Family Trust v Christchurch City Council* C26/2003 (unrep) (NZEnvC); and *Campbell v Christchurch City Council* [2004] NZRMA 254 (NZEnvC).

'noxious or polluting'[183] when pollution is a 'relative concept not an absolute').[184] Decision-makers are required to assess degrees by, for example, considering 'less harmful' practices, or to prevent 'contamination'.[185] Or they are required to take into account 'significant' impacts[186] where significance is an open-textured notion. Whether something is significant is a value question: it embraces opinion and fact, comparison and contextualisation, and impacts may be significant in ecological, socio-cultural and/or economic terms, and in a public or private, spatial or temporal sense.

The increasing use of flexible standards and relativistic concepts in environmental law put new demands on legal reasoning because, 'value questions are necessarily posed when standards are set'.[187] Standards requires different forms of knowledge to merge – strands of fact, expert opinion, legal philosophies, lay values and political ideologies are all woven together with primary law. Specialist environment courts have developed new methods to manage this interplay between law, policy, facts, opinions and values. For example, the NZEnvC developed a schema to help address whether a wetlands was a 'significant' habitat ('significance' being the statutory test for protection) in a series of cases culminating in *Friends of Shearer Swamp Inc v West Coast Regional Council*.[188] The dispute had to be decided in accordance with legal tests but an important feature of these cases was the influence that scientific expertise had on legal reasoning. Expert ecologists proposed, and the Court accepted, that to qualify as 'significant' a wetland must satisfy at least one of four criteria, namely, ecological context; representativeness; rarity; and distinctiveness, and the Court expanded upon the test for each.[189] In effect, the Court created a legal

[183] Environmental Permitting (England and Wales) Regulations 2010, Sch 21(3)(1)(a)(i); and see W Howarth, '"Poisonous, Noxious or Polluting": Contrasting Approaches to Environmental Regulation' (1993) 56 *MLR* 171. See also RMA, s 322(1)(a)(ii) 'noxious, dangerous, offensive, or objectionable'.

[184] J Steele, 'Private law and the environment: nuisance in context' (1995) 15 *Legal Studies* 236, 245; *R v Dovermoss Ltd* UKCA (Criminal Division) 3 February 1995, 5, 6 'it will of course be a matter of fact and degree whether the matter does pollute the waters'.

[185] *Attorney-General v Lower Hutt City* [1965] NZLR 116), 116–25 (PC ('does addition of fluorine constitute a foreign element or impurity and impact wholesomeness?'– answered in the negative).

[186] Environmental Planning and Assessment Act 1979 (NSW), s 5.7(1): 'A determining authority shall not carry out an activity, or grant an approval in relation to an activity, being an activity that is a prescribed activity, an activity of a prescribed kind or an activity that is likely to significantly affect the environment (including critical habitat) or threatened species, populations or ecological communities, or their habitats'.

[187] E Fisher, B Lange and E Scotford, *Environmental Law: Text, Cases, and Materials* (Oxford University Press, 2013) 34.

[188] *Friends of Shearer Swamp Inc v West Coast Regional Council* [2012] NZEnvC 162 endorsed by the High Court, see *West Coast Regional Council v Friends of Shearer Swamp Inc* [2012] NZRMA 45 (HC).

[189] ibid, HC noting at [10] that the schema developed by the NZEnvC also includes: (i) representativeness: extent of range of genetic and ecological diversity; (ii) diversity and pattern in relation to ecosystems, species and landforms; (iii) rarity factors and/or special features; (iv) naturalness/intactness: size and shape (affecting the long-term viability of species, communities and ecosystems, and amount of diversity); (v) inherent ecological viability/long-term sustainability; (vi) relationship

framework for the evaluation of evidence in order to both interpret and apply statute law. In establishing the schema, the Court directed the future administrative behaviour of local authorities (which have a statutory duty to identify and protect significant habitats via planning documents) and also established a guide for future litigation (by directing what evidence will be legally relevant and providing a decision-making frame in relation to the substantive issue). This example neatly illustrates the necessary interplay between law and facts in environmental adjudication, and the need for different forms of legal reasoning to manage that interchange.

Further, while indeterminancy of language is always a problem with law this contestability is perhaps even more pronounced in the environmental context. Of necessity, environmental legislation has to include discrete but complex ecological and socially constructed concepts.[190] For example, Part 2 of New Zealand's Resource Management Act requires all decision-makers to 'recognise and provide for ... the protection of outstanding natural features and **landscapes** ... [and] the relationship of Maori and their culture and traditions with their ancestral lands, water, sites, **waahi tapu**, and other taonga' (emphasis added).[191] Once again, value-laden concepts such as 'landscapes' and 'waahi tapu' (akin to sacred sites) will not yield to a simple process of statutory interpretation,[192] nor are they capable of being proven by witnesses as a matter of primary fact[193] because they reflect 'competing understandings'.[194] Nevertheless, statutory terms have to be translated into something that is legally meaningful in order for people to regulate their behaviour, resolve disputes and determine legal rights. There are 'numerous examples of the NZEnvC attempting to craft environmental or ecological phenomena into concepts that can be used in legal contexts, and translating Māori cultural ontologies into a common language'.[195] For example, after hearing one heavily contested case the Court acknowledged the difficulty in attributing a simple meaning to such an ecologically complex term as 'landscape'.[196] At best, it could create a legal framework

between natural areas and other areas of mere modified character; and (vii) vulnerability of site: management input required to maintain or enhance an area's significance (see, eg, *Minister of Conservation v Western Bay of Plenty District Council* A71/2001 (NZEnvC), [20] endorsed by *Royal Forest & Bird Protection Society Inc v Central Otago District Council* A128/2004 (unrep) (NZEnvC), [32]).

[190] R Somerville, *Submissions on: Striking the Balance – Appeal Processes – The Specialist Environment Court* (A Review of the New Zealand Court System, New Zealand Law Commission, Wellington, 2002).

[191] RMA, s 6 (b)–(e).

[192] Davis (n 62) 402; Somerville (n 190) 24.

[193] *Comptroller of Customs v Gordon & Gotch (NZ) Limited* [1987] 2 NZLR 80, 93 (HC).

[194] Fisher, Lange and Scotford (n 187) 670.

[195] C Warnock, 'Reconceptualising the Role of the New Zealand Environment Court' (2014) 26 *JEL* 507, 510; *Winstone Aggregates Ltd v Franklin District Council* A080/02 (unrep) (NZEnvC); *Ngati Hokopu Ki Hokowhitu v Whakatane District Council* (2002) 9 ELRNZ 111, [34]–[46] (NZEnvC).

[196] *Wakatipu Environmental Society Inc v Queenstown Lakes District Council* [2000] (No 1) NZRMA 59 (NZEnvC). See also *Wakatipu Environmental Society Inc v Queenstown Lakes District Council* [2003] NZRMA 289 (NZEnvC).

for managing fact-finding in future adjudication that takes into account the wording and structure of the Act and relevant case law, incorporated policy directives, and marshalled evidence, so managing the interchange between law, policy and fact. The resulting methodology took into account not just romantic-pastoral perceptions of aesthetic quality (considerations reflected in the policy framework), and the scientific evidence of expert witnesses, but also called for evidence to include the historical associations of the land and its importance in Māori tikanga (constitutional considerations)[197] – crafting a meaning to 'landscape' that reflected the identity of the New Zealanders who inhabited it. This approach merged the strands of sustainability (the statutory imperative), while also reflecting that 'finding facts is only partly a matter of discovery, observation and description of data about the world; it is also a matter of analysis, classification and interpretation'.[198]

In sum, the inherent nature of environmental problems forces the greater use of principles, standards and value-laden terminology in environmental law, that in turn act to blur the distinction between law, policy and facts. Chayes noted that the 'continuous and intricate interplay between factual and legal elements' in public law disputes (of which environmental law is considered a subset) justifies a court having a greater control over the evidence.[199] But this factor also helps to explain the specialist nature of many ECs, including the NZEnvC and NSWLEC. Epistemic complexity can prove challenging for generic courts. New epistemic communities that blend knowledge from different disciplines can help, but institutional forms need to adapt to facilitate this transformation.[200]

The inherent nature of environmental problem-solving has forced both a regulatory and institutional reconfiguration. A complex regulatory layering blurs the distinctions between law and policy in environmental law, and functionally distinct institutions (where 'regulatory, policy-making and adjudicative' roles are siloed) have of necessity been replaced with more dynamic, problem-solving bodies with merged functions. As the higher courts have opined, it is precisely for these reasons that the specialist Environment Court of New Zealand exists.[201]

Just this brief survey shows how the inherent nature of *environmental problems* forces *environmental law* to be written in a particular way, that in turn presents challenges for *environmental adjudication*. Environmental regulation is not alone in requiring new structural forms or content – other areas of modern ordering present similar challenges – but these difficulties are immutable in the environmental context because of the very nature of environmental problems.

[197] Tikanga is the 'right way to behave': it has been described as Māori customary law, or sometimes lore.
[198] Cane, *Administrative Tribunals and Adjudication* (n 71) 12–13, referring to Jerome Franks' description.
[199] Chayes (n 36) 1297.
[200] GN Gill, *Environmental Justice in India: The National Green Tribunal* (Routledge, 2016).
[201] eg, *New Zealand Rail Ltd v Marlborough District Council* (n 181).

For all these reasons and more, attempting to make environmental adjudication fit within a pure separation of powers frame might appear futile. The separation of powers struggles in setting limits for legal institutions in the context of environmental adjudication and repeated as a mantra, it risks turning into 'a suffocating straitjacket'[202] that might serve to undermine the functionality of the Court. This frame fails because it splices the raison d'etre for ECs from normative legitimacy, and it ignores the particular nature of environmental adjudication. But its pervasiveness provides an important lesson for pre-theory building. In order to foster normative legitimacy, environmental adjudication has to be referable back to some conceptual limits and this is a challenge that any theory for environmental adjudication would have to address.

V. DEVELOPING A FRAME THAT WE CAN AGREE ON?

Without doubt, ECs raise complex issues of governance and power and foster differing conceptions of legitimacy. This chapter has explained that we may view ECs through competing frames of reference. These frames can act to legitimise or alternatively render illegitimate various functions and powers of ECs and in turn, constitute and limit ECs' legal nature. However, this chapter also argues that the three frames being used within the New Zealand and NSW debates all appear inadequate for the tasks of analysing ECs in particular and environmental adjudication more generally. Critically, the use of these ill-fitting frames has a real impact by directing policy debates about the appropriate forms, functions and powers of ECs and their continuing existence, and influencing adjudicative outcomes, as chapter two illustrated.

In an attempt to make the theoretical divergence constructive, we need a new conceptual model, one that explains and more properly accommodates environmental adjudication. A model for environmental adjudication might surmount the present divisions and foster a more reflective dialogue about ECs. It might enable us to take environmental adjudication seriously, allowing us to draw the limits properly, while also acknowledging the significance of these important bodies in many nations' constitutional arrangements. Such a frame might help tease out the adjudicatory nature of the NZEnvC, NSWLEC and other ECs rather than suppressing their legal nature within a separation of powers

[202] Berlin (n 17) 19.

discourse or simply subsuming them within the messy administrative justice landscape.

Undertaking pre-theory building and exploring existing frames that are being used to make sense of environmental adjudication enables us to see what a theory would need to address. In order to foster normative legitimacy some conceptual limits must be established, but any valid theory must also acknowledge the relationship and embrace the interaction between the nature of environmental disputes and the form, functions and powers of environmental adjudicators. Responsiveness matters. There is a need to adopt a pragmatic but principled approach to theory-building, one premised upon the importance of considering four factors as indivisible parts of the whole: the distinct characteristics of environmental disputes; commensurate challenges for law and dispute resolution; the resulting development of environmental law principles and pragmatic and justified procedural responses; and institutional forms that can respond to these forces. Adopting this approach would help to explain the complexity of environmental dispute-resolution, show how ECs have in the past and might in the future respond to those complexities in a way that has legal integrity, and provide the basis for building a detailed frame for environmental adjudication. The next chapter begins the process of theory-building by considering the idea of adjudication and normative legitimacy in greater detail.

4

Developing the Theory: Adjudicative Integrity

As chapters two and three demonstrated, the paucity of theory in the literature on environment courts (ECs) means that scholars have omitted to develop any conceptual models or frames that make sense of ECs' roles, functions and unusual legal nature. This omission is problematic because it leaves ECs vulnerable to criticism, particularly (as we saw in previous chapters) from government and policymakers interested in reforming or disestablishing ECs, and it may impact the creation of new ECs. Exploring these criticisms and the wider debates surrounding the Environment Court of New Zealand (NZEnvC) and the New South Wales Land and Environment Court (NSWLEC) revealed three themes. First, people tend to have fixed views about adjudication: what it is, what it can do and what it should not do. Second, people employ different conceptual frames in an attempt to legitimise or delegitimise the form and functions of adjudicative bodies, but we also saw that none of the frames used in the debates about the NZEnvC and NSWLEC (in isolation or together) adequately explain ECs. Third, using Beetham's framework of legitimacy, we saw that conceptual frames were being employed to address the *normative* justifiability of the ECs.

Beetham explains normative justifiability as a shared belief or understanding that justifies the rules establishing power.[1] Importing this definition into the EC context, normative justifiability means that what ECs are and what they do can be justified in accordance with shared beliefs. Shared beliefs eventuate from sources seen as authoritative – such as religion, natural law doctrine, philosophy, or science etc – and from the moral persuasiveness of their content.[2] Such beliefs manifest both in tradition – which Beetham describes as 'accumulated wisdom[3] … built up over time through processes of struggle and compromise'[4] – and continuing practice, ie, the beliefs are still intact and relevant to social functioning.[5]

[1] D Beetham, *The Legitimation of Power*, 2nd edn (Political Analysis, 2013) 17.
[2] ibid, 70.
[3] ibid, 74.
[4] ibid, 35.
[5] ibid, 74–75.

The pertinent question for the rest of this book is, how do we build a conceptual frame based on shared beliefs that justifies the legal nature of ECs?

There are a number of possible ways to undertake this exercise. Drawing on legal and political philosophy we could, for example, attempt to *replace* the maladjusted frames employed at present – the administrative justice, separation of powers, generic instrumentalism frames – with a singular, meta-frame that better explains the constitutional arrangements of modern government, that in turn accommodates multifunctional ECs. We could take up Elias CJ's challenge to better 'map the constitution';[6] and employ different conceptual metaphors to explain modern governance arrangements (such as Vibert's new separation of powers,[7] Rubin's network imagery,[8] and Loughlin's new ephorate).[9] The difficulty with this approach – and it is perhaps trite to say so – is that it would be highly divisive. There is little chance of creating a normative frame *capable of common acceptance*. This is because existing metaphors based on particular versions of constitutionalism are so highly entrenched, as indeed the discussion in chapter three demonstrated, and so the core aim of creating a *shared belief* by replacing constitutional meta-frames is unlikely to be obtainable, certainly in the medium term.

The solution therefore is to adopt a more modest aim: developing a frame directly focused on environmental adjudication that allows us to avoid some great constitutional reimagining, but one that nevertheless transcends the disputes discussed in chapter three. In this chapter, I argue that a belief capable of perhaps near universal acceptance is that of *integrity* in adjudication matters. Adjudication is a social service, set up to do a specific job, ie, to resolve legal disputes. My core argument is that in order to have integrity, adjudication must be created in a way that addresses or can respond to the nature of the problems (both legal and factual) it is tasked with resolving, rather than ignoring that nature. Responsive adjudication will have integrity, in turn shoring up legitimacy. Unresponsive or ill-fitting adjudication will not be fit for purpose. With environmental adjudication, if the form of adjudication cannot respond to deal with the immutable nature of environmental problems and the nature of environmental law (that in turn is a response to the nature of environmental problems), it will not be fit for purpose – it won't have integrity.

Thus, the shared belief that I argue should underpin norm-justifiability in environmental adjudication is that *adjudication must have integrity and an essential component of adjudicative integrity is responsiveness*. My interactional theory is therefore premised on integrity and responsiveness, and we can

[6] S Elias, 'Mapping the Constitutional' [2014] *NZLR* 1.

[7] F Vibert, *The Rise of the Unelected: Democracy and the New Separation of the Powers* (Cambridge University Press, 2007).

[8] EL Rubin, *Beyond Camelot: Rethinking Politics and Law for the Modern State* (Princeton University Press, 2005).

[9] M Loughlin, *Foundations of Public Law* (Oxford University Press, 2010).

use that theory to build a frame for environmental adjudication. If people can agree on this modest theory and the resulting frame, we can begin to make sense of ECs and importantly the existence of ECs will be buttressed conceptually.

The second part of this chapter considers the importance of integrity in adjudication and I interrogate that premise from various perspectives to show its robustness. Support is drawn from legal and political philosophy to illustrate integrity as an ideal standard; from historical developments and tradition to illustrate integrity as an ideal practice; and I conclude the chapter by returning to Beetham's framework to test the idea more expansively. However, in order to make my argument, I have to first dissuade the reader of any misconception that there is one unassailable form of adjudication. While there are undoubtedly core components of adjudication (and I discuss these below), we can create novel forms of adjudication that *do* respond to the nature of disputes without transgressing one homogeneous, correct standard and acknowledging this reality helps counteract thinking that would trip my argument at the first hurdle.

I. THE MALLEABILITY OF ADJUDICATION

A. Misconceptions

For many lay people, and possibly lawyers, reference to adjudication tends to trigger an automatic image – drawn from traditional prototypes – of a bilateral dispute, heard in a court of law and determined by a judge in accordance with litigious procedures. In this traditional form, adjudication entails 'the impartial application of determinate existing rules of law in the settlement of disputes'.[10] The parties present evidence and make submissions as to the applicable law. The judge determines the facts, applies the law to those facts and imposes a suitable remedy. Civil and criminal disputes are dealt with in a similar way, albeit with the presence of a jury to decide disputed facts in some types of dispute.[11] As an image, this adjudicatory form is self-explanatory – a clear meme – and it tends to satiate enquiry: a dispute is resolved and there is a winner and loser. It also helps to provide a natural legitimacy to dispute resolution by aligning the institution and its processes with traditional conceptions of the separation of powers. But an unthinking response fails to acknowledge the reality of adjudication as a heavily contested and contestable practice neither constituted nor constrained by any single form, theory or definition.

In a typological sense, adjudication is hard to confine. We can define adjudication in the negative, ie, it is not a means of resolving disputes through negotiation,

[10] HLA Hart, 'American Jurisprudence Through English Eyes: The Nightmare and the Nobel Dream' [1976–77] 11 *Georgia Law Review* 969, 971.

[11] More serious criminal offences and (in some jurisdictions) certain tort cases, for example.

mediation, voting, contracting or conciliation for example, but crafting something with substance is trickier. Definitions are not universally consistent, nor necessarily stable within particular jurisdictions; usage is neither restricted to court processes, reliant on the presence of a legally trained judge,[12] or linked to any constitutional delineation. Cane notes that in the UK adjudication tends to be used in a legally formalist sense and reserved for decision-making by the judicial branch,[13] but in the US – where there are clear constitutional placements for the courts of generalist jurisdiction as opposed to other dispute-resolution bodies[14] – the term is used expansively and encompasses initial executive decision-making.[15] In Australia, the situation is the opposite,[16] and in other jurisdictions, such as New Zealand – where no clear constitutional demarcation exists – adjudication is used to refer to decision-making in ordinary courts, specialist courts, tribunals and other forms of dispute resolution, and it is possible to see these bodies collectively as 'species of adjudicative institution'.[17] In England, the restrained usage is a relatively modern phenomenon and concepts of adjudication, administration and courts have transposed over time. 'Court' used to signify a place that was the seat of executive power (the Court of St James, for example, where the monarch resided).[18] And, as Maitland commented in the 1880s, in England 'the [administrative and the judicial] have for ages been inextricably blended'[19] (and in fact state-sponsored adjudication 'began as a mode of administration'),[20] so we can see the shifting and amorphous nature of adjudication. Indeed, common typology may be shifting again in the UK with the increasing prominence of tribunal justice following the introduction of the Tribunal, Courts and Enforcement Act 2007,[21] a phenomenon that reveals the

[12] *cf* J Gardner, 'The Twilight of Legality' (2018) University of Oxford Legal Research Paper Series Paper number 4/2018, available at: www.ssrn.com/link/oxford-legal-studies.html.

[13] P Cane, *Administrative Tribunals and Adjudication* (Hart Publishing, 2010) 48.

[14] Constitution of the Commonwealth of Australia, Chapter III; Constitution of the United States of America Art III and see literature on Art. 1–III courts in the US: E Pfander, 'Article I Tribunals, Article III Courts and the Judicial Power of the United States' (2004) 118 *Harvard Law Review* 645; TE Baker, 'Federal Court Practice and Procedure: A Third Branch Bibliography' (1999) 30 *Texas Tech Law Review* 909; (although this is not completely clear cut in the US, see Cane, *Administrative Tribunals and Adjudication* (n 13) 5).

[15] P Cane, *Controlling Administrative Power: An Historical Comparison* (Cambridge University Press, 2016) 283 and see ch 9 more generally.

[16] ibid, 283, 341.

[17] Cane, *Administrative Tribunals and Adjudication* (n 13) 48.

[18] WA Robson, *Justice and Administrative Law*, 2nd edn (Stevens, 1947) 39.

[19] FW Maitland, 'The Shallows and Silences of Real Life' in HAL Fisher (ed), *The Collected Papers of Frederic William Maitland: Downing Professor of the Laws of England*, vol 1 (Cambridge University Press, 1911) 478.

[20] P Cane, 'Public Law in the Concept of Law' (2013) 33 *OJLS* 649, 660–61.

[21] Albeit the Franks Committee included tribunals as part of the judicial branch in 1957, see Franks Committee, *Report of the Committee on Administrative Tribunals and Enquiries* (Cmnd 218, 1957). See *R (on the application of Cart) v The Upper Tribunal* [2011] UKSC 28 for the differing views about the Upper Tribunal's position and role in the judicial hierarchy expressed by the UK Supreme Court, Court of Appeal and High Court.

separation of powers frame is not a particularly useful one when thinking about specialist forms of adjudication.[22]

Surmounting these etymological difficulties, Shapiro notes in essence that adjudication simply constitutes a triadic structure, and 'whenever two persons come into a conflict that they themselves cannot solve, one solution appealing to common sense is to call upon a third for assistance in achieving a resolution'.[23] If we use this wide rubric, adjudication takes place at a multitude of different points – geographical, temporal, within and between social groups and peoples; it occurs in different institutional forms and employs different problem-solving mechanisms.[24] As a social phenomenon it prompts analysis by political theorists and scientists,[25] sociologists,[26] economists,[27] historians[28] and legal scholars from all disciplines. Adjudicative forms may be evaluated for institutional competence[29] and efficacy.[30] They may be critiqued for constitutional legitimacy, so bringing in to play constitutionalism.[31] Or they may be cast within wider ethnographic frames and evaluated as viscid social phenomena.[32] Each discrete evaluation will be located within different contexts, jurisdictions and legal cultures[33] between which there may be differing conceptions of the

[22] Some are comforted by a clear distinction between tribunals and courts in the UK as this aligns with a functionalist separation of powers conception (see, eg, R Craig, 'Black Spiders Weaving Webs: The Constitutional Implications of Executive Veto of Tribunal Determinations' (2016) 79 *MLR* 166) but this attempt to erect silos does not reflect the real impact of tribunal justice in promoting consistency between decisions, that may reflect a growing a body of precedent (see, eg, Carnwath LJ's comments in *Jones (By Caldwell) v First Tier Tribunal* [2013] UKSC 19, [2013] 2 AC 48, [41]).

[23] M Shapiro, *Courts: A Comparative and Political Analysis* (University of Chicago Press, 1981) 1 (specifically Shapiro uses this definition for 'court-ness').

[24] eg, just looking at 'classic' courts, compare the constitution, functions, powers and processes of the International Court of Justice; European Court of Justice; national generic courts; specialist international courts such as the International Tribunal for the Law of the Sea or World Trade Organisation Appellate Body; specialist national courts (eg, that in the New Zealand context include the Employment Court, Māori Land Court, Māori Appellate Court, Family Court, and Environment Court) etc.

[25] Shapiro, *Courts: A Comparative and Political Analysis* (n 23); M Shapiro, *Who Guards the Guardians? Judicial Control of Administration* (University of Georgia Press, 1988); CG Gehy, *Courting Peril: The Political Transformation of the American Judiciary* (Oxford University Press, 2016).

[26] B Latour, *The Making of Law: An Ethnography of the Conseil D'Etat* (M Brilman and A Pottage trans, Polity 2010).

[27] W Landes and R Posner, 'Adjudication as a private good' (1979) 8 *Journal of Legal Studies* 235.

[28] C Stebbings, *Legal Foundations of Tribunals in Nineteenth Century England* (Cambridge University Press, 2006).

[29] L Fuller, 'The Forms and Limits of Adjudication' (1978–79) 92 *Harvard Law Review* 353.

[30] See, eg, G Richardson and H Genn, 'Tribunals in Transition: Resolution or Adjudication?' [2007] *PL* 116; H Genn, 'Tribunals and Informal Justice' (1993) 56 *MLR* 393.

[31] J Jowell, 'Of vires and vacuums: the constitutional context of judicial review' [1999] *PL* 448.

[32] Latour, *The Making of Law* (n 26).

[33] Cane, *Controlling Administrative Power* (n 15) 283, 325. Note, legal culture is taken to mean 'a set of beliefs and attitudes (implicit and explicit) which give meaning to and condition activity. Many of these are inherited from tradition and are consciously transmitted, eg by legal education, but they can be forcibly changed' – see J Bell and D Ibbetson, *European Legal Development: The Case of Tort* (Cambridge University Press, 2012) 45.

adjudicative function.[34] As chapter two explained, debate as to the appropriate role for adjudication in governance exists between the judges heading up the different divisions of the NSWLEC. Alternative views of adjudication – and adjudication's place within a constitution – may even exist between different judges sitting in the same court, as Allan's analysis of *Evans v Attorney General*, a UK Supreme Court case, demonstrates.[35] In that case, divergent attitudes to the relationship between the courts and the executive, and to parliamentary sovereignty and the rule of law, resulted in the five justices employing subtly different reasoning to the interpretation of a statutory provision.[36] Allan opines that in eschewing literal statutory interpretation, some privileged

> moral deliberation ... as the defining characteristic of a system of law grounded on defensible principles of justice or fairness – principles that judges have a duty to develop and articulate in the course of adjudication.[37]

Whereas others

> were willing to take the statutory instructions at face value, swallowing their discomfort over such a dubious interference with the normal separation of powers, were also keen to insist on clear distinctions between law – and hence the judicial role – and moral or political judgment acceptably reserved for politicians.[38]

Scholarship mirrors this dispute. Fuller regarded adjudication as inherently limited.[39] Rubin regards adjudication as constituting law's empire.[40] Certainly, arguing about adjudication brings into play the whole contested body of jurisprudence, stretching from the 'command theory of law'[41] to 'realism',[42] 'textual originalism'[43] to 'judicial activism'.[44] But this is the point. Adjudication is an essentially contested concept.[45] Equally rational people will appraise adjudication's legitimate social function and associated benefits differently; differing

[34] J Miles, 'Standing under the Human Rights Act 1998: Theories of Rights Enforcement & the Nature of Public Law Adjudication' (2000) 59 *CLJ* 133, 152.

[35] *R (Evans) v Attorney General* [2015] UKSC 21; TRS Allan, 'Law, Democracy, and Constitutionalism: Reflections on Evans v Attorney General' (2016) 75 *CLJ* 38.

[36] Freedom of Information Act 2000 (UK), s 53. The question for the Court was whether the statute allowed a government minister to veto a judicial decision he disapproved of.

[37] Allan, 'Law, Democracy, and Constitutionalism: Reflections on Evans v Attorney General' (n 35) 39.

[38] ibid, 39.

[39] Fuller, 'The Forms and Limits of Adjudication' (n 29).

[40] Rubin, *Beyond Camelot* (n 8); see also R Dworkin, 'Does Law Have a Function? A Comment on the Two-Level theory of Decision' (1965) 74 *Yale Law Journal* 640, 640.

[41] eg, J Austin, *The Province of Jurisprudence Determined* (J Murray, 1832).

[42] eg, OW Holmes, 'The Path of the Law' (1897) 10 *Harvard Law Review* 457; J Frank, *Law and the Modern Mind* (Stevens, 1949).

[43] eg, A Scalia and BA Garner, *Reading Law: The Interpretation of Legal Texts* (West, 2012).

[44] eg, M Kirby, *Judicial activism: Authority, Principle and Policy in the Judicial Method* (Sweet & Maxwell 2004).

[45] WB Gallie, 'Essentially Contested Concepts' (1955–56) 56 *Proceedings of the Aristotelian Society* 167, 171–72.

perspectives may be genuinely held, justified and arguable but ultimately the debate is irresolvable. This conclusion helps inform debate about ECs. In particular, critics of the NZEnvC and NSWLEC who saw court-based adjudication as fixed and homogenous appear misguided because privileging a monocultural approach to adjudication does not reflect reality.

B. Core Characteristics

Despite this contestability, it is still possible to identify a number of core characteristics of adjudication capable of universal acceptance, albeit given the plurality of this exercise necessarily focuses on higher-level abstractions. Each characteristic is apparent in specialist environmental adjudication undertaken in the NZEnvC and NSWLEC. The quote taken from Shapiro paints adjudication as dispute *resolution* and this component is undoubtedly foundational. Adjudicating legal disputes, via a process that tests competing claims, is intended to lead to a decision. As the US Supreme Court in *Daubert v Merrel Dow Pharmaceuticals* opined (albeit in a different legal context),

> there are important differences between the quest for truth in the courtroom and the quest for truth in the laboratory. Scientific conclusions are subject to perpetual revision. Law, on the other hand, must resolve disputes finally and quickly.[46]

A second foundational aspect that differentiates adjudication from other forms of dispute resolution is that proffered by Gardner: 'the rule in the case, even if it has just been created to resolve the case, could in principle be re-applied in future'.[47] In common law systems this characterisic aligns with *stare decisisi*, the doctrine of precedent, but even in different legal systems (such as civil law jurisdictions) or within courts at the same level in a court hierarchy, consistent reasoning techniques between similar-fact cases and equitable treament of disputants is seen as important.[48] In this sense, adjudicative decisions are regarded as the *correct* way to resolve legal disputes.

But quite how adjudication resolves disputes, the integrity, wider ramifications and resonance of this process, are not incontrovertible. One premise of this book is that expansive approaches in which adjudicative processes are required to predict the future, assess and manage risk, and resolve normative conflicts – ie, all characteristics of ECs – are not outliers, and I want to suggest some additional core characteristics of adjudication that help support this contention. The first abstraction concerns 'truth', the second, 'futurity' and the

[46] *Daubert v Merrel Dow Pharmaceuticals* 509 US 579 596, 597 (1993).

[47] Gardner (n 12) 18.

[48] TG Watkin, *An Historical Introduction to Modern Civil Law* (Routledge, 2017) 8–9. In the context of tribunal justice see *Jones (By Caldwell) v First Tier Tribunal* (n 22) [41]–[47] (Carnwath LJ) explaining the role of consistency in tribunal decision-making.

third, 'interaction'. All these points are of critical relevance in how we resolve disputes about the environment, a contention developed further throughout the book.

C. Truth in Adjudication

In thinking about the *resolution* of disputes *Daubert* suggests one function of adjudication is discovering truth.[49] But Latour cautions that 'law should not be asked to pronounce truth'[50] and many scholars contest the traditional paradigm that adjudication is concerned with truth in any absolute sense.[51] Rather, rules of evidence have been developed to produce a certain kind of truth – acceptable truth.[52]

Over time, adjudication has employed various methods to produce an acceptable form of the truth. Trial by combat in the Middle Ages was seen as 'a definitive method for determining truth' by drawing on God's revelation.[53] This form of 'judicial combat' was replaced with the adjudicatory system that we retain to date that is, Rubin notes, 'equally problematic for ascertaining definitive truth' (although the 'defects, injustices and oddities' of our present system are not so readily apparent).[54] Frank dispelled the myth of 'finding facts' in the 1930s: facts 'are guesses' he wrote, and the truth capable of distortion in a myriad of ways once it is cast asunder and left to the foibles of litigation.[55] Categorising litigious procedures as the 'rules' of evidence carries a heavy connotation, but the moniker gives a false impression of the causal relationship between procedural clarity and the integrity of substantive results. Witnesses may forget or be mistaken,[56] experts may be (unintentionally but inherently) selective,[57]

[49] I understand truth in this context to mean descriptions of physical reality. Truth is a contestable idea (see, eg, J Habermas, *The Theory of Communicative Action: Reason and Rationalization of Society* (T McCarthy trans, Beacon Press, 1984) critiqued in E Rubin, 'The New Legal Process, the Synthesis of Discourse and the Microanalysis of Institutions' (1995–96) 109 *Harvard Law Review* 1393, 1421, 1435) but we do not need to explore these arguments for the purposes of this book.

[50] Latour, *The Making of Law* (n 26) 242.

[51] For opposing positions see, eg, D Leonard, 'The Use of Character to Prove Conduct: Rationality and Catharsis in the Law of Evidence' (1986–87) 58 *University of Colorado Law Review* 1, 2–3 (stating that the dominant paradigm underlying a modern trial is 'rational truth-seeking'); *cf* C Nesson, 'The Evidence or the Event? On Judicial Proof and the Acceptability of Verdicts' (1985) 98 *Harvard Law Review* 1357, 1359.

[52] S Jasanoff, 'Serviceable Truths: Science for Action in Law and Policy' (2014–15) 93 *Texas Law Review* 1723.

[53] Rubin (n 8) 232–33.

[54] ibid.

[55] Frank, *Law and the Modern Mind* (n 42).

[56] J Frank, *Courts on Trial: Myth and Reality in American Justice* (Princeton University Press, 1949) 17–19.

[57] S Jasanoff, 'Law's Knowledge: Science for Justice in Legal Settings' (2005) 95 *American Journal of Public Health* S49, S53–4.

knowledge can be partial, facts socially construed,[58] documents selective, representation unequal,[59] and decisions may be impressionistic.[60] Certainly, we can no longer 'call on divine assistance' to guide us towards adjudicative truth.[61]

Some suggest at best we might hope for objectivity in adjudication – aspiring 'to knowledge that bears no trace of the knower'.[62] And yet Latour charts the procedure and rituals of adjudication as often being some futile effort at objectivity, when the only evaluative tool the adjudicator has is their own mind.[63] In any event, objectivity is 'not the same as truth or certainty'.[64] Truth in adjudication might at times be a legal fiction or at best, a hit-and-miss affair. Finding truth in past events cannot therefore be an essential requirement for adjudication; adjudication is not reliant upon or constrained to this purpose for its functionality. Rather, adjudication can be called upon to provide the 'best answer to a practical problem'.[65]

This actuality is a critical factor when we consider environmental adjudication, so much of which is concerned with uncertainty. Specialist environment courts are seldom asked simply to find what occurred in the past (as criminal and civil courts are): the 'fact-finding' exercise in environmental adjudication is often not so much about finding facts as opposed to predicting what might happen in the future[66] and there are no guarantees that predictions will come true. But this predictive function does not, in and of itself, render specialist environmental courts illegitimate.

If adjudication cannot be relied upon to determine truth, how does it resolve disputes? What credibility can it claim? Scholars argue that adjudication can be seen as a legitimisation mechanism for creating an acceptable version of the truth.[67] Shapiro talks of the 'politics of fact finding', suggesting that the actual truth of a fact is not necessarily as important as following a process that

[58] S Jasanoff, *Science at the Bar: Law, Science, and Technology in America* (Harvard University Press, 1997).

[59] S Kós, 'Public participation in environmental adjudication: some further reflections' (2017) 29 *Environmental Law & Management* 60.

[60] Frank, *Courts on Trial* (n 56) 153, 174.

[61] Rubin, *Beyond Camelot* (n 8) 232–33.

[62] L Daston and P Galison, *Objectivity* (Zone Books, 2007) 17.

[63] Latour, *The Making of Law:* (n 26) 236–37; note also his comment that in this book he shows in 'great detail the complete implausibility of [the objects of law] being socially explained' (noted in B Latour, 'Why Has Critique Run Out of Steam? From Matters of Fact to Matters of Concern' (2004) 30 *Critical Inquiry* 225, 232). Of course, the Critical Legal Studies movement criticises the whole notion of objectivity in law for indeterminacy, claiming that no adjudication can be wholly objective – see G Postema, 'Objectivity Fit for Law' in B Leiter (ed), *Objectivity in Law and Morals* (Cambridge University Press, 2001).

[64] Daston and Galison (n 62) 17, 51.

[65] T Bustamante, 'The Ongoing Search for Legitimacy: Can a "Pragmatic yet Principled" Deliberative Model Justify the Authority of Constitutional Courts?' (2015) 78 *MLR* 372, 373.

[66] Or, as I explained in ch 3, about making sense of legislative terminology to ascertain how those 'facts' are to be employed in the decision-making process.

[67] See, in general, Jasanoff, 'Serviceable Truths' (n 52).

is legitimate from the parties' perspective.[68] Or, he posits, adjudication may support a legitimate social policy from the state's perspective, employing different processes and standards for fact-finding *depending on the issues at stake* (for example, adopting 'strict liability' for regulatory offences). Shapiro notes that adjudication was legitimised initially by parties' discrete consent to the 'big man' resolving the dispute.[69] In the modern state (in the absence of explicit consent) adjudicative forms remain tethered to legitimacy by institutional neutrality and their role of assuming responsibility, removing from individuals the burden of seeking revenge or reparation.[70] Moreover, by allowing 'competing claims to confront and engage with one another in an orderly process'[71] – employing measured deliberation and calm reason – adjudication avoids familial feuds, bloodshed, internecine warfare[72] and 'shouting match[es]'.[73] Specialist environment courts undoubtedly provide a site for resolving legal disagreements, allowing opponents to confront each other's arguments in an orderly fashion. In writing of Athena's transformation of the Furies to the Eumenides, and the creation of legal institutions in fifth-century BC Athens to replace bloody vengeance, Nussbaum sets out starkly, binary alternatives. But she also sets the parameters for possibility – the Furies' past destruction and brutality could not be obliterated, their transformation can only impact future justice: 'justice focuses not on a past that can never be altered but on the creation of future welfare and prosperity'.[74] This leads to a second core characteristic – adjudication impacts the future.

D. Futurity

In fact, as Sanchirico suggests, the real value of adjudication can lie more in shaping the future than in sorting out factual events from the past.[75] How adjudication impacts the future is multifaceted – from the imposition of remedies that directly impact the behaviour of the parties (payment of damages, injunctions, incarceration, permitting activities) or create on-flow effects (deterring future behaviour) to the wider role of adjudication in norm-creation that extends beyond the specific parties to the dispute.[76] Certainly, adjudicators are

[68] Shapiro, *Courts: A Comparative and Political Analysis* (n 23) 35–46.
[69] ibid.
[70] M Nussbaum, *Anger and Forgiveness: Resentment, Generosity, Justice* (Oxford University Press, 2016) 4.
[71] J Waldron, 'Thoughtfulness and the Rule of Law' (2011) 18 *British Academy Review* 1, 7.
[72] Or the death of 'star-cross'd lovers' (William Shakespeare, *Romeo and Juliet* (Simon & Schuster, 2011) opening prologue).
[73] Waldron, 'Thoughtfulness and the Rule of Law' (n 71) 7.
[74] Nussbaum (n 70) 5.
[75] C Sanchirico, 'Character Evidence and the Object of Trial' (2001) 101 *Columbia Law Review* 1227.
[76] G Spann, 'Expository Justice' (1983) 131 *University of Pennsylvania Law Review* 585.

required to deliberately predict the future in many instances. For example, in sentencing offenders, judges have to predict what penalty will have the greatest deterrent effect.[77] In making an order for a child to live with one parent over the other, judges have to predict which scenario will best meet the welfare of the child.[78] As mentioned, environmental adjudicators are required to predict the future by assessing the impact of proposed activities on the environment in order to resolve disputes. When specialist environment courts undertake merits review and determine permitting applications, the relief granted very definitely impacts the future.

In distinguishing adjudication from other forms of dispute resolution, Gardner relies on futurity: an adjudicative ruling impacts future cases, whereas an arbitral decision does not.[79] In creating norms, adjudication becomes part of 'expository justice'.[80] Expository justice accepts that the legitimate development of the law occurs through adjudication,[81] whether that process develops wider common law principles[82] or is constrained to a 'dependent common law': that is, 'the creation of 'norms generated during adjudication as a by-product of the application of statutory and constitutional norms'.[83] Whether the judiciary merely find or are instrumental in making the law is of long-standing dispute in common law systems, but few would now contest the norm-making role of *court-based* adjudication. Van Hoecke believes that the meaning of law can never be 'entirely determined by its author, but is constantly refined and sometimes thoroughly changed' through adjudication.[84] But other adjudicatory forms also impact norm-development in an expansive sense – affecting the behaviour and

[77] eg, Sentencing Act 2002 (NZ), s 7.

[78] eg, Children Act 1989 (UK), s 1.

[79] Gardner (n 12). Gardner must mean that the rule could be reapplied in the future *within the adjudicative sphere*. Other forms of dispute resolution impact norm-development in a more expansive sense – affecting the wider behaviour and customs of peoples and communities (and commercial arbitration is an obvious example: see P Devlin, 'The Relation Between Commercial Law and Commercial Practice' (1951) 14 *MLR* 249) but Gardner is distinguishing the wider societal impact of a decision from what must happen in the *adjudicative context* in the future. Adjudicators cannot, Gardner claims, declare what a rule is or will be and then decline to apply it in the particular case. This is the core feature of legal reasoning that distinguished adjudication from generic dispute resolution (see also Jasanoff, 'Law's Knowledge' (n 57) S49: 'adjudication is dispute resolution bounded by legality'). To justify this logic, Gardner relies upon the oath taken by judges in many jurisdictions to do justice 'according to law'. His argument relies upon the fact that adjudication can only be performed by judges (see 18: 'When the judge takes an oath to do justice according to law she binds herself to do justice first and foremost, and to modify the law as she goes along to make it possible to do justice. The words "according to law" are there to determine *how* – under what constraints – she modifies the law to make it more just'). Note, this explanation is less comprehensive than it first appears: adjudicative rulings bind – except, he says, when they don't: judges *can* create a new rule; and other forms of dispute resolution may be undertaken by judges without that activity becoming adjudication.

[80] O Fiss, 'The Forms of Justice' (1979) 93 *Harvard Law Review* 1.

[81] ibid.

[82] Holmes (n 42).

[83] Cane, *Controlling Administrative Power* (15) 333.

[84] M Van Hoecke, *Law as Communication* (Hart Publishing, 2002) 204.

customs of peoples and communities. Commercial arbitration is an obvious example.[85] As I have written elsewhere, specialist environment courts also play this norm-creating role regardless of their status in the court hierarchy.[86]

Thus, adjudication has a role impacting futurity. The natural corollary to this thinking, as Sanchirico observes, is that adjudication is best regarded as 'one mechanism by which the state regulates behaviour in the real world'[87] – and dispute resolution between the state and the public, directly so. The question becomes, however, one of intent and scope. Is adjudication merely responsive and passively so, in which case the future impacts of adjudicative decision-making are a natural by-product of determining a dispute (like the sentencing example) or can adjudication look towards and draw upon the future to resolve disputes – can it be predictive, deliberately regulative and catalytic?[88]

This is a critical question in determining whether court-based adjudication is suited to determining the merits review of applications to use or develop the environment. Fuller and Chayes address this conundrum in their writings on normative adjudicatory scope, with each taking a different position. It's a debate undertaken posthumously on Fuller's part, but worth considering in some detail nevertheless because Fuller's writing is used to justify criticisms of courts dealing with environmental law disputes.[89] Court-based adjudication, as Fuller famously said, was not suited to determining polycentric disputes because courts 'cannot encompass and take into account the complex repercussions that may result'.[90] Disputes that in effect serve to allocate public resources to one user or another – such as taking water, allocating space in the marine environment, polluting into an environment, or damaging biodiversity etc – are polycentric disputes. Polycentric debates involve 'a complex network of relationships, with interacting points of influence. Each decision made communicates itself to other centres of decision, changing the conditions, so that a new basis must be found for the next decision'.[91] Polycentric decision-making requires consideration of diverse yet interdependent factors (such as environmental, socio-cultural and economic wellbeing), creates effects beyond the confines of the immediate factual dispute, and so encompasses futurity.[92] By way of example, a dispute

[85] Devlin (n 79).

[86] C Warnock and O Pedersen, 'Environmental Adjudication: Mapping the Spectrum and Identifying a Fulcrum' [2017] *PL* 643.

[87] Sanchirico (n 75) 1227.

[88] J Scott and S Sturm, 'Courts as Catalysts: Re-thinking the Judicial Role in New Governance' (2006–07) 13 *Columbia Journal of European Law* 565.

[89] J Jowell, 'Legal Control of Administrative Discretion' [1973] *PL* 178; S Rivers-McCombs, 'Planning in Wonderland: The RMA, Local Democracy and the Rule of Law' (2011) 9 *New Zealand Journal of Public International Law* 43.

[90] Fuller, 'The Forms and Limits of Adjudication' (n 29) 394.

[91] *Bulga Milbrodale Progress Association Inc v Minister for Planning and Infrastructure and Warkworth Mining Limited* [2013] NSWLEC 48, [31].

[92] ibid, [31]–[42]; see also MA Eisenberg, 'Participation, responsiveness, and the consultative process: an essay for Lon Fuller' (1978) 92 *Harvard Law Review* 410.

as to whether to permit coal mining – that may impact local human communities, endanger biodiversity, contribute to climate change, but produce economic wealth – is a polycentric debate.[93] The need to consider the public welfare in determining an application (as both the NSWLEC and NZEnvC are legislatively mandated to do)[94] will mean that a dispute is polycentric.

A common argument is that adjudication is unsuited to determining resource allocation because of its polycentric, predictive nature. Critics argue the dispute may extend beyond the evidential remit of the (generalist) court and the analytical capabilities of the judiciary, an argument proffered by many[95] but based on Fuller's analysis. Jowell draws upon 'The Forms and Limits of Adjudication' to argue that planning disputes in particular are not suited to adjudication.[96] But this analysis appears to misunderstand Fuller's initial (and perhaps not finessed) thinking reflected in that essay. If you look deeper to Fuller's core beliefs – particularly the influence that custom, consensual relations and the formation of contractual arrangements had upon his thinking[97] – one can see a more fundamental approach that helps inform the present debate. His conception of legal ordering was that it was created from the 'bottom up' and the main province of law is the facilitation of this human *interaction*.[98] His point was that context morphs and moulds different forms of legal ordering in order to facilitate that interaction. Seen from this perspective, Fuller's philosophy does not prohibit adjudication from resolving complex problems; it just excludes traditional prototypes of court-based adjudication from this role. As Cane points out, Fuller's analysis is concerned with two particular forms of adjudication: civil and criminal adjudication, with all the associated constitutive, functional and procedural constraints that apply.[99] He was not concerned with the administrative justice system or with public law adjudication. Nor was he concerned with environmental adjudication – a form of (public law) adjudication that, as I argue throughout this book, *of necessity* constitutes a completely different species.

[93] *Bulga Milbrodale Progress Association Inc v Minister for Planning and Infrastructure and Warkworth Mining Limited* (n 91); *Royal Forest and Bird Society of New Zealand Inc v Buller District Council* [2006] NZRMA 193 (HC).

[94] eg, Environmental Planning and Assessment Act 1979 (NSW), s 1.3; Resource Management Act 1991 (NZ), s 5.

[95] Jowell, 'Legal Control of Administrative Discretion' (n 89) 213–15; S De Smith, H Woolf and J Jowell, *Judicial Review of Administrative Action*, vol 5 (Sweet & Maxwell 1995) 311–12; TRS Allan, *Constitutional Justice: A Liberal Theory of the Rule of Law* (Oxford University Press, 2001) 188–90; *cf* JA King, 'The pervasiveness of polycentricity' [2008] *PL* 101; JWF Allison, 'Fuller's Analysis of Polycentric Disputes and the Limits of Adjudication' (1994) 53 *CLJ* 367.

[96] Jowell, 'Legal Control of Administrative Discretion' (n 89) 213–15.

[97] Fuller's research was predominantly in private contract law.

[98] L Fuller, 'Human Interaction and the Law' (1969) 14 *American Journal of Jurisprudence* 1; RS Summers, 'Professor Fuller's Jurisprudence and America's Dominant Philosophy of Law' (1978–79) 92 *Harvard Law Review* 433, 447 referring to L Fuller, 'Law as an Instrument of Social Control and Law as a Facilitation of Human Interaction' [1975] *Brigham Young University Law Review* 89.

[99] Cane, *Administrative Tribunals and Adjudication* (n 13) 9–11.

Yet as early as 1947 (following the expansion of the administrative state and development of administrative law)[100] Robson cemented the existence of public law adjudication, writing '[w]e must now regard the public as very definitely a "party" to certain kinds of proceedings which are decided judicially'.[101] Long before 'Forms and Limits' was published, adjudication had become one tool in the public law dispute-resolution box with correlative impacts on adjudicatory form.[102] For Robson, the 'socialisation of government' in the early twentieth century had of necessity to 'be accompanied by the socialisation of law'.[103] Universal suffrage altered people's expectations as to the role they could and should play within political democracies, and this extended to executive and administrative decision-making, and the forms of dispute resolution that emerged as a consequence.[104]

This reality does not escape Chayes. In the equally influential essay, 'The Role of the Judge in Public Law Litigation', Chayes describes a morphology of adjudication that 'reverses many of the crucial characteristics and assumptions of the traditional concept of adjudication'.[105] I have touched upon these points above but they are worth repeating here. Chayes notes that in such adjudication the relief is flexible; the administration of the decree may require 'the continuing participation of the court'; and the decision may have 'important consequences for many persons including absentees'.[106] In Chayes' conception, adjudication is deliberately forward-looking and involves the judge in actively 'organizing and shaping the litigation to ensure a just and viable outcome'.[107] In this sense, certain forms of adjudication become part of the wider governance landscape, capable of constituting 'sites of democracy'.[108] Specialist environment courts align neatly with this understanding.

The differing perspectives of Chayes, Robson and Fuller illustrate the multifaceted nature of adjudication and its pluralism, and they highlight that different

[100] *Board of Education v Rice* [1911] AC 179 (HL); *Local Government Board v Arlidge* [1915] 1 AC 120 (HL); AV Dicey, 'The Development of Administrative Law in England' (1915) 31 *LQR* 148; HW Arthurs, 'Rethinking Administrative Law: A Slightly Dicey Business' (1979) 17 *Osgoode Hall Law Journal* 1; J McLean, *Searching for the State in British Legal Thought: Competing Conceptions of the Public Sphere* (Cambridge University Press, 2012); TT Arvind and L Stirton, 'The Curious Origins of Judicial Review' (2017) 133 *LQR* 91.

[101] Robson *Justice and Administrative Law* (n 18) 69.

[102] Cane, *Administrative Tribunals and Adjudication* (n 13) 9–11.

[103] WA Robson, *Justice and Administrative Law: A Study of the British Constitution*, 1st edn (Macmillan, 1928) 254.

[104] P McAuslan, *The Ideologies of Planning Law* (Pergamon Press, 1980).

[105] A Chayes, 'The Role of the Judge in Public Law Litigation' (1975) 89 *Harvard Law Review* 1281, 1302.

[106] ibid, 1302.

[107] ibid, 1302.

[108] J Resnik, 'Reinventing Courts as Democratic Institutions' (2014) 143 *Daedalus* 9, 11. For a different although compatible approach see J Mashaw, *Reasoned Administration and Democratic Legitimacy: How Administrative Law Supports Democratic Government* (Cambridge University Press, 2018).

contexts and forms impact views as to institutional competence.[109] But in order to abstract a universal characteristic from this discussion we have to draw back a bit, and the third abstraction I want to address concerns the essentially interactional nature of adjudication.

E. Interaction

Adjudication is interactional generally in (at least) two senses. First, it facilitates debate between people, structuring and providing a frame for discourse. Second, form and function interact within institutional frames to create diverse types of adjudication. In explaining the first aspect – which is discussed in detail below – I am going to rely upon the works of Arendt and Waldron. The second point is introduced here but developed throughout the rest of the book.

In thinking about adjudication as a frame for discourse, Waldron draws upon the idea of thoughtfulness and opines:

> [W]e want to be ruled thoughtfully. Thoughtfulness – the capacity to reflect and deliberate, to ponder complexity, and to confront new and unexplained circumstances flexibly, with an open mind, and to do so articulately (sometimes argumentatively or even adversarially) in the company of others – these are amongst the dignifying attributes of humanity.[110]

A recurrent theme in Arendt's work is that a lack of thoughtfulness in public life is deeply problematic, leading to disconnections between people, an inability to broach disagreements or broker agreements, and the silencing of peoples' lived experiences.[111] Thoughtfulness to Arendt is necessarily interactional. In favouring Socratic dialogue over Plato's solitary philosophical reflection, Arendt emphasises the importance of conversation for negotiating between the plural position of others in a communal space, articulating disagreements, and understanding new variables that might result in a shift in position: '[m]en in the plural … can experience meaningfulness only because they can talk with and make sense to each other and themselves'.[112] She suggests that only through conversation can transformation occur, a process and outcome seemingly harder to do in our troubled and divided world. But adjudication sets a frame for this interaction and law enables disputants to converse together.

In explaining this idea, Waldron suggests that when we argue we each start from the set of premises that we find compelling (God, utility or whatever) and

[109] Cane, *Administrative Tribunals and Adjudication* (n 13) 9–11.

[110] Waldron, 'Thoughtfulness and the Rule of Law' (n 71) 1.

[111] eg, H Arendt, *Eichmann in Jerusalem: A Report on the Banality of Evil* (Viking Press, 1964) Postscript 280–98; H Arendt, *The Origins of Totalitarianism* (Harcourt Brace Jovanovich, 1973) ch 10 and 307, 310, 315–16 in particular.

[112] H Arendt, *The Human Condition* (University of Chicago Press, 1958) 3–4 (Arendt believed Plato troublingly turned away from a political and pluralist society, favouring the 'singular').

this can lead to 'a cacophony as people talk across each other, following different and often mutually unintelligible trajectories'.[113] But law sets the parameters for the debate. It provides common meanings and establishes a set of shared premises as a starting point, preventing us from continually returning to first principles, and providing a way for us to 'argue together without immediately talking at cross purposes'.[114] Fuller expressed a similar view in 'Human Interaction and the Law'.[115] Metaphors and frames can assist this process, providing a common reference point that disputes are referable back to.

Critically, adjudication provides an institutional structure for this thoughtful discourse. By refining meanings, telling us what is legally relevant or irrelevant (and see chapter three for examples), adjudication helps us to talk together. This factor is especially important in environmental law, where standards are commonly used and the objective is often sustainability (whatever that might mean). Resnik has written that courts are 'active and disciplined sites of public exchange'[116] and the political scientist, Elster has drawn analogies between 'deliberative democracy' and adjudication,[117] stating that both facilitate a procedure for public interaction in which 'interchanges can serve to weed out falsehoods and inconsistencies and thus enable the [decision maker] to make a good decision'.[118] These forms of public interaction are imperative for healthy human functioning – fostering the political self as opposed to productive-man[119] – and enabling humans to live with dignity.[120] Cohen reports that discursive forms of interaction provide 'a basis for self-respect ... encouraging the development of a sense of political competence, and ... contribute to the formation of a sense of justice'.[121] To this extent, adjudication with its requirements for impartiality, *audi alteram partem*, transparency and the giving of reasons has some significant advantages over non-public administrative decision-making or political processes[122] that 'might handle it poorly or with doubtful integrity'.[123]

[113] Waldron, 'Thoughtfulness and the Rule of Law' (n 71) 8 citing J Rawls *Political Liberalism* (Columbia University Press, 1996).

[114] ibid, 16.

[115] Fuller, 'Human Interaction and the Law' (n 98) 2.

[116] Resnik (n 108) 9.

[117] J Elster (ed), *Deliberative Democracy* (Cambridge University Press, 1998) 8 – deliberative democracy revolves around 'the transformation rather than simply the aggregation of preferences' necessitating collective decision-making by all who will be affected by the decision or their representatives: this is the democratic part ... and includes decision-making by means of argument offered by and to participants who are committed to the values of rationality and impartiality: this is the deliberative part'.

[118] ibid, 2.

[119] Arendt, *The Human Condition* (n 112).

[120] Waldron, 'Thoughtfulness and the Rule of Law' (n 71).

[121] J Cohen, 'Deliberation and Democratic Legitimacy' in J Bohman and W Regh (eds), *Deliberative Democracy: Essays on Reason and Politics* (MIT Press, 1997) 69.

[122] Note, political decision-making is ideologically based (and in turn, generally divisive) and if it is not then what is the point of having a politician making the decision.

[123] E Scotford, *Environmental Principles and the Evolution of Environmental Law* (Hart Publishing, 2017) 39 quoting J Crawford, 'The Constitution' in T Bonyhady (ed), *Environmental Protection and Legal Change* (Federation Press, 1992) 21.

The public are said to 'prefer institutions in which the connections between deliberation and outcomes are evident, to ones in which the connections are less clear'.[124] The UK Supreme Court referred to participation in decision-making as fostering human dignity and the rule of law: procedural requirements that decision-makers should listen to persons who have something relevant to say 'promote congruence between the actions of decision-makers and the law which should govern their actions'.[125]

The foregoing connotes adjudication as harmonising discord and reconciling the incommensurate, ie, it identifies and favours the 'ideal self' thus attaining a collective consciousness based on sociological construct over selfish individualism.[126] The transparent and deliberative process is a balm to conflict and all sides emerge better off than before. In forms of adjudication concerned with collective action problems – like environmental adjudication – harmonisation is an ideal to be obtained. But this belief is seen as naïve by some.[127] An alternative view is that adjudication draws upon the energy of discord and uses tension as its creative driver.[128] It draws upon the opposing stances of parties, and results in favouring one side or the other, or it carves a compromise from the positions they present; an approach more reflective of Hayek's thinking that we are only ever motivated by self-interest (although not necessarily in an Epicurean hedonistic sense).[129] Much environmental law is public law – affecting relations between the state and individuals – and Loughlin says that we need to see public law as 'born of a compromise affected between antagonists who cannot defeat one another'.[130] In this sense, forms of public law adjudication can be seen as derivatives of an irreconcilable conflict.

[124] Cohen (n 121) 73.

[125] *R (Osborn) v Parole Board*; *R (Booth) v Parole Board* [2013] UKSC 61, [67]–[72] (see also *John v Rees* [1970] Ch 345, 402 with Megarry J describing 'the feelings of resentment that will be aroused if a party to legal proceedings is placed in a position where it is impossible for him to influence the result'). The rule of law values identified by the UK Supreme Court – promoting participation and thereby fostering responsive decision-making and respecting human dignity – are normative in environmental justice and, as will be explored in ch 6 of this book, promoting greater participation in environmental management has been a dominant theme in international treaty-making, case law and the writing of jurists over the last three decades: see BJ Preston, 'The effectiveness of the law in providing access to environmental justice: an introduction' in P Martin et al (eds), *The Search for Environmental Justice* (Edward Elgar, 2015) 24.

[126] McLean (n 100) ch 6.

[127] Critiquing Habermas' 'communicative action' in particular – Rubin states this sounds more 'like the guiding principle of academic scholarship, not political or social interaction' see EL Rubin, 'From Coherence to Effectiveness: A Legal Methodology for the Modern World' in R Van Gestel, H-W Micklitz and EL Rubin (eds), *Rethinking Legal Scholarship: A Transatlantic Dialogue* (Cambridge University Press, 2017) 345.

[128] For this idea in different contexts, see CR Sunstein, *Designing Democracy: What Constitutions Do* (Oxford University Press, 2001) 8; M Cohn, 'Tension and Legality: Towards a Theory of the Executive Branch' (2016) 29 *Canadian Journal of Law and Jurisprudence* 321.

[129] FA Hayek, *Individualism and Economic Order* (University of Chicago Press, 1958) (especially ch 1) taken to the extreme in 'public choice' theory, see JL Mashaw, *Greed, Chaos and Governance: Using Public Choice to Improve Public Law* (Yale University Press, 1997).

[130] Loughlin (n 9) 465.

The two approaches I have painted above seem oppositional (and both lead to interesting possibilities in the context of environmental adjudication) but it is not necessary to explore them further here. Both support a view of adjudication as a form of creative disagreement, and interactional regardless of the combative or conciliatory nature of that interaction – albeit the process might not necessarily prove transformational for the parties to the immediate dispute.[131] Regardless, specialist environment courts are clearly 'active and disciplined sites of public exchange'.[132] The ramifications that can flow from the resolution of environmental law disputes point to the appropriateness of this role. For instance, individuals, companies or government may wish to develop, destroy or pollute part of an ecosystem that in turn restricts access to public resources for private gain or prevents individuals using their property as they wish. In doing so they may be imposing risks and restrictions on people inhabiting particular environments that could impact upon their psychological and physiological health, socio-cultural and economic wellbeing, and upon their children and future generations.[133] Environmental adjudication allows the risk-takers and the risk-bearers to confront each other 'thoughtfully', in an orderly and transparent process subject to the rule of law.[134]

There is a second, equally important way to think about adjudication as interactional. With adjudication, form and function interact: that is, the inherent nature of the dispute will have ramifications for the appropriate form of the adjudication.[135] Nature in this context means the fundamental characteristics of the problem, that in turn impacts normative form, ie, who should make decisions and how they make those decisions, what tools do they have to investigate and what remedies can they employ to resolve the dispute. For example, arbitration is preferred by commercial entities that aim to preserve future business relationships.[136] Care proceedings concerning vulnerable children seek to promote the child's welfare as the paramount consideration[137] and this policy leads to a certain form of adjudication.[138] Chayes' conception of public law adjudication is another example of form and function interacting. Forms of

[131] It may, however, contribute to a 'gradually transforming continuum' see Cohn (n 128) 325 citing L Zadeh, *Fuzzy Sets and Applications: Selected Papers* (Wiley, 1987).

[132] Resnik (n 108) 9.

[133] C Warnock, 'Understanding the Objective: Psychological Effects in Environmental Decision-Making' (2011) 24 *New Zealand Universities Law Review* 574.

[134] Legal theorists argue that risk-bearers should be able to challenge the imposition of risk upon them (certainly in the private law field), see B Fried, 'The Nonconsequentialist Approach to Torts' (2012) 18 *Legal Theory* 231.

[135] HW Arthurs, *Without the Law: Administrative Justice and Legal Pluralism in Nineteenth-Century England* (University of Toronto Press, 1985) 202, stating 'institutional design should also reflect the special qualities of the specific activity being addressed'.

[136] J Effron, 'Alternatives to Litigation: Factors in Choosing' (1989) 52 *MLR* 480.

[137] eg, Children Act 1989 (UK), s 1.

[138] eg, in the UK context a Guardian-ad-litem represents the child, the court proceedings are relatively informal (eg, the strict rules of evidence do not apply), the court retains hold of the litigation (and can for example order a sequence of interim care orders etc).

adjudication morph by responding to the inherent nature of the dispute, and this interactional quality of adjudication leads to adjudicative plurality. This aspect is core to my argument and I discuss the inherent features of environmental problems and explain their normative impact on adjudicatory forms in more detail in chapters five and six.

The discussion so far has emphasised that while adjudication is contestable and contested we can extract core features, all of which characterise adjudication in ECs. Specialist environmental adjudication provides a public site for 'thoughtful' interaction: arguments can be tested in an orderly fashion and disputes resolved. Environmental adjudication can often be predictive with adjudicators called upon to assess the possible impacts of activities on the environment – and there are no guarantees as to whether predictions will eventuate – but adjudication in general is concerned with producing an acceptable form of truth, rather than pronouncing definitive truth. Further, environmental adjudication often plays a deliberate role in environmental governance but general adjudication impacts the future in a multitude of ways and, scholars opine, can be considered a part of governance in that sense. If we focus on the core *features* of adjudication, rather than privileging particular *forms* of adjudication – focusing on adjudication's role in determining acceptable truth, impacting the future and facilitating interaction – it is clear that ECs are not normatively illegitimate per se.

To summarise the argument in chapter four at this point: thinking about adjudication is like plotting co-ordinates on a schematic, albeit a multidimensional one that plots forms, impacts (individual and cumulative impacts of decisions), relational aspects (with other institutions of government), and legitimacy. Each of those co-ordinates interact with and influence the others. So, while adjudication can be seen in mechanistic terms by considering the 'ordinary, technical nature of adjudication'[139] (focusing on form, constitution, procedures and jurisdiction) these technical aspects actually serve to create multidimensional institutional structures, and these structures have implications for how we might conceive of adjudication in more abstract terms. Adjudication might be viewed in a limited sense, as mere bi-party dispute-resolution,[140] and instrumentally as a mechanism for the *enforcement* of social norms – a recipient and transmitter forward of signals.[141] Or it may be viewed more expansively as providing a frame for discourse[142] in which 'the norm sender, norm receiver and norm text mutually presuppose each other and co-determine the meaning of the norm' – constituting in Van Hoeke's

[139] Rubin, *Beyond Camelot* (n 8) 232.
[140] Fuller, 'The Forms and Limits of Adjudication' (n 29).
[141] J Smillie, 'Who wants Juristocracy?' (2006) 11 *Otago Law Review* 183.
[142] In the Socratic tradition, reflecting Hannah Arendt's writing, and applied directly to adjudication by Waldron: Waldron, 'Thoughtfulness and the Rule of Law' (n 71).

terminology, a form of 'dialectic communication'.[143] To repeat my core point: expansive approaches that perceive adjudication as norm generating, premised on deliberative discourse, forward-looking, and part of wider governance – ie, the form taken by many ECs – are not outliers. They are well traversed and justified intellectually, a thought necessarily carried through into the rest of my argument.

II. NORMATIVE JUSTIFIABILITY AND ADJUDICATIVE INTEGRITY

The first part of this chapter demonstrated that adjudication is flexible, both conceptually and in practice. The next part explains that the particular form, functions and powers given to or assumed by adjudicative bodies – ie, their legal nature – are important in terms of ensuring adjudicative *integrity*. The actual word 'integrity', has a particular resonance in my theory building. The dictionary definition of integrity is 'soundness; uprightness; honesty' and most interestingly, 'wholeness'.[144] Its root is the Latin adjective – *integer*, meaning whole or complete (think of 'integral' to). The interactional theory necessitates seeing certain components as integral parts of the whole,[145] and I argue that it is the relationship between the parts – their responsiveness to each other – that underpins the integrity of specialist environmental adjudication.

The idea that *integrity in adjudication is important* is not controversial (although as I explain below, the particular meaning and emphasis to be placed on integrity exercises legal philosophers) and I argue that this premise is capable of supporting a shared belief underpinning the normative justifiability presently lacking with ECs, *if* we can agree what integrity in environmental adjudication looks like. As stated above, my argument is that adjudication must respond to, rather than ignore, fundamental context in order to promote integrity. I develop this idea in the specific context of environmental adjudication in chapters five and six. In the remainder of this chapter, I consider the general idea of 'integrity-responsiveness-legitimacy' in greater detail and explore the idea from various perspectives in order to demonstrate its robustness.

A. Philosophical Support for Adjudicative Integrity

Previously, I explained that the shared beliefs underpinning normative justifiability eventuate from sources seen as authoritative (such as religion, natural law

[143] Van Hoecke (n 84) 82.

[144] J Coulson and et al (eds), *The Oxford Illustrated Dictionary*, 2nd edn (Redwood Burn, 1981) 436.

[145] ie, identifying the distinct characteristics of environmental problems; acknowledging commensurate challenges for dispute resolution; developing environmental law doctrine, procedure and

doctrine, philosophy, or science etc), from the persuasiveness of their content, and that they manifest both in tradition and continuing practice. Legal and political philosophy can provide an authoritative and persuasive source for shared beliefs – the separation of powers is a classic example – and as I discuss below, the philosophical literature provides strong support for the idea that integrity in adjudication promotes legitimacy.[146] It is worth noting that political philosophers tend to approach legitimacy differently from political scientists like Beetham, believing that power is legitimate 'if it meets certain standards of the right and the good'.[147] This is a subtly different test from that employed by political scientists, that emphasise the importance of people acknowledging the rightfulness of the institution's power.[148] Philosophers' standards are objective and external, so identifying common themes in the philosophical literature helps to address the 'moral persuasiveness' of my theory – an essential component of normative justifiability.[149] Within that discourse, there is general agreement that integrity in adjudication matters, with Dworkin being the most famous proponent.[150] However, as with much in the field of jurisprudence, integrity does not constitute a singular term of art. Rhode notes that 'in common usage, integrity often functions as an all-purpose term for moral approval'[151] but beyond that, philosophers attribute a wide range of meanings to and uses for the idea.[152] The purpose here is not to enter the fray, arguing for various conceptions over others. Rather, I reinforce my argument – an argument that derives from another place – with correlative thinking drawn from the philosophical literature.

Integrity is most readily aligned with personal morality.[153] We say someone has integrity when their acts are justified by reference to their principles; they apply those principles consistently; those principles are coherent amongst themselves and have some intelligibility to outsiders (with intelligibility being 'context sensitive'); and people's actions are 'based on the set of principles one

appropriate remedies that *respond* to those distinct characteristics; and considering the impact on normative institutional form, including the constitutional makeup of any adjudicative body.

[146] See, eg, G Postema, 'Integrity: Justice in Workclothes' (1997) 82 *Iowa Law Review* 821, 855.

[147] Beetham (n 1) x.

[148] ibid.

[149] ibid, 70.

[150] R Dworkin, *Law's Empire* (Harvard University Press, 1987) chs 6 and 7. Dworkin qualified integrity as an independent principle on a par with justice and fairness (176–77); his ideas of political and legal integrity are derived from parallel ideals of personal morality (166); the fictional judge Hercules embodies integrity in adjudication (239–40); and for Dworkin adjudicative integrity meant deciding cases in the manner prescribed, ie, generating interpretative options that fit the relevant legal materials, and then selecting as optimal the interpretation that put the legal system 'in the best light', based on the coherence of underlying principles (226).

[151] D Rhode, 'If Integrity is the Answer what is the Question?' (2003–04) 72 *Fordham Law Review* 333, 336.

[152] See the wide range of conceptions evident in the special edition of the *Fordham Law Review* 72 (2003–04).

[153] G Taylor, *Pride, Shame, and Guilt: Emotions of Self-assessment* (Clarendon Press, 1985) 109.

believes to be best'.[154] Colhoun identifies three possible perceptions of personal integrity:

> On the integrated-self view, integrity involves the integration of 'parts' of oneself – desires, evaluations, commitments – into a whole. On the identity view, integrity means fidelity to those projects and principles which are constitutive of one's core identity. On the clean-hands view, integrity means maintaining the purity of one's own agency, especially in dirty-hands situations.[155]

Colhoun emphasises the importance of integration, fidelity and wholeness, as does Taylor.[156] Postema regards integrity as fostering an 'intelligibility, a unity of vision'.[157] Besson uses 'integrity' and 'coherence' as interchangeable, using coherence in the sense of principled consistency.[158] For Dworkin, people behave with integrity if they act 'according to convictions that inform and shape their lives as a whole, rather than capriciously or whimsically'.[159] There is also, as Zipursky terms it, a 'grounded-ness' or 'solidness' to integrity. Integrity does not present a façade; it is not vacuous, and Zipursky aligns integrity with honesty.[160] Colhoun agrees.[161] There has to be a real substance or solidness to the values that actions are based on, because they act as a bedrock – anchoring integrity. They have got to be clearly formulated, firm and fixed. A common theme derived from the literature is that integrity requires linkages between acts, reasoning and core principles that form part of one's identity.[162] It's the relationship between the components – their responsiveness to each other that matters – but the foundational values have to have a stability and 'rootedness'. Otherwise, one is simply considered vacuous and superficial.

Personal integrity finds a natural home in adjudication through the expected behaviour of lawyers and judges. Judicial integrity, Zipursky notes, is the 'opposite of corruption, duplicity, dishonesty, or manipulativeness';[163] the 'opposite of bad faith'.[164] For Fuller, acting with integrity requires judges to listen to litigants and 'the advocate can play an important role in preserving the integrity of adjudication' by 'presenting proofs and reasoned argument' that in turn heightens the

[154] L Alexander and K Kress, 'Against Legal Principles' (1997) 82 *Iowa Law Review* 739, 770–71; Taylor (n 153) 113.

[155] C Colhoun, 'Standing for Something' (1995) 92 *Journal of Philosophy* 235, 235.

[156] Taylor (n 153) 109.

[157] Postema, 'Integrity: Justice in Workclothes' (n 146) 827.

[158] S Besson, *The Morality of Conflict: Reasonable Disagreement and the Law* (Hart Publishing, 2005) 378 and ch 11 (whilst acknowledging that 'it is possible to distinguish seven properties of ideas or theories that make them coherent: consistency, comprehensiveness, completeness, monism, unity, articulateness and justifiedness', 379).

[159] Dworkin, *Law's Empire* (n 150) 166.

[160] B Zipursky, 'Conflicts of Integrity' (2003) 72 *Fordham Law Review* 395, 402; see also Taylor (n 153) 126.

[161] Colhoun (n 155) 250.

[162] Taylor (n 153) 131.

[163] Zipursky (n 160) 395.

[164] ibid, 397.

participation of the litigant.[165] He opines that 'whatever destroys the meaning of that participation destroys the integrity of adjudication itself'.[166] In *Justice in Robes*, Dworkin aligns integrity with procedural fairness.[167] Judicial opinions tend to support this conception – following due process, conducting proceedings fairly, will enable adjudicators to 'command the respect and confidence of the public'.[168] In this sense, ajudicative integrity is linked to the adjudicator behaving impartially and ensuring equal treatment of parties (neither side is favoured because of their identity; applicants cannot be excluded; there are no secrets; and *audi alterma partem* and *nemo iudex in causa sua* apply).[169]

But the application of integrity in adjudication can widen beyond the personal integrity of the actors. It can also be seen as indicating a technical legal mechanism, denoting features of Feinberg's comparative justice[170] through doctrinal consistency, the application of *stare decisis*[171] and 'treating like cases alike'.[172] The linkage here is between the present case and past decisions. For Dworkin though, legal integrity is not just concerned with *stare decisis*: '[i]ntegrity is a more dynamic and radical standard than it first seems, because it encourages a judge to be wide-ranging and imaginative in his search for coherence with fundamental principle'.[173] Famously Dworkin extends integrity outwards from being an aspect of personal morality and a function of common law adjudication, to becoming a political virtue.[174] To have integrity the state should 'act on a single, coherent set of principles even when its citizens are divided'.[175] Waldron explains Dworkinian integrity as a way of reconciling the losing side in democratic politics – the past matters and the winners can't tear it up and start afresh.[176] In this way, integrity helps us to become a true community. Besson describes this wider application of integrity not as a political but as a 'moral' value that makes law 'more justifiable' and worthy of respect.[177] Regardless, both the narrow and the wide conceptions of comparative rely upon 'solidness' – linking action to something of solidity. As Postema explains,

> [j]ust as we value integrity in others, in part because it allows us to know what we are contending with, so do we value integrity in the law, in part because our freedom and

[165] Fuller, 'The Forms and Limits of Adjudication' (n 29) 390.
[166] ibid, 364.
[167] R Dworkin, *Justice in Robes* (Harvard University Press, 2008) 171.
[168] *Connelly v Director of Public Prosecutions* [1964] AC 1254, 1353 (HL).
[169] W Lucy, *Law's Judgement* (Hart Publishing 2017).
[170] J Feinberg, 'Noncomparative Justice' (1974) 83 *Philosophical Review* 297, 310.
[171] C Peters, 'Foolish consistency: On equality, integrity, and justice in stare decisis' (1996) 105 *Yale Law Journal* 2031.
[172] J Waldron, 'The Rise and Decline of Integrity' [2019] New York University School of Law Public Law and Legal Theory Research Paper Series Working Paper No 19-49, 16.
[173] Dworkin, *Law's Empire* (n 150) 220.
[174] Postema agrees: 'integrity is an important value of political morality – perhaps the most immediately important such value governing law and its administration', Postema, 'Integrity: Justice in Workclothes' (n 146) 824.
[175] Dworkin, *Law's Empire* (n 150) 166.
[176] Waldron, 'The Rise and Decline of Integrity' (n 172) 15.
[177] Besson (n 158) 393.

> our sense of equal worth are enhanced if we can count on the rules and the system actually being solid and coherent.[178]

Zipursky uses an ecological metaphor to make the same point: integrity connotes a 'sort of continuity and stability and rootedness [that] we value in a legal system'.[179]

There are some common themes that can be extracted from the brief discussion above that are helpful in thinking about the interactional theory for environmental adjudication. The first concerns coherence.[180] Integrity is about linkages: there are logical relations flowing between act and justification. Coherence is important because while we may not agree with our neighbour's decision we can respect it if it coheres with their foundational values; that coherence is logically intelligible to us. The interactional theory for environmental adjudication provides a coherence that is intelligible too. It requires four factors to be considered as integral parts of the whole: identifying the distinct characteristics of environmental problems; acknowledging the impact those characteristics have on law and dispute resolution, and the challenges they create for adjudication; developing environmental law doctrine, procedure and remedies that respond to those challenges; and acknowledging that particular adjudicative forms and functions facilitate this process.

The second theme concerns solidity. In the adjudicative setting, litigants (whether they win or lose) respect the approach the court has taken when it coheres with something solid, or that has 'rootedness' as Zipursky describes it. In the interactional theory for environmental adjudication, that *rootedness* is provided by acknowledging and responding to the immutable structural features of environmental problems. Everything else flows from that acknowledgement. This proposition inevitably raises further questions. One issue that has taxed legal philosophers is 'what does practice need to cohere *with* in order to have integrity?' Dworkin says there needs to be a coherence with principles established by past political decisions[181] which Waldon takes to mean 'legislative events' and particular case law.[182] But if integrity requires coherence with fundamental legal principles, critics say it has no stand-alone character. It will always be reliant on substantive justice, political fairness and procedural due process for its force.[183] Of course, coherence within adjudication can, should and even must be to underlying political or legal principles, to the written texts

[178] Zipursky (n 160) 402.

[179] ibid, 397, 402; as does Taylor in the context of personal integrity, that has 'roots in the past' (see Taylor (n 153) 114).

[180] Note, although it is not for this book to explore, the meaning of 'coherence' is also contestable (see Besson, (n 158) 378–79. Here coherence is given the normal dictionary meaning of 'the quality of forming a unified whole'.

[181] Dworkin, *Law's Empire* (n 150) ch 6.

[182] Waldron, 'The Rise and Decline of Integrity' (n 172) 12.

[183] D Reaume, 'Is Integrity a Virtue? Dworkin's Theory of Legal Obligation' (1989) 39 *University of Toronto Law Journal* 380; Alexander and Kress (n 154).

of the law.[184] That is 'justice'. Can integrity be an independent value? In the context of adjudication, I think it can – depending of course on what additional principles adjudicative practice coheres with.

In my theory, integrity has work to do on its own two feet. What is cohering is not necessarily 'past legal text' and present practice, rather the theory is based on the substrata below, the bedrock upon which legal doctrine and principles emerge and develop. In the interactional theory for environmental adjudication, identifying and acknowledging the inherent characteristics of environmental problems provides the base for coherent action. I use this base because I am addressing the problems that occur when legal texts are incomplete, they are unable to account for the particular challenges of adjudicating over the environment, or where courts are left to fill in the gaps – where existing written law wasn't able to be predictive. In those circumstances, adjudication must be anchored to something else that is solid in order to have integrity. According to Zipursky, integrity guides the development of substantive content[185] and that is how I use it here. The interactional theory is a manifestation of integrity and the application of that theory guides the development of a frame that provides substantive legal content.

My approach may be critiqued as developing a theory based not on law but on sociology (albeit adjudication *is* a form of sociological practice) or perhaps more accurately, the accommodation of law and science. That may be true.[186] But I am focused on providing content for a shared belief underpinning normative justifiability. Legal text does not hold a monopoly on that. Further, if we consider the *implementation* of the interactional theory, that first component (or bedrock consideration) does permit the rational development of law: iterative problem-solving in adjudication, developing procedure and doctrine that *respond* to the inherent characteristics of environmental problems, crystallises into law (certainly in common law jurisdictions). Moreover, my theory aligns with core fundamentals that we require of law; the solidity that we require of law; the stabilisation of preferences; the reference to something else authoritative that anchors the present dispute and provides an intelligible basis for decision-making. Integrity explains how the structural challenges of environmental problems 'yield present practical directives … [and] provide rational support' for the generative capacity of practice and doctrine in environmental adjudication.[187] Coherence with an inherent structural reality provides fidelity in this context that can bring the community together.

The first two themes derived from the philosophical literature on integrity concerned coherence and solidity. The third theme is that to have integrity,

[184] eg, see Scotford (n 123).

[185] Zipursky (n 160) 402–03.

[186] ie, my theory does not depend on 'rules or principles drawn from past *political* decisions of the community, as recorded in the books and reflected in the practices of its law' (Postema, 'Integrity: Justice in Workclothes' (n 146) 825).

[187] ibid, 825.

what courts do and how they do it is fundamental – a view highlighting the importance of self-validation. Judicial integrity has been described as 'leading by example'.[188] This point reinforces the value of courts *employing* the interactional theory. Hübner Mendes argues that 'a court will be more or less legitimate for what it does, not the power that it has formally received'.[189] Bustamante concurs: a court 'is more or less legitimate depending upon how well it is able to discharge its deliberative duties'.[190] If we consider how a court is best 'able to discharge its deliberative duties',[191] the importance of context becomes clear. To deliberate means giving a matter intentional and careful consideration. Hübner Mendes suggests there are four kinds of deliberative achievement: epistemic, communitarian, psychological and educative, and

> from the epistemic point of view, deliberation would promote, at least, clarity about what issues are at stake; at most, it would arrive at the true and best answer. From the communitarian perspective, deliberation would encourage consensus (or at least minimize dissensus), nurture social legitimacy, and deepen a sense of community. Third, it would instill in deliberators the feeling of being respected. Last, it would educate deliberators both about the respective subject matter and about the deliberative skills themselves. These outcomes may co-exist and reinforce each other. They are not unambitious bets. Their merits are not exclusive of deliberation either. Advocates, however, give credence to deliberation as a more powerful means to foster them.[192]

An adjudicator will be better able to discharge their deliberative duties if they respond to rather than ignore the inherent nature of the problems they are tasked with resolving. In the context of environmental problem-solving, they will better meet the epistemic, communitarian, psychological and educative promises of Hübner Mendes' conception by acknowledging context.

I want to give a simple example to illustrate that point (note: this is just a heuristic so there is no need to get tied up in what court, type of proceedings, or statutory provisions we are concerned with). Imagine there is a dispute concerning the discharge of waste water from industry to a river system. The river system is a habitat for endangered flora and fauna, and supplies water downstream for domestic purposes. The factory has a filtration system that prevents toxic pollutants entering the river with the waste water. However, practice shows that these filtration systems are susceptible to operational and mechanical failure, the possibility of breakdown is real and calculable albeit small, and if pollution entered the river the harm would be significant, killing the fauna and flora.

[188] R Bloom, 'Judicial Integrity: A call for its re-emergence in the adjudication of crime' (1993) 84 *Journal of Criminal Law and Criminology* 462, 464.

[189] C Hübner Mendes, *Constitutional Courts and Deliberative Democracy* (Oxford University Press, 2013) 225.

[190] Bustamante (n 65) 375.

[191] ibid, 375.

[192] Hübner Mendes (n 189) 22–23.

If adjudication of the dispute followed generic civil litigation – like the kind Fuller was writing about in 'The Forms and Limits of Adjudication'[193] – the risk might not factor in the deliberation because those wishing to protect the fauna might not have standing; applying the balance of probabilities test, the court might not accept the risk of breakdown as a 'fact' to be cognisant of; opinion evidence might be discounted and so on. However, if adjudication responds to the nature of the dispute it is tasked with resolving (ie, it follows Chayes' conception of public law litigation): a wide *locus standi* test would apply, encompassing all those impacted; the adjudicators could receive opinion evidence about the risk of breakdown and the adverse ecological effects (and have the expertise to understand it); they might arrange for Alternative Dispute Resolution (ADR) to see if other discharge methods could be proposed (such as discharge to land) and may organise witness caucusing for the same end; evaluate the risk without holding it to a balance of probabilities test and/or apply the precautionary principle; and they may impose additional conditions on the grant of a permit that neither party had asked for, including adaptive management that would better educate the court as to the way forward. In discharging their deliberative duties, the adjudicators would be able to focus on the most contentious issue – the risk of harm to the environment, and the mode of adjudication will enable that issue to be rigorously scrutinised. I explore all these ideas (and more) in chapter six by returning to the practices, procedures and doctrine developed by the NZEnvC and the NSWLEC, but this brief illustration helps to make the point – adjudication will have greater integrity if it is responsive to context.

Similar thinking has been applied to the wider law-state, linking purpose and responsive practice with legitimacy. In *Law as Communication*, Van Hoecke writes 'if power is exercised in certain ways then it becomes socially acceptable',[194] and Duguit believed that as administration 'no longer retains a necessary connection with sovereign will', we should be looking to its purpose to sustain its legitimacy.[195] In drawing analogies between the legitimacy of the 'new ephorate' (as he terms specialist, often independent, unelected agencies) and adjudicative legitimacy, Loughlin emphasises the importance of *integrity*: 'the judiciary's authority derives not from delegation from the people but from the integrity of its own procedures'.[196] Loughlin develops a more detailed idea of integrity in the context he's concerned with stating, for example, that the new ephorate 'feeds scientifically acquired evidence into governmental processes'[197] – but certain wider themes can be extrapolated that are useful to the present discussion. In particular, integrity of procedure means that particular

[193] Fuller, 'The Forms and Limits of Adjudication' (n 29).
[194] Van Hoecke (n 84) 63.
[195] Loughlin (n 9) 458 citing L Duguit, *Law in the Modern State* (F Laski and H Laski trans, Allen and Unwin 1921) 142–43.
[196] Loughlin (n 9) 454.
[197] ibid.

processes have been devised for the entity's distinct role; those that respond to and make sense of the context it works within.[198] And while Loughlin's new ephorate helps establish a demarcation between 'professional judgments founded on specialized knowledge and political judgments based on values and principles' it also has the 'ability to instil co-ordination', fostering a coherence that can underpin contemporary government.[199]

The discussion above emphasises three main themes: integrity as coherence; the need for solidity in values or principles that anchor action; and the idea that what courts do matters in terms of normative legitimacy. All are critical in shoring up the interactional theory for environmental adjudication because '[t]heories that refuse to recognize the demands and discipline of integrity deprive official decisions and actions of legitimacy at precisely the point at which it is needed most'.[200]

B. Historical Developments and Tradition

Historical developments also show that integrity in adjudication is important – taking integrity to constitute responsiveness that in turn promotes legitimacy. In chapter three, I briefly surveyed the effect that the development of the administrative state had upon forms of adjudication. As explained, generalist courts were seen as ill-suited to adjudicating the problems of modernity and their failings led to different forms of adjudication and dispute-resolution methods emerging. However, to emphasise the point I want to also consider the matter from a positive angle, to show how adjudicative bodies that *do* respond to context are socially well supported and have longevity. A good illustration is provided by the swanimotes, the ancient forest courts of England and Wales. I describe the swanimotes in some detail below because they make the point about integrity and responsiveness so well.

Swanimotes (also swainmotes) and woodmotes are 'amongst the oldest English forums of local self-determination'.[201] They were established in Crown forests[202] throughout England and Wales to help maintain 'a delicate balance

[198] ibid.

[199] ibid.

[200] Postema, 'Integrity: Justice in Workclothes' (n 146) 855.

[201] G Jones, 'Swanimotes, Woodmotes, and Courts of "Free Miners"' in J Langton and G Jones (eds), *Forests and Chases of England and Wales c1500–c1850* (St John's College Research Centre, 2005) 41.

[202] In historical legal terms – as opposed to in a physical sense – a forest was an area of land over which the Crown exercised rights of hunting and timber crop, and forest law applied, see O Rackham, *Woodlands* (Harper Collins, 2006). Crown forests were maintained by the Crown predominantly as game reserve to protect the *vert* and the *venison* for the hunt but also contained coppices, villages and agricultural land with many different inhabitants often reliant upon their surrounding environment for their existence, see P Large, 'From swanimote to disafforestation: Feckenham Forest in the early seventeeth century' in R Hoyle (ed), *The Estates of the English Crown 1550–1640* (Cambridge University Press, 1992) 389.

of rights and restrictions for the Crown and the inhabitants'[203] and to determine disputes in accordance with both custom and the laws of the Forest Charter 1217.[204] What can we take from the swanimotes to support the importance of adjudicative integrity and responsiveness?

The first point is that these dispute-resolution bodies developed iteratively over time. The first documented evidence of swanimotes was from 1189, but historians speculate that given their name they were potentially in existence from before the Norman invasion and Magna Carta.[205] This is an important point because it suggests that these dispute-resolution bodies were not *imposed* on communities, rather they grew up from *within* those communities. Remarkably, however, swanimotes, now named Verderers' Courts, still exist in the New Forest[206] and the Forest of Dean.[207] Although their role is now placed on a statutory footing,[208] their powers and functions remain surprisingly unchanged from centuries before.[209]

Second, the swanimotes facilitated a harmonious interaction between the community and the environment that it relied upon through the social ordering (in the form of customs or 'law') and dispute resolution. The swanimotes helped protect different forms of medieval liberties, commons use rights and the customary practices of the forest inhabitants[210] (including pannage (releasing foraging animals), estover (collecting firewood) and turbary (cutting turf) that had existed for centuries prior to the Norman invasion, and were referred to in the Forest Charter,[211] the companion document to the Magna Carta) predominantly

[203] ibid, Large, 393; Jones (n 201) 42.

[204] The Charter of the Forest 1217 was the companion document to the Magna Cart. 1215 (and later reincorporated within the Magna Carta in the Confirmation of Charters 1297).

[205] Jones (n 201) 43–44.

[206] See: www.verderers.org.uk/court.html.

[207] See: www.deanverderers.org.uk; CE Hart, *The Verderers and Speech-court of the Forest of Dean* (Bellows, 1950); CE Hart, *The Verderers and the Forest Laws of Dean* (Lightmoor Press, 2005). Note that other Forest Courts continued into the later 17th century, eg, Cliff in Rockingham Forest, see Jones (n 201) 42. For reasons for their demise see Large (n 202) 391; EP Thompson, *Whigs and Hunters: The Origin of the Black Act* (Allen Lane, 1975).

[208] eg, Dean Forest (Mines) Act 1838; with amendments contained in a series of later statutes including the New Forest Act 1877, New Forest Act 1959, and associated regulations: Regulations Of The Verderers Of The New Forest Relating To The Courts Of Swainmote For The Dispatch Of Administrative And Judicial Business As Provided For In Section 24 Of The New Forest Act 1877 As Amended. The 1927 Forestry Act created the Forestry Commission, which is now the main governmental body concerned with forest management, but the Forestry Commission is constrained by the commoners' rights and requires consent from the Verderers for activities that might impinge upon these rights.

[209] Regulations Of The Verderers Of The New Forest Relating To The Courts Of Swainmote For The Dispatch Of Administrative And Judicial Business As Provided For In Section 24 Of The New Forest Act 1877 As Amended, regs 14 and 17.

[210] Note Holdsworth's view that there had been confusion by some writers, including Manwood, who conflated the role of the swanimotes and the separately held inquisitions that managed offences against the vert and the venison – see WS Holdsworth, *A History of English Law Volume 1*, 7th edn (Methuen, 1956) 97.

[211] Charter of the Forest, 1217, ch 8.

through what historians describe as a form of 'controlled exploitation',[212] and which lawyers would recognise now as a licensing scheme created to sustain the commons.[213]

Third, swanimotes were multifunctional bodies, merging administrative, regulatory and adjudicative roles, so creating mini-governance regimes for their local environments. They regulated communal use rights and made decisions concerning warrants and grants, but also collected any payments due (for example, in accordance with the Forest Charter, they 'ought to receive our pannage-dues').[214] A localised history noted that by the early sixteenth century, the Feckenham Swanimote was issuing by-laws and ordinances and had a wide jurisdiction with a surprisingly communitarian ethos.[215] Forest courts could be seen (while undoubtedly a forum protecting Crown property) as 'a forum in which local social regulation was achieved'.[216] The swanimotes were never brought within a centralised decision-making system under the authority of the Exchequer (although there were attempts to do so in 1616).[217] This adjudicatory specialisation and wide remit has been described as a particular feature of natural resource management: miners' courts ('stanneries'), for example, were said to have made the environments where they operated 'semi-independent states'.[218] Echoes of this merged, multifunctional role can be seen in the specialist NZEnvC, that has powers to amend proposed policy statements and plans (ie, local regulations) on their merits.[219]

Fourth, the procedures adopted by the swanimotes appear to respond more carefully to the collective action nature of commons dispute. Writing in the sixteenth century, Manwood reported that decision-making was *communitas*[220] (Manwood's phrase was 'enquired into')[221] and 'the judgment rendered was a judgment of the whole territorial community'.[222] From the sixteenth century, the adjudicators were not drawn from the aristocratic elite, but were comprised of yeomen who lived within and depended upon the environment that they were adjudicating over. Again, this *communitas* decision-making has modern

[212] Large (n 202) 399.

[213] *Aoraki Water Trust v Meridian Energy Limited* [2005] 2 NZLR 268 (NZHC); *Harper v Minister for Sea Fisheries* (1989) 168 CLR 314 (HCA).

[214] Charter of the Forest 1217, ch 8.

[215] Large (n 202) 395. Large notes, at 396, that the composition of the regarders changed from knights to local yeoman over the sixteenth century.

[216] Jones (n 201) 43. Note however it was unlikely that the swanimotes were concerned with trespasses to the *vert* and *venison*, certainly before the sixteenth century, see Holdsworth (n 210) 97.

[217] R Hoyle, 'Disafforestation and drainage: The Crown as Entrepreneur?' in R Hoyle (ed), *The Estates of the English Crown 1558–1640* (Cambridge University Press, 1992) 356.

[218] Jones (n 201) 47.

[219] RMA Act 1991 (NZ), s 293.

[220] J Manwood, *Manwood's Treatise of the Forest Laws* (W Nelson ed, 5th edn, London 1741) 339–40.

[221] Jones (n 201) 44.

[222] JP Dawson, *A History of Lay Judges* (Harvard University Press, 1960) 116.

parallels. Specialist environment courts such as the NSWLEC and NZEnvC tend to have open standing provisions, have created procedures to facilitate public participation, and have a mixed bench where legal and lay members work together to adjudicate over disputes.

Swanimotes are bodies that have existed for over a thousand years, pre-existing any manifestation of the modern English legal system, and despite several centuries now of seismic upheavals in law and politics they sustain in a form that is shockingly unchanged in all fundamental senses. Although it is not within the remit of this book to explore examples from other jurisdictions, they were clearly not alone in this.[223] This heritage is important: our 'interest in the past is for the light it throws upon the present'.[224] Clearly, these legal bodies have a normative function because they impact upon the behaviour of people and the organisation of social life[225] – and they have done so for a millennium.[226] Swanimotes and their like never fitted within the conceptual frames being employed by modern critics of ECs; they are clear exceptions, falling outside a functionalist separation of powers. Arguably, their longevity and efficacy allowed them to transcend the conceptual constraints suggested by this frame.

Today, specialist environment courts might be seen as the ultimate 'modern court', and as Resnik observes:

> [T]oday's judges are independent actors in complex and critical relationships with the government and the public ... courts have themselves become sites of democracy

[223] eg, a community organisation was formed in 1483 in the Swiss village of Torbel to resolve disputes concerning the commons; it takes a *communitas* form, and merges regulatory, administrative and adjudicative roles. The organisation still operates today to oversee the 1517 'Cow Law'. See E Ostrum *Governing the Commons: The Evolution of Institutions for Collective Action* (Cambridge University Press, 1991); R McNetting *Balancing on an Alp: Ecological Change and Continuity in a Swiss Mountain Community* (Cambridge University Press, 1981).

[224] Holmes (n 42) 474.

[225] J Raz, 'The Institutional Nature of Law' (1975) 38 *MLR* 489, 490.

[226] *Contra* Weber one might argue that longevity alone does not amount to a *res ipsa loquiter* argument for legitimacy. Dicey posited that 'the possible weakness at any rate of the historical method as applied to the growth of institutions, is that it may induce men to think so much of the way in which an institution has come to be what it is, that they cease to consider with sufficient care what it is that an institution has become' see AV Dicey, *Introduction to the Study of the Law of the Constitution*, 3rd edn (Macmillan, 1889) vii–viii; and Holmes wryly observed, when commenting on the role of historical analysis in the law, that we may find out 'the practical motive for what now best is justified by the mere fact of its acceptance and that men are accustomed to it' and that history must be 'the first step toward an enlightened skepticism ... [a] 'blind imitation of the past' is 'revolting', see Holmes (n 42) 469. There may be too much of a difference between the small, localised communities characterised by the need for ongoing relationships amongst disputants that were serviced by the swanimotes, and the dispute-resolution mechanisms that best address modern environmental conflicts (for a fuller discussion of this point in general see RL Abel, 'Western Courts in Non-Western Settings: Patterns of Court Use in Colonial and Neo-Colonial Africa' in SB Burman and BE Harrell-Bond (eds), *The Imposition of Law* (Academic Press, 1979)). Longevity may well however create a displaceable presumption of legitimacy or may support Beetham's third criterion for legitimacy: action which provides evidence of consent – see further text below.

> because the particular and peculiar practices of adjudication produce, redistribute, and curb power among disputants who disagree in public about the import of legal rights.[227]

But looking at the heritage of disputes about natural resource management we see this manifestation is an entrenched one. Environmental adjudication has taken unusual forms of dispute resolution for centuries – this is not a modern phenomenon, it has always been so; and those bodies that operate with integrity, responding to the nature of the problems they are tasked with resolving, were protected from the ruptures that rocked the rest of the law-state.

C. Integrity, Responsiveness and Legitimacy

Considering legal and political philosophy – and also historical developments – supports the idea that integrity in adjudication is important and that responsiveness in adjudication upholds integrity. But I want to test the linked idea of 'integrity-responsiveness-legitimacy' in a different way. The discussion in chapter three showed how useful Beetham's multidimensional conception of legitimacy was in the context of ECs. I return to it now to demonstrate how adjudicative integrity achieved through responsiveness can provide the catalyst or rationale for each of Beetham's three criteria, thus demonstrating just how pervasive this ideal is.

To recap briefly, ECs will be legitimate if their legal nature is acquired and exercised in accordance with established rules. Those rules may be written laws (as in the case of the NSWLEC and NZEnvC, that are empowered by statute) or conventions, custom and practice (as was the case with the swanimotes before they were put on a statutory footing). The rules constituting and empowering the NZEnvC and NSWLEC enable responsive adjudication. For example, the specialist constitutions, the flexibility given in relation to process and procedure, and the possibility of creating alternative dispute-resolution processes[228] all enable the courts to adjudicate in a way that takes account of the nature of the problems they are tasked with resolving. The Cripps Review into the NSWLEC made a number of recommendations to develop rules to further these ideals (for example, widening the material available to the Court, enabling the Court to facilitate ADR, and expanding the range of qualifications that enabled experts to become commissioners).[229]

Second, actions of the subject community must provide evidence of consent in order to reinforce the other criteria for legitimacy. With the NSWLEC and

[227] Resnik (n 108) 9–10.

[228] See ch 2.

[229] JS Cripps et al, *Report of the Land and Environment Court Working Party* (Government of New South Wales, 2001) ix–xiii.

NZEnvC, active consent is apparent through the day-to-day functioning of the courts: people bring cases to be adjudicated over, attend and participate in hearings, and (most) comply with orders of the courts.[230] With the swanimotes, their sheer longevity evidences the subject communities support for the bodies. The ability of the courts to respond to the legal problems brought before them secures community support.

Third, their legal nature must be justified in terms of beliefs shared by both dominant and subordinate groups – there must be justification grounded on *shared beliefs*. As Beetham notes, 'there is no ultimate authority to settle such questions; nevertheless, clear limits are set by logic and the beliefs of a given society to what justifications are plausible or credible within it'.[231] The discourse in relation to the NZWLEC and NZEnvC demonstrated how important this aspect of legitimacy is. Political scientists (like Beetham) emphasise the importance of people acknowledging the rightfulness of the institution's power (*cf* political philosophers).[232] Beetham justifies this focus by explaining that if the surrounding social conditions, ideas or beliefs change, an institution may start to lose normative legitimacy regardless of how well it had functioned previously. Consider, for example, the Holy Roman Empire or, as Beetham suggests, hereditary rule, male power, or 'first-past-the-post' electoral systems.[233] As the number of people 'who do not accept the norms underpinning the rules of power' becomes more widespread, legitimacy erodes.[234] This is why it is critical to identify norms that are in the common interest in the widest possible sense and that rise above fragmentary, divisive or transient discourses.

At present, a shared belief in relation to ECs is lacking. In this chapter, I have argued that a belief capable of common acceptance is that integrity in adjudication matters, and to have integrity, adjudication has to be able to respond to the nature of the problems it seeks to resolve. This shared belief is founded in authoritative sources such as legal and political philosophy, and it manifests in both tradition and present practice. In the context of environmental adjudication, this shared belief can be used to underpin the interactional theory, supplying the necessary foundations. In turn, it can help to construct the more detailed frame for environmental adjudication.

The next chapter considers what environmental adjudication has to respond to in order to have integrity. In particular it examines the inherent nature of environmental problems, that forces law to adopt particular forms (as discussed

[230] New Zealand Environment Court, *Annual Review by Members of the Court* (Environment Court, Wellington, New Zealand, 2017); Land and Environment Court of New South Wales, *Annual Review* (Department of Justice, New South Wales, 2017).

[231] Beetham (n 1) 17.

[232] ibid.

[233] ibid, 17–18.

[234] ibid, 20.

in chapter three), and the challenges this nature presents for fact-finding in adjudication that specialist environmental adjudication must respond to in order to have integrity. In a sense, it shores up shared belief with another authoritative source – physical science – helping to build a stable frame that is politically neutral,[235] capable of widespread acceptance, and that in turn legitimises environmental adjudication.

[235] I acknowledge the argument that science cannot be wholly objective (Daston and Galison (n 62); S Jasanoff, *The Fifth Branch: Science Advisers as Policy Makers* (Harvard University Press, 1990)) and address this further in ch 5, but the literature on co-production does not undermine my core thesis, because my argument is not premised upon particular scientific results but rather on the structural or natural state of things, ie, ecosystems are complex and dynamic, and I demonstrate this point in the analysis throughout the book and particularly in ch 5.

5

Developing the Theory: Contextual Foundations

THE LAST CHAPTER established that adjudication will attract normative legitimacy if it has integrity and that integrity will be promoted if adjudication responds to the nature of the disputes it is tasked with resolving. Adjudicative forms that are constituted and empowered to deal with the type of legal and factual disputes they receive – and critically, that employ those powers to develop legal doctrine, processes and procedures that respond to inherent challenges – will be used, supported and respected in the communities they are set up to serve.[1]

This chapter moves from the general to the specific by considering what challenges are created for adjudication by the inherent nature of environmental problems. Chapter three touched upon this issue briefly. It explained that the inherent nature of environmental problems has led to statute law being written in a particular way, that in turn impacts the type of *legal* disputes adjudication has to address. To illustrate this point, it described the common use of framework statutes; principles and flexible standards; statutory terminology that is both descriptive and evaluative; and the greater reference to soft law and policy guidance in environmental statute law. I argued that the architecture and content of modern environmental law put new demands on legal reasoning.[2] For example, interpreting statutory terminology that contains competing ecological, socio-cultural and legal ontologies (such as 'landscape' and 'waahi tapu') has led to novel forms of legal reasoning being created within adjudication itself (for instance, the need for adjudicators to draw upon expert opinion to create evaluative schematics that in turn facilitated the interpretation and application of the law).[3]

[1] See ch 2 referring to the negative response of the wider community to government suggestions that the Environment Court of New Zealand (NZEnvC) be disbanded and in respect of the New South Wales Land and Environment Court (NSWLEC), Stein J mused that the Court had survived various political attacks because of its general popularity with the public, business and environmental groups (see P Stein, 'Specialist Environment Courts: the Land and Environment Court of New South Wales Australia' (2002) 4 *Environmental Law Review* 5, 7).

[2] See also C Rose, 'Environmental Law Grows Up (More or Less), And What Science Can Do To Help' (2005) 9 *Lewis and Clark Law Review* 273.

[3] eg, *Friends of Shearer Swamp Inc v West Coast Regional Council* [2012] NZEnvC 162 (endorsed by the High Court in *West Coast Regional Council v Friends of Shearer Swamp Inc* [2012] NZRMA 45 (HC)) discussed in ch 3.

Chapter five develops this idea from a different perspective. Employing a bottom-up approach, it explores the inherent nature of environmental problems in greater detail and considers how this nature impacts factual determination in adjudication, which in turn moulds legal reasoning. In doing so, it returns directly to the theory-building exercise and establishes the first two components of the interactional theory. It identifies two inherent and immutable features of environmental problems – 'interaction' and 'change' – and notes a third feature as characteristic – 'uncertainty', and it highlights the challenges for environmental adjudication that these features pose and that adjudication must respond to in order to have integrity. I explain why interaction and change are immutable features of environmental problems and uncertainty is characteristic, and I explore the ramifications of this reality for adjudication.

One caveat: in talking about the reality of environmental problems, I acknowledge that environmental problems are always framed by the surrounding discourse (by policy responses, judicial reasoning and academic scholarship etc). There is a certain malleability in the way that we frame environmental problems: to call a problem polycentric is a framing device, for example. But this malleability has limits. There is an immutability based on the *structural* features of environmental problems that we cannot avoid.[4] So, we might argue about what precisely is scientifically uncertain – how much we know and can be sure about – but no one doubts that scientific uncertainty is a feature of environmental problems. What I attempt to do in the first part of this chapter is strip away, as far as possible, the (political and legal) framing to look at the essential physical nature of environmental problems that create challenges for fact-finding in adjudication.[5] In order to do this, I approach the issue with a degree of artificiality, splicing ecological complexity from the complexity of social systems before bringing them back together. 'Bracketing off nature'[6] appears somewhat perverse when I am highlighting interactional complexity, but doing so demonstrates the challenges for adjudication that flow from the natural state of things[7] that fundamentally we cannot change, or rather cannot change with any ease or speed.

Accordingly, the first part of the chapter adopts a layered approach, addressing (1) ecological complexity without humans; (2) considering humans as actors of change; (3) adding humans as impacted; and finally (4) thinking about the wider relevance of humans' relationship with the environment. The layered method adopted in this chapter helps explain why environmental adjudication is of necessity different from disputes that flow from social orderings we have created in their entirety (for example, disputes in tax or trust law). No matter how complex those human constructs might be, at a fundamental level we

[4] E Fisher, 'Environmental Law as "Hot" Law' (2013) 25 *JEL* 347.

[5] And that has forced regulatory form – see ch 3.

[6] B Latour, *We Have Never Been Modern* (C Porter trans, Harvard University Press, 1993) 104.

[7] Ecological relations, as it is termed by A Lowenhaupt Tsing, *The Mushroom at the End of the World: On the Possibility of Life in Capitalist Ruins* (Princeton University Press, 2015) or Latour's 'things in themselves' – see Latour, *We Have Never Been Modern* (n 6) 104.

can change their inherent features, but we cannot do this with environmental problems. The chapter explores the immutable physical structures that set the context and at each stage of the analysis I explain the particular ramifications for environmental adjudication that this reality presents.

The concluding part of this chapter summarises the implications of the analysis for the interactional theory and resulting frame. As I argue throughout the book, we can construct a detailed normative frame in environmental adjudication by recognising the immutable structural features of environmental problems; acknowledging the challenges they present for adjudication and the need to respond to them; and ensuring adjudicative bodies are constituted, empowered and actually use those powers to respond to these inherent structural features. Using the theory to construct a more detailed frame will help guide the development of new environmental courts (ECs); reforms to existing ECs; and the legal reasoning within ECs where legislative direction is incomplete or uncertain, or where ECs have been deliberately endowed with wide discretion. As indicated above, the theory and frame will be relevant to decision-makers who have to determine factual and legal disputes (such as the Environment Court of New Zealand (NZEnvC) and the New South Wales Land and Environment Court (NSWLEC) in their merits review role) *and* those concerned solely with legal disputes (for example, courts confined to legality appeals from ECs). Legality review is impacted because the inherent features of environmental problems create pressures on adjudicative procedure (the forms of knowledge to be adduced in evidence and ways to evaluate that evidence); party status (who should be able to contribute to environmental adjudication); approaches to decision-making in the face of uncertainty; and possible remedies, all leading to the development of new legal doctrine. Contextual forces also impact approaches to statutory interpretation, so thickening environmental law. Accordingly, the frame for legitimacy can impact legal reasoning and in turn appeals on points of law.[8] I introduced this argument in chapter three, develop it further below, and return to it in chapter six.

I. THE INHERENT FEATURES OF ENVIRONMENTAL PROBLEMS

Talking of the inherent features of environment problems might appear unduly generic. After all, environmental problems are 'diverse',[9] their causes multiple, impacts are of variable nature, and they are spatially and temporally

[8] Compare, eg, the New Zealand High Court cases of *Royal Forest and Bird Society of New Zealand Inc v Buller District Council* [2006] NZRMA 193 (HC) and *RJ Davidson Family Trust v Marlborough District Council* [2017] NZHC 52, with the Court in the latter case accepting the NZEnvC must make predictions as to environmental effects that will inevitably influence standards of evidential proof.

[9] J Kooiman, 'Societal Governance: Levels, modes, and orders of socio-political interaction' in J Pierre (ed), *Debating Governance* (Oxford University Press, 2000).

'multi-scalar'.[10] Environmental problems may be seen to range from the local or temporary – such as disagreements concerning business operations in a residential area,[11] removing trees,[12] or discharging treated sewage to water bodies[13] – up to disputes concerning significant or irreversible impacts on the global environment, for example, fossil fuel mining[14] or other activities that will contribute to climate change,[15] or species destruction.[16] Environmental law as a subject matter certainly resists neat classification and refuses to have its parameters set,[17] and perhaps it is unsurprising that perceptions as to what constitute environmental problems vary over time, within different contexts and between peoples. Attempts to create a formula defining environmental problems are therefore wide and flexible.[18] Fisher, Lange and Scotford argue that environmental problems involve 'a situation where there is a collective judgment that environmental quality is not acceptable, or that there is a threat to accepted environmental quality' while acknowledging that all the individual features of that definition are multifaceted and contestable – a complexity that mirrors the nature of the problems themselves.[19] But to call something complex is conclusory and we need to unpack that conclusion in our search for inherent characteristics. If we do so, we will discover the core features that exert normative force on environmental adjudication.

A. Two Inherent Features and a Characteristic

Despite the fluctuating scope of environmental problems, two features inhere in *all* environmental problems and a third feature is characteristic.[20] Each of these

[10] M Lockwood et al, 'Governance Principles for Natural Resource Management' (2010) 23 *Society & Natural Resources* 986, 987.

[11] eg, *Lindsay v Dunedin City Council* [2013] NZEnvC 302.

[12] eg, *Barker v Kyriakides* [2007] NSWLEC 292.

[13] eg, *Te Runanga O Taumarere v Northland Regional Council* [1996] NZRMA 77 (PT).

[14] eg, *Bulga Milbrodale Progress Association Inc v Minister for Planning and Infrastructure and Warkworth Mining Limited* [2013] NSWLEC 48.

[15] eg, *Genesis Power Ltd v Greenpeace* [2008] NZSC 112.

[16] eg, *Royal Forest and Bird Society of New Zealand Inc v Buller District Council* (n 8); *Friends of Tumblebee Inc v ATB Morton Pty Ltd (No 2)* [2016] NSWLEC 16. Note, that I have referred to cases decided in the NZ and NSW contexts to make these points above but of course there are many illustrations from other nations (for a particularly famous US case on 'taking endangered fauna' see *National Association of Homebuilders v Babbit* 130 F 3d 1041 (1997) (DC Cir)).

[17] T Aagaard, 'Environmental Law as a Legal Field: An Inquiry in Legal Taxonomy' (2010) 95 *Cornell Law Review* 221; AD Tarlock, 'Is There a There There in Environmental Law?' (2004) 19 *Journal of Land Use & Environmental Law* 213.

[18] Note the difficulties of defining 'environment': Tarlock (n 17) 221: '[T]he term "environmental" has become so all-encompassing that it has been robbed of any operative meaning; it needs contours'; World Commission on Environment and Development, *Our Common Future* (Oxford University Press, 1987) xi – defining the environment as simply 'where we all live'.

[19] E Fisher, B Lange and E Scotford, *Environmental Law Text, Cases, and Materials* (Oxford University Press, 2013) 22.

[20] Aagaard reaches a similar conclusion as to uncertainty being a secondary feature reliant on core features, although he categorises those core features differently from the way that I do, see Aagaard

features has particular relevance to my argument because in order to operate with integrity, environmental adjudication must respond to them. I argue that the two inherent, albeit interrelated, features concern 'interaction' and 'change' – that is, the environment consists of multiple elements, constantly interacting, resulting in changing conditions. These two features of environmental problems can be regarded as inherent because they persist regardless of the knowledge-producing or knowledge-evaluating context (ie, whether assessed in the laboratory or court room, for example), and they are not obliterated by context and scale. In turn, they impact the quality of environmental knowledge, so leading to a characteristic third feature: knowledge of environmental problems tends to be incomplete and uncertain. This feature *does* change depending on scale and context, and the knowledge-arena and test of sufficiency employed:[21] law may accept sufficient knowledge of environmental problems in circumstances where science would not. I leave the discussion about uncertainty until the end of this chapter. The next part explains why interaction and change are inherent features of environmental problems – factors that can never be completely avoided in environmental adjudication no matter how hard we try. As a warning, this part of the chapter is densely written and it takes the legally trained reader into subject areas that they might feel less comfortable with but it is a critical basis for the argument.

II. INTERACTION AND CHANGE

In large part the complexity of environmental problems flows from the interactive nature of the ecosystem.[22] The ecosystem, or nature, has been described as 'perhaps the most complex term in the language'[23] by including

> the entire physical universe … animate and inanimate worlds … physical changes (such as thermodynamic processes) … living organisms and their interactions

(n 17) 264–73; see also H Doremus, 'Constitutive Law and Environmental Policy' (2003) 22 *Stanford Environmental Law Journal* 295, 319–29 who suggests a similar list of characteristics – pervasive uncertainty, intractable value conflicts, the need for collective action – but adds a fourth, the need for durable and dynamic solutions, and argues that all fundamentally flow from uncertainty.

[21] Thanks to Brian Preston for prompting this observation.

[22] Explaining the 'wicked' nature of many environmental problems: see HWJ Rittel and MM Webber, 'Dilemmas in a general theory of planning' (1973) 4 *Policy Sciences* 155. Wicked problems are 'difficult to clearly define and are often not stable; have many interdependencies and are often multi-causal; there is often disagreement about the causes of the problems and the best way to tackle them; attempts to address wicked problems often lead to unforeseen consequences; they usually have no clear solution; are socially complex; and go beyond the capacity of any one organisation to understand and respond to them' – see Australian Public Service Commission, *Tackling wicked problems: A public policy perspective* (Canberra, 2012), available at: www.enablingchange.com.au/wickedproblems.pdf.

[23] R Williams, *Keywords: A Vocabulary of Culture and Society*, 2nd edn (Oxford University Press, 1983) 219.

> with their physical surroundings and the ways in which components pass across boundaries ... humans and human activities ... human social, political, and cultural institutions as well as an individual entity's character or qualities.[24]

Thinking carefully about environmental problems requires thinking about those individual elements and all of the interactions between those elements.[25] Environmental problems are found at the intersection of two massively complex systems: the natural world and human social systems. One should therefore 'expect them to be doubly complex [as] [t]he more complex a situation, the larger the number of plausible perspectives upon it'.[26] This interaction between complex systems explains why the causes of environmental problems can be 'multi-dimensional'[27] and cumulative, impacts tend to be 'dynamic'[28] and 'non-linear',[29] and '[w]hen a change occurs in one part of the [ecosystem], many other parts must adjust themselves to it'.[30] Paradoxically, with environmental problems interdependency is core[31] but indeterminacy is rife. But in order to illustrate the dynamism of environmental problems, and to demonstrate clearly that environmental adjudication often has to operate against an unstable factual backdrop regardless of what *we* do, the following discussion disassociates connections between the social and natural worlds.

A. Ecological Complexity

> As the First Law of Ecology says, everything is connected to everything else.[32]

The inherent structural features of environmental problems – interaction and change – begin at the ecological layer. Natural ecosystems have a huge number of interacting parts, starting from the basic building blocks of life (the sub-atomic particles explored in quantum physics, and atoms and molecules) up to large complicated systems like the atmosphere. I want to explore this point in detail because lawyers are apt to forget why establishing a comprehensive and stable ecological data set, ie, establishing a clear factual backdrop against which to adjudicate environmental disputes, is often impossible.

[24] C Merchant, *Autonomous Nature: Problems of Prediction and Control from Ancient Times to the Scientific Revolution* (Routledge, 2016) 8.

[25] F Müller, 'Hierarchical approaches to ecosystem theory' (1992) 63 *Ecological Modelling* 215, 216.

[26] J Dryzek, *The Politics of the Earth*, 2nd edn (Oxford University Press, 2005) 9.

[27] ibid, 8.

[28] Kooiman (n 9).

[29] Lockwood et al (n 10).

[30] A Leopold, *A Sand Country Almanac: And Sketches Here and There* (Oxford University Press, 1977) 216.

[31] MC Lemos and A Agrawal, 'Environmental Governance' (2006) 31 *Annual Review of Environmental Resources* 297.

[32] Z Plater et al, *Environmental Law and Policy: Nature Law and Society*, 3rd edn (Wolters Kluwer, 2004) xxx.

In order to understand complex biological systems, scientists first tend to employ reductionism and then try to reconcile individual parts. So, base biological processes are determined first; then the impacts of multiple variables within each scale are assessed; and finally, scientists attempt to reconcile how each scale 'talks to other scales'.[33] Functioning ecosystems depend on maintaining important sub-assemblies, ie, those parts that are 'tightly connected within themselves', so it is important to know 'who is connected to whom and how'.[34] Simply listing the biological scales illustrates the enormity of this task and gives some idea of the sheer number of elements and interactions. The scales range sequentially upwards from the atomic scale, to the molecular, cell, tissue, organ, organ systems, organisms, population-scale, up to the whole environment. Reconciliation is made more difficult by the fact that 'information is lost as you go up though the scales'.[35] Often lower-order laws of nature (for example, that operate at cell level) cannot be extrapolated to higher-order levels (for example, organism levels) in order to predict collective behaviour. Rather, different laws of nature apply at each scale. And some scales such as the microscopic (as quantum physics shows) or at the highest order (as special relativity suggests) are characterised by chaos and unpredictability, not mechanistic processes.[36] Thinking about climate change makes sense of this disparity for legally trained readers. While analytical scientists are well aware of the base chemical processes that cause climate change, forensic or environmental scientists have greater difficulty pinpointing the precise effects that climate change will wreak on particular environments, other than in relatively general terms.

But natural systems, even in the absence of human intervention, are in constant flux, evolving and adapting,[37] and that interactional nature manifests in different behaviours. Darwinian evolution is not a heterogeneous process. For example, elements within each scale may follow 'emergence' behaviours (ie, evolution is forced by the interactions between lower-level elements in the system) or 'co-evolution' (the modification of elements in the same scale create changes) or 'self-organisation' (where systems adapt to their environment by spontaneous modification).[38] Nor does evolution constitute a perfect progress story. As the evolutionary biologist Ernst Mahr opined, 'there is only one universal law

[33] R McLachlan, *Prediction is difficult, especially about the future* (Royal Society of New Zealand Lecture Series 2013).

[34] C Holling (ed), *Adaptive Environmental Assessment and Management* (Wiley, 1978) 27.

[35] McLachlan (n 33).

[36] Merchant (n 24) 10–11.

[37] D Botkin, *Discordant Harmonies: A New Ecology for the Twenty-First Century* (Oxford University Press, 1990); W Rodgers, 'Where Environmental Law and Biology Meet: Of Pandas' Thumbs, Statutory Sleepers, and Effective Law' (1993) 65 *University of Colorado Law Review* 25, 51: 'there are no definite directions, no strict causal determinism producing identical results in similar circumstances. The path of environmental change through time is tortuous and undirected'.

[38] A Macintosh and D Wilkinson, 'Complexity Theory and the Constraints on Environmental Policymaking' (2016) 28 *JEL* 65, 66.

in biology: "all biological laws have exceptions'"[39] – maladaption, randomness, mutation, pleiotropy and the like, all play a role. Each organic system is 'rich in feedbacks, homeostatic devices, and potential multiple pathways'.[40] Further, complex systems can reach points of self-organised criticality where they permanently change their state to a new state of normality, but this point is not always capable of prediction.[41] Nature is after all, 'autonomous'.[42]

Pausing for one moment, we can see that even when we silo ecological complexity – ignoring human interactions with the environment – the challenges for adjudication are immense. Environmental problem-solvers are surveyors of time. They cannot ignore the (data-rich but incomplete knowledge of the) past, the (unsatisfactory) present and critically, the future – a future that will change in some way and that they are trying to impact in a positive manner. But because of ecological interaction and change they do not have a comprehensive existing data set, may often be dealing with instability and uncertainty, and so may be without a sound factual basis upon which to apply the law. So, in adjudicating over a dispute concerning the discharge of pollutants into the environment for example, the receiving environment will seldom be fixed nor will information about that environment be comprehensive.[43] The interactional frame for environmental adjudication must be drawn with this feature in mind because it will impact responsive processes, doctrine and remedies in environmental adjudication as the discussion in chapter six demonstrates. However, these problems of interaction and change become even more complex when we add humans to the mix.

B. Humans as Actors of Change

Environmental adjudicators may be tasked with determining whether a new activity should proceed and, as part of the evaluation, must consider the effects

[39] E Mahr, *The Growth of Biological Thought: Diversity, Evolution, and Inheritance* (Belknap Press 1982) 37-38; see also DF Peat, *From Certainty to Uncertainty: The Story of Science and Ideas in the Twentieth Century* (Joseph Henry Press, 2002).

[40] Rodgers (n 37) 47.

[41] *cf* P Bak, *How Nature Works: The Science of Self-Organized Criticality* (Copernicus, 1996) (arguing for the existence of universal laws in criticality).

[42] Merchant (n 24) 8 (nature 'cannot be predicted or controlled except in very limited domains'); *cf* McKibben who takes the thinking to the ultimate abstraction in claiming that any clear distinction between nature and the socio-cultural world has ended because 'the idea of nature will not survive the new global pollution … we have deprived nature of its independence … we have ended the thing that has, at least in modern times defined nature for us – its separation from human society' B McKibben, *The End of Nature* (Anchor, 1989) 58, 64 quoted in D Westbrook, 'Liberal Environmental Jurisprudence' (1993–94) 27 *UC Davis Law Review* 619, 656.

[43] If the legal command is to avoid 'significant pollution' this feature becomes problematic. I accept it is less *legally* problematic in a dispute concerning a clear quantifiable rule regulating point source pollution, and while uncertainty in that case may hinge upon technological processes, monitoring or measurement, I accept that form of uncertainty does not fit within my 'beyond human control' point.

of this activity on the environment. This predictive role proves challenging because of the dynamism of ecosystems as explained above (ie, the environmental backdrop is not fixed) but also because human interventions imposing external stimuli on the environment may take scientific assessment and predictions outside the range of normal variations. As Leopold noted '[e]volutionary changes … are usually slow and local. Man's invention of tools has enabled him to make changes of unprecedented violence, rapidity, and scope'.[44]

Human disturbance of complex systems can produce 'counterintuitive results'[45] that with hindsight range from the simple and observable – such as the land erosion observed by Leopold in the American south west[46] – to the untraceable and malevolent, such as the insidious toxicity of chemical pollution captured by the marine biologist, Rachel Carson. In her seminal work, *Silent Spring*, Carson described how,

> chemicals spayed onto croplands or forests or gardens lie in soil, entering into living organisms, passing from one to another in a chain of poisoning and death. Or they pass mysteriously by underground streams until they emerge and, through the alchemy of air and sunlight, combine into new forms that kill vegetation, sicken cattle, and work unknown harm on those who drink once pure wells.[47]

None of these adverse impacts were intentional or foreseen. They were unpredicted, sometimes untraceable, and often unattributable to a single cause or actor, and they impacted many people and multiple species.[48] In both scenarios, changes can be irreversible: species become extinct and once chemical pollution has infiltrated living tissues, Carson writes, it can penetrate 'the germ cells to shatter or alter the very material of heredity upon which the shape of our

[44] Leopold (n 30) 217.

[45] Dryzek (n 26) 201.

[46] Leopold (n 30) 206: '[t]his region, when grazed by livestock, reverted though a sense of more and more worthless grasses, shrubs, and weeds to a condition of unstable equilibrium. Each recession of plant type bred erosion; each increment to erosion bred a further recession of plants. The result today is a progressive and mutual deterioration, not only of plants and soils but of the animal community subsisting thereon'.

[47] R Carson, *Silent Spring* (Houghton Mifflin, 1962) 6.

[48] On unintended consequences see Aagaard (n 17) 48, citing J Huffman, 'Marketing Biodiversity' (2002) 38 *Idaho Law Review* 421, 425 (noting that domestic environmental regulation of industry may export environmental degradation to other countries); JB Ruhl and J Salzman, 'Mozart and the Red Queen: The Problem of Regulatory Accretion in the Administrative State' (2003) 91 *Georgetown Law Journal* 757 (noting the problem of 'media-shifting' in which 'pollution-control laws protecting one environmental medium (for example, air, water, or land) … generat[e] … pollution in alternative media'); E Ryan, 'New Orleans, the Chesapeake, and the Future of Environmental Assessment: Overcoming the Natural Resources Law of Unintended Consequences' (2006) 40 *University of Richmond Law Review* 981, 984–85 (noting that, when 'Virginia resource managers attempted to protect inter-tidal wetlands by establishing a development-free jurisdictional boundary … landowners then built all the way to the legal side of the line … [which] inadvertently doomed the protected wetlands by disconnecting them from the natural shoreline systems that sustain them during such periods of sea-level rise' and thereby 'accomplished the exact opposite of what policymakers had hoped for')).

future depends'.[49] The Nobel prize-winning chemist Ilya Prigogine and philosopher Isabelle Stengers wrote that irreversibility in complex systems mean that they are non-deterministic;[50] 'instability breaks time symmetry'[51] – the present cannot be privileged and the past cannot determine the future.[52] Human agents of change in particular can force acute breaks between the past and future behaviour of ecosystems. This dynamism and stochasticism in particular, creates significant challenges for scientific assessment that is trying to predict future behaviour.

Understanding these higher-level physical constraints is particularly important for the interactional theory because it helps link together the first two components of the theory, ie, the challenges created for adjudication by the inherent nature of environmental problems. In attempting to assess environmental impacts, adjudication relies heavily upon scientific *opinion* evidence as to the future. As judges of the NZEnvC have written, 'fact-finding routinely includes extensive adjudication on conflicting expert opinion about management of future states and risks'.[53] Yet absolute scientific guarantees of the future based on the past, are impossible[54] and to suggest otherwise would be a logical fallacy science simply does not recognise.[55] Scientists may express high confidence in relation to some predictions, for example, where there is lengthy actuarial evidence or systems with periodic behaviours return to the same state (for example, the orbit of planets)[56] and in other scenarios, predictions may still be explained statistically or may be expressed in terms of varying confidence. But human impacts on non-linear and chaotic systems such as biological ecosystems, create predictive problems of a different magnitude. We might know the starting conditions and understand the stimuli or forces exerted on these chaotic systems but tiny discrepancies can multiply incredibly quickly, leading to massive differences in results thus creating inherent contestability with scientific modelling.[57] Further, assessments are spatially and temporally multi-scalar,[58] and accurately charting change is complicated by the wide-ranging orders of magnitude capable of being employed – from nanoseconds to millennia. As systems get more complex

[49] Carson (n 47) 8. Widespread pesticide use in the US from 1945 to 1972 led to health and fertility problems, damage to plant life, population reduction in many species, and death, and remains problematic: see D Pimentel, 'Is Silent Spring Behind Us?' in G Marco, R Hollingworth and W Durham (eds), *Silent Spring Revisited* (American Chemical Society, 1987).

[50] I Prigogine and I Stengers, *The End of Certainty: Time, Chaos and the New Laws of Nature* (The Free Press, 1997).

[51] ibid, 5.

[52] ibid, 6.

[53] L Newhook, D Kirkpatrick and J Hassan, 'Issues with Access to Justice in the Environment Court of New Zealand' (2017) 29 *Environmental Law & Management* 125, 126.

[54] Mahr (n 39) 137: '[w]hen I say: "A territory-holding male songbird has a 98.7% … chance to be victorious over an intruder", I can hardly claim to have established a law'.

[55] J Steele, *Risks and Legal Theory* (Hart Publishing, 2004) 169.

[56] McLachlan (n 33).

[57] ibid.

[58] Lockwood et al (n 10) 987.

and transpose over time, and as stimuli alter, scientists have to rely on generalisations to predict future effects and it is at this point in particular that science becomes contestable. As Bohr purportedly said, 'prediction is very difficult, especially about the future'.[59]

In these non-linear scenarios, scientists may draw on different methodologies to make predictions of future behaviour.[60] For example, they may be in a position to undertake epidemiological studies of actual effects in the real world; or statistical analysis of human populations that relate degree of exposure to a risk; and/or create dose-response curves, 'which show how risks to health and life varies with the amount of exposure to a hazard'.[61] If epidemiological evaluations are not possible or available, there may be 'persuasive animal studies or other bio-mechanistic evidence'[62] (although the assumption is that these studies can yield useful information about how human or other species' physiology will react).

The inherent limitations of scientific prediction and the use of variable scientific methodologies, create significant challenges for environmental adjudicators. There may be relatively high levels of agreement between experts with opinions coalescing, even where different methodologies are employed.[63] But where there is disagreement, adjudicators have to decide which opinion to prefer. In order to do so, classic judicial assessment methods such as 'which witness gave evidence in the most compelling way' can be misplaced (science is seldom concerned with the plausibility of one person). Rather, adjudicators may have to look behind expert opinion to methodology.[64] But even that evaluative technique must be approached with caution. As the Environmental Resources and Development Court of South Australia accepted in the *Tuna Boat Owners* case:

> The scientific method does not necessarily give the quality of certainty to the opinion or assessment of a scientist. Indeed, one writer has suggested that a scientific opinion might be best evaluated for reliability by testing it against seven types of uncertainty he identified as being likely to be found in any scientific assessment or opinion, namely conceptual uncertainty, measurement uncertainty, sampling uncertainty, mathematical modelling uncertainty, causal uncertainty, testing uncertainty and communicative and cognitive uncertainty.[65]

[59] McLachlan (n 33).

[60] Steele (n 55) 23; see also the NSWLEC's consideration of various types of scientific uncertainty in *Telstra Corporation v Hornby Shire Council* [2006] NSWLEC 133, [141], [146]–[148].

[61] Dryzek (n 26) 85.

[62] *Shirley Primary School v Christchurch City Council* [1999] NZRMA 66, [175] see also [10]–13].

[63] A good example concerns climate change and the work of the IPCC collating and peer reviewing global research on climate change (RK Pachauri and LA Meyer, *Synthesis Report. Contribution of Working Groups I, II and III to the Fifth Assessment Report of the Intergovernmental Panel on Climate Change* (IPCC, Geneva, 2014)).

[64] eg, *Friends of Tumblebee Inc v ATB Morton Pty Ltd (No 2)* (n 16) [105].

[65] *Conservation Council of South Australia v Development Assessment Committee and Tuna Boat Owners Association (No 2)* [1999] SAERDC 86, [22] (*Tuna Boat Owners*) (case developed the application of the precautionary principle in that jurisdiction).

In essence, the Court acknowledged that while scientific research aspires to follow certain epistemic virtues (such as objectivity and precision achieved by a transparent and systematic methodology; adopting due scepticism to challenge pre-existing biases; 'quality control by peer review, professional independence and accountability'; and critically, replicability),[66] these aspirations are not always met.[67] Methodological *approaches* reflect choices and methodological *choices* are underpinned by different rationales, conditions, values and beliefs; they can be highly subjective and 'there is every reason to think that the biases affecting expert risk assessment are as systematic as those affecting lay responses'.[68]

A particularly good illustration is provided by *Royal Forest and Bird Society v Buller District Council*,[69] a case decided by the NZEnvC and appealed on a point of law to the High Court. The facts of the case are relatively stark. Coal miners proposed removing and relocating 12 hectares of habitat from the surface of a planned opencast mine, along with the resident Great Spotted Kiwi – New Zealand's national bird and an endangered species – and the critically endangered and endemic Powelliphanta Snail. If the translocation failed, the endangered species were at risk but the value of the coal was thought to be NZ$850 million. Translocation of an entire wetlands habitat had never been attempted before and much of the conflict concerned the feasibility of this mitigation plan.[70] Ecologists employed by the miner expressed greater confidence than the expert instructed by the NGO that the translocation would succeed, yet their assessments were based on agreed facts: the experts were interpreting the same data, looking at the same research, and had similar experiences, however they reached different opinions concerning the risk. The NZEnvC permitted the mining and sanctioned the mitigation plan.[71] The High Court appeal on a point of law illustrates the problems with trying to fit environmental problems within ill-fitting adjudicatory frames. For example, the Court criticised the NGO's lawyers for not putting their case fully to one of the miner's experts but did not

[66] L Daston and P Galison, *Objectivity* (Zone Books, 2007) 32.

[67] There is a whole body of literature critiquing scientific process (see, in particular, S Jasanoff, *The Fifth Branch: Science Advisers as Policy Makers* (Harvard University Press, 1990)). Suffice to say there are inherent challenges that make perfect objectivity difficult, particularly if knowledge is 'generated for a particular purpose' because 'rather than being objective and value free, environmental knowledge is being co-produced alongside policy' – Fisher, Lange and Scotford (n 19) 32, 35. The neo-liberalisation of the academy and the use of rigid research quality evaluations, militates against University-based researchers undertaking replicability research (thanks to Bokyong Mun for this observation).

[68] Steele (n 55) 166, citing P Slovic, *The Perception of Risk* (Earthscan, 2000) 390.

[69] *Solid Energy NZ Ltd v West Coast Regional Council* C74/2005 (unrep) (NZEnvC); *Royal Forest and Bird Protection Society NZ Inc v Buller District Council* [2006] NZRMA 193 (NZHC) (*Buller* case) (decision upheld on appeal).

[70] Note, however, the NZEnvC's analysis of this conflict is extremely limited see *Solid Energy NZ Ltd v West Coast Regional Council* (n 69) paras [123]–[128].

[71] *Solid Energy NZ Ltd v West Coast Regional Council* (n 69).

remit the matter back to the trial court, choosing instead to draw adverse implications (against the argument that hydrological conditions would not support the direct transfer of vegetation).[72] So rather than pursuing the need for clarity, the High Court adopted an adjudicatory technique often used in other forms of litigation to create a shortcut or legal fiction. Fundamentally, the appeal failed because the Court found that (regardless of the values at stake) there was 'only one standard of evidential proof – the balance of probabilities' and the risk of failure had not been proven to that standard.[73] The High Court misunderstood the role of the first-tier adjudicator in this case – that is, the case was concerned with assessing risk, not fact-finding as to the past, an issue discussed at length in chapter six. Unfortunately, the case does not have a happy outcome. Eight hundred of the snails froze to death following a technical malfunction at the Department of Conservation site established to house them while their habitat was relocated.[74] The remaining snails experienced a mortality rate of 30 per cent over the natural mortality rate and it was not known whether the population could sustain such a loss.[75]

The *Buller* case demonstrates the 'close interrelationship between facts and values'[76] in environmental adjudication because knowledge and values in the scientific assessments became entangled. Further, while the knowledge base in that case was incomplete, the strong rational underpinning dispute resolution – for a decision to be reached regardless – dominated. Incomplete knowledge is particularly problematic in adjudication that can adversely impact, sometimes forever, the conditions of the natural world. Accordingly, environmental adjudicators need to know when science has gaps or is uncertain and to take omissions seriously because even so-called calculated risks can go horribly wrong, wiping out a species or leading to a large-scale pollution incident.

Before moving on to consider the next layer of 'interaction and change', it is worth drawing some threads together at this point. Environmental adjudicators must often identify the effects on the ecosystem likely to be imposed by a human activity and in order to do so scientific opinion evidence will often be valuable. But scientific assessments do not come in neat packages. Scientific predictions can reflect varying possibilities from relative confidence, to diminishing degrees

[72] *Royal Forest and Bird Society of New Zealand Inc v Buller District Council* (n 69) [56].

[73] ibid, [73].

[74] *BBC World News*, 'Mishap freezes to death 800 rare New Zealand snails' (11 November 2011), available at: www.bbc.co.uk/news/world-asia-15691701.

[75] R Morris, *An Unfortunate Experiment* (The Royal Forest and Bird Protection Society, August 2010) 337: 14–18. Note, in another tragic example of prediction being no guarantee, the miners went bankrupt when the market for coal dropped dramatically wiping out the value of coal reserves (see *Reuters Intel*, 'NZ State-owned coal miner put into administration' (*Thomson Reuters*, 13 August 2015), available at: www.reuters.com/article/newzealand-solidenergy/nz-state-owned-coal-miner-put-into-administration-idUSL3N10O1KP20150813.

[76] Fisher, Lange and Scotford (n 19) 29, describing this phenomenon as 'the most significant aspect of environmental problems'.

of confidence, to complete uncertainty, and predictions can be premised on widely differing methodologies. In the event of conflict, adjudicators may be presented with a range of methodologies to unpick in determining which opinion to accept. Further, adjudicators must be able to distinguish the scientific fact or omission from the sociological frame that imports values, philosophies and ideologies into scientific opinions. Failing to do so would mean that objective facts are devalued in environmental adjudication, creating significant socio-political imbalances because merging facts, values and opinions act to hide power structures.[77] Finally, as the *Buller* case clearly illustrated, subjecting uncertain facts or contested scientific predictions to the straitjacket of adjudicatory techniques developed in other contexts is especially problematic in environmental adjudication.

All these factors contribute to the construction of the detailed frame for environmental adjudication. They point in particular towards the need for a specific type of judicial expertise, combining ideally with scientifically trained members of the court – so creating new epistemic communities.[78] But they also suggest the need for flexible evidential processes, for example, the ability for *courts* to instruct expert witnesses if there is a lacuna; the employment of different methods for evaluating evidence rather than reliance on the more traditional methods of proof (such as which witness was more compelling in the witness box etc); the use of different standards of evidence; and the rejection of adjudicative techniques that use legal fictions in order to resolve disputes.

C. Direct Impacts on Humans

I want to consider the inherent features – interaction and change – from another perspective now, by thinking about environmental impacts *on* humans. Environmental adjudicators are often tasked with assessing the direct effects of activities (for example, the use, development or pollution of the environment) upon the health and wellbeing of people and communities.[79] Activities in the environment can impact humans' physiological health, psychological wellbeing and sensibilities (so affecting taste, smell, sound, visual or aesthetic experiences, and people's sense of amenity and wellbeing) and all three aspects are interlinked. For example, emotional arousal causes profound physiological changes by secreting hormones from the cortex and medulla of the adrenal

[77] B Latour, 'Why Has Critique Run Out of Steam? From Matters of Fact to Matters of Concern' (2004) 30 *Critical Inquiry* 225.

[78] GN Gill, 'Environmental Justice in India: The National Green Tribunal and Expert Members' (2016) 5 *Transnational Environmental Law* 175.

[79] eg, decisions of the NZEnvC must enable 'people and communities to provide for … health and safety' (Resource Management Act 1991 (NZ) (RMA), s 5(2)); decisions of the NSWLEC under the Environmental Planning and Assessment Act 1979 (NSW) (s 1.3) must promote the 'health and safety' of building occupants etc.

glands and 'when too much of any hormone is secreted into the bloodstream, or if these hormones remain in the body for too long, they can result in harm to the tissues'.[80] Once again, the very *nature* of the problems they are tasked with resolving creates particular challenges for environmental adjudicators with regard to identifying who might be impacted, the actual impacts and assessing those impacts.

I could choose any number of devastating human–ecological encounters to show the multilayered effects on humans, the difficulties in accurately assessing those impacts and the challenge this creates for adjudication.[81] But small things can often best illuminate big problems,[82] so I am going to rely on unpleasant smells to make the point. The nauseating stench of pigswill prompted the first recognisably environmental case in the common law world,[83] and objectionable odours continue to found the basis for environmental disputes while creating challenges for adjudicators.[84] Odour and other examples of second-order quality distinctions (for example, light and noise) are less 'clearly and distinctly perceived in the mind' than primary distinctions such as size, figure and duration.[85] Smell, has been described as a 'confusing mix of elusiveness and certainty'.[86] For some an odour 'draws us into the entangled threads of memory and possibility' while for others the same smell repulses, forcing us to move 'out of its range'[87] and if we cannot, it can lead to litigation. In *Waikato Environmental Protection Society Inc v Waikato Regional Council (Meadow Mushrooms)* the NZEnvC – faced with malodorous but economically productive mushroom-growing operations in a neighbourhood – explained the inherent difficulties in undertaking odour assessments: 'Put briefly, the difficulty lies in the fact that there is no equipment or mathematical formula that can determine whether or not any given odour has an offensive or objectionable effect'.[88]

Not capable of quantitative calculation, odour assessment requires complex, qualitative assessments that mix the objective and subjective.[89] Of course,

[80] RS Lazarus and BN Lazarus, *Passion and Reason: Making Sense of our Emotions* (Oxford University Press, 1994) 183–84, and further see ch 12 'Emotions and our health' at 239–61 in particular.

[81] For an unusual example, see the famous Japanese case of *Toshogu Shrine Religious Organisation v Minister of Construction* 710 HANREI JIHO, 23 (Tokyo HC) that was concerned with forest clearances for a road project that destroyed cultural sites.

[82] Lowenhaupt Tsing (n 7) 119.

[83] *Aldred's Case* (1610) 9 Co Rep 57b; (1610) 77 ER 816; [1558–774] All ER Rep 622 (possibly the first nuisance case; concerned odours from a pigsty).

[84] eg, Ministry for the Environment, *Good Practice Guide for Assessing and Managing Odour in New Zealand* (MfE, 2016).

[85] Daston and Galison (n 66) 32, citing Descartes.

[86] Lowenhaupt Tsing (n 7) 45.

[87] ibid, 46.

[88] *Waikato Environmental Protection Society Inc v Waikato Regional Council* [2008] NZRMA 431 (NZEnvC), [34]; see also *Northcompass Inc v Hornby Shire Council* [1996] NSWLEC 213.

[89] *Bulga Milbrodale Progress Association Inc v Minister for Planning and Infrastructure and Warkworth Mining Limited* (n 14) [296].

qualitative assessment is a factor in other areas of the law – this is the whole point about the 'reasonable man'.[90] But interactions in environmental disputes stress even the relative stability of that concept. In the *Meadow Mushrooms* case the Court accepted that persons exposed to chronic odours (ie, moderate odours that occur frequently over a long period) can suffer from a slow accumulation of stress that makes them more sensitive to the odour.[91] Further, interactions between the activity, those impacted and the wider atmospheric conditions were dynamic and accordingly, impacts varied. Employing the objective so-called 'reasonable man test' derived in criminal and civil disputes before the ordinary courts, may not therefore achieve appropriate levels of environmental protection.[92] In this context, assessment depends not solely on the frailties and foibles of individual humans[93] or even on the impacts and intensity of others' activities, but the fluctuating conditions in the wider receiving environment and critically, the dynamic interactions between all three. In this interactional reality we need a combination of information to accurately determine effects, including evidence of subjective effects from lay people and expert knowledge from various disciplines.[94]

Another mushroom-growing case illustrates an additional challenge for adjudication created by the interactional nature of environmental problems: identifying who might be affected. During the course of the litigation in *Haslam v Selwyn District Council*[95] the parties pondered whether the proposed mushroom composting operation should be located on a different part of the site and if so whether other people in the surrounding environment would be adversely affected. If they were, should they become party to the proceedings?[96] This case highlights, in a very simple way, the collective nature of environmental problems.[97] In terms of air pollution, and in fact *any* use of the commons[98] (air, water, public lands, biodiversity), impacted persons can be wide-ranging geographically and also temporally, by including present and future generations. As discussed further in chapter six this point has implications not only for the

[90] M Moran, *Rethinking the Reasonable Person: An Egalitarian Reconstruction of the Objective Standard* (Oxford University Press, 2003) 146; see also Lord Hoffmann, 'Anthropomorphic Justice: The Reasonable Man and his Friends' (1995) 29 *Law Teacher* 127.

[91] *Waikato Environmental Protection Society Inc v Waikato Regional Council* (n 88), [38]–[39].

[92] Within this legal landscape, we have moved into and out the far side of classic 'eggshell skull' territory.

[93] The 'messy individualism of humanity' as described by Susan Bandes: S Bandes (ed), *The Passions of Law* (New York University Press, 1999) 7–8.

[94] Rose, 'Environmental Law Grows Up' (n 2) (arguing environmental problems put new demands on knowledge).

[95] *Haslam v Selwyn District Council* (1993) 2 NZRMA 628 (PT).

[96] *Waikato Environmental Protection Society Inc v Waikato Regional Council* (n 88).

[97] E Ostrom, *Governing the Commons: The Evolution of Institutions for Collective Action* (Cambridge University Press, 1990).

[98] G Hardin, 'The Tragedy of the Commons' (1968) 162 *Science* 1243.

forms of knowledge required to determine disputes, but also for *locus standi*.[99] Again, both of these factors are important in helping to construct the frame for normative legitimacy: environmental adjudication that operates with integrity must provide a site that accepts and evaluates different forms of knowledge, and allows for the impacted to participate in some way. Moreover, in considering how the core features of environmental problems impact the forms of knowledge required in adjudication, we can add a further layer of interactional complexity: socio-cultural wellbeing, economic functioning and ethical pluralism.

D. Social-cultural and Economic Complexity

At the beginning of this chapter I quoted Dryzek's observation that environmental problems are 'doubly complex' because they are found at the intersection of the natural and human-made realms. Conditions in either realm impact those in the other. In *Bulga Milbrodale Progress Association Inc v Minister for Planning and Infrastructure*,[100] the NSWLEC noted this interdependence, the range of interests affected and accordingly characterised disputes before the Court as 'polycentric'.[101] In describing polycentric problems, Preston CJ draws on Fuller's analysis to explain that,

> [a] polycentric problem involves a complex network of relationships, with interacting points of influence. Each decision made communicates itself to other centres of decision, changing the conditions, so that a new basis must be found for the next decision.[102] Fuller uses the concept of a spider web to assist in visualising the kind of situation presented by a polycentric problem.[103] A pull of one strand of the web will distribute tensions, after a complicated pattern of adjustment, throughout the web as a whole. Doubling the original pull will not simply double each of the resulting tensions but will rather create a different, complicated pattern of tensions. This would occur if the doubled pull caused one of the weaker strands to snap. This is a

[99] Legal theorists argue that risk-bearers should be able to challenge the imposition of risk upon them: see B Fried, 'The Nonconsequentialist Approach to Torts' (2012) 18 *Legal Theory* 231 (although note, the context of this article is private law); G Walker, *Environmental Justice: Concepts, Evidence and Politics* (Routledge, 2012) 49. There is a huge literature reviewing standing in environmental law, particularly in light of the Convention on Access to Information, Participation in Decision-making and Access to Justice in Environmental Matters (Aarhus Convention) 1998, UNTS vol 2161, 477 – see, eg, C Poncelet, 'Access to Justice in Environmental Matters – Does the European Union Comply with its Obligations?' (2012) 24 *JEL* 287; and in the US context see, eg, JG Miller, 'Case law analysis. The standing of citizens to enforce violations of environmental statutes in the United States' (2000) 12 *JEL* 370.

[100] *Bulga Milbrodale Progress Association Inc v Minister for Planning and Infrastructure and Warkworth Mining Limited* (n 14).

[101] ibid, [31].

[102] J Jowell, 'Legal Control of Administrative Discretion' [1973] *PL* 178, 213.

[103] L Fuller, 'The Forms and Limits of Adjudication' (1978–79) 92 *Harvard Law Review* 353, 395.

> polycentric problem because it is many centred, each crossing of strands is a distinct centre for distributing tensions.[104]

I discussed polycentric decision-making in chapter three but it is important to note here that this interactional reality presents significant challenges for fact-finding in adjudication. Adjudicators may be required to identify, assess and weigh the effects of activities in the environment on the wider socio-cultural and economic functioning of communities.[105] And ecological, socio-cultural and economic interests often come into conflict in environmental adjudication. Proponents or opponents of activities will adduce different types of evidence, argue that different evaluative mechanisms should be employed (such as cost–benefit analysis), and also present different legal arguments based on the particular values that they hold. Accordingly, environmental adjudication is a site for ethical pluralism. A good example is provided by the NSWLEC case, *Gloucester Resources Ltd v Minister for Planning*[106] that concerned the merits review of an application to establish a coal mine. In the face of climate change concerns, the proponents of the coal mine submitted that the Court should adopt 'the principle of efficiency in greenhouse gas abatement' as a legal test.[107] This principle was described as making emissions reductions 'where they count most and generate the least economic and social harm'.[108] The proposed mine would produce coking coal for steel production. The miners' adduced evidence to support their argument that there was no reasonable substitute to this form of steel production and rather than refusing consent for the mine, greenhouse gas abatement could be achieved in other ways that were not so essential to the well-being of the community (albeit those projects were not before the Court). They also used cost–benefit analyses to support their conception of the efficiency principle. However, those analyses calculated local economic efficiencies but excluded the global efficiencies of making wholesale emissions cuts quickly.[109] The miners wanted the Court to employ 'the principle of efficiency' as a legal consideration in the final decision-making process but the way that they framed this so-called principle and the evidence they called in support of it demonstrates the pervasive role of ethical pluralism and how it infuses legal reasoning in environmental adjudication.

I want to drill down to consider ethical pluralism in some detail because it is an immutable feature in environmental adjudication and the challenges for

[104] *Bulga Milbrodale Progress Association Inc v Minister for Planning and Infrastructure and Warkworth Mining Limited* (n 14) [31].

[105] eg, decisions of the NZEnvC must enable 'people and communities to provide for their social, economic, and cultural well-being' (RMA, s 5(2)); decisions of the NSWLEC under the Environmental Planning and Assessment Act 1979 (s 1.3) must promote the 'social and economic welfare of the community'.

[106] *Gloucester Resources Ltd v Minister for Planning* [2019] NSWLEC 7.

[107] ibid, [459].

[108] ibid, [459].

[109] ibid, [485].

adjudicators are magnified by this reality. However, it is important to be clear at the outset that I am not concerned with advancing particular values, morals or ethics in this book. I am not arguing that humans should treat or interact with the ecosystem or other species in particular ways. So, for example, I do not argue that those seeking to preserve the environment are morally superior to those wishing to use ecosystems for financial gain, with the result that the former's values should be privileged. Rather, I am arguing that pluralism is an inherent feature of environmental problems and needs to be accommodated and addressed if environmental adjudication is to have normative legitimacy.

E. Ethical Pluralism

All communities need some form of environmental dispute-resolution because we will always argue about the environment and we will do so primarily for three reasons. First, the environment is of critical importance to everyone: it feeds and waters us, houses us, surrounds us and provides not just for our physiological needs[110] but also our psychological wants.[111] Second, as mentioned above, environmental problems have a collective nature: they impact more than single individuals alone and may transcend present generations.[112] Third, whether environmental conditions are problematic and if so, how this should be resolved will always be contestable because of ethical pluralism. To really understand the role of ethical pluralism in environmental adjudication, we need to stake a step back to consider why it is such an embedded feature.

When we argue about the environment we are debating the ultimate question of ethical philosophy, that is, how we ought to live. In answer, philosophers tell us that people seek the good life, described by Allott as

> a sense that they and their family are succeeding in integrating satisfactorily their own daily lives, and realising their human potentiality as much as possible in all four existential realms of the human condition [i.e. the personal, social, supernatural and nature].[113]

Allott recognises that the good life includes creating some kind of relationship with the (non-human) natural world. But the conduct of that relationship will

[110] That is, our sustenance and health.

[111] Including economic profit, amenity values, aesthetic pleasure, and it can supply a sense of moral wellbeing. Nature acts as a muse for artists and poets and provided the context for Kant's philosophising on reason, morality, aestheticism and the sublime – see M Warnock, *Critical Reflections on Ownership* (Edward Elgar, 2015) chs 6 and 9 in particular; *cf* Westbrook (n 42) 678: '[w]ith the dissolution of the opposition between nature and culture, much that we looked to nature to find, a sense of wildness, humility, irrationality, mystery, or religion, may be found in the unpredictable combinations of markets'.

[112] E Ostrom, 'Polycentric Systems for Coping With Collective Action and Global Environmental Change' (2010) 20 *Global Environmental Change* 550.

[113] P Allott, *Eutopia: New Philosophy and New Law for a Troubled World* (Edward Elgar, 2016) 83.

vary between people and will be impacted by differing motivations,[114] specific end-goals and understanding as to how to reach those goals, degrees of knowledge about the natural world, beliefs and values.[115] As a result, environmental philosophy 'cannot provide a single determinative account' of how one ought to live.[116] Further, there is no one value *inherent in nature*[117] and '[t]here is no necessary bridge between fact and value, there is only choosing to act according to our understanding of nature – because of a commitment to an ethical value'.[118]

This prevalent ethical pluralism has led scholars to corral and catalogue core foci, and name various ideologies.[119] For example, 'anthropocentricism' and 'liberal individualism'[120] sees humans as separate and apart from the natural world, and superior to it.[121] As Todd pithily retorted to accusations of human arrogance, 'man bloody well is the measure of the being and value of all things, and that's an end on it'.[122] So-called economic rationalists, committed to perpetual economic growth,[123] may also separate out and privilege (short-term) financial wealth over ecological health, adopting a kind of them and us thinking. Others align separatist thinking with a Christian religious ethic[124] based on a particular interpretation of Genesis (let man have 'dominion over … all the earth, and over every creeping thing that creepeth

[114] M Warnock (n 111) ch 9 (discussing the different motivations of fear of cataclysmic climate change as opposed to love for wilderness).

[115] Westbrook (n 42) 682 (statements of value as to 'what is best' are ultimately statements of personal opinion); see also M Oelschlaeger, *The Idea of Wilderness: From Prehistory to the Age of Ecology* (Yale University Press, 1991); J Habermas, *Justification and Application: Remarks on Discourse Ethics* (MIT Press, 1993) 122–23.

[116] T Barraclough, 'How far can the Te Awa Tupua (Whanganui River) proposal be said to reflect the rights of nature in New Zealand?' (LLB (hons), University of Otago, 2013) 35.

[117] And if there were, this may not help the conservationist cause: as Brian Baxter mused, 'nature does not contain harmony and balance; … death and suffering are integral to it, not optional extras' – B Baxter, 'Naturalism and Environmentalism: A Reply to Hinchman' 15 *Environmental Values* 64, 65; or, as Mark Sagoff provocatively asks '[w]hy wouldn't Mineral King [mountain] want to host a ski resort, after doing nothing for a billion years?' – M Sagoff, 'On Preserving the Natural Environment' (1974) 84 *Yale Law Journal* 205, 222.

[118] Barraclough (n 116) 36–37.

[119] C Stone, 'Moral Pluralism and the Course of Environmental Ethics' (1988) 10 *Environmental Ethics* 139.

[120] L Tribe, 'Ways Not to Think About Plastic Trees: New Foundations for Environmental Law' (1974) 83 *Yale Law Journal* 1315, 1325–35.

[121] R Eckersley, *Environmentalism and Political Theory: Towards an Ecocentric Approach* (University of New York Press, 1992) 2–3.

[122] DD Todd, 'The Arrogance of Humanism, by Ehrenfeld David. New York, NY: Oxford University Press. 1978. Pp Viii, 286' (1981) 20 *Canadian Philosophical Review* 620, 624.

[123] Dryzek (n 26) 35, 52 (*cf* to 'ecological economics' that conceptualises ecosystems 'as the fundamental entities within which human economic systems are embedded' and 'treats natural systems as finite', 34).

[124] L White, 'The Historical Roots of Our Ecological Crisis' (1967) 155 *Science* 1203; *cf* Papa Francesco 'Enciclica Laudato Si' (2015) (en: Pope Francis 'Encyclical Letter of the Holy Father Francis on the Care for Our Common Home' (2015)).

upon the earth').[125] In contrast, various schools of thought such as 'ecological feminism',[126] 'bio-centric egalitarianism',[127] 'deep ecology',[128] ideas concerning 'stewardship'[129] and 'rights of nature',[130] all focus more on human responsibilities to nature than rights to own, use and take the environment. Indigenous beliefs such as the Māori worldview of 'whakapapa' regard humans and nature as inextricably linked.[131] Dame Mary Warnock suggests that foregoing Cartesian dualism enables us to embrace our kinship with the natural world, seeing ourselves as 'part' rather than 'apart' from the wider environment[132] (we are, after all, host to an essential 1.5 kgs of bacteria).[133] In *The Politics of the Earth*, Dryzek charts what he considers to be the dominant environmental discourses and their sub-categories.[134] Dryzek shows how each discourse is dependent on different data sets and models different variables,[135] leads to different policy prescriptions and legal doctrine, favours different institutional forms (markets, government bureaucracies, legal systems etc) and employs different assessment tools and evaluative techniques.[136]

Dryzek's premise can be illustrated by tracing one discourse through to the development of legal doctrine and its impact on adjudication. For example, entrenched ideas of human superiority and domination over nature lead naturally to ownership and property thinking.[137] Writing in the 1970s, Lord

[125] King James Bible, Book of Genesis 1:26. *cf* Adam and Eve being part of the natural world in the Garden of Eden (and vegetarians – Genesis 1:29, 30) with the Garden described as a climatic paradise before the 'fall of man' and 'original sin'.

[126] K Warren and J Cheney, 'Ecological Feminism and Ecosystem Ecology' (1991) 6 *Hypatia* 179.

[127] P Taylor, *Respect for Nature: A Theory of Environmental Ethics* (Princeton University Press, 1986).

[128] A Naess, 'The Deep Ecology Movement: Some Philosophical Aspects' (1986) 8 *Philosophical Inquiry* 10.

[129] E Barritt, 'Conceptualising Stewardship in Environmental Law' (2014) 26 *JEL* 1.

[130] Leopold (n 30); C Stone, 'Should Trees Have Standing? Towards Legal Rights for Natural Objects' (1972) 45 *Southern California Law Review* 450.

[131] G Harmsworth and S Awatere, 'Indigenous Māori Knowledge and Perspectives of Ecosystems' in J Dymond (ed), *Ecosystem Services in New Zealand* (Manaaki Whenua Press, 2013).

[132] M Warnock (n 111) ch 7.

[133] Bruce Munro, 'Germs are Us' *Otago Daily Times* (27 May 2017) (quoting microbiologist Rob Knight).

[134] Dryzek (n 26) 13–15. In opposition to unthinking 'industrialism' Dryzek identifies four core themes namely: 'problem solving' (that includes the three sub-categories of administrative rationalism, democratic pragmatism and economic rationalism); 'survivalism'; 'sustainability'; and 'green radicalism'. He argues that many different discourses exist at once rather than a single discourse dominating at any given time, and he notes how they sometimes complement but more often than not compete with each other (22). See also Habermas (n 115) 122–23.

[135] Dryzek (n 26) 53, 60–61. For example, so-called 'survivalists' chart the interaction of particular elements such as natural resources and population but tend to omit technology and market-price influences. Whereas 'prometheans' (anthropocentrics who believe there are no limits to man's ingenuity) ignore nature and often present single variable trends – eg, economic theory that ties price to scarcity, and analysis that shows the price of natural resources has consistently fallen or that life expectancy is increasing – to extrapolate the conclusion that 'all is well' with the environment.

[136] ibid, especially 20.

[137] C Rose, 'Possession as the Origin of Property' (1985) 52 *University of Chicago Law Review* 73, 87–88; Stone, 'Should Trees Have Standing?' (n 130) (particularly the discussion on slavery).

Scarman acknowledged that for environment law 'a traditional lawyer reads "property": English law reduces environmental problems to questions of property'.[138] Economic rationalists often advocate for environmental policy to adopt property-based approaches[139] because reducing nature to property facilitates market-based strategies reliant on commodity exchange.[140] Their aim is to translate the disparate considerations in environmental decision-making (considerations premised upon inherently incommensurable values) into common units capable of quantification and full fungibility, so creating arithmetic solutions to environmental problems.[141] Within adjudication, economic rationalists argue that particular assessment tools, such as cost–benefit analysis, input–output assessments, choice modelling and contingent-valuation methodologies,[142] can best determine public welfare.

Because of ethical pluralism, people may oppose the values that market-based mechanisms privilege.[143] For the philosopher Mary Warnock, economic cost–benefit analyses are not intelligible to humans who oppose the destruction of nature on moral grounds.[144] Market-based mechanisms also assume that goods are fully fungible and transactions are reversible, but such assumptions are 'incompatible with ecologists' conception of evolution and the uniqueness of ecosystems'.[145] As Warnock posits, an absolute loss, such as the demise of the lark, cannot ever be compensated.[146]

However, while those ideologically opposed to the use of market-based mechanisms may disagree with their use because of the values they privilege, they tend to attack them in adjudication on methodological grounds. At a

[138] L Scarman, *English Law: The New Dimension* (Stevens, 1974) 51.

[139] Dryzek (n 26) ch 6; K Baker, 'Consorting with Forests: Rethinking our Relationship to Natural Resources and How We Should Value Their Loss' (1995) 22 *Ecology Law Quarterly* 677, 691.

[140] R Coase, 'The Problem of Social Cost' (1960) 3 *Journal of Law & Economics* 1.

[141] D Anderson, *Environmental Economics*, 2nd edn (Pensive Press, 2006) 239.

[142] For an explanation of these tools see ibid, ch 10; see also *Bulga Milbrodale Progress Association Inc v Minister for Planning and Infrastructure and Warkworth Mining Limited* (n 14) [454], and for criticisms of input-output methodology see [463].

[143] Deep ecologists argue that all 'economic models have limitations' in the environmental context; optimal *environmental* outcomes are not their point, rather, they have a solely anthropocentric focus, see *Bulga Milbrodale Progress Association Inc v Minister for Planning and Infrastructure and Warkworth Mining Limited* (n 14) [462]; D Pearce, *Economics and Environment* (Edward Elgar, 1998) 15, 17. See also: R Eckersley, 'Rationalising the market: How much am I bid?' in S Rees et al (eds), *Beyond the Market: Alternatives to Economic Rationalism* (Pluto Press, 1993), opining that economic tools are concerned with optimal allocation based on human want not need and hence foster social inequality.

[144] M Warnock (n 111) 138–39. Note further, Preston CJ in *Bulga Milbrodale Progress Association Inc v Minister for Planning and Infrastructure and Warkworth Mining Limited* (n 14) [490]: '[t]he clearing and open cut mining of the [endangered ecological communities] and habitats would unacceptably disturb "the integrity, stability, and beauty of the biotic community". There is an ethical dimension to these land use impacts on the biotic community; it is not exclusively an economic problem'. Fried concurs, and adds that cost–benefit analysis just gives the sheen of legitimacy to a seriously flawed process, see Fried (n 99) 231–62.

[145] Fisher, Lange and Scotford (n 19) 42.

[146] M Warnock (n 111) 138–39.

fundamental level, the greater the uncertainties or dynamism in any given situation – a common feature of complex environmental disputes – the less the possibility of undertaking 'calculable' assessments,[147] and where 'no stable information or shared predictions on the future exist' market theory falls short.[148] Contingent valuation methodology (CVM) and Choice Modelling attract particular criticism.[149] These methodologies are used when no market exists and natural goods do not have a real exchange value: endangered biodiversity provides a good example. CVM creates pretend market conditions, valuing environmental media by conjecture through surveys of hypothetical questions. Survey participants estimate the monetary value of various goods or benefits, such as the transportation ease offered by a motorway or the preservation of an endangered species.[150] Preferences are then calculated as if goods were being traded. CVM relies upon the assumption that people are 'rational maximisers of preferences'[151] but many have questioned this premise.[152] Critics also argue that CVM does not assess the 'intrinsic value [of nature] rather it assesses the value that humans place on the instrumental (even if that is the non-use) value to them of the environment'.[153] Contestation can lead to lengthy and complex trials[154] (the judgment on contested cost–benefit analyses in *Gloucester Resources Ltd v Minister for Planning*[155] for example, runs to over 120 paragraphs).

[147] M Callon, 'An essay on framing and overflowing: economic externalities revisited by sociology' in M Callon (ed), *The Laws of the Markets* (Blackwell, 1989) 260–63. Despite significant work on this issue, economists are unable to reach a consistent view on how to address this flaw – a problem that highlights 'the dismal science of economics', see M Lines, 'Dynamics and Uncertainty' in H Folmer et al (eds), *Principles of Environmental and Resource Economics* (Edward Elgar, 1995) 102; R Ready, 'Environmental Value Under Uncertainty' in D Bromley (ed), *The Handbook of Environmental Economics* (Blackwell, 1996); Pearce (n 143) 63; see also John Rapley, 'How economics became a religion' *The Guardian* (11 July 2017).

[148] M Callon, 'Introduction: The embeddedness of economic markets in economics' in M Callon (ed), *The Laws of the Markets* (Blackwell, 1998) 1, 6; see also Anderson (n 141) 245–46.

[149] For a comprehensive analysis of Choice Modelling see *Bulga Milbrodale Progress Association Inc v Minister for Planning and Infrastructure and Warkworth Mining Limited* (n 14) [464]–[496].

[150] Anderson (n 141) 239. Various methods can be employed – eg, stating a 'Willingness to Pay' (ie, if they do not possess the resource – what is the largest amount a person would be willing to pay in exchange for the resource?) or 'Willingness to Accept' (ie, they already have the resource – what is the smallest amount of money they would accept to forego the resource?).

[151] Steele (n 55) 177.

[152] H Simon, *Administrative Behavior: A Study of Decision-Making Processes in Administrative Organizations*, 1st edn (Macmillan 1947); D Kahnemann and A Tversky (eds), *Choices, Values and Frames* (Cambridge University Press, 2000); D Kahnemann, *Thinking, Fast and Slow* (Farrar, Straus and Giroux, 2011); Baker (n 139) 715; M Sagoff, *The Economy of the Earth* (Cambridge University Press, 1988); P Slovic, 'The Construction of Preference' in D Kahnemann and A Tversky (eds), *Choices, Values and Frames* (Cambridge University Press, 2000); Anderson (n 141) 239–43.

[153] Baker (n 139) 685. Some have accused these mechanisms of simply calculating human selfishness, or allowing short-term personal gains to be the driving force behind assessment, see T Hayward, *Ecological Thought: An Introduction* (Polity Press, 1995) 92.

[154] eg, *Bulga Milbrodale Progress Association Inc v Minister for Planning and Infrastructure and Warkworth Mining Limited* (n 14) [446]–[496].

[155] *Gloucester Resources Ltd v Minister for Planning* (n 106) [557]–[685]. The applicant presented two economic assessment reports from different consultants containing different tools (cost–benefit

Alternatively, opponents may seek to persuade adjudicators to use different measures of community wellbeing, reflecting moral[156] and spiritual stances,[157] cultural impacts,[158] intrinsic value,[159] amenity,[160] personal anxieties[161] and intra-generational equity.[162] Suffice to say, such foci can prove equally troublesome for adjudication.[163] For example, submitting that adjudicators should have regard to the 'intrinsic value' of nature[164] brings into play difficult questions of ontology[165] and epistemology,[166] and creates evaluative challenges because intrinsic values are difficult to define,[167] assess[168] or compare with other issues.[169] Scholars have

analyses and localised effects analyses) and the Minister obtained a separate economic assessment that challenged the assumptions made by the applicant. The NSWLEC was required to address the parties' debates about: the direct economic benefits of the proposal (including net producer surplus attributable to the NSW community, royalties, rates and income tax – all requiring analysis of coal price forecasts); indirect benefits (such as worker, supplier and landowner benefits); direct costs (such as the opportunity cost of resources including land, labour and capital used for the project); and indirect costs (eg, net environmental, social and transport costs, net public infrastructure costs and indirect costs to other industries).

[156] *McQueen v Waikato District Council* A45/94 (unrep) (PT) (nudist camp).

[157] For relatively early and interesting New Zealand cases considering the importance of Māori spiritual and cultural factors in environmental decision-making, see *Huakina Development Trust v Waikato Valley Authority* [1987] 2 NZLR 188 (HC); *Bleakley v Environmental Risk Management Authority* [2001] 3 NZLR 213 (HC); *Te Runanga O Taumarere v Northland Regional Council* (n 13). See also C Warnock and M Baker-Galloway, *Focus on Resource Management Law* (LexisNexis, 2015) 106–18. For criticism, see R Ahdar, 'Indigenous Spiritual Concerns and the Secular State: Some New Zealand Developments' (2003) 23 *OJLS* 611. Also *cf Grunke v Otago Regional Council* C8/1996 (unrep) (PT), an application for an interim enforcement order. The judge did not dismiss out of hand Sister Grunke's objection to the use of pesticides near rivers on the basis of spiritual concerns. The Roman Catholic nun regarded 'water as a symbol of baptism and therefore life, and for her polluting it turns it into a symbol of death' (at 3). Although the judge stated, '[a]s for Sister Grunke's spiritual beliefs, while I accept them as genuine from her point of view, I cannot accept on an objective basis that they should carry the weight that again would be necessary to enable either application to succeed' (at 8).

[158] eg, *Waiheke Marinas Ltd v Auckland Council* [2015] NZEnvC 218, [432]–[457].

[159] *Kuku Mara (Forsyth Bay) v Marlborough District Council* W25/2002 (unrep) (NZEnvC) (intrinsic value of endangered bird species).

[160] *Van Brandenburg v Queenstown Lakes District Council* C121/2001 (unrep) (EnvC); *Shell NZ Ltd v Auckland City Council* [1996] NZRMA 189 (NZCA) (aesthetic concerns).

[161] *Shirley Primary School v Christchurch City Council* (n 62) (fear for children's health); *Orica Mining Services NZ Ltd v Franklin District Council* W32/2009 (unrep) (NZEnvC) (stress); *AA Knight v Wairoa District Council* W37/90 (unrep) (PT) (fear for personal safety); see also C Warnock, 'Understanding the Objective: Psychological Effects in Environmental Decision-Making' (2011) 24 *New Zealand Universities Law Review* 574.

[162] *Gloucester Resources Ltd v Minister for Planning* (n 106) (climate change).

[163] Legal mechanisms such as forms of trusteeship and co-management have developed but bring their own difficulties to adjudication.

[164] RMA, s 7(d).

[165] A Naess, 'The Shallow and the Deep, Long-range Ecology Movement: A Summary' (1973) 16 *Inquiry* 95; K Bosselmann, 'A Vulnerable Environment: Contextualising Law with Sustainability' (2011) 2 *Journal of Human Rights and the Environment* 45, 61.

[166] L Code, 'Ecological Responsibilities: Which trees? Where? Why?' in A Grear (ed), *Should Trees Have Standing? 40 Years On* (Edward Elgar, 2012).

[167] Mary Warnock argues that moral reasoning about the environment, rather than a reliance on economic rationality, should be reflected in legislation (see M Warnock (n 111) 139). In some jurisdictions, legislation requires decision-makers to take into account the 'intrinsic values of nature'.

observed that adjudicators can struggle reconciling arguments based on quantifiable data with those based on qualitative measures,[170] and Tribe notes that qualitative values may be overshadowed by quantifiable values.[171] Suggestions that environmental adjudication should develop procedural approaches – such as appointing a Guardian ad Litem to represent nature – puts these concerns into stark relief.

In summary, different perspectives create a tension in environmental adjudication. Regardless of the reality, our understanding of environmental problems and our approach towards resolving them is socially construed and varied.[172] And inherent pluralism means that parties to environmental adjudication may draw on different discourses, employing different reasoning strategies resting on different 'definitions, judgments, assumptions, and contentions'.[173] In turn, those parties will advocate that particular forms of evidence and assessment techniques should be privileged and influence judicial evaluation to a greater degree as the *Gloucester Resources* case discussed above demonstrates.[174] In the event of conflict, adjudicators may be required to interrogate different mechanisms and scrutinise methodologies. Importantly, the inherent features of environmental problems can undermine the validity of certain tools. As with scientific evidence, adjudicators will need to understand the weaknesses and flaws in these tools, and see where the gaps are and need to be supplemented with additional forms of knowledge.[175] Adjudicators must understand the respective contributions that mechanisms such as cost–benefit analysis can make

RMA, s 7(d) does and s 2 loosely defines 'intrinsic values': 'in relation to ecosystems, means those aspects of ecosystems and their constituent parts which have value in their own right, including – (a) their biological and genetic diversity; and (b) the essential characteristics that determine an ecosystem's integrity, form, functioning, and resilience'.

[168] New Zealand guidance on assessment has been relatively sparse. Environmental Risk Management Authority, *Interpretation and Explanation of Key Concepts* (NZ Policy Series: Protocol 3, Wellington, 2011) [2.5] suggests decision-makers assessing the release of new organisms consider whether organisms are likely to 'destabilise the natural evolution of ecosystems which are valued for their own sake'.

[169] No decision of the NZEnvC has yet attempted to grapple with the difficult metaphysical discourse accompanying a true understanding of the concept of 'intrinsic value' and in some cases the NZEnvC has submerged intrinsic value into human spiritual or amenity values, or simply conflated it with scenic views or the beauty of unspoilt environments (see, eg, *Waitakere Ranges Protection Society Inc v Waitakere City Council* A89/2000 (unrep) (NZEnvC); *Gill v Rotorua District Council* [1993] 2 NZRMA 604 (PT); *Beadle v Minister of Corrections* W018/02 (NZEnvC)).

[170] T Black, 'Defending the Environment' (1978) 8 *NZLJ* 153; N Wheen, 'The Resource Management Act 1991: A "Greener" Law for Water?' (1997) 1 *New Zealand Journal of Environmental Law* 165.

[171] Tribe (n 120).

[172] Dryzek (n 26) 12; R Brulle, 'Habermas and Green Political Thought: Two Roads Converging, Environmental Politics' (2002) 11 *Environmental Politics* 1.

[173] Dryzek (n 26) Preface.

[174] *Gloucester Resources Ltd v Minister for Planning* (n 106).

[175] eg, see acknowledgement in the hazardous substances risk assessment context: Hazardous Substances and New Organisms (Methodology) Order 1998 (NZ) Schedule, cls 31 and 33 'Approach to Risk'.

to decision-making, while being aware that the use of one mechanism rather than another may draw the decision towards particular ethical positions so privileging those values over others. Adjudicators must also appreciate that technical assessments – be they cost–benefit analyses or cultural impact statements – cannot replace the evaluative judgement of the person who has been tasked with the ultimate decision-making. Some have suggested that cost–benefit analysis could substitute for the final decision-making process[176] but the propriety of doing so poses a particular problem in environmental adjudication.[177] Much economic analysis tends to present selective, single variable trends that may be limited in time and geographical scope,[178] a linear approach that does not fit well with polycentric problem-solving.[179] More generally, economic modelling is unconcerned with justice and equality.[180] As Preston CJ opined in *Bulga*, assigning weight to various legislative criteria is a subjective task, granted to the ultimate decision-maker, '[who] needs to evaluate the relative importance of the relevant matters, each compared to the others. The decision-maker cannot delegate that task to others or subordinate it to the marketplace'.[181] If adjudicators rely unduly upon one or other of the assessment tools adduced by parties, they risk favouring one discourse or ethical position over others. More critically they will fail to understand and address the interactional nature of environmental problems. Different preferences create tensions, but the greater risk with ethical pluralism is that we talk past each other. Environmental adjudication has to provide a forum for finding common ground, enabling us to talk together.[182] This later aspect is foundational in constructing the frame. It draws together all the points addressed in the first part of this chapter so far because in order

[176] See Preston CJ rejecting such assertions in *Bulga Milbrodale Progress Association Inc v Minister for Planning and Infrastructure and Warkworth Mining Limited* (n 14) [39]: assigning weight to various legislative criteria is a subjective task, granted to the ultimate decision-maker, who 'needs to evaluate the relative importance of the relevant matters, each compared to the others. The decision-maker cannot delegate that task to others or subordinate it to the marketplace'. The NZEnvC has previously suggested that 'resource management is a subset of economics' (*Marlborough Ridge Ltd v Marlborough District Council* [1998] NZRMA 73 (NZEnvC)) but the High Court found that it was wrong in law to reduce the test of 'efficiency' in s 7(b) of the RMA to a quantitative cost–benefit analysis (*Meridian Energy Ltd v Central Otago District Council* [2011] 1 NZLR 482 (HC)).

[177] *Telstra Corporation v Hornby Shire Council* (n 60) [174]–[175].

[178] Dryzek (n 26) 60; *Bulga Milbrodale Progress Association Inc v Minister for Planning and Infrastructure and Warkworth Mining Limited* (n 14) [496].

[179] *Bulga Milbrodale Progress Association Inc v Minister for Planning and Infrastructure and Warkworth Mining Limited* (n 14) [490].

[180] As Preston CJ opined in *Bulga Milbrodale*, ibid, [491]: '[t]he [cost benefit analysis] and Choice Modelling … are concerned only with the aggregation of costs and benefits, not how or why these are allocated … [they] did not address the equity or fairness in either the distribution of the benefits and burdens of these entities or the nature and extent of the distributed benefits and burdens'. Note, justice and equality, Hulme argues, are 'artificial virtues' created by particular civil ordering and effected through law and democracy, see M Warnock (n 111) 27.

[181] ibid, *Bulga* [39].

[182] J Waldron, 'Thoughtfulness and the Rule of Law' (2011) 18 *British Academy Review* 1. Note the similarity with systems-thinking that maintains different spheres of society must find a common language to converse (eg, G Teubner, *Law as an Autopoietic System* (Blackwell, 1993)).

to provide a forum 'enabling us to talk together', adjudicators must be highly skilled: they must understand, embrace and manage complex pluralism yet be able to rise above the messiness of environmental conflicts to exercise objective adjudicative judgement.

Before moving on to summarise how the immutable features of environmental problems help construct the detailed frame for legitimacy, I want to consider what I identified at the outset of this chapter as a *characteristic* feature of environmental disputes, ie, uncertainty. From the analysis above it is clear that a lack of knowledge will be a feature of many environmental disputes. The unstable factual backdrop; dynamic conditions in the ecosystem, socio-cultural and economic realms; importance of opinion evidence (from multiple disciplines); and need for prediction, all contribute to environmental disputes being characterised by uncertainty. However, as I indicated above 'law may accept sufficient knowledge of environmental problems in circumstances where science would not' and I want to explain this idea in a little more detail because it has particular ramifications for environmental adjudication and the development of the normative frame.

III. UNCERTAINTY

There are different ways of conceiving of knowledge, or perhaps more accurately *truth* as a description of physical reality. This idea is well traversed in the social science discourse[183] but for present purposes, it is worth recalling that the knowledge-arena will impact on truth: that is, the knowledge-arena is transformative because different contexts approach truth differently.[184]

As I have explained above, physical science does not make claims of absolute knowledge or truth. While scientists strive to be objective, in doing so 'even the most fervent advocate of objective methods in the sciences – be they statistical, mechanical, numerical or otherwise, would hesitate to claim that they generate the truth of a finding'[185] because of the real ramifications of mistakes. Within science, findings and in particular predictions as to possible futures are always qualified – and this is acceptable in the context because science 'places an

[183] K Popper, *The Open Society and its Enemies*, 4th edn (Routledge, 1962); K Popper, *The Logic of Scientific Discovery*, 4th edn (Routledge, 1980); K Popper, *Conjectures and Refutations: The Growth of Scientific Knowledge*, 5th edn (Routledge, 1989); T Kuhn, *The Structure of Scientific Revolutions*, 3rd edn, Chicago University Press, 1996); B Wynne, 'Uncertainty and environmental learning: reconceiving science and policy in the preventative paradigm' (1992) 1 *Global Environmental Change* 111.

[184] For acknowledgment in case law see *Daubert v Merrel Dow Pharmaceuticals* 509 US 579 (1993) 951F 2d1128 (1991) 485; *Darroch v Whangarei Disrict Council* A18/93 (PT) 5; *Canterbury Regional Council v Canterbury Frozen Meat Company* A14/94 (PT) where the Tribunal stated (at 21) their role was a judicial one and not 'in the sense that scientists might seek after absolute truth about a subject'.

[185] Daston and Galison (n 66) 51. Truth in this context is taken to mean 'descriptions of physical reality'.

emphasis on continual learning'.[186] Accordingly, indeterminacy is a motivating factor not a disciplinary flaw.

The test of sufficiency is complex in law, as it varies. Truth is a conclusion impacted by legal tests for evidence and different legal contexts adopt different tests of sufficiency in order to affect different social purposes (for example, the adverse inference rule or employing strict liability in the context of regulatory offences). Suffice to say truth has been a more slippery concept in adjudication – rather more *pravda* than *istina*, as the Russians would say.[187] This is because a key characteristic of adjudication is the need to resolve a dispute – the need for finality in some sense.[188] There is more use for artificial certainty in adjudication, and the same knowledge might enable a legal finding of fact in circumstances where the scientific community would hesitate to claim absolute knowledge.

I can use a rather extreme example as a heuristic to help explain why uncertainty is characteristic in adjudication not inherent, and also to show that scope and scale is important.[189] By way of example, consider the erection of a building that disrupts the soil through earthworks and the laying of subterranean infrastructure. This development will interact with the existing environment and create change by possibly destroying or damaging existing flora, fauna and productive soil; preventing the establishment of new ecological communities in the footprint of the building; requiring the use of natural resources; creating pollution from the construction and operation of the building; maybe interfering with the water table and so on. A scientist would not claim absolute or definitive knowledge about the full impacts of the building because of the nature of science as a discipline. And by way of a simple illustration we can consider mycelium. It is only in the last decade that scientists have discovered the ability of mycelium (an underground fungal mesh) to act as a critical neurological network for the surrounding natural environment, sending signals warning nearby plants of approaching pests, and scientists are still exploring mycelium's role and the effects of its removal on ecological health.[190] In the adjudicative context however, it is unlikely that this development, with its seemingly minor ecological disruption would be characterised by a lack of knowledge.

[186] Fisher, Lange and Scotford (n 19) 43.

[187] In Russian two words mean truth: 'pravda' which is 'subjective and infinitely malleable' and 'istina' which reflects the 'underlying cosmic unshakeable truth of things' see Andrew Rosenthal, 'To Understand Trump, Learn Russian' *New York Times* (16 December 2016).

[188] C Jones, *Expert Witnesses: Science, Medicine, and the Practice of Law* (Clarendon Press, 1994) 69.

[189] The adjudicative approach is impacted by the scope and scale of the development and the risk an adjudicator is prepared to take, *cf* for example the development of a coal mine in *Bulga Milbrodale Progress Association Inc v Minister for Planning and Infrastructure and Warkworth Mining Limited* (n 14) to the heuristic example I use in the text.

[190] P Stamets, *Mycelium Running: How Mushrooms can Help Save the World* (Ten Speed Press, 2005).

To be clear, I am not arguing that the 'concept of objective truth is fading out of the [legal] world'.[191] Rather, I am arguing that truth takes on a different significance in different forms of adjudication. Establishing the social purpose to truth or certainty in environmental adjudication is important because it is not concerned with an artificial world created by law (like, say, trusts.)[192] It is concerned with ecological reality, and it is often more concerned with the future than the past because of the very nature of environmental law.[193] Environmental adjudicators are frequently tasked with assessing effects on the environment that include past, present and predicted future effects. Often they are required to find an acceptable medium between environmental degradation and human development, or as Baxter describes it 'optimal pollution',[194] and of course, there is some need for pragmatic proportionality. But if we get environmental decision-making wrong, the effects can be irreversible, and in some cases widespread and catastrophic.[195] For example, adjudicators might be tasked with deciding whether an offshore oil well should be consented to, or whether a development that might impact an endangered species should proceed. Significant environmental risks are inherent in those decisions. The well may fail, leading to a large-scale pollution incident; the species might be so adversely impacted it becomes extinct. Potentially, the risks inherent in environmental adjudication make the transformation of evidence into truth even more delicately fraught in this legal context and questions the desirability of adjudicative finality hurried along by pragmatic artifice and good-enough notions of truth. Thus, the implications for environmental adjudication are twofold. First, remedies must be able to respond to this feature, providing a degree of flexibility that can accommodate uncertainty. Second, the test for sufficiency may well vary within environmental adjudication itself, depending on contextual variables: risks of large-scale or irreversible impacts on ecosystems may necessitate greater caution in decision-making. The frame for legitimacy must acknowledge these features and in order to operate with integrity, environmental adjudication must be able to respond to them.

To summarise, while uncertainty cannot be said to be an *inherent* feature of all environmental disputes because contexts and contingencies are formative, it *is* a commonly found feature (as the discussion of the case law from the NZEnvC and NSWLEC in chapter six demonstrates). Environmental adjudicators must determine the disputes that appear before them: they must be able to

[191] George Orwell, 'Looking back on the Spanish War' in A Comfort and J Bayliss (eds), *New Road: New Directions in Art and Writing*, vol 1 (Grey Walls Press, 1943).

[192] S Elias, 'Righting Environmental Justice' (The Salmon Lecture, Auckland, 25 July 2013).

[193] Although I accept that much adjudication imposes future *impacts* on parties often based on a determination of past behaviour.

[194] W Baxter, *People or Penguins: The Case for Optimal Pollution* (Columbia University Press, 1974).

[195] As the Dutch court observed in the famous climate change case: *Urgenda Foundation v The State of the Netherlands* (unreported) C/09/456689/HA ZA 13-1396 (DC).

cope with all disputes falling within their jurisdictional remit that may include cases where lack of knowledge becomes a defining feature and the potential for environmental harm is significant. They cannot refuse to address problems about which there is insufficient knowledge, but they must also confront the social purpose to truth or certainty in environmental adjudication, and the ramifications of getting it wrong. This characteristic feature impacts how we think about environmental adjudication – its normative form, and the evaluative procedures employed and doctrine developed – and this is explored in greater detail in chapter six.

IV. DRAWING THE THREADS TOGETHER

Exploring the immutable nature of environmental problems in detail reveals the challenges for fact-finding in adjudication, that in turn creates challenges for legal reasoning. Static forms of adjudication, mired in traditional forms and methods, can prove maladaptive in addressing the messy contextual reality.[196] Traditional forms of adjudication work best within a neat classificatory approach to law:[197] with factual certainty slotting between clear 'legal yardsticks';[198] linear causality; confined effects; clearly identified parties; binary opposing arguments; the apparent exclusion (whether disingenuous or not) of opinions and values; and syllogistic reasoning.[199] In contrast, in environmental adjudication there are no neat boundaries.[200] The factual backdrop is seldom fixed; dynamism is prevalent; effects can be diffuse, difficult to identify and assess because environmental problems are polycentric problems.[201] There can be many impacted parties (including those that are difficult to identify or those not yet born) and so environmental disputes often transcend traditional bi-party conflicts.[202] Disputes may concern 'the commons' or public resources, but environmental problems can also impact individual rights, including property rights.

[196] Rodgers (n 37); C Warnock and Ole Pedersen, 'Environmental Adjudication: Mapping the Spectrum and Identifying a Fulcrum' [2017] *PL* 643.

[197] R Lazarus, 'Meeting the Demands of Integration in the Evolution of Environmental Law: Reforming Environmental Criminal Law' (1994–95) 83 *Georgetown Law Journal* 2407; R Lazarus, 'Survey Says: Court Doesn't Get It' (2000) 17 *Environmental Forum* 44; J Williams, 'The Collision of Two Worlds: Law and Lore' (Matauranga Māori, RMLA Conference 2015, Tauranga, 24–26 September 2015).

[198] *Curtis v Minister of Defence* [2002] 2 NZLR 744 (NZCA), [27].

[199] *cf* Neil MacCormick, *Rhetoric and the Rule of Law: A Theory of Legal Reasoning* (Oxford University Press, 2005) Ch 3.

[200] Fisher, 'Environmental Law as "Hot" Law' (n 4).

[201] eg, *Bulga Milbrodale Progress Association Inc v Minister for Planning and Infrastructure and Warkworth Mining Limited* (n 14) (discussing the polycentricity of a mining proposal).

[202] eg, *Waiheke Marinas Ltd v Auckland Council* (n 158) (an unusual judgment where the Court included a 'Preamble' advising the community how to read the decision as the case had 'divided, indeed even polarised, a sizeable portion of the population', 'involved a basket of highly complex issues' and could not be 'viewed through a single issue lens').

They may therefore have 're-distributive force',[203] or allocate risk-burdens[204] and address normative conflicts.[205]

Of necessity, adjudicators must be open to receiving and assessing different forms of knowledge, including from those impacted. Adjudicators are frequently required to make predictive decisions about the future as opposed to fact-finding in relation to the past and so adjudication may be expert-opinion heavy.[206] Scientific evidence is important but not monolithic and adjudicators may need to identify the sociological frames underpinning expert opinions. Further, adjudicators must develop confidence in employing and critiquing economic tools (such as CVM), other evaluative mechanisms (like cultural impact statements) and possibly creating different assessment mechanisms within adjudication (like evaluative schema that marshal legally relevant factors). They must understand how the methodologies underpinning these mechanisms fit or jar in the particular context, recognising their uses and limitations. Importantly, adjudicators are forced to confront the ideologies at work behind those tools, to consider the possibility of the final evaluation being skewed towards a particular value if too much reliance is placed upon one or another mechanism, and to recognise that legal arguments may disguise the different ideologies and values at work (as the discussion on *Gloucester Resources* demonstrated).

Moreover, the inherent characteristics of environmental problems impact legal reasoning in multiple ways. Absolute knowledge or truth is not static in environmental adjudication and, if this test is not provided by legislation, adjudicators may need to decide what should be the test for sufficiency in the context they are concerned with. Legal reasoning may be unable to rely upon syllogism because polycentric problems 'cannot be resolved by identifying each issue and sequentially resolving it; the resolution of one issue has repercussions on the other issues'.[207] Remedies may need to import a degree of flexibility to account for changing conditions and uncertainty.

Finally, it is important to add that the sheer factual complexity of the subject demands a particular type of expertise from adjudicators.[208] Decision-makers

[203] Lazarus, 'Meeting the Demands of Integration in the Evolution of Environmental Law' (n 197) 2427.

[204] eg, *Shirley Primary School v Christchurch City Council* (n 62) (considered risks of electromagnetic frequency on schoolchildren from the siting of a telecommunications mast).

[205] eg, *Te Runanga O Taumarere v Northland Regional Council* (n 13) (determining whether to permit development of community sewage treatment facility that would impact Māori cultural values).

[206] eg, *Royal Forest and Bird Society of New Zealand Inc v Buller District Council* (n 69) (expert evidence was crucial to predicting the survival of a species if a development progressed but the evidence conflicted).

[207] *Bulga Milbrodale Progress Association Inc v Minister for Planning and Infrastructure and Warkworth Mining Limited* (n 14) [483]; see also *R (Mott) v Environment Agency* [2016] EWCA Civ 564, [75].

[208] As the higher courts have at times acknowledged, see for example: *Environmental Defence Society Incorporated v Marlborough District Council* [2014] NZSC 38, [150]; *New Zealand Rail Ltd v Marlborough District Council* [1994] NZRMA 70, 86 (HC).

must have specialist knowledge about environmental problems. Moreover, environmental disputes can impact people's legal rights, accordingly decision-makers should have legal expertise and bodies may need to be independent from government. Thus, in order to adjudicate over environmental problems, responsive adjudicatory forms must emerge that can address both the legal and factual complexities, with the constitutional make-up and functions of adjudicatory bodies being designed to accommodate this need. New epistemic communities that bring together scientific and legal expertise in the decision-making process may best address this challenge.

Returning to the interactional theory for normative legitimacy, this chapter has established the core contextual foundations upon which to build the frame for environmental adjudication. In particular, it has addressed the first two components, ie, it has identified the immutable structural features of environmental problems and explained some of the challenges that these features create for adjudication. It has also touched upon the third and fourth components of the interactional theory, suggesting *how* adjudication should respond to these features in order to have integrity and *which* constitutional forms will best achieve this end. In doing so, it has begun to construct the internal criteria for the frame for environmental adjudication. The next chapter continues with this process, adding detail to the frame. It tests the theory against actual practice in the NZEnvC and NSWLEC and shows how those courts have (in the main) developed environmental law doctrine, procedure and remedies that respond to the challenges of adjudicating over the environment, often in the absence of specific legislative direction.

6

The Interactional Theory in Practice

THIS CHAPTER DIRECTLY addresses the last two components of the interactional theory, ie, the development of environmental law doctrine, procedure and remedies that respond to the adjudicative challenges created by environmental problems, and the contribution of different adjudicative forms and functions to this process. The chapter tests the theory by considering how legal reasoning in the Environment Court of New Zealand (NZEnvC) and the New South Wales Land and Environment Court (NSWLEC) has responded to the challenges created by the inherent nature of environmental problems, and in doing so it continues the process of filling in the detail of the normative frame. It is important to note at the outset that this chapter does not provide an exhaustive exploration of environmental adjudication, rather it provides illustrations of the interactional theory in action.

The NZEnvC and NSWLEC provide good laboratories for testing the theory because both determine factual disputes through merits review and in this way are made aware of the contextual intricacies through the receipt and evaluation of evidence. They also have broad, flexible powers. For example, they are not constrained by the processes and rules of evidence created within and for other forms of litigation[1] (a critical point, as rigid procedural rules have significantly hindered environmental problem-solving in some other environment courts (ECs)),[2] and although the default position of both courts is to follow normal

[1] The NSWLEC is 'not bound by the rules of evidence', 'may inform itself on any matter in such manner as it thinks appropriate' and can receive fresh evidence, Land and Environment Court Act 1979 (NSW) (LECA), ss 38, 39(3). The NZEnvC 'may regulate its own proceedings in such manner as it thinks fit' and can receive any evidence, Resource Management Act 1991 (NZ) (RMA), ss 269, 276.

[2] eg, in relation to the Environment Court of Santiago, Chile, Chief Justice Asenjo has written: 'Regarding procedural aspects, the court faces rules that are inconsistent with the flexibility and agility required by the adequate resolution of environmental conflicts. We have also faced difficulties involved in applying procedures from classical legal institutions that are inconsistent with the characteristics of environmental legal processes. In this aspect, the issues that the court has faced when applying the default rules of legally determined evidentiary weight in a process characterised by a more flexible evaluation of evidence have been significant. The court has made efforts in determining the applicability and form of application of these rules, but as long as our country fails to update its general rules of civil procedure, this task remains incomplete' – see R Asenjo, 'Environmental Justice in Chile: three years after the establishment of the Environmental Court of Santiago' (2017) 29 *Environmental Law & Management* 110, 114.

adjudicatory processes, they can adapt them where appropriate.[3] Further, their empowering legislation contains standards and principles guiding (but not prescribing) action,[4] and they are also able to craft remedies to do justice on the facts.[5] In terms of their constitutions, both courts have benches comprised of judicial and expert lay members, addressing in part the need to develop new epistemic communities in environmental adjudication.[6] Nevertheless, as I explain below, while non-legal expertise informs legal reasoning, that process is taking place within courts and so is constrained, shaped and guided by the legal processes employed by those institutions.[7] Accordingly, advances in doctrine are a product of these institutional forms.

The first part of this chapter explains that the NSWLEC and NZEnvC have acknowledged the challenges of adjudicating over environmental disputes and the need to adjust adjudicative technique accordingly. This awareness provides a link, connecting together the four parts in the interactional theory in practice. The second part of the chapter considers how those courts have developed a comprehensive jurisprudence that responds to 'the dark cave of the factual and contingent world'[8] in which they must work. The analysis shows that the challenges of fact-finding in environmental adjudication *has* impacted legal reasoning: in response to factual uncertainty, the NZWLEC operationalised

[3] See *Darkinjung Local Aboriginal Land Council v Minister for Planning and Infrastructure; Australian Walkabout Wildlife Park Pty Ltd v Minister for Planning and Infrastructure* [2015] NSWLEC 1465, [31]–[33]: 'While the Court is not bound by the rules of evidence but may inform itself on any matter in such manner as it thinks appropriate and as the proper consideration of the matters before the Court permits – the rules of evidence, for obvious reasons, are still relevant [in light of objections about hearsay and relevance] … our general position was to accept the evidence tendered, noting the objections were generally as to form or relevance, and assigning appropriate weight'. To like effect see L Newhook, 'The Constitution, Work, Powers and Practices in Trial and Pre-Trial Work of the Environment Court of New Zealand' (International Forum of Environment Judges, IUCN AEL Colloquium, Oslo, June 2016).

[4] eg, in the NZ context the NZEnvC must 'promote sustainable management of natural and physical resources' in all it decisions (RMA, s 5); and in the context of merits appeals, LECA, s 39(2) states 'the Court shall have regard to this or any other relevant Act, any instrument made under any such Act, the circumstances of the case and the public interest'.

[5] eg, the NZEnvC has all the powers of the original decision-maker (RMA s 290(1)), has wide scope to impose different forms of conditions on consents (RMA, s 108) and has expansive enforcement powers (RMA, Pt 12). The NSWLEC has all the powers of the original decision maker in class 1–3 appeals (LECA s 39(2)), and can dispense with any requirement of the rules if appropriate (LECA, s 75) thus allowing the Court, 'to mould the manner of its intervention in such a way as will best meet the practicalities as well as the justice of the situation before it', *F Hannan Pty Ltd v Electricity Commission of New South Wales [No 3]* (1989) 66 LGRA 306 (NSWSC), 311.

[6] Although this feature is more developed in the NZEnvC context where expert lay commissioners sitting with judges are the norm. Joint benches are reserved for particularly complex factual disputes in the NSWLEC.

[7] This interaction is well illustrated in *Telstra Corporation v Hornby Shire Council* [2006] NSWLEC 133. Preston CJ begins his judgment with this question and general answer: 'The case raises questions about fear, rationality and the law. How should a responsible decision-maker respond to public fear? Responsiveness to public fear entails a commitment to rational deliberation, in the form of reflection and reason-giving' [9].

[8] *Clifford Bay Farms Ltd v Marlborough District Council* C131/2003 (unrep) (NZEnvC), [51].

'the precautionary principle' within adjudication and the NZEnvC crafted 'a precautionary approach' to evaluating environmental effects. Both developments are well traversed in the scholarly literature[9] and so provide a good backdrop against which to test the theory. This part concludes that the interactional theory is well illustrated within this jurisprudence: the two courts respond to the inherent nature of environmental problems in a way that makes sense of their role and shores up adjudicative integrity. In focusing on the precautionary principle, some might accuse me of cherry-picking – ie, selecting jurisprudential developments that support my theory – and indeed, I do. Viewed in a different light, showing the theory in action allows me to identify good practice in environmental adjudication.

However, in order to test the theory in another way, the final part of the chapter addresses the collective-action nature of environmental problems, briefly exploring how the NZEnvC and NSWLEC have responded to this feature by expanding access to justice where possible (ie, when not prohibited by legislation from doing so). The chapter concludes that the courts' approach to standing is in part but not always supportive of the interactional theory. In particular, the NZEnvC has interpreted statutory text narrowly to restrict standing on occasion and *locus standi* is an area where better alignment between the theory and doctrinal development could occur.

I. ACKNOWLEDGING THE CHALLENGES IN ENVIRONMENTAL ADJUDICATION

Both the NSWLEC and NZEnvC have explicitly acknowledged that environmental problems create particular challenges for adjudication and there is a need for legal reasoning to respond appropriately. This acknowledgement is important because it helps link together the four component parts of the interactional theory, ie, identifying the distinct characteristics of environmental problems; the

[9] eg, C Barton, 'The Status of the Precautionary Principle in Australia: Its Emergence in Legislation and as a Common Law Doctrine' (1998) 22 *Harvard Environmental Law Review* 509; E Fisher and R Harding, 'The Precautionary Principle in Australia: From Aspiration to Practice?' in T O'Riordan, J Cameron and A Jordan (eds), *Reinterpreting the Precautionary Principle* (Cameron May, 2001); BJ Preston, 'The Role of the Judiciary in Promoting Sustainable Development: The Experience of Asia and the Pacific' (2005–06) 9 *Asia Pacific Journal of Environmental Law* 109; J Peel, 'When (Scientific) Rationality Rules' (2007) 19 *JEL* 103; J Peel, *The Precautionary Principle in Practice: Environmental Decision-Making and Scientific Uncertainty* (Federation Press, 2005); E Scotford, *Environmental Principles and the Evolution of Environmental Law* (Hart Publishing, 2017); B Preston, 'The Judicial Development of the Precautionary Principle' (Queensland Government Environmental Management of Firefighting Foam Policy Implementation Seminar, Brisbane, 21 February 2017); R Somerville, 'Policy adjudication, adaptive risk management and the Environment Court' [2013] *Resource Management Theory & Practice* 13; A Gillespie, 'Precautionary New Zealand' (2011) 24 *New Zealand Universities Law Review* 364; G Severinsen, 'Letting our standards slip? Precaution and the standard of proof under the Resource Management Act 1991' (2014) 18 *New Zealand Journal of Environmental Law* 173.

creation of commensurate challenges for dispute resolution; developing environmental law doctrine, procedures and remedies that respond to those distinct characteristics; and recognising that particular institutional forms and functions facilitates this process.

A selection of cases from both courts demonstrates this contextual awareness. For example, in *Long Bay–Okura v North Shore City Council*, the NZEnvC described the ecosystem as 'an interacting system of living and non-living parts' and by drawing attention to the 'heterogenity of ecosystems and their dynamic constituent components' acknowledged that background facts are seldom fixed in environmental adjudication.[10] And in *Clifford Bay Farms Ltd v Marlborough District Council*, the NZEnvC mused:

> In the dark cave of the factual and contingent world in which the Environment Court works, the evidence tends to illuminate very few certitudes about the future, and reveals instead many more potential effects (some of greater, some of lesser probability) … all cumulative effects are conditional … [and] the Courts, when dealing with cause and effect in environmental law, have turned away from categorising causes according to 'abstract metaphysical theory': *Alphacell Ltd v Woodward [1972]* 2 All ER475 at 489–490.[11]

The NSWLEC and NZEnvC have differentiated decision-making in environmental disputes from the causal linearity-tests seen in other areas (such as tort litigation) by, for example, noting the importance and challenges of cumulative effects.[12] In *Friends of Tumblebee Inc v ATB Morton Pty Ltd*, the NSWLEC found that localised impacts can constitute significant effects on a threatened species (the statutory test) because they accumulate with effects from existing activities unrelated to the proposal, so magnifying the impact.[13] In environmental disputes, indirect impacts can prove to be as damaging as direct impacts, as the NSWLEC explained when discussing the climate change forcing impact of a coal mine in *Gloucester Resources Ltd v Minister for Planning*.[14] Other cases discuss the adjudicative challenges presented by the polycentric nature of environmental disputes. In *Bulga Mibrodale*,[15] the NSWLEC highlighted

[10] *Long Bay–Okura Great Park Society v North Shore City Council* A78/2008 (unrep) (NZEnvC), [303], drawing on the New Zealand Biodiversity Strategy.

[11] *Clifford Bay Farms Ltd v Marlborough District Council* (n 8) [51].

[12] eg, *Bulga Milbrodale Progress Association Inc v Minister for Planning and Infrastructure and Warkworth Mining Limited* [2013] NSWLEC 48; *Newcastle & Hunter Speleological Society Inc v Upper Hunter Shire Council* [2010] NSWLEC 48, [104]; *BT Goldsmith Planning Services v Blacktown City Council* [2005] NSWLEC 210 [89]–[90]; and in the New Zealand context see *Kuku Mara (Forsyth Bay) v Marlborough District Council* W25/2002 (unrep) (NZEnvC), [651]: 'we anticipate difficulties in being able to attribute any adverse effects on King Shags to a particular marine farm site and difficulties in differentiating between site specific effects and accumulated effects from any other farms that may impinge on King Shag feeding areas'.

[13] *Friends of Tumblebee Inc v ATB Morton Pty Ltd (No 2)* [2016] NSWLEC 16, [113], [83].

[14] *Gloucester Resources Ltd v Minister for Planning* [2019] NSWLEC 7, [494]–[524].

[15] *Bulga Milbrodale Progress Association Inc v Minister for Planning and Infrastructure and Warkworth Mining Limited* (n 12) [31]–[42].

the difference between traditional adjudication – where it is often possible to identify a single criterion through which to ascertain the rights of the parties, or where a list of statutory criteria could be 'objectively weighed and choices were not interdependent' – and polycentric environmental disputes.[16] The Chief Judge explained that environmental disputes require 'consideration, weighting and balancing of the environmental, social and economic impacts', encompass a range of complex issues, affect multiple parties, and, '[a] decision about one issue raised by the carrying out of the project is linked by interacting points of influence to decisions about other issues, necessitating readjustment of the project.[17] His Honour set out the necessary decision-making steps in environmental disputes that required identifying the 'relevant matters'; 'fact-finding for each relevant matter'; 'determining how much weight each relevant matter is to receive'; and 'balancing the weighted matters to arrive at a managerial decision'.[18] The final 'balancing' stage constituted a qualitative and not quantitative exercise' involving an 'intuitive synthesis of the various matters'.[19]

It is precisely this need for 'intuitive synthesis' that has led the superior courts in New Zealand to justify the specialist nature of the NZEnvC.[20] In discussing the need for environmental adjudicators to be across the wider policy guidance contained in and underpinning the Resource Management Act 1991 (RMA), the High Court stated, 'indeed it is for that purpose that the [Environment Court], with specialist expertise and skills, is established and appointed to oversee and to promote the objectives and the policies and the principles under the Act'.[21] However, at times the NZEnvC's acknowledgment of and response to the reality of environmental problems has brought it into conflict with the generalist courts on appeal, and this disjunct illustrates the impact that different forms of adjudication has on legal reasoning in this context. In *Clifford Bay Farms v Tasman District Council*,[22] the NZEnvC discussed the difficulties with a Court of Appeal decision that took an unhelpfully literal approach to statutory interpretation, leading to future cumulative effects being disregarded in a decision.[23] The NZEnvC observed, 'in our respectful view, [*Dye v Auckland*

[16] ibid, [35] drawing on academic scholarship in support: MA Eisenberg, 'Participation, responsiveness, and the consultative process: an essay for Lon Fuller' (1978) 92 *Harvard Law Review* 410.

[17] *Bulga Milbrodale Progress Association Inc v Minister for Planning and Infrastructure and Warkworth Mining Limited* (n 12) [33].

[18] ibid, [36].

[19] ibid, [41].

[20] eg, *Environmental Defence Society Incorporated v Marlborough District Council* [2014] NZSC 38, [150].

[21] *New Zealand Rail Ltd v Marlborough District Council* [1994] NZRMA 70, 86 (HC).

[22] *Clifford Bay Farms Ltd v Marlborough District Council* (n 8).

[23] *Dye v Auckland Regional Council* [2002] 1 NZLR 337 (NZCA). To distinguish the Court of Appeal decision that interpreted the legislation in a literal manner so preventing future cumulative effects from being considered by decision-makers, the NZEnvC identified another category of pertinent effects that the inclusive definition of effects in s 3 of the Resource Management Act 1991

Regional Council] shows that in two important and related areas the case law under the RMA is losing touch with the natural world of ecosystems in all its confusion and uncertainty'.[24] The two related areas were the Court of Appeal's understanding of 'the concept of effects' and determining what 'the appropriate standard of proof for alleged effects' should be.[25] In the case under discussion (*Dye v Auckland Regional Council*), the Court of Appeal appeared to misunderstand the wider factual and regulatory complexity within which the NZEnvC must work (and ignored the impact of plan provisions on legal reasoning in particular).[26] It seemed to treat legal doctrine as fully fungible, and law immured from the social systems it operated within. In *Outstanding Landscape Protection Society Inc v Hastings District Council*, the NZEnvC noted the effect of *Dye* could be environmentally harmful, explaining that the combination of effects from the proposal with future changes to the environment already sanctioned but not yet actioned, would be ignored if *Dye* was followed: 'a consent authority could never say "[t]his site has reached saturation point, it can take no more"'.[27] Certainly, *Dye* served to distort the factual evaluation in environmental decision-making. As a result, the NZEnvC has tended to distinguish the case.[28]

In its merits review role, the NZEnvC cannot treat legal reasoning as an exercise immured from the factual context, and the Court's form and its functions helps frame its legal approach. The Court's immersion in the 'confusion and uncertainty'[29] of environmental problems and the need to resolve disputes with integrity, prevents it from treating law as generic or fixed and unyielding. And the need for law and (the immutable nature of) ecology to work symbiotically creates different reasoning approaches in ECs as the rest of this chapter demonstrates, impacting, for example, decisions on standing; the admission and evaluation of evidence; the weight to give to various findings; statutory interpretation; the development of legal principles; and the imposition of remedies. Thus, legal reasoning in ECs is 'shaped by [their] own logic and normative concerns',[30] which in turn is formed by an immutable contextual reality.

(NZ) allowed for: 'accumulative effects', see *Clifford Bay Farms Ltd v Marlborough District Council* (n 8) [53].

[24] *Clifford Bay Farms Ltd v Marlborough District Council* (n 8) [65]–[66].

[25] ibid, [53]. Later High Court decisions affirmed the NZEnvC approach to the appropriate standard of proof – see *RJ Davidson Family Trust v Marlborough District Council* [2017] NZHC 52.

[26] For a detailed description of *Dye v Auckland Regional Council* (n 23) see C Warnock and Maree Baker-Galloway, *Focus on Resource Management Law* (LexisNexis, 2015) 219–22.

[27] *Outstanding Landscape Protection Society Inc v Hastings District Council* [2008] NZRMA 8 (NZEnvC), [51].

[28] eg, ibid, [51]–[52]; *Emerald Residential Ltd v North Shore City Council* A31/2004 (unrep) (NZEnvC); *Cashmere Park Trust v Canterbury Regional Council* C48/2004 (unrep) (NZEnvC).

[29] *Clifford Bay Farms Ltd v Marlborough District Council* (n 8) [65]–[66].

[30] E Fisher, *Risk Regulation and Administrative Constitutionalism* (Hart Publishing, 2007) 17.

A. The Scope for Creativity

The responsiveness described above might seem at odds with the legal realms the NZEnvC and NSWLEC operate within. After all both are the products of legislation[31] and operate within a complex regulatory web. But as chapter three explained, environmental legislation is particularly interstitial because of the very nature of the subject. The tendency in modern environmental statute law is to include principles and standards that are open-textured (allowing for decision-makers to respond to the different ecological, socio-cultural and economic concerns in any given scenario) but the legislation may not provide methods for those ideals to be operationalised within adjudication.[32] Nevertheless, courts are charged with resolving legal disputes and cannot resile from the role if the regulatory regime fails to provide adequate direction.[33] Given their jurisdiction is bestowed by statute, doctrinal developments by the NSWLEC and NZEnvC can be categorised as a form of dependent common law, that is 'the creation of norms generated as a by-product of the application of statutory and constitutional norms' during adjudication.[34] Certainly, some decisions of the NSWLEC have drawn on wider constitutional frames in order to underpin legal reasoning.[35] The problem as we saw in chapter three, is that these frames may differ, come into conflict with each other, or are not particularly helpful in the environmental context.

Australian common law doctrine provides that if the statute does not set out relevant considerations they are to be derived from 'the subject-matter, scope and purpose' of the legislation.[36] And legislative scholars opine that while general interpretative principles are important, 'the sources are not all legal … philosophical, and economic doctrine enters in … [c]ommon sense and savoir faire bind the whole together':[37] a critical element with environmental legislation that tends to guide rather than prescribe. In the New Zealand context, some superior court judgments explicitly acknowledge wider interpretative frames in environmental law beyond the statutory confines. For example, in *Friends of Turitea Reserve Society Inc v Palmerston North City Council*, Baragwanath J found the High Court could take judicial notice of increasing environmental concerns in society and that 'statutes are no longer considered in isolation but,

[31] RMA, Pt 11; LECA.

[32] BJ Preston, 'The judicial development of ecological sustainable development' in D Fisher (ed), *Research Handbook on Fundamental Concepts of Environmental Law* (Edward Elgar, 2016) 477.

[33] ibid, 476.

[34] P Cane, *Controlling Administrative Power: An Historical Comparison* (Cambridge University Press, 2016) 333.

[35] See ch 2.

[36] *Minister for Aboriginal Affairs v Peko-Wallsend* (1986) 162 CLR 24, 39–40 (HCA).

[37] F Bennion, *Understanding Common Law Legislation: Drafting and Interpretation* (Oxford University Press, 2001) 95.

where reasonably possible, as forming part of a wider and seamless public policy' that includes sustainable development.[38]

My argument is that the interactional theory provides a wider interpretative frame in the context of environmental adjudication. As chapter four established, the doctrinal developments of the NSWLEC and NZEnvC *of necessity* have to take in to account this wider interpretative frame because of the need for adjudication to *respond* to the inherent features of environmental problem-solving. The next part of the chapter explores examples of ingenuity employed by the NSWLEC and NZEnvC in making sense of environmental adjudication, and demonstrates their leadership in breaking with entrenched adjudicative traditions. In doing so, it shows the interactional theory in action.

II. RESPONDING TO UNCERTAINTY

As the previous chapters have explained, environmental adjudicators often determine disputes against an uncertain *factual* backdrop, making it challenging to follow traditional adjudicative practices of applying the law to the facts. Further, they may be deciding disputes against an uncertain *legal* backdrop that is interstitial, sets down legal guidance but not necessarily legal prescription, or that requires decision-makers to take into account multiple statutory criteria that push and pull decision-making in different directions.

A good illustration is provided by *Crest Energy Kaipara Ltd v Northland Regional Council*.[39] That case concerned an application to build an array of tidal turbines in a harbour, which would significantly advance the use of new technology and contribute renewable energy to the national grid. But the development also had the potential to impact the critically endangered Māui dolphins, of which there were only about 100 left at that time. The statutory requirement was for the NZEnvC to 'promote the sustainable management of the resource' (ie, the harbour) which specifically included taking into account the need to promote renewable forms of energy *and* the need to protect the habitat of endemic fauna.[40] Marine scientists gave opinion evidence that the dolphins might be adversely impacted by noise, habitat loss, collision with the turbines and other effects unforeseen at present. That evidence was suppositional however. Due to their rarity, there was very little knowledge of Māui dolphins' migratory patterns, limited sightings of dolphins in the area and (it goes without saying) there had been no field trials to demonstrate the likelihood of all or any of the adverse impacts occurring. Nevertheless, the statute required the NZEnvC to make predictions about the positive and negative environmental

[38] *Friends of Turitea Reserve Society Inc v Palmerston North City Council* [2008] 2 NZLR 661 (HC), [22].

[39] *Crest Energy Kaipara Ltd v Northland Regional Council* A132/2009 (unrep) (NZEnvC).

[40] RMA, Pt 2.

effects that would flow from the project, including the impacts on Māui dolphins, in determining whether to give consent to the application.[41]

Clearly, the procedures and doctrine employed by the Court would have a significant impact on the outcome of the case. For example, if the Court simply applied standard adjudicative methods – required evidence of past harm upon which to base findings of future harm; refused to accept expert opinions of a reasoned hypothesis; subjected the evidence to a balance of probabilities test; refused to apply precautionary thinking; or failed to understand the causes and relevance of species extinction – the risks to the dolphins would not be factored into the decision-making. If the Court had subjected the 'sustainable management' purpose of the Act to close statutory interpretation, attempting to extract a clearer direction from the list of principles it had to promote, the importance of conserving the dolphins' habitat might have been diminished in the overall decision-making.[42] And if the Court was confined to simply granting or refusing the application, with no scope for developing creative remedies to the problem, the significant advance in renewable energy proposed by the project would be stymied. But the way that the Court framed the issues became critical. The Court's understanding of itself as a problem-solving court allowed it to employ its wide, flexible powers (ie, it is not bound by rules of evidence and has power to impose novel remedies) to surmount these challenges. For example, it accepted that there was a real risk to the dolphins' habitat and it developed an adaptive management regime that allowed for greater knowledge of the relevant ecosystem to be gathered while the development proceeded in stages (see further discussion below). The main argument is *how* the litigation is framed and managed can impact legal reasoning and outcome. The discussion below analyses the approaches taken by the NSWLEC and NZEnvC to respond to factual uncertainty and develop precautionary thinking in order to make this point.

A. The Kernel of Precautionary Thinking in the New South Wales Land and Environment Court

Famously, the NSWLEC employed a precautionary approach to uncertainty *before* any reference to the precautionary principle was incorporated into relevant statute law. In *Leatch v National Parks and Wildlife Service*, the Court described precautionary thinking in cases of factual uncertainty as

[41] RMA, s 104(1)(a): ('When considering an application for a resource consent and any submissions received, the consent authority must, subject to Part 2 [ie the promotion of sustainable management] have regard to – (a) any actual and potential effects on the environment of allowing the activity').

[42] eg, the courts *could* have interpreted the statutory management purpose of the RMA in Pt 2 as establishing a hierarchy that privileged certain national values over others (for a general discussion, see D Fisher, 'Clarity in a little while' (1991) 11 *Terra Nova* 50).

'common sense'[43] and in *Nicholls v Director-General of National Parks and Wildlife Service* as 'a practical approach which this court finds axiomatic in dealing with environmental assessments'.[44] *Leatch* in particular, demonstrates the interactional theory at work and is a good example of how the institutional features of the NSWLEC enabled legal reasoning to respond to the features of environmental problem-solving.

Leatch concerned an appeal against the decision of the Director-General to grant a licence under the National Parks and Wildlife Act 1974 (NPWA) permitting endangered fauna – the Yellow-bellied Glider and Giant Burrowing Frog – to be taken or killed for the purposes of building a road. The NPWA made the Director-General the authority for the 'protection and care of fauna'[45] but nevertheless empowered him/her to grant licences allowing endangered fauna to be taken or killed. Reports before the Director-General stated that there was a likelihood of the fauna being killed by the development 'even though precise estimates cannot be given as to current population distribution and abundances'.[46] The appeal to the NSWLEC took the form of a merits review and the Court had all the statutory functions and discretions of the Director-General.[47] Opponents to the proposal submitted that the Court should apply the precautionary principle in the case and refuse the licence. The Court allowed the appeal and drew on precautionary reasoning to do so.

Stein J accepted that there was no express reference to the precautionary principle (or even to ecological sustainable development, that was later found to encompass the precautionary principle)[48] in the legislation.[49] However, the Court noted that the Director-General and Court on appeal must have regard to the Land and Environment Court Act, any other relevant Act or instrument, 'the circumstances of the case and the public interest',[50] and the list of criteria in the NPWA including 'any other matter which the Court considers relevant'.[51] The question (one of statutory interpretation) became 'what was a relevant matter?' While the Court noted the range of international treaties that incorporated the precautionary principle, the legal reasoning in the case does not rely upon the incorporation of international law into domestic law with Stein J stating, 'it seems to me unnecessary to enter this debate. In my opinion the precautionary principle is a statement of common sense'.[52]

[43] *Leatch v National Parks and Wildlife Service* (1993) 81 LGERA 270, 282 (NSWLEC).

[44] *Nicholls v Director-General of National Parks and Wildlife Service* [1994] 84 LGERA 397, 419 (NSWLEC).

[45] At the time, s 92 of the National Parks and Wildlife Act 1974 (NSW) (NPWA).

[46] *Leatch v National Parks and Wildlife Service* (n 43) 277.

[47] LECA, s 39(2).

[48] eg, *Telstra Corporation v Hornby Shire Council* (n 7) [124]–[127].

[49] *Leatch v National Parks and Wildlife Service* (n 43) 281, 282.

[50] LECA, s 39(4).

[51] At the time, s 92A(6)(e) of the NPWA.

[52] *Leatch v National Parks and Wildlife Service* (n 43) 282.

Stein J observed that a matter may be relevant 'if an examination of the subject matter, scope and purpose (of the Act) shows it not to be an extraneous matter'.[53] The relevant part of the NPWA (then Part 7), specifically allowed for the taking and killing of endangered animals, but Stein J found that the purpose of Part 7 more generally was 'the protection and care of endangered fauna'.[54] Setting the legislative scope widely – as one of environmental conservation, as Stein J did – clearly maximised the opportunity to take into account different matters, but it does not necessarily explain the use of a precautionary approach. It is the Court's knowledge of environmental problems, taken from evidence and policy documents, that explains the importation of precaution. As Stein J noted:

> While there is no express provision requiring consideration of the 'precautionary principle', consideration of the state of knowledge or uncertainty regarding a species, the potential for serious or irreversible harm to an endangered fauna is clearly consistent with the subject matter, scope and purpose of the Act.
>
> Upon an examination of the available material relevant to the Giant Burrowing Frog (Heleioporus australiacus) and the knowledge of the frog in this particular habitat, one is driven to the conclusion that there is a dearth of knowledge.[55]

In the circumstances, Stein J opined that precaution was necessary, and described the precautionary principle as,

> a statement of common sense … directed towards the prevention of serious or irreversible harm to the environment in situations of scientific uncertainty. Its premise is that where uncertainty or ignorance exists concerning the nature or scope of environmental harm (whether this follows from policies, decisions or activities), decision makers should be cautious.[56]

Stein J's approach *is* 'common sense'[57] as he describes it *but only* in the context of understanding the nature of environmental problems. The legal reasoning in this case (ie, to adopt a precautionary approach) is undoubtedly driven by environmental understanding (ie, what the risks of the uncertainty were; the relevance of sustainable population size; and the implications of potential geographical reach or habitat restrictions; and why species extinction is problematic). Thus, the Court bolstered the 'scope and purpose of the Act' by taking the features of environmental problems into account. This is subtle, but important because the inherent nature of environmental problems impacted statutory interpretation.[58]

[53] ibid, 282 (citing *Minister for Aboriginal Affairs v Peko-Wallsend* (1986) 162 CLR 24).

[54] ibid, 282.

[55] ibid.

[56] ibid.

[57] Reflecting a long-standing acknowledgement that 'a certain amount of common sense must be applied in construing statutes', see *Barnes v Jarvis* [1953] 1 All ER 1061, 1063 (HL).

[58] In a different jurisdictional context see *Conservation Council of South Australia v Development Assessment Committee and Tuna Boat Owners Association (No 2)* [1999] SAERDC 86, [22], where the Court relies on scholarly articles that explain the ecological value of precaution,

Importantly, the particular constitution, powers and functions of the NSWLEC enables that environmental understanding, and you see clear evidence of that understanding throughout. Environmental knowledge was introduced to the Court though recognisably legal channels (ie, through expert evidence, albeit that evidence was not constrained by the rules of evidence derived in other legal contexts) but it also came from the Court's own, specialist nature. For example, at one point Stein J commented that

> it is somewhat strange that under State law rare and endangered plants are not accorded similar protection to rare and endangered fauna, especially since flora is important for biological diversity and advances in medical science sometimes involve the application of rare plants.[59]

His Honour also suggested that the statutory requirements for Fauna Impact Statements were lacking: they should require information on how the proposed development would impact the wider species population and its chances of survival,[60] and additional evidence was received by the Court on this point. Accordingly, the fact that the NSWLEC is a trial court – with a specialist bench determining facts, and with wide powers enabling the receipt of additional evidence – is not insignificant, rather this feature directly impacts legal doctrine.[61] We can clearly see the four components of the interactional theory at work in *Leatch*: the features of environmental problems (here, scientific uncertainty created by the complexity of ecosystems) and the recognition of the challenges they create for adjudication, led to the embryonic development of new doctrine (the precautionary principle), a process that was facilitated by the merging of legal and non-legal expertise.

Following *Leatch*, many other decisions of the NSWLEC referred to and employed precautionary thinking in order to respond to uncertainty before the precautionary principle was included in legislation.[62] For example, in *Nicholls v Director-General of National Parks and Wildlife Service*, the Court saw a general need to be cautious, which it described as a 'practical approach'.[63] This approach to reasoning influenced the remedies in the case, with conditions

'the environment could not assimilate all the consequences of activities impacting upon it. Implicit in this recognition is an acknowledgment that science and the scientific method have limitations'.

[59] *Leatch v National Parks and Wildlife Service* (n 43) 275.

[60] ibid, 283–84.

[61] See also E Fisher, 'Is the Precautionary Principle Justiciable?' (2001) 13 *JEL* 315, 327; A Edgar, 'Institutions and Sustainability: Merits Review Tribunal and the Precautionary Principle' (2013) 16 *Australasia Journal of Natural Resources Law and Policy* 61, 64: suggesting that 'merits review has institutional characteristics that make it highly suited to operationalising precautionary decision-making'.

[62] eg, *Nicholls v Director-General of National Parks and Wildlife Service* (n 44); *Simpson v Ballina Shire Council* [1994] NSWLEC 43; *Greenpeace Australia Ltd v Redbank Power Co Ltd* (1994) 86 LGERA 143 (NSWLEC); *Alumino (Aust) Pty Ltd v Minister Administering the Environmental Planning and Assessment Act 1979* [1995] NSWLEC 177; *KA Cox v Concord Council* [1995] NSWLEC 24; *Northcompass Inc v Hornby Shire Council* [1996] NSWLEC 213.

[63] *Nicholls v Director-General of National Parks and Wildlife Service* (n 44) 419.

being imposed on the order 'to take account of the need for ongoing survey, research and assessment',[64] a response enabled by the Court's wide power to impose remedies. Precautionary thinking influenced the evidential burden and standard of proof in *Simpson v Ballina Shire Council*,[65] which occurred because the Court is not restricted to the classic rules of evidence. The Court rejected an error of law appeal after the initial Assessor refused to permit a development on a deep slope that released effluent to the soil in a sensitive area.[66] The developer said the design enabled the effluent to percolate safely down through the ground, and although there was no scientific risk assessment contesting the developer's evidence (or actually supporting it) the Assessor found that, 'the percolation argument for the disposal of effluent seems to involve an "out of sight out of mind" attitude. In dealing with such a sensitive ecosystem, this is not only anthropocentric but unrealistic'.[67]

In *Greenpeace v Redbank Power*,[68] the Court found that the precautionary principle 'dictates that a cautious approach should be adopted in evaluating the various factors' (in this case, the emission of greenhouse gases) but did not accept that a cautious approach should colour the overall decision-making, stating that 'it is for state and national governments to take into account the competing economic and environmental issues raised by the enhanced greenhouse gas effect and to set policy in the light of those issues'.[69] *Greenpeace v Redbank* can be categorised as an example of formalist thinking, with the Court appearing to erect clear, binary divisions between the branches of government involved in 'the environmental justice system',[70] so distancing itself from any conception of the Court as an 'innovative experiment'.[71] But the case neatly illustrates that the way the Court frames its role impacts legal reasoning and the ultimate outcome.[72]

In these early cases, there was undoubtedly an inconsistent approach to the issue of precaution. However, the important point for my argument is that

[64] ibid, 398; see also *Alumino (Aust) Pty Ltd v Minister Administering the Environmental Planning and Assessment Act 1979* (n 62).

[65] *Simpson v Ballina Shire Council* (n 62).

[66] ibid. Specifically, Pearlman J found that the appellants were really arguing about an error of fact. The Assessor had to consider impacts on the environment and he had done so. As there was no risk analysis that disturbed his findings, the Assessor did not make an error of law.

[67] ibid, 393.

[68] *Greenpeace Australia Ltd v Redbank Power Co Ltd* (n 62).

[69] ibid, 153.

[70] P Ryan, 'Court of Hope and False Expectations: Land and Environment Court 21 Years On' (2002) 14 *JEL* 301, 301.

[71] NSW Parliamentary Debates, 21 November 1979, 3345, Second Reading Speech of the Hon Paul Landa MP, Minister for Planning and Environment quoted in S Smith, *A Review of the Land and Environment Court: Briefing Paper No 13/01* (NSW Parliamentary Library Research Service, 2001) 1.

[72] *cf Gloucester Resources Ltd v Minister for Planning* (n 14), a much later decision of the NSWLEC but one that adopts a much more expansive role for the Court in environmental governance and climate change.

adjudicating in situations of factual uncertainty led to the NSWLEC striving to respond, and that development was not catalysed by any express legislative requirement. It came rather from the need to react in a principled but pragmatic way to the adjudicative challenges created by environmental problems. From the mid-1990s, amendments were made to various NSW statutes in order to incorporate reference to ecological sustainable development[73] (which the Court found encompassed the precautionary principle)[74] and at times, direct reference to the principle itself often in the form of statutory objectives.[75] Nevertheless, very little guidance was given as to how the principle should be operationalised within adjudication, leaving the Court to develop legal tests and procedures iteratively.[76]

The case of *Telstra Corporation v Hornby Shire Council*[77] is perhaps regarded as the apex of that development. Summarising other cases and a wide array of academic scholarship (forms of knowledge that demonstrate the wide problem-solving methods available to the Court), *Telstra* addressed the threshold conditions for the application of the precautionary principle (that there are threats of serious or irreversible damage and a lack of full scientific certainty as to the nature and scope of the threat of environmental damage); standards of evidentiary proof and shifting the burden of proof; preventative measures (including adaptive management); and determining the proportionality of response. The Court heard and had to make findings in relation to complex evidence from physics, engineering and epidemiology, and the legally trained judge sat with an expert commissioner. The decision clearly shows the interactional links between 'problem-challenge-response-institutional form'. However, *Telstra* was an unusual case because it paralleled the interactional theory almost in the abstract: the Court set down a comprehensive guide to the

[73] eg, Environmental Planning and Assessment Act 1979 (NSW) was amended in 1998 to incorporate the objective of ecological sustainable development in s 5(a)(vii) (now see s 1.3).

[74] eg, *Hub Action Group Inc v Minister for Planning* [2008] NSWLEC 116, [1]; *Carstens v Pittwater Council* (1999) 111 LGERA 1 (NSWLEC); *BGP Properties Pty Limited v Lake Macquarie City Council* [2004] NSWLEC 399; *Minister for Planning v Walker* [2008] NSWCA 224; *Telstra Corporation v Hornby Shire Council* (n 7); *Friends of Tumblebee Inc v ATB Morton Pty Ltd (No 2)* (n 13); and see Scotford (n 9) for a comprehensive treatment of the issue.

[75] eg, Protection of the Environment Administration Act 1991 (NSW), s 6(2).

[76] P Stein, 'Specialist Environment Courts: the Land and Environment Court of New South Wales Australia' (2002) 4 *Environmental Law Review* 5, 19; Preston, 'The Role of the Judiciary in Promoting Sustainable Development Pacific' (n 9); B Preston, 'Leadership by the Courts in Achieving Sustainability' (2010) 6 *Resource Management Theory & Practice* 17. For other cases decided prior to *Telstra Corporation v Hornby Shire Council* (n 7) and post-legislative incorporation see, eg, *Providence Projects Pty Ltd v Gosford City Council* [2006] NSWLEC 52; *Port Stephens Pearls Pty Limited v Minister for Infrastructure and Planning* [2005] NSWLEC 426; *Murrumbidgee Ground-Water Preservation Association v Minister for Natural Resources* [2004] NSWLEC 122; *Gales Holdings Pty Ltd v Tweed Shire Council* [2006] NSWLEC 85; *BT Goldsmith Planning Services v Blacktown City Council* (n 12); *BGP Properties Pty Limited v Lake Macquarie City Council* (n 74); *Anderson & Anor v Director-General of the Department of Environment & Conservation & Anor* (2006) 144 LGERA 43 (NSWLEC).

[77] *Telstra Corporation v Hornby Shire Council* (n 7).

operationalisation of the precautionary principle without necessarily needing to do so in the particular circumstances of the case.[78] To that end, it reveals the Court's view of itself as a problem-solving court, with a role to play in environmental governance and having a wider societal influence. But as a result, it makes sense to consider the development of these procedures as they come up in specific fact contexts in the New Zealand case law, drawing on the NSWLEC jurisprudence as appropriate.

B. Developing a Precautionary Approach in the Environment Court of New Zealand

The development of precautionary thinking in the NZEnvC followed a slightly different path from that taken by the NSWLEC in order to reach a similar result. In particular, the NZEnvC has described 'a precautionary approach' flowing from legislative interpretation, rather than from separate judge-made doctrine.[79] Interestingly, despite this categorisation, there are no explicit textual references to caution, precaution or the precautionary principle in New Zealand's main environmental statute, the RMA 1991;[80] very few references to risk[81] or uncertainty;[82] and the New Zealand Supreme Court has expressly declined to

[78] *Telstra Corporation v Hornby Shire Council* (n 7) concerned a merits appeal of a refusal to grant development consent for a telecommunications mast in a residential area that was classed as a heritage conservation area. Residents' primary opposition was based on the purported health risks from radio frequency electromagnetic energy (RF EME). The expert evidence on the health effects of RF EME was provided by a court-appointed witness. This evidence was unchallenged and the Court found that the RF EME from the mast would 'not cause any adverse biological or health effects to the general public', [90]. The emissions also met the relevant Australian Standard for RF EME by a significant margin, [88]. Accordingly, there was not really a live issue that justified the Court's expansive analysis of the precautionary principle in the case. See Edgar (n 61) 72–73.

[79] *Shirley Primary School v Christchurch City Council* [1999] NZRMA 66 (NZEnvC), [223].

[80] As noted by the Court in *Wratten v Tasman District Council* W8/98 (unrep) (NZEnvC), 17. Certain policy instruments now contain reference to precaution, eg, New Zealand Coastal Policy Statement 2010 and the precautionary principle is referenced in some other environmental legislation including the Fisheries Act 1996 (NZ) and the Hazardous Substances and New Organisms Act 1996 (NZ) (although both statutes concern ministerial decision-making challengeable by judicial review only).

[81] In essence, a discrete operational provision concerning the content of 'Section 32 Reports' (that contain cost–benefit evaluations of proposed local authority planning rules) evinces a precautionary approach by stating, s 32(1): An evaluation report required under this Act must – ss(2)(c) assess the risk of acting or not acting if there is uncertain or insufficient information about the subject matter of the provisions. Other than the use of the term in s 32, decision makers must take into account the 'risk of natural hazards' or risks from 'hazardous installations' see RMA ss 6(h), 65, 106, Sch 4, cl 6. The only other reference to 'risk' is the requirement for the Minister in determining the contents of the New Zealand Coastal Policy Statement to take into account 'anything which, because of its uniqueness, or the irreversibility or potential magnitude or risk of its actual or potential effects, is of significance to the environment of New Zealand' (see RMA s 45(2)(g)).

[82] The singular reference to uncertainty concerns the ability of the NZEnvC to amend planning documents if there is any 'uncertainty' (see RMA, s 292(1)(a)). 'Uncertain' is used once, in s 32, as discussed above.

comment on whether a precautionary 'approach' can be derived from the legislation itself.[83] Decision-makers under the RMA are however required to take into account 'effects' on the environment,[84] and oblique references to prediction and precaution in the Act are found in the definition of 'effects' in section 3, which includes '(e) any potential effect of high probability; and (f) any potential effect of low probability which has a high potential impact'. Nevertheless, with only two scant statutory references upon which to draw the Court has developed an expansive jurisprudence to address factual uncertainty[85] – drawing on that pithy sub-section as a way of responding legally to the challenges of environmental problems – and has done so often in the face of confused and confusing higher court precedent.[86]

The NZEnvC is concerned with assessing past facts and the state of the present environment, but much of its substantive work requires predicting future impacts. It has specifically drawn on the discourse of risk, explaining its predictive role as one of risk assessment and management.[87] In *Clifford Bay Farms*, the Court saw the 'huge literature on risk assessment' as a useful check in managing risk.[88] It warned against sloppy thinking, categorising effects simply as 'high risk' or 'low risk', explaining that assessing risk encompasses two components: determining (1) probability of likelihood and (2) severity of consequence.[89] Further, in *Land Air Water Association v Waikato Regional Council*,[90] the NZEnvC distinguished between 'uncertainty', 'ignorance' and 'risk' in a way that implicitly accords with Wynne's typography that corrals various forms of knowledges and experience in order to predict future behaviour.[91] In a similar vein, the NSWLEC has also referred to evaluating uncertainty as involving

[83] *Sustain Our Sounds Inc v New Zealand King Salmon Company Ltd* [2014] NZSC 40, [102] despite endorsing precautionary remedies.

[84] eg, in deciding resource consent applications (RMS s 104), plan changes (eg, RMA ss 30–32), and designations (ss RMA 168A(3)).

[85] For comprehensive treatment see: *Shirley Primary School v Christchurch City Council* (n 79); *Golden Bay Marine Farmers v Tasman District Council (Second Interim Report)* W19/2003 (NZEnvC); *Clifford Bay Farms Ltd v Marlborough District Council* (n 8).

[86] eg, *Dye v Auckland Regional Council* (n 23); *Royal Forest and Bird Society of New Zealand Inc v Buller District Council* [2006] NZRMA 193 (HC).

[87] Risk is understood to express something about the possibility that harm will occur (The Royal Society, *Risk: Analysis, Perception, Management*, The Royal Society, 1992, 2). Risk assessment includes identifying areas of uncertainty, if possible assessing the prospects of the uncertainty manifesting, and looking at the potential ramifications (*Clifford Bay Farms Ltd v Marlborough District Council* (n 8) [72]); and a risk-management process decides on what action to take, having reference to those affected and the relevant values framework (Somerville (n 9) 23).

[88] eg, *Clifford Bay Farms Ltd v Marlborough District Council* (n 8) [71].

[89] ibid, [55].

[90] *Land Air Water Association v Waikato Regional Council* A110/01 (unrep) (NZEnvC), [519].

[91] B Wynne, 'Uncertainty and environmental learning: reconceiving science and policy in the preventative paradigm' (1992) 1 *Global Environmental Change* 111. Wynne distinguishes between indeterminacy (causal chains are open, greater science may not solve); ignorance (we don't know what we don't know); uncertainty (we may know the parameters but not the odds); and risk (we have statistics to calculate the odds).

'an assessment of risk in its usual formulation'.[92] Case law developed by the NZEnvC as a response to uncertainty covers the evaluation of evidence (for example, the admissibility and weight to be given to expert evidence premised on different methodologies,[93] and the standards and burdens of 'proof)',[94] and the development of novel remedies (such as adaptive management programmes that respond to uncertainty with continual information-gathering and the consequential adjustment of permit conditions).[95] Each of these developments are discussed in more detail below to demonstrate the importance of adjudicative form, functions and framing in this context, and to show support for the interactional theory.

C. Evaluating Evidence

The interactional theory can be shown in action by analysing a line of cases demonstrating how the NZEnvC altered its approach to the evaluation of evidence. In the jurisprudence, one can clearly trace the Court's acknowledgment of the challenges created by environmental problems and the need for legal reasoning to respond accordingly. Further, the resulting doctrinal developments were facilitated by the specialist form and functions of the Court.

In cases prior to the 1999 decision of *Shirley Primary School v Christchurch City Council*,[96] the NZEnvC subjected all evidence of environmental effects – past, present and future – to a standard of proof test on the balance of probabilities, the usual standard in civil litigation.[97] Standards of proof 'instruct the factfinder concerning the degree of confidence our society thinks he should have in the correctness of factual conclusions'[98] and the different degrees of proof required in different contexts 'allocate the risk of error between the litigants'[99] (or considered in a different light, 'minimises expected losses').[100] Employing the balance of probabilities standard means that the risk of error is allocated equally between the parties. However, as later decisions of the Court realised, there are a number of difficulties with subjecting evidence in environmental disputes to a balance of probabilities test.

[92] *Telstra Corporation v Hornby Shire Council* (n 7) [161].

[93] *Shirley Primary School v Christchurch City Council* (n 79) [68].

[94] ibid, [68].

[95] *Golden Bay Marine Farmers v Tasman District Council* W42/2001 (unrep) (NZEnvC); *Crest Energy Kaipara Ltd v Northland Regional Council* [2011] NZEnvC 26; *Sustain Our Sounds Inc v New Zealand King Salmon Company Ltd* (n 83).

[96] *Shirley Primary School v Christchurch City Council* (n 79).

[97] eg, *McIntyre v Christchurch City Council* [1997] NZRMA 289 (PT); *Wratten v Tasman District Council* (n 80); *Telecom v Christchurch City Council* W165/96 (unrep) (PT).

[98] *In re Winship* 397 US 358 (1970) (US Supreme Court).

[99] *Addington v Texas* 441 US 418, 423 (1979) (US Supreme Court).

[100] *Clifford Bay Farms Ltd v Marlborough District Council* (n 8) [65] citing D Kaye, 'The error of equal error rates' (2002) 1 *Law Probability & Risk* 3.

First, as the Court found in *Shirley Primary School*, there was an important conceptual difference between ascertaining past facts and making predictions as to possible future effects. Quoting the Privy Council case of *Fernandez v Government of Singapore*[101] the Court explained that an approach to the evidence based on the balance of probabilities 'is inappropriate when applied not to ascertaining what has already happened but to prophesying what, if it happens at all, can only happen in the future'.[102] At some point in the future, predictions will be proved right or wrong. As a result, the NZEnvC has described predictions as 'more real than the findings of the Court about past events', and described findings of probability in this context as 'simply a statement of our uncertainty when making a prediction'.[103]

Second, employing the balance of probabilities standard causes problems in the environmental context where a court could be dealing with serious and irreversible risks (for example, the extinction of Māui dolphins). The Court in *Clifford Bay Farms* explained that the rationale behind the balance of probabilities test (ie, allocating error equally between the parties) was perverse when errors can result in abject inequality to one side or another.[104] Refusing consent in that particular case would have resulted in profits foregone to the applicant company but granting consent may have led to the extinction of a species. The Court explained the problem using a heuristic in *Long Bay–Okura Great Park Society Inc v North Shore City Council* to help those of a more anthropocentric bent understand the concept:

> Consider a proposed activity which may endanger human lives. Assume the consent authority finds that the probability of the alleged effect is 16.67% (the roll of a dice). If the authority applied a 'balance of probabilities' standard of proof, that effect would be disregarded.[105]

Further, employing classic approaches to evidence to determine the *present* state of the environment can also cause difficulties. The case of *Long Bay–Okura Great Park Society Inc* concerned a proposed development in an area of outstanding natural beauty and some of the most contentious issues in the case related to where the outstanding natural landscape began or ended. The Court noted, that on these issues:

> [T]he civil standard expressed as 'on the balance of probabilities' is not apt because it really becomes just a metaphor about the scales of justice. Instead the Court should

[101] *Fernandez v Government of Singapore* [1971] 1 WLR 987 (PC).

[102] *Shirley Primary School v Christchurch City Council* (n 79) [117]; although the NZEnvC later acknowledged that 'relying on a fact/judgement distinction overlooks that the finding of a fact by a Court is not a scientific exercise; it is itself quintessentially a matter of judgement' see *Long Bay–Okura Great Park Society v North Shore City Council* (n 10) [314].

[103] *Long Bay–Okura Great Park Society v North Shore City Council* (n 10) [314].

[104] *Clifford Bay Farms Ltd v Marlborough District Council* (n 8) [66].

[105] *Long Bay–Okura Great Park Society v North Shore City Council* (n 10) [310]. See also *Shirley Primary School v Christchurch City Council* (n 79).

> decide such subjective, value-laden issues on the more formal (but here more useful) standard of proof of facts. That is, a fact is determined on the preponderance of the evidence having regard to the seriousness of the allegation.[106]

In acknowledging the value-laden character of the evidence, the Court highlighted the challenge created by merged fact and opinion, and the overlap between the ecological, socio-cultural and economic spheres – an inherent feature of environmental disputes.

In each of these examples the NZEnvC adjusted its evaluative techniques to respond to the nature of the disputes it is tasked with resolving, and its institutional form and functions allowed for this response (for example, it is not bound by the formal rules of evidence). These cases clearly show the interactional theory in action. But the Court's approach to evidentiary tests initially encountered difficulties within the higher generalist courts.[107] At times, the NZEnvC has had to re-clarify and explain its evaluative approach. For example, in referring to an earlier (and somewhat confusing) High Court decision, the Court in *Clifford Bay Farms* noted that

> one issue was whether certain land was waahi tapu – *Ngati Maru Iwi Authority v Auckland City Council* (AP18/02 [High Court]) Doogue J confirmed that '... the appropriate standard of proof upon someone asserting a fact, ... [is] the balance of probabilities. I do not read *Shirley Primary School* as in conflict with what is common to so many decisions of the Environment Court'.
>
> We take it that the second sentence in that passage shows that Doogue J was carefully confining his statement to the standard of proof of facts. He was not stating anything about the standard of proof of the judgements about possible future events and their effects which is the principal task of decision makers under the RMA.[108]

Nevertheless, the NZEnvC also counselled that '[s]imply differentiating between facts and judgements and the placing of predictions either in the category of "facts" or in the category of "judgements" is overly simplistic': neither constitute scientific exercises; both require matters of judgement.[109]

The NSWLEC reached similar conclusions in the way it frames the evaluation of evidence. In *Plum v Penrith City Council*, the Court made it clear that determining future effects on the environment 'can never truly be an objective

[106] *Long Bay–Okura Great Park Society v North Shore City Council* (n 10) [48].

[107] eg, *Royal Forest and Bird Society of New Zealand Inc v Buller District Council* (n 86).

[108] *Clifford Bay Farms Ltd v Marlborough District Council* (n 8) [58]; see also *Long Bay–Okura Great Park Society v North Shore City Council* (n 10) [47]–[48]. Note, as an aside, the interrelationship between specialist environment courts and the ordinary appellate courts provides scope for greater investigation. At times, the higher courts can confirm and stabilise creative legal developments, so enhancing ECs legitimacy; on other occasions, the disjunct between 'problem solving' approaches and legal formalism becomes irresolvable. While I do not address the issue in this book, questions naturally arise as to 'whether ordinary courts should defer to specialist courts interpretations of the statute and attempts to fill in statutory lacunae' and/or 'should appeals go to specialist appellate bodies'?

[109] *Long Bay–Okura Great Park Society v North Shore City Council* (n 10) [313].

fact – it must always be a matter of opinion',[110] and a statutory test of likelihood (for example, 'likely to be a significant effect on threatened species') means 'a real or not remote chance or possibility regardless of whether it is less or more than a fifty per cent chance'.[111] In *Friends of Tumblebee Inc v ATB Morton Pty Ltd*, the NSWLEC rejected the evidence of an expert witness that a proposed development was unlikely to impact the Regent Honeyeater, a threatened species, because they had misunderstood the test of likelihood (amongst other reasons). Pepper J found that '[i]n cross-examination [the expert] stated initially that he believed that "likely" (wrongly) meant "more chance than not" … [and] stated, also incorrectly, that the words "more likely than not" were equivalent to a "more than 50% probability"'.[112]

Further, both the NZEnvC and the NSWLEC have emphasised quite *what* probability of likelihood should suffice will depend upon the context, and here again we see the courts responding to the nature of environmental problems. In *Clifford Bay Farms Ltd*, the NZEnvC stated that, 'there is no Procrustean – one size fits all – principle for risk assessment and the standard of proof of risks under the RMA':[113] ecological context helps form the legal response. *Aquamarine Ltd v Southland Regional Council*[114] provides a good example. In that case, the NZEnvC declined an application to extract water for mass export from Deep Cove in the pristine Doubtful Sound. The applicant proposed to manoeuvre 200-metre tankers into the Sounds. Opposition to the proposal was primarily based on the potential harm to the fragile ecosystem from foreign organisms that could be introduced by the ships' ballast, and the risks of an oil spill if a ship were to founder. The Court found that both events would be catastrophic in that particular environment, and even though the probabilities of them occurring was very low the Court was not prepared to say they were so remote they could be put to one side altogether.[115] Thus although the Court found there was a very small likelihood of both risks eventuating, consent was refused because of the distinct and special nature of the ecosystem. Likewise, in the context of the NSWLEC's formation of the precautionary principle, the combined effect of the degree of seriousness and irreversibility of the environmental threat (ie, the ecological context), and the degree of uncertainty (ie, the lack of scientific knowledge), impacts the legal approach taken to evaluating the evidence. The more significant and uncertain the threat, the greater the degree of

[110] *Plumb v Penrith City Council* [2002] NSWLEC 223, [16] (Pearlman J).

[111] eg, *Lend Lease Developments Pty Ltd v Manly Council* [1998] NSWLEC 136, [24] quoting *Matthews v Goulburn Wool Processing Pty Ltd* NSWSC, Smart J, 6 November 1986 (unrep) (NSWSC) 15 that interpreted the meaning of 'likely' in s 16(2)(a) of the Clean Waters Act 1970 (NSW), and applying that interpretation to 'likely' in the context of the Environmental Planning and Assessment Act 1979 (NSW) (EPAA).

[112] *Friends of Tumblebee Inc v ATB Morton Pty Ltd (No 2)* (n 13), [105].

[113] *Clifford Bay Farms Ltd v Marlborough District Council* (n 8) [68].

[114] *Aquamarine Ltd v Southland Regional Council* C126/97 (unrep) (NZEnvC).

[115] ibid, 121.

precaution required.[116] This responsive approach to the evaluation of environmental risk – an approach that breaks with traditional adjudicative process – is possible because of the Court's institutional features but also because of the way the Court framed its role.

The New Zealand and New South Wales ECs have also had to address the required quality and form of scientific information upon which to base a finding of risk, and again their particular institutional form and powers to receive 'any evidence' has facilitated a responsive approach. Given the inherent features of environmental problems, at times expert opinions about a particular risk may be derived from hypotheses, rather than experiential evidence. A litigious red-line, separating legal dispute-resolution from other forms of problem-solving, is that evidence must be 'reliable',[117] and the two ECs have not crossed this line. Accordingly, allegations that a proposed activity could harm the environment must be based on 'real evidence',[118] rather than uninformed suspicion or mere innuendo, and the courts have explained that phantom risks would not be factored into decision-making.[119] However, in setting the test for 'real evidence', the NZEnvC has responded to the inherent challenges of environmental problems by finding that a 'scintilla'[120] of 'reliable'[121] evidence will suffice, and that well-justified hypotheses can constitute reliable evidence.

In *Shirley Primary School v Christchurch City Council*[122] the NZEnvC heard the merits appeal of an application to erect a telecommunications mast next to a primary school. The community were concerned about the adverse health risks of electro-magnetic frequency. The Court found that it is not only 'proven actual effects that need to be considered but also scientifically possible effects'.[123] Informed by scientific expertise, it developed a legal matrix within which to assess expert evidence and support a finding of a 'real' risk, stating that,

> an effect must not simply be a hypothesis: there must be some evidence supporting the hypothesis. This evidence may consist of at least one of:
>
> (1) consistent sound statistical studies of a human population; or
> (2) general expert acceptance of a hypothesis; or

[116] *Telstra Corporation v Hornby Shire Council* (n 7) [161].

[117] *R v Mohan* [1994] SCR 9 (SCC), 25.

[118] *McIntyre v Christchurch City Council* (n 97) 104, citing *R v Mohan* [1994] SCR 9 and focusing on the need for scientific evidence to meet a basic threshold of 'reliability'. For a critique of *Mohan* see B Limpert, 'Beyond the Rule in Mohan: A New Model for Assessing the Reliability of Scientific Evidence' (1996) 54 *University of Toronto Faculty of Law Review* 65.

[119] *Telstra Corporation v Hornby Shire Council* (n 7). For a critique of this approach, see Peel, 'When (Scientific) Rationality Rules' (n 9).

[120] *Shirley Primary School v Christchurch City Council* (n 79) [142].

[121] *McIntyre v Christchurch City Council* (n 97) 104.

[122] *Shirley Primary School v Christchurch City Council* (n 79).

[123] ibid, [179].

(3) persuasive animal studies or other bio-mechanistic evidence accompanied by an explanation as to why there is no epidemiological evidence of actual effects in the real world; or
(4) (possibly) a very persuasive expert opinion.[124]

In the case the Court found that there was some 'very tenuous epidemiological evidence' of adverse health effects impacting children's learning and sleep and the finding was factored into the decision-making (albeit this risk was of very low probability and did not ultimately prove determinative in the final decision-making analysis).[125] In *Clifford Bay Farms Ltd v Marlborough District Council*, the NZEnvC noted that there was a lack of research into the possible effects on Hector's dolphins from marine farming but that expert opinion evidence 'should be accepted as beyond mere suspicion ... they rank as expert hypotheses with some analogic evidential backing'.[126]

The NSWLEC has adopted a similar approach. For example, in *Newcastle & Hunter Speleological Society Inc v Upper Hunter Shire Council*,[127] the Court was concerned with a merits appeal against a development consent for a limestone quarry. Objections were based on the impacts to the endangered ecological community on the land surface and also karst formations and fauna in the underground caves. Although there was no site-specific evidence of cave dwelling fauna, there was evidence of biota in caves nearby and generalist studies that established the presence of biota in limestone, 'make it scientifically likely that some form of biota will be found within the limestone on the site'. Accordingly, the Court found that '[w]ithout being able to predict the particular species which would be present, *it is beyond a mere possibility that biota will be present* (emphasis added)'.[128] This possibility was sufficient to engage the application of the precautionary principle and, given the circumstances of the case, an adaptive management regime was imposed on the consent.[129] In all these cases, the courts required some probative evidence upon which to establish legal claims (of benefit or harm), and so the evaluation met recognisable legal tests for fairness and transparency, preventing arbitrariness, ensuring objective evaluation and anchoring the decision in reliable evidence. But the courts widened the forms of acceptable evidence and adapted evaluative approaches in order to respond to the nature of environmental problems.

Contextual uncertainty in environmental disputes has also altered the courts' approach to the burden of evidentiary proof. Once adequate evidence of a risk of harm has been adduced, both the NZEnvC and NSWLEC have found that the

[124] ibid, [147].
[125] Although, this was only one factor in the overall decision-making and the Court consented to the application.
[126] *Clifford Bay Farms Ltd v Marlborough District Council* (n 8) [79].
[127] *Newcastle & Hunter Speleological Society Inc v Upper Hunter Shire Council* (n 12).
[128] ibid, [177].
[129] ibid, [178]–[189].

evidential burden shifts to the applicant to disprove the risk or to show that any harm can be adequately mitigated.[130] In *Providence Projects Pty Ltd v Gosford City Council*[131] – a case in which there was scientific uncertainty as to whether a threatened ecological community, the Umina Coastal Sandplain Woodland, was widely distributed over the development site or present in limited areas only – the NSWLEC employed the precautionary principle to shift the burden of proof onto the applicant. Bignold J held that the precautionary principle justified a margin of error approach 'which avoids the risk of serious or irreversible environmental damage by assuming the existence of the wide distribution of [Umina Coastal Sandplain Woodland] over the development site'.[132] It was for the applicant to tender expert evidence disproving this assumption.

In all the cases discussed above, the NZEnvC and NSWLEC demonstrated an awareness of the adjudicative challenges presented by the nature of environmental problems. They developed new doctrine in response, and their particular form and functions facilitated this creative legal reasoning. The cases clearly show the interactional theory in action. This responsive approach to the development of jurisprudence is echoed in the courts' approach to environmental law remedies, as the following part explains.

D. Crafting Remedies

Once the ECs have found that there is a risk of environmental harm, or the precautionary principle is activated, they must decide what to do. Both courts have a wide remit to impose suitable remedies in their merits review jurisdiction, and can affirm, amend or cancel the decision being appealed against;[133] adjourn and retain control of proceedings;[134] grant injunctions;[135] employ ADR processes;[136] impose enforcement measures and make declarations.[137] Some environmental risks are deemed wholly unacceptable. For example, even a small risk 'of annihilation of an endangered species'[138] may result in a

[130] *Shirley Primary School v Christchurch City Council* (n 79) [142]; *Telstra Corporation v Hornby Shire Council* (n 7) [150]. Note this is not a complete shifting of the burden of proof that a strong approach to environmental conservation would require.

[131] *Providence Projects Pty Ltd v Gosford City Council* (n 76).

[132] ibid, [77]; see also *SHCAG Pty Ltd v Minister for Planning and Infrastructure and Boral Cement Ltd* [2013] NSWLEC 1032, [90]: 'The burden of proof that the proposal is not harmful falls on the proponent [Colliery]'.

[133] RMA, s 290; eg, EPAA, s 8.14.

[134] RMA, s 269; eg, Civil Procedure Act 2005 (NSW), ss 66–67.

[135] RMA, s 320; eg, (LECA), s 23.

[136] RMA, s 267; eg, LECA, s 34, 34A; Civil Procedure Act 2005 (NSW) s 26.

[137] RMA, Pt 12; eg, LECA, ss 20–21.

[138] *Sustain Our Sounds Inc v New Zealand King Salmon Company Ltd* (n 83) [139]. For an example of a refusal see *Kuku Mara (Forsyth Bay) v Marlborough District Council* (n 12) (endangered King Shag at risk). In the NSW context, see, eg, *Darkinjung Local Aboriginal Land Council v Minister for Planning and Infrastructure & Anor; Australian Walkabout Wildlife Park Pty Limited*

development being refused in its entirety. However, the legislative regimes that the NSWLEC and NZEnvC operate under are not 'no-risk' statutes, nor are they premised solely upon environmental conservation.[139] In its merits review role, the NZEnvC must promote the sustainable management of natural resources and an objective of the Environmental Planning and Assessment Act 1979 (NSW) (EPAA) is for the NSWLEC to facilitate ecological sustainable development. Both concepts encompass environmental, socio-cultural *and* economic wellbeing.[140] If a proposal will create positive economic effects but uncertainty about environmental harm remains, simply granting or refusing the application may not promote sustainability (as *Crest Energy* demonstrated above). Further, attempting to predict adverse effects and managing them through conditions on consents can be problematic because predictions may prove to be wrong.[141] The NZEnvC has also noted that the need for finality, a policy that informs other types of adjudication (as we saw in chapter four, an essential characteristic of adjudication by the US Supreme Court in *Daubert* was speedy finality)[142] is not so dominant in the environmental sphere where other policy imperatives such as mitigating ongoing environmental harm come to the fore.[143] As a result of this reasoning, the ECs have crafted remedies in environmental cases that respond to the nature of the problems they are tasked with resolving. It is worth noting that this approach stands in stark contrast to the one adopted in judicial review proceedings before the ordinary courts, where a finding of illegality might be made but the public body is generally left to choose how to respond.[144]

Early cases in the NSWLEC and NZEnvC tended to increase conditions on consents for monitoring and reporting, which increased the possibility for enforcement actions if harm occurred.[145] Some cases dealt with uncertainty by

(ACN 115 219 791) as Trustee for the Gerald and Catherine Barnard Family Trust v Minister for Planning and Infrastructure & Anor (n 3) (possible destruction of cultural heritage landscapes; proposed adaptive management inadequate because once harm discovered it would be too late to remedy, [461]).

[139] eg, *Shirley Primary School v Christchurch City Council* (n 79) [106]: the RMA is 'not a "no risk" statute'.

[140] RMA, s 5 (2); EPAA, s 1.3(b).

[141] eg, *Tranz Rail New Zealand v Marlborough City Council* W001/08 (unrep) (NZEnvC) (fast ferry case); *Meridian Energy Ltd v Wellington CC* [2011] NZEnvC 232.

[142] *Daubert v Merrel Dow Pharmaceuticals* 509 US 579, 596–97 (1993).

[143] *Long Bay–Okura Great Park Society v North Shore City Council* (n 10) [316].

[144] *cf R (on the application of Client Earth) No 3 v Secretary of State for Environment, Food and Rural Affairs* [2018] EWHC 315, an English case which perhaps reflects the limits of how a judge of the administrative court might respond to an environmental dispute. In the English context, the Environment Bill 2019–21 creates some interesting complexities in this regard. Enforcement appeals from the proposed Office for Environmental Protection are likely to go to the Upper Tier Tribunal and require the Tribunal to determine how compliance should be achieved. This role will move the Tribunal closer to that of the NSWLEC and NZEnvC and may, in turn, lead to similar debates about the legitimacy of the Upper Tier Tribunal. Thank you to an anonymous reviewer for this observation.

[145] eg, *Carter Holt Harvey Ltd v Te Rūnanga O Tūwharetoa Ki Kawerau* [2003] 2 NZLR 349 (NZHC).

focusing on the flexibility of conditions to stop the activity if it was shown to be damaging.[146] For example in *Nicholls v Director-General of National Parks and Wildlife*, the NSWLEC granted a licence to take or kill endangered species during logging operations,

> subject to conditions specifying the particular fauna and taking into account the need for ongoing survey research and assessment to enable the Director-General to be kept up to date so that the conditions could be varied or the licence revoked according to the evolving circumstances.[147]

In the New Zealand context, the NZEnvC began to employ so-called 'conditions precedent', requiring the satisfaction of certain conditions *before* the substantive activity consented to was allowed to occur. In *Director-General of Conservation v Marlborough District Council*, the Court required the applicant to conduct a two-year survey to satisfy the authorities that the project site was not of special significance for Hector's dolphins 'in terms of breeding, nursing, feeding or sheltering', *before* the aquaculture activity could commence.[148] This approach created a legal conundrum based on property law doctrine: if conditions have to be fulfilled before a grant or legal right passes, what is the legal vehicle to which the conditions are attached? But the High Court found that such conditions could legally be attached to resource consents – consents could provide for a number of activities not just the core substantive activity – so differentiating environmental permits and licences from property doctrine.[149] In this instance, the High Court agreed with the solution crafted by the NZEnvC in response to the nature of the problem before it, even though it stretched traditional policy with regard to adjudicative finality. But the High Court found that the NZEnvC had to reserve the matter to itself. It could not delegate to the council the final decision as to whether the activity could proceed because that was a 'judicial function'.[150] Interestingly, therefore, the High Court authorised continuing *mandamus* in the environmental context. To this extent, the higher court stabilised environmental problem-solving within the wider legal system.

With the feed-in of evidence from environmental managers and recourse to wider environmental policy – again, made possible because of the institutional features of the courts – the NZEnvC and NSWLEC developed highly refined

[146] eg, *Port Stephens Pearls Pty Limited v Minister for Infrastructure and Planning* (n 76) [81] (the extensive nature of the conditions shows the willingness of one division of the Court to allow much latitude to the applicant and regulators to manage the effects rather than seeing this as a judicial function; *cf* with *Director-General of Conservation v Marlborough District Council* [2004] 3 NZLR 127 (HC) where the High Court required the NZEnvC to retain control of final decisions).

[147] *Nicholls v Director-General of National Parks and Wildlife Service* (n 44) 398.

[148] *Director-General of Conservation v Marlborough District Council* C113/04 (unrep) (NZEnvC), [6].

[149] ibid.

[150] *Director-General of Conservation v Marlborough District Council* (n 148) [27]–[28].

remedies such as financial and environmental compensation,[151] biodiversity offsetting[152] and adaptive management regimes. Both courts developed legal tests as to when these remedies might appropriately be employed – emphasising their use depends upon ecological context[153] – and they created detailed frameworks as to the various components of these remedies.[154] None of these concepts were included in the relevant statutory regimes but they made sense in the context of environmental adjudication and the specialist expertise of the bench facilitated these developments. Drilling down and considering adaptive management in a little more detail provides a good example of the interactional theory in practice because its development as a legal remedy is directly related to the institutional form of ECs, ie, scientific expertise fed ideas to the courts that responded by transforming scientific practice into legal doctrine through the adjudicative process.

An adaptive management regime allows for an activity to proceed in incremental stages, with monitoring, reporting and assessment of any adverse effects taking place before the next stage of the activity progresses. Because of the dynamic nature of environmental problems, 'few, if any can be solved by action taken at a single point in time' and adaptive management enables institutional learning through experimentation and feedback.[155] Adaptive management rejects a hierarchical approach to problem-solving and the centralisation of knowledge and instead encompasses flexibility and plurality of information from different sources.[156] If a court imposes an adaptive management regime, this is in one sense a resolution to the dispute and so fulfils a core objective of adjudication.

The NZEnvC first used adaptive management in a succession of cases concerning pollution to the seas from aquaculture.[157] It is no coincidence that many adaptive management cases in New Zealand concern activities in

[151] eg, *JF Investments Ltd v Queenstown Lakes District Council* C48/2006 (unrep) (NZEnvC).

[152] eg, *Royal Forest and Bird Protection Society v Gisborne District Council* W26/2009 (unrep) (NZEnvC); *Sanctuary Investments Pty Ltd v Baulkham Hills Shire Council* [2006] NZWLEC 733.

[153] eg, *Long Bay–Okura Great Park Society v North Shore City Council* (n 10) [302] (in correcting an expert witness, who had assumed no need for any environmental compensation through the restoration of a stream the NZEnvC responded: '[w]e consider that is not correct as a matter of law: it all depends on the ecological context').

[154] For a detailed explanation of financial and environmental compensation and biodiversity offsetting in the New Zealand context see Warnock and Baker-Galloway (n 26) 245–49.

[155] H Doremus, 'Constitutive Law and Environmental Policy' (2003) 22 *Stanford Environmental Law Journal* 295, 327.

[156] J Dryzek, *The Politics of the Earth*, 2nd edn (Oxford University Press, 2005) 95–96.

[157] *Golden Bay Marine Farmers v Tasman District Council (Second Interim Report)* (n 85); *Minister of Conservation v Tasman District Council* HC Nelson CIV-2003-485-1072, 9 December 2003 (unrep); *Golden Bay Marine Farmers v Tasman District Council (Final Report)* W89/2004 (unrep) (NZEnvC); *Lower Waitaki River Management Society Inc v Canterbury Regional Council* C80/09 (unrep) (NZEnvC); *Geotherm Group Ltd v Waikato Regional Council* A47/06 (unrep) (NZEnvC); *Crest Energy Kaipara Ltd v Northland Regional Council* (unrep) (n 39); *Biomarine Ltd v Auckland Regional Council* A14/07 (unrep) (NZEnvC); and *Clifford Bay Farms Ltd v Marlborough District Council* (n 8).

or pollution of the oceans, a realm considered to be the last great unexplored frontier on earth. In *Clifford Bay*, the Court acknowledged that, 'our knowledge of the sea relative to terrestrial systems is extremely poor',[158] and in the New Zealand context, adaptive management was a direct response to resolving disputes about this relatively unknown environment.

The practice of adaptive management was first introduced to the Court through expert ecological evidence in cases such as *Kuku Mara (Forsyth Bay) v Marlborough District Council*.[159] Environmental scientists used adaptive management as a management technique in the field. But it was adopted and adapted as a legal remedy in the New Zealand context in *Golden Bay Marine Farmers v Tasman District Council*.[160] In *Golden Bay*, the Court accepted a staged approach for an aquaculture development would be appropriate due to the uncertain effects on coastal ecology, explicitly terming this an 'adaptive management' approach.[161] The Court order initially provided for the parties to develop this regime but they could not reach agreement and the Court was tasked with developing the detail, again emphasising the importance of a specialist bench and the merging of legal and scientific expertise in developing legal responses to the challenges of environmental problems. After synthesising the expert evidence, the Court laid down clear criteria for staged adaptive management in an order that included undertaking baseline assessments (to determine the state of the existing environment before development); a detailed management plan; collaboration, co-management and transparency (that includes monitoring, information gathering and establishing causal relationships, reporting, and feedback to a scientific panel – an 'Ecological Advisory Group' in the present case); identifying trigger events or unanticipated harm, and requiring the cessation of activities and restoration in that event; and providing for the parties to return to Court. The applicant was required to lodge financial bonds and the process was set out in legal conditions on the consent, providing a route for enforcement if necessary.[162]

In *Sustain Our Sounds Inc v New Zealand King Salmon Co*, the NZ Supreme Court endorsed the legal development of adaptive management by the NZEnvC and agreed that certain core features were important. For example, thresholds must be set in adaptive management regimes to trigger remedial action in the event of any harm becoming apparent.[163] The Supreme Court also confirmed

[158] *Clifford Bay Farms Ltd v Marlborough District Council* (n 8) [38]. Further, the aquaculture industry closes off the public commons for private interests and so attracts much opposition from wider members of the public, meaning that applications tend to be fully challenged before the Court.

[159] *Kuku Mara (Forsyth Bay) v Marlborough District Council* (n 12).

[160] *Golden Bay Marine Farmers v Tasman District Council (Second Interim Report)* (n 85); *Golden Bay Marine Farmers v Tasman District Council (Final Report)* (n 157).

[161] *Golden Bay Marine Farmers v Tasman District Council (Second Interim Report)* (n 85) [415].

[162] ibid, [406]–[422]; *Golden Bay Marine Farmers v Tasman District Council (Final Report)* (n 157) [98].

[163] *Sustain Our Sounds Inc v New Zealand King Salmon Company Ltd* (n 83) [108].

that adaptive management would not be appropriate if effects cannot be remedied before becoming irreversible.[164] Once again, we see the superior generalist courts stabilising in law the innovative practices developed by the Environment Court, in turn shoring up the legitimacy of the NZEnvC.

The NSWLEC has also developed an extensive jurisprudence in adaptive management.[165] In *Newcastle & Hunter Speleological Society Inc v Upper Hunter Shire Council*, the Court cautioned that 'adaptive management is not a "suck it and see", trial and error approach' to environmental management, rather it is 'an iterative approach involving explicit testing of the achievement of defined goals':

> Through feedback to the management process, the management procedures are changed in steps until monitoring shows that the desired outcome is obtained. The monitoring program has to be designed so that there is statistical confidence in the outcome. In adaptive management the goal to be achieved is set, so there is no uncertainty as to the outcome and conditions requiring adaptive management do not lack certainty, but rather they establish a regime which would permit changes, within defined parameters, to the way the outcome is achieved.[166]

The need to avoid a 'suck it and see' approach poses a conundrum with regard to baseline information. The courts require baseline studies of the existing environment upon which to construct adaptive management regimes[167] but there may be insufficient knowledge about a particular environment and no way to obtain the necessary data through external channels (for example, there may be no interest in or resources available from government or independent researchers). At times, the NZEnvC has required applicants to undertake and fund baseline studies before any consented-to activity could commence,[168] explaining that adaptive management regimes can enable research and knowledge about the ecosystem that might not otherwise be obtained.[169] This rationale takes environmental dispute-resolution far outside the confines of other litigious processes, but it makes sense as a response to the adjudicative challenges presented by environmental problems. And once again, we see clear evidence of the interactional theory at work.

This part of the chapter has looked at the complexity of adaptive management as a legal remedy in some detail because the cases show how expert scientific evidence has been translated into legal doctrine via the institutional setting. In terms of the interactional theory, the courts' response to

[164] ibid, [139]–[140].

[165] eg, *Telstra Corporation v Hornby Shire Council* (n 7); *Newcastle & Hunter Speleological Society Inc v Upper Hunter Shire Council* (n 12); *Port Stephens Pearls Pty Limited v Minister for Infrastructure and Planning* (n 76); *Ulan Coal Mines Ltd v Minister for Planning* [2008] NSWLEC 185; *Rivers SOS Inc v Minister for Planning* [2009] NSWLEC 213.

[166] *Newcastle & Hunter Speleological Society Inc v Upper Hunter Shire Council* (n 12) [184].

[167] *Clifford Bay Farms Ltd v Marlborough District Council* (n 8) [89] [136].

[168] ibid, [89], [136].

[169] ibid, [153]–[155].

environmental uncertainty shows a clear linkage between the four component parts of the theory: problem-challenge-response-institutional form. Moreover, the special institutional context – permitting the testing of evidence, close interrogation and oversight of environmental management mechanisms, and interaction between legal and scientific expertise – has enabled the NZEnvC in particular to play a wider role in environmental *governance*. For example, the legal tests crafted by the Court have been utilised by government in other regulatory regimes (for example, adaptive management remedies were included in the Exclusive Economic Zone (Environmental Effects) Act 2012)[170] and the Court has suggested amendments to government policy documents (that have application beyond court proceedings), in order to refine components of adaptive management regimes.[171] A similar feedback loop has occurred in the New South Wales context with adjudicative solutions to legal problems influencing the legislature. By way of example, in *Corkhill v Forestry Commission*[172] the NSWLEC found that the 'taking' of endangered species in the NPWA should also be triggered by habitat modification not just direct action (again, a view informed by the Court's knowledge of ecosystems) and this judgment led in part to the principal Act being amended.[173] Thus, we see a synergist process: court-created responses to environmental problems have in turn informed other branches of government that draft legislation accordingly. In validating the ECs' wider influence in norm-development, perhaps we 'find ourselves with a new and richer understanding of what we mean by "law"' in this context.[174] Law has been created through a three-way dialogue between the courts, scientific experts and the legislature.

The next part of the chapter provides another example of how the interactional theory works in practice, by considering the courts' response to the collective action nature of environmental problems. This issue is not explored in the same level of detail as the risk strand because its inclusion is to simply show that the theory can be tested in multiple ways. As explained at the outset, the courts have responded to this feature of environmental problems by facilitating access to justice in many ways, but an expansive approach to standing has not always been followed. This part focuses to a greater extent on those

[170] Exclusive Economic Zone and Continental Shelf (Environmental Effects) Act 2012 (NZ), s 64.

[171] *Crest Energy Kaipara Ltd v Northland Regional Council* (unrep) (n 39) [100]. The Court considered the explanation of adaptive management in the New Zealand Biodiversity Strategy, finding that '[w]e are inclined to the view that the definition in the Strategy might be deficient in a failure to focus on the need on such occasions for robust baseline monitoring.'

[172] *Corkhill v Forestry Commission* [1991] 73 LGERA 126 (NSWLEC); decision confirmed on appeal *Corkhill v Forestry Commission* [1991] 73 LGERA 247 (CA).

[173] P Stein, 'New directions in the prevention and resolution of environmental disputes – specialist environmental courts' (South-East Asian Regional Symposium on the Judiciary and the Law of Sustainable Development, Manila, 6 March 1999) [60]–[61], available at: www.lawlink.nsw.gov.au/sc/sc.nsf/pages/stein_2.

[174] D Trubek and L Trubek, 'Hard and Soft Law in the Construction of Social Europe: the Role of the Open Method of Co-ordination' (2005) 11 *European Law Journal* 344, 364.

disjuncts, ie, where practice has not always paralleled the interactional theory, and it suggests that there is scope for better alignment.

III. RESPONDING TO THE COLLECTIVE ACTION NATURE OF ENVIRONMENTAL PROBLEMS

Given that environmental effects can extend over space and time, the range of those impacted by particular uses of the environment may extend beyond a single respondent. Sometimes wide swathes of the present population and/or future generations may be impacted. Some have argued that the rule of law requires that those impacted by decisions – ie, the risk-bearers – must be involved in decision-making in some way, and that it is problematic if the only voices heard are those who benefit from imposing risks on others.[175] Within adjudication, this feature raises specific issues of *locus standi* and access to justice more generally.

Determining standing has traditionally been the preserve of the courts and the common law[176] but within legislative regimes governing planning law and the environment, party status can be prescribed and limited. English planning law provides a good example. While applicants are entitled to a merit appeals before the Planning Inspectorate, third parties can only appeal the legality of first-instance decisions via judicial review,[177] an approach that is said to reflect a strong emphasis on the preservation of property rights.[178] The legitimacy of restricting third-party appeal rights is the subject of much debate in the planning literature.[179] At its simplest, it represents a divergent cultural emphasis on the relative values of representative democracy (ie, community wellbeing is protected by the executive branch) versus participatory democracy;[180] an emphasis that

[175] B Fried, 'The Nonconsequentialist Approach to Torts' (2012) 18 *Legal Theory* 231; G Walker, *Environmental Justice: Concepts, Evidence and Politics* (Routledge, 2012) 49; see also D Beetham, *The Legitimation of Power*, 2nd edn (Political Analysis, 2013) 90: 'in denying the subordinate all independent means of expressing or defending their interests, there is nothing to stop it degenerating into the exercise of power in the interests merely of the powerful'.

[176] eg, P Cane, 'Open Standing and the Role of Courts in a Democratic Society' (1999) 23 *Singapore Law Review* 23, 35.

[177] Town and Country Planning Act 1990 (UK), s 78; and see R Duxbury, *Telling and Duxbury's Planning Law and Procedure*, 15th edn (Oxford University Press, 2012) 449–51.

[178] C Armeni and H Tegner Anker, 'Public participation and appeal rights in decision-making on wind energy infrastructure: a comparative analysis of the Danish and English legal framework' (2020) 63 *Journal of Environmental Planning & Management* 842, 845.

[179] ibid; JP Clinch, 'Third Party Rights of Appeal: Enhancing Democracy or Hindering Progress?' (2006) 7 *Planning Theory & Practice* 327; M Purdue, 'The Case for Third Party Planning Appeals' (2001) 3 *Environmental Law Review* 83; C Towns, 'The Right of Third Party Appeal in New Zealand Land-use Planning: An Outsider's Perspective' (2006) 10 *New Zealand Journal of Environmental Law* 329; S Willey, 'Planning Appeals: Are Third Party Rights Legitimate? The Case Study of Victoria, Australia' (2006) 24 *Urban Policy and Research* 369.

[180] C Warnock, 'Differing conceptions of environmental democracy in New Zealand resource management law' (2016) 31 *Australian Environment Review* 253.

can be influenced by (and indeed influence) public trust in government.[181] More recently, academics have questioned whether it is possible to justify this dichotomy other than on a purely pragmatic basis,[182] and have provided empirical evidence to support the argument that expanding third-party appeal rights leads to better environmental decision-making.[183]

Access to the NSWLEC and NZEnvC is in large part regulated by statute too, albeit appeal rights are significantly wider than in the UK context. In New Zealand, parties who were involved with a dispute at first instance have a right to be joined as parties to any merits appeal and others may be joined with the leave of the Court.[184] Under the New South Wales EPAA a similar approach exists, and appeals against development consents may be made by objectors who submitted at first-instance level.[185] Further, the EPAA provides that 'any person may bring proceedings in the Court for an order to remedy or restrain a breach of this Act, whether or not any right of that person has been infringed by or as a consequence of that breach',[186] allowing any person to ensure public rights and duties are complied with. Similar open-standing provisions exist in other NSW statutes such as the Heritage Act 1977, Fisheries Management Act 1994, Wilderness Act 1987, and Protection of the Environment Operations Act 1997.[187] Arguments from counsel that these open-standing 'restraint' provisions should be interpreted narrowly were rejected by the NSWLEC and NSW Court of Appeal,[188] and older restrictive common law cases such as *Australian Conservation Foundation Inc v Commonwealth of Australia*[189] (that has been described as 'posing an intellectual problem' by a previous Chief Justice,[190] distinguished in many lower courts decisions,[191] and led in part to the legislative intervention) were not followed by the NSW courts.[192] The Court has enabled

[181] eg, the 2020 International Society of Public Law Annual Conference 'Public Law (Dis)Trust and Dissent', University of Wroclaw, Poland (postponed to 2021) explored the idea that governments who allow dissent foster trust.

[182] eg, E Buitelaar, M Galle and W Salet, 'Third-party appeal rights and the regulatory state: Understanding the reduction of planning appeal options' (2013) 35 *Land Use Policy* 312.

[183] eg, M Figg, 'Protecting third party rights of appeal, protecting the environment: A Tasmanian case study' (2014) 31 *Environmental and Planning Law Journal* 210.

[184] RMA, ss 273, 274.

[185] EPAA, s 8.8 (previously s 98); other parties can be joined under s 8.25.

[186] EPAA, s 9.45 (previously s 123).

[187] Heritage Act 1977 (NSW), s 153; Fisheries Management Act 1994 (NSW), s 282; Wilderness Act 1987 (NSW), s 27; Protection of the Environment Operations Act 1997 (NSW), s 252.

[188] eg, *Rowley v New South Wales Leather and Trading Co Pty Ltd and Woolahra Municipal Council* (1980) 46 LGRA 250 (NSWLEC); *Building Owners and Managers Association of Australia Ltd v Sydney City Council* (1985) 55 LGRA 444 (NSWLEC); see also P McClellan, 'Access to Justice in Environmental Law – An Australian Perspective' (Commonwealth Law Conference, London, 11–15 September 2005).

[189] *Australian Conservation Foundation Inc v Commonwealth of Australia* (1981) 146 CLR 493 (AHC).

[190] McClellan, 'Access to Justice in Environmental Law – An Australian Perspective' (n 188) 2.

[191] ibid, 3–6.

[192] ibid, 6–7.

parties to be joined so as to 'inform itself' on matters.[193] In *Maritime Services Board of New South Wales v Citizens Airport Environment Association Inc*, the NSW Court of Appeal observed that the open-standing provisions 'reflect the high social importance of protecting the environment by the processes of law'[194] and as a result, the NSWLEC has been described by the Chief Justice as playing a role in administering 'social justice … a task that travels far beyond administering justice inter partes'.[195]

However, jurists noted that despite these legislative provisions significant procedural hurdles remained to increasing access to environmental justice, such as the possibility of punitive costs orders and litigious complexity.[196] Both the NSWLEC and NZEnvC have demonstrated ways to overcome these procedural hurdles where possible.[197] For example, they have protected public interest litigants from costs orders,[198] capped costs,[199] have excused the necessity for undertakings as to damages in injunctive proceedings[200] or declined to order security for costs,[201] and justified such decisions by the need to encourage actions aimed at protecting the environment. The courts have facilitated the involvement of unrepresented parties by providing for 'submitters' friends' (who help multiple, unrepresented parties to manage the litigious process);[202] court appointed experts;[203] simplified pleadings and technology-based processes (to ease the filing and management of applications and evidence);[204] a roaming court (that travels to the site of the dispute);[205] and alternative dispute-resolution processes.[206] All these doctrinal and procedural approaches recognise

[193] *Double Bay Marina Pty Ltd v Woollahra Municiple Council* (1985) 54 LGRA 313, 314–15 (NSWLEC).

[194] *Maritime Services Board of New South Wales v Citizens Airport Environment Association Inc* (1993) 83 LGERA 107, 111 (NSWCA).

[195] *F Hannan Pty Ltd v Electricity Commission of New South Wales [No 3]* (n 5) [59].

[196] Stein, 'Specialist Environment Courts' (n 76) 10.

[197] For an overview of costs orders in the Australian climate change context see N Pain and R Pepper, 'Legal Costs Considerations in Public Interest Climate Change Litigation' (2019) 30 *King's Law Journal* 211.

[198] eg, *Oshlack v Richmond River Shire Council* (1994) 82 LGERA 236 (NSWLEC), upheld on appeal *Oshlack v Richmond River Shire Council* (1998) 163 CLR 72 (HCA).

[199] *Blue Mountains Conservation Society Inc v Delta Electricity (Blue Mountains)* (2009) 170 LGERA 1 (NSWLEC).

[200] eg, *Walden v Auckland City Council* [1992] 1 NZRMA 101, 103 (NZEnvC).

[201] eg, *Mahanga E Tu Inc v Hawkes Bay Regional Council* [2011] NZEnvC 21, [14]; *Byron Shire Businesses for the Future Inc v Byron Shire Council* (1994) 83 LGERA 59 (NSWLEC).

[202] eg, New Zealand Environment Court, *Practice Note 2014* (2014), [3.2].

[203] eg, RMA, s 259; and see *Telstra Corporation v Hornby Shire Council* (n 7) for an example from NSW.

[204] eg, NZ Environment Court, *Practice Note 2014* (2014), [Appendix 1]; the NSWLEC has an 'Online Court', see, eg, NSW Land and Environment Court, *Practice Note Class 1 Development Appeals* (NSW, 2018), [40].

[205] eg, NZ Environment Court, *Practice Note 2014* (2014), [6.4]; LECA, s 34A–D.

[206] eg, NZ Environment Court, *Practice Note 2014* (2014), [5.1]; Land and Environment Court, *Practice Note Class 1 Development Appeals* (n 204), [46].

and respond to the nature of environmental problems as impacting many different people.

However, the NZEnvC has not always responded expansively to the collective action nature of environmental problems, and has at times drawn back to more traditional thinking and doctrine developed in other contexts.[207] Under section 274(1)(da) of the RMA, the Court has the power to grant standing to non-submitters[208] if they have an interest in the proceedings 'greater than the interest the general public has',[209] and the NZEnvC has interpreted the statutory wording narrowly. *Purification Technologies Ltd v Taupo District Council*[210] sets out the general test. Adding a gloss to the statutory wording, the Court in *Purification* found there must be 'some advantage or disadvantage, such as that arising from a right in property, directly affected which is not remote' and opined that economic impacts would demonstrate a 'quality of interest' while general concern for the environment would not:

> We also hold that an interest in proceedings in seeking to enforce the public law as a matter of principle, a belief that activity of a particular kind ought to be prevented, or as part of an endeavour to achieve the objects of an association, or uphold the values which it was formed to promote, would not be an interest in the proceedings greater than that of the public generally. Nor would an interest in the preservation of a particular environment, or an intellectual or emotional concern, the satisfaction of righting a wrong, an interest in upholding a principle, a sense of grievance or the risk of being ordered to pay costs.[211]

The Court refused to join Greenpeace, Friends of the Earth, or Mangakino Concerned Citizens Inc, a group of residents who would be 'living with the risk', to an appeal concerning the development of an irradiation plant.[212] In its reasoning, the Court drew heavily on cases from other jurisdictions (often decided in very different contexts),[213] and directly imported wording into the

[207] *Purification Technologies Ltd v Taupo District Council* [1995] NZRMA 197 (PT).

[208] ie, those who did not make submissions at the local council stage but want to become parties to an appeal before the Court. Submitters to the first-stage dispute before the local authority are automatically granted standing in the appeal to the NZEnvC (RMA s 274(1)(e)).

[209] Note the wording of s 274(1)(d) changed in 2013 and it was renumbered s 274 (1)(da). It previously read: an interest in the proceedings 'greater than general public'. Different divisions of the Court disagree as to the impact: eg, *Genera Ltd v Bay of Plenty Regional Council* [2018] NZEnvC 171, [12] (the change in wording does not require a different approach to previous case law); *cf Treble Tree Holdings Ltd v Marlborough District Council* [2012] NZEnvC 88, [5] ('the new wording in the Simplifying Act is arguably a dilution of the previous test. The interest of the general public is often apathetic').

[210] *Purification Technologies Ltd v Taupo District Council* (n 207).

[211] ibid, 204.

[212] ibid, 209.

[213] ibid, the Court drew on cases from Australia, Canada and the US, such as *Re McHatton and Collector of Customs* (1977) 18 ALR 154 (whether customs agent gave correct advice); *QIW Retailers v David Holdings* (1992) 109 ALR 377 (contravention of trade practices); *Re Control Investment and Australian Broadcasting Tribunal (No 1)* (1980) 3 ALD 74 (review of a decision refusing acquisition of shares in a media company); *Empire Gas & Fuel Co v Railroad Commission of Texas*

test from *Australian Conservation Foundation v Commonwealth of Australia*[214] that as I explained above had proved problematic and led to legislative intervention in the NSW context. The Court also drew on an *absence* of statutory text (the fact that the criteria, 'any body or person representing some relevant aspect of the public interest' was not included in section 274 of the RMA as it had been in previous Town and Country Planning Acts)[215] to justify a narrow interpretative approach, and noted 'Parliament's evident intent to restrict the classes of persons entitled to appear and call evidence in proceedings'.[216] It opined that its discretion was curtailed 'even if [the Planning Tribunal] considers that the statutory purpose, or the interests of justice would be advanced by considering submissions or evidence' from other people.[217]

One way to conceive of *Purification* is that it situates the Court neatly within a 'pure' separation of powers frame and underscores legal formalism. That is certainly the argument proffered by the Court – it is just following Parliament's direction. But the fact that the Court added a gloss to the test suggests otherwise. More interesting still is the fact that in its reasoning the Court conflated 'greater interest' with those who might be directly affected in some tangible way (property or economic interests, for example). In doing so, the Court reveals a marked preference for Dryzek's economic rationalism discourse. As Dryzek explains:

> Notably missing from economic rationalism are citizens ... environments do not exist in any strong sense. At most 'the environment' is only a pathway for some human decisions to have effects on other people ... The existence of ecosystems, let alone ecosystems that often defy understanding, cut across chunks of private property, and impose constraints on human activity, is not perceived. There is no such thing as wilderness.[218]

The highly restrictive[219] *Purification* test was endorsed by the High Court[220] and followed in many cases, often being used to confine standing to individuals with

90 So West Rep (2d) 1240 (1936) (gas leases in 1930s America); *Australian Conservation Foundation Inc v Commonwealth of Australia* (n 189) (whether a Federation had standing to challenge the validity of government action without the Attorney General being a party).

[214] *Australian Conservation Foundation Inc v Commonwealth of Australia* (n 189).

[215] eg, Town and Country Planning Act 1977 (NZ) (TCPA), s 2(3)(d).

[216] *Purification Technologies Ltd v Taupo District Council* (n 207) 204. Of course, interpreted literally the RMA s 274(1)(d) test ('interest greater than the public') could encompass the TCPA test ('body or person representing some relevant aspect of the public interest').

[217] ibid, 199.

[218] Dryzek (n 156) 133.

[219] Described in *Treble Tree Holdings Ltd v Marlborough District Council* (n 209) [20] as 'very rigorous. It does not even allow for a combination of the elements to meet a test. So, if a person is interested in preserving a particular environment, and has intellectual and emotional concerns about the proceeding, and is upholding a principle in the RMA, it appears that combination is not sufficient to bring him or her under section 274(1)(d) of the RMA'.

[220] *Ngatiwai Trust Board v New Zealand Historic Places* Trust [1998] NZRMA 1, 10 (HC); *Meadow 3 Limited v van Brandenberg* [2008] NZHC 830, [34].

adversely impacted property[221] or business interests[222] and to exclude representative groups.[223] Given there is no public environmental defenders office in New Zealand (*cf* NSW), nor any other formal system for guardians ad litem to represent nature in litigation, this exclusion is troubling. Scholars have criticised these cases because individuals tend to lack the resources or the skills of dedicated public interest groups, making the information and arguments placed before the Court all the poorer.[224]

More recently however, there has been a loosening of the test in certain divisions of the Court. In *Lindsay v Dunedin City Council*[225] the Court expressly disagreed with *Purification* and found the exclusion of representative groups 'as part of an endeavour to achieve the objects of an association' to be an overgeneralisation: it depended on what the objectives of the organisation were. The Court found that an association with a specific interest which can be clearly defined and identified is more likely to qualify.[226] Nevertheless, even the more liberal cases demonstrate that in order to be granted standing groups have to show a very specific interest in the relevant environment through their objectives of corporation.[227] For example, in *Sandspit Yacht Club Marina Society Inc v Auckland Regional Council*,[228] an Incorporated Society that had been set up to maintain and enhance public access to the islands in the Hauraki Gulf was refused section 274 status in relation to a proposed marina development on a nearby spit on the mainland, as the constitutional objectives of the Society

[221] Despite the Court routinely stating property interest are not a prerequisite for standing, most s 274(1)(d)/(da) status appears founded on property interests, eg, *Answer Service Holdings Ltd v Auckland City Council* [2010] NZEnv C142 [34]; *Meadow 3 Limited v Van Brandenberg* (n 209) (adverse visual impact from property founded s 274 status); *Mt Christina Ltd v Queenstown Lakes District Council* [2018] NZEnvC 190.

[222] eg, *Aratiatia Livestock Ltd v Southland Regional Council* [2018] NZEnvC 218, [16] (farmers granted standing – 'water is an essential constraint on and enabler of agricultural production and ultimately, business profitability, resilience and value'); *West Coast ENT Inc v Buller District Council* [2010] NZEnvC 332.

[223] eg, *Genera Ltd v Bay of Plenty Regional Council* (n 209) (health action group concerned with methyl bromide use whose members were local residents refused standing in a resource consent application that included the use of methyl bromide); *Toomey v Thames-Coromandel District Council* [2017] NZEnvC 199 (Coromandel Watchdog formed in opposition to open cast coal mining on the Coromandel refused standing in plan change application impacting the natural character of the Coromandel coast); *Water and Environmental Care Association Inc v Manawatu-Wanganui Regional Council* [2012] NZEnvC 217 (an active interest in the good workings of the resource management system and regular participation in community planning processes was insufficient to found *locus standi*).

[224] S Nolan, 'Affected persons under the Resource Management Act 1991' (2007) 13 *Canterbury Law Review* 120; see also E Mok, 'No leg to stand on: a critique of s 274 of the Resource Management Act 1991' (2014) 10 *Butterworths Resource Management Bulletin* 153.

[225] *Lindsay v Dunedin City Council* [2013] NZEnvC 302, [11].

[226] ibid, [18]. See also *Trustees of the Neville Crawford Family Trust v Far North District Council* [2013] NZEnvC 141 (Russell Protection Society Inc had a specific interest in Russell and development in the area –granted standing).

[227] *Lindsay v Dunedin City Council* (n 225).

[228] *Sandspit Yacht Club Marina Society Inc v Auckland Council* [2011] NZEnvC 25.

and the application were deemed to be too legally remote. In other cases, local community groups demonstrating a clear and specific interest in a particular environment have been granted standing but had their involvement curtailed. For example, the Court limited the involvement of a community group, Keep Okura Green Inc, in proceedings related to the Okura Estuary to issues that directly related to the objectives listed in their constitution, ie, preventing river sediment and siltation.[229]

Other cases have challenged the *Purification* exclusion of 'intellectual interests'.[230] In *Treble Tree Holdings Ltd v Marlborough District Council*,[231] the Court granted standing to a scientist with expertise relating to the endangered King Shag stating:

> 'Intellectual' is used [in *Purification*] with a pejorative whiff: it suggests 'academic', 'non-practical', and 'not engaging in the real world' … Are practical scientific researchers – people who carry out painstaking, mind and body numbing data collection and research in the open air and waters of New Zealand – mere 'intellectuals' in the *Purification Technologies* sense? I consider they are not: scientists should be accorded more respect than that, at least when it comes to giving them status to appear. Robust scientific evidence is about the best evidence a court can ever hope for … It often takes a researcher to recognise what others (especially applicants who do not want to see) cannot and so it becomes important to leave open the door for such persons.[232]

Te Rūnanga O Ngāti Awa v Bay of Plenty Regional Council[233] followed suit. In that case, people with special customary knowledge were granted standing. In *Federated Farmers of New Zealand Inc Mackenzie Branch v Mackenzie District Council*[234] the Court joined two public interest societies, the Environmental Defence Society and Mackenzie Guardians Inc, to a plan change concerning the outstanding natural landscape of the Mackenzie Basin, noting their participation would ensure evidence on ecological issues was adduced and they would give 'adjudicative assistance' to the Court.[235] A feature in all these cases is the assistance that the Court would derive from joining the party. In these cases one senses the Court's image of itself as a problem-solving body informing the legal analysis, again suggesting the influence of conceptual frames.

Overall however, the standing cases are surprising for a number of reasons. First, the legislative text could bear a wider meaning – 'interest' could be interpreted more expansively to include those with a demonstrated commitment

[229] *Schippers Cleanfill Ltd v Auckland Council* [2011] NZEnvC 74.

[230] *Purification Technologies Ltd v Taupo District Council* (n 207) 204.

[231] *Treble Tree Holdings Ltd v Marlborough District Council* (n 209).

[232] ibid, [25].

[233] *Te Rūnanga O Ngāti Awa v Bay of Plenty Regional Council* [2018] NZEnvC 169.

[234] *Federated Farmers of New Zealand Inc Mackenzie Branch v Mackenzie District Council* [2016] NZEnvC 80.

[235] ibid, [35], [42]. (This factor seemed particularly important as the District Council in the case was small and had limited resources.)

to environmental conservation[236] – and the narrow interpretative approach adopted is at odds with the general approach of the NZEnvC to encouraging access to environmental justice (see the innovations described above). The cases are also at odds with New Zealand case law in other areas of public law, for example, in judicial review where the High Court has more or less done away with restrictive standing rules.[237] Nor do they align with approaches developed in other ECs such as the NSWLEC,[238] or the global trajectory in environmental law over the last 30 years, where public participation has been promoted wherever possible.[239] Better environmental decision-making is said to flow from increased participation because it results in the receipt of fuller information (including potential effects); enables decision-makers to better determine the 'public interest', particularly in relation to discrete, localised, or novel issues; gives substance to legal principles; legitimises decisions and reduces possible future challenges.[240] When decision-makers have to determine disputes against a legal backdrop characterised by contestable principles and incommensurate values, participation becomes increasingly critical. Because environmental problems are collective action problems, a wider approach to *locus standi* is seen to be justified and the Victorian ideology that affected persons primarily constitute those with property rights that can in turn show economic damage really has no place in modern understandings of environmental law.[241] Most interestingly, however, the cases are at odds with each other.[242] The rarefied formalism evident in *Purification* is hard to reconcile with the 'getting-to-the-truth-of-the-matter' approach in *Treble Tree*, a robust approach that perhaps better reflects the sustainable management purpose of the governing Act.

Of course, pragmatists will point to the administrative burden of allowing all-comers a voice, but that is a concern for government resourcing not legal reasoning. Perhaps the best way for courts to reconcile the theory for

[236] A more expansive definition along these lines would not render the provision meaningless, as the Court has sometimes feared. By analogy with *Treble Tree Holdings Ltd v Marlborough District Council* (n 209) the Court could require evidence of conservation action rather than just intention.

[237] *Great Christchurch Buildings Trust v Church Property Trustees* [2012] NZHC 3045.

[238] McClellan (n 188).

[239] A point reflected in numerous scholarly contributions, national and international treaty law, and some judicial opinions in the higher courts in NZ, see, eg: *Murray v Whakatane District Council* [1999] 3 NZLR 276, 281, 283, 284 (HC); *King v Auckland City Council* [2000] NZRMA 145 (CA); *Westfield (New Zealand) Ltd v North Shore City Council* [2005] 2 NZLR 597 (NZSC), [10], [25]–[27], [45]–[46], [105], [145].

[240] P McAuslan, *The Ideologies of Planning Law* (Pergamon Press, 1980), ch 1.

[241] For a counter-argument that justifies more restrictive standing rules as a way to preserve the separation of powers see Cane, 'Open Standing and the Role of Courts in a Democratic Society' (n 176).

[242] For another example of variance, compare *Genera Ltd v Bay of Plenty Regional Council* (n 209) [19] ('the threshold of interest in relation to a [plan change] is likely to be lower') with *Mt Christina Ltd v Queenstown Lakes District Council* (n 221) (in plan changes one would expect the general public to have a high interest in the matter, accordingly the applicant has an even higher hurdle to cross).

environmental adjudication and *locus* decisions is to employ the principle of legality: regarding access to environmental justice as a fundamental right to be preserved in the absence of explicit statutory language to the contrary, and so requiring 'Parliament to squarely confront what it is doing and accept the political cost'.[243]

IV. TESTING THE THEORY

This chapter has analysed two strands of jurisprudence in the NSWLEC and NZEnvC in order to test the interactional theory in practice and show the linkages between the four component parts of the theory (that are: (1) the inherent nature of environmental problems; (2) the challenges these features present for traditional forms of adjudication; (3) the need for legal reasoning to respond appropriately; and (4) the advantages provided by particular adjudicative forms and functions). In particular, it has analysed the third and fourth components of the theory, ie, the development of responsive doctrine and the contribution that particular institutional form and functions make to those developments. The results show some variance.

In terms of *locus standi* in the NZEnvC, the cases jar with the interactional theory by providing an example of where the Court has *not* always responded to the nature of environmental problems when it had the opportunity to do so. If the NZEnvC had been able to draw on the normative framework created by the interactional theory the cases may well have been framed in a different light. Certainly, a greater range of environmental interests could have been acknowledged and accommodated by the Court, but most importantly the use of a uniform frame may have promoted greater coherence. In terms of my argument and the methodological approach that I have taken to theory building, the discussion on standing cases in the NZEnvC is particularly valuable. As actual practice has not *always* accorded with the interactional approach suggested by the theory, this disjunct shows that my theory building is not just expository, masquerading as normative. Rather, the New Zealand *locus standi* cases serve as a critical foil against which to assess the interactional theory.

In terms of the risk strand, the interactional theory is well illustrated in the jurisprudence. The case law developed by the courts responds well to the inherent features of environmental problems, in turn promoting adjudicative integrity. Analysing this jurisprudence tells us that the legal nature of adjudicatory institutions is important because it impacts legal reasoning. Specialist environment courts are an infusion of the traditionally conceived legal and non-legal;[244] these

[243] *R v Secretary of State for the Home Department, Ex parte Simms* [2000] 2 AC 115, 131 (UKHL).

[244] A more general observation is that studying the jurisprudence from ECs forces us to re-evaluate binary structures that silo tribunal-type justice from legal reasoning and exclude decisions in

institutions enable environmental adjudication to respond to the nature of problems themselves, and through these institutional forms, environmental problems have (at times) created normative force on the law. A further critical point is that these jurisprudential developments have taken place with extremely limited guidance from the regulatory regime, and to this extent, the courts are contributing detail to the normative frame for legitimacy themselves.

Finally, it is important to note, that this chapter provides two illustrations of how the interactional theory works in practice but testing the theory can be conducted in many other ways. One could, for example, analyse how ECs have responded to the inherent nature of environmental problems by exploring how the courts have addressed the polycentricity of environmental problems through the admissibility and evaluation of various forms of knowledge in evidence; analysing ECs' interpretation of principles and standards in environmental legal instruments, and their approach to the content of and interactions between different types of legal instruments in environmental law;[245] assessing their response to the various facets of environmental justice, such as distributive justice;[246] considering how they have gone beyond positivist state law to draw on indigenous, customary law thereby drawing on an expanded range of legal principles; mapping how enforcement actions have morphed; or scrutinising more closely the interaction of legal and non-legal expertise in the development of legal reasoning in environmental dispute resolution.[247] Exploring and testing the jurisprudence in these ways would help to construct a more comprehensive frame for normative legitimacy. I cannot fill in the frame in its entirety in this book, but it can undoubtedly be done.

merits review from having legal force (see for example, R Craig, 'Black Spiders Weaving Webs: The Constitutional Implications of Executive Veto of Tribunal Determinations' (2016) 79 *MLR* 166). Siloed-thinking perceives (and is comforted by) a sharp division between the legal character of courts and non-legal administrative decision-making, erecting barriers between fact-finding and the application of the law to those facts once they are found.

[245] T Hester, 'Green statutory interpretation by environmental courts and tribunals' (2017) 29 *Environmental Law & Management* 92; Scotford (n 9).

[246] *Gloucester Resources Ltd v Minister for Planning* (n 14) [398].

[247] An exercise already undertaken in the context of the Indian National Green Tribunal: see GN Gill, *Environmental Justice in India: The National Green Tribunal* (Routledge, 2016).

7

Conclusion

IN THE INTRODUCTORY chapter of this book, I invited readers to suspend their judgement until the end. Now I can remake the argument that we need a new theory explaining environmental adjudication with greater force. This last chapter assembles core findings from the research, provides a synopsis of the interactional theory, makes suggestions as to potential uses of that theory, and identifies remaining issues.

My original enquiry into environmental adjudication was prompted by two discordant phenomena. The first concerns the exponential growth in specialist environment courts worldwide – a development accompanied by a large body of literature that overwhelmingly promotes environmental courts (ECs) as a 'good thing' but lacked any conceptual underpinnings for that position. The second concerns the criticisms by ministers, policymakers and scholars about the specialist Environment Court of New Zealand (NZEnvC) – criticisms that were echoed in debates about the New South Wales Land and Environment Court (NSWLEC), and that led to proposals to abolish, reform or downgrade those courts. The conflict between these two lines of thought becomes even more pronounced when one considers the esteem afforded to the NZEnvC and NSWLEC in the international literature: both courts are identified as role models for other jurisdictions to follow.[1] It would be easy to dismiss this tension as simply reflecting differing political ideologies, but my analysis shows that conflict was occurring because specialist environmental adjudication has no theoretical underpinnings.

I. FINDINGS

Attempting to understand the various discourses surrounding ECs led to five main findings. First, many ECs can be conceived of as an important part of environmental governance in their nations. Thinking about their de facto roles illustrates this point. As I have explained in this book, ECs are often asked to

[1] M Grant, *Environmental Court Project: Final Report* (DETR, 2000); G Pring and C Pring, *Greening Justice: Creating and Improving Environmental Courts and Tribunals* (World Resources Institute, 2009).

resolve problems that have multiple causes and impacts, involving a wide range of actors and those impacted upon, and as a result they undertake polycentric decision-making; they may oversee participatory and consultative processes that have the effect of creating structures for construing the law while simultaneously giving substantive content to the law; they are frequently required to make predictions about the future as opposed to fact-finding in relation to the past; disputes may concern 'the commons' or public resources but can also impact individual rights, including property rights, and so decisions may have redistributive force or allocate risk-burdens and address normative conflicts. Moreover, the decisions of ECs cumulatively have significant impact upon future environmental, economic and socio-cultural conditions in their nations and further afield. The mapping exercise in chapter two shows that ECs tend to be multifunctional bodies with flexible powers, enabling them to achieve creative solutions to environmental disputes. Yet many are independent judicial bodies. Accordingly, their legal form combined with their de facto role raises complex issues about adjudication, governance, constitutionalism and legitimacy. My work reconciles the associations between these practices, structures and ideas in the context of environmental adjudication.

Second, debates about ECs centre on the legitimacy (or more commonly, illegitimacy) of particular adjudicative forms, functions, powers and responsibilities, but properly understood those debates are concerned with *normative* legitimacy. Chapter three explained legitimacy as a multidimensional concept. Analysis of the debates concerning the NZEnvC and NSWLEC revealed that while these institutions have so-called legal validity (ie, they were created by and are operating in accordance with legislation enacted by Parliament) and that citizens tend to comply with their authority (ie, aspects of recognition exist), normative legitimacy is lacking. Normative legitimacy means that the acquisition and exercise of authority is well grounded in the shared beliefs of the relevant population.[2]

Third, in order to capture shared beliefs and address normative legitimacy, we are drawn into sketching frames. Conceptual frames are models that help make sense of complex phenomenon: they are often unacknowledged by those who draw upon them to make arguments but they play a significant role in influencing thinking. Frames can be superficially simple (taking the form of metaphors, like the 'separation of powers') or more detailed with their internal structures better articulated (like Chayes' conception of public law litigation).[3] The analysis in chapter three revealed that the use of different conceptual frames of normative legitimacy was a major reason for the discord surrounding the NZEnvC and NSWLEC. Participants in the debates were talking across each other because they were drawing on different frames of reference that were (often) hidden,

[2] D Beetham, *The Legitimation of Power*, 2nd edn (Political Analysis, 2013) ch 3.
[3] A Chayes, 'The Role of the Judge in Public Law Litigation' (1975) 89 *Harvard Law Review* 1281.

pervasive and contestable. Three main conceptual frames were being used in the debates about the courts: the 'administrative justice and legal pluralism' frame; a frame based on 'generic instrumentalism'; and a final frame premised upon a 'pure conception of the separation of powers'. Commentators were using these frames to argue for the normative legitimacy of particular adjudicative forms and functions. That is, frames were being used to set the parameters for debate about the courts' legal nature.

Fourth, as the analysis in chapter three showed, the frames being employed in the debates about the NZEnvC and NSWLEC failed to make sense of specialist environmental adjudication. Each of the frames had particular weaknesses. The 'administrative justice-adjudicative pluralism' frame was poor at establishing limits. The 'generic instrumentalism' frame did little to help explain or constitute the discrete legal nature of ECs. And a pure 'separation of powers' frame, was unable to address the challenges created for adjudication by the very nature of environmental problems. As I explained in chapter three, the inherent nature of environmental problems has created a particular legal context for environmental adjudication to operate in, one in which the lines between law, policy, discretion and fact are often blurred and one which a pure separation of powers frame struggles to accommodate. Fundamentally none of the frames were able to set parameters for constituting, empowering and limiting ECs, either in isolation or in combination with the others, while also preserving their ability to adjudicate over environmental disputes.

Fifth, in order to illuminate the literature on environmental adjudication and to foster more productive discussions about ECs, the analysis concluded that we need to construct a new frame for normative legitimacy. In order to cross present divides, a new frame would have to rise above political ideologies; contestable moral stances, beliefs or goals that would result in an instrumentalist approach to environmental adjudication; and particular versions of constitutionalism.

II. DEVELOPING THE THEORY

Those five findings led naturally to the following question: how can we construct a normative frame of legitimacy for environmental adjudication? That question raised both methodological and substantive challenges. Substantively, any valid frame would need to reflect shared beliefs and so (somewhat paradoxically) needed to be neutral and objective. Methodologically, the challenge was to identify a valid process through which to develop the frame.

In addressing those challenges, it helped to identify the premises and preoccupations identified in the frames being employed at present. The use of the 'administrative justice-adjudicative pluralism' frame demonstrated that a frame for environmental adjudication must acknowledge the relationship between the inherent nature of the problem adjudicators are seeking to resolve and the legal nature of the adjudicatory body. The use of the 'generic instrumentalism frame' illustrated that adjudicative efficiency is important. Developing a frame capable of common acceptance would help promote efficiency. It would avoid commentators returning constantly to squabble about essential underpinnings, or subjecting ECs to the futile loop of reforms and reversals. And it would enable a progressive dialogue to take place about ECs, one that accepted the inevitability of legal disputes about the environment and focused on refining an adjudicative method to best address those disputes. Finally, the use of the pure 'separation of powers' frame established both that conceptual limits are critical – a frame needs to be established that the form, functions and powers of ECs can be referable back to, thus helping to constitute and constrain the legal nature of the body – and a frame must also be based on a theory with much deeper legal resonance. Few would disagree with the fundamental aim of the separation of powers, that is the avoidance of despotism. Accordingly, a frame premised on a core social purpose with universal appeal will foster normative legitimacy.

That last point – ie, the need to identify the essential foundation that would attract substantial agreement, became the basis for theory building. In thinking about adjudication more generally, what can we agree on? What constitutes a shared understanding about adjudication? Chapter four deconstructed the concept and practice of adjudication in order to address that question. The answer proposed was that adjudication must have integrity, and to have integrity adjudication must be both constrained *and* responsive to the inherent nature of the problems it is tasked with resolving (both legal and factual) rather than ignoring that nature.

From this core essence of integrity and responsiveness, it became possible to develop the interactional theory. In the context of environmental adjudication, the interactional theory is premised upon the response, or more accurately the interaction between four components: (1) identifying the distinct characteristics of environmental problems; (2) acknowledging the commensurate challenges for law and dispute resolution that this nature poses; (3) developing environmental law principles, procedures and remedies that respond to rather than ignoring that nature; and (4) understanding how each of the preceding developments will be facilitated by particular adjudicative forms, functions and powers. Critically, the interactional process must start from the bottom up by identifying the inherent and immutable features of environmental problems, deducing how these features will impact law and adjudication, and then considering how legal reasoning in adjudication might respond to these challenges and how particular adjudicative forms and functions will facilitate that process. Addressing each of those components in detail will enable a more robust frame for environmental adjudication to be constructed. Thus, the theory developed in this book does two main things: it helps set the parameters for debate about ECs; and it enables the construction of a more detailed frame that establishes an exemplar for environmental adjudication.

III. FILLING IN THE FRAME

Chapters three, five and six each contribute detail that helps to build the frame for environmental adjudication. In essence, the internal components of the frame are premised upon Chayes' morphology of public law adjudication that I described in chapter three:

> [T]he party structure is not rigidly bilateral but sprawling and amorphous ... the fact inquiry is not historical and adjudicative but predictive and legislative ... [relief is] flexible ... having important consequences for many persons including absentees ... [and] requires the continuing participation of the court ... the judge is active, with responsibility not only for credible fact evaluation but for organizing and shaping the litigation to ensure a just and viable outcome.[4]

However, using the interactional theory enables a much thicker and more contextually based description to accrue. Chapter three demonstrated that the inherent nature of environmental problems has impacted the legal context within which adjudicators must work, and it noted the correlative impact on interpretative methodology.

Chapter five is an exercise in deductive reasoning. It identified two inherent features of environmental problems that environmental adjudication must respond to in order to have integrity – 'interaction and change' – and a third characteristic feature – 'uncertainty' (while acknowledging that there are inevitably more). In particular, it considered how the theory might impact legal reasoning in the fact-finding process, leading to the development of particular doctrine, procedural responses and remedies, and how particular adjudicative forms and functions can facilitate those developments.

Chapter six acted as a critical foil, testing the theory against actual practice in the NZEnvC and NSWLEC, and in that sense it employs inductive reasoning to bolster the theory. It draws on two strands of jurisprudence to illustrate the links between the four component parts of the theory and begin the process of constructing a detailed frame. The first strand that I traced addresses risk. In relation to the first and second components of the theory, the inherent features of environmental problems – interaction, change and uncertainty – create particular challenges for traditional forms of adjudication because the facts upon which to apply the law are often not fully known or stable. In relation to the third component of the theory, the legal reasoning of the NSWLEC and NZEnvC responded to this challenge by developing doctrine – ie, the precautionary principle (or 'precautionary approach' in the New Zealand context); different ways to test and evaluate evidence; and remedies such as adaptive management that could accommodate changing conditions. In relation to the fourth component, the fact that legal disputes were taking place immersed in

[4] ibid, 1302.

evidence about environmental problems proved legally formative. Responsive doctrine was facilitated by the merging of specialist legal expertise with scientific expertise. For example, adaptive management was first used as a tool by environmental managers operating in the field, introduced to ECs through evidence in contested cases, and later transformed and refined into a legal remedy (and thereafter imported into legislation in the New Zealand context). Further, empowering the courts to create their own procedures (neither court is bound by the rules of evidence, for example) facilitated legal reasoning that responded to rather than ignoring context. The risk strand clearly illustrated the interactional theory at work. As the doctrinal developments in the NZEnvC and NSWLEC demonstrated, where legislation is interstitial, unclear or affords discretion to the decision-maker and existing doctrine ill-fitting, these ECs are developing legal reasoning that responds to the environmental context in order to resolve disputes. Accordingly, the risk jurisprudence from these courts helps to construct the detail of a frame for environmental adjudication.

The second strand of jurisprudence that I traced concerned the collective action nature of environmental problems. The process follows that outlined above. In relation to the first component of the theory, the interactional nature of environmental problems (that merges the ecological, socio-cultural and economic realms) results in polycentricity. As a result, it is seldom possible to draw clear lines around all the impacts of activities in the environment: they may be far-reaching or insidious; affect many people (in both future and present generations); and bring into play ethical pluralism. In relation to the second and third components of the theory, the collective action nature of environmental problems transcends traditional bi-party approaches to litigation. This feature forces more expansive approaches to access to justice, that in turn impacts legal reasoning in relation to *locus standi*, costs orders, injunctions and practical procedures. Testing the theory showed that the legal reasoning developed by the NSWLEC paralleled the interactional theory (for example, the Court has developed an expansive approach to standing by refusing to read down statute law); whereas the approach of the NZEnvC paralleled the theory in part but not fully. The NZEnvC has developed creative procedures to help existing parties play an effective role in litigation (and developed a 'public interest litigation' approach to costs orders, for example), but has failed to adopt a generous approach to *locus standi* when it had the opportunity to do so. Many of the New Zealand standing cases appeared to read down the legislative text, albeit there was some variation between the reasoning in the cases that was difficult to reconcile. These variations perhaps reflected a tension between different judicial visions of the Court and the use of different (albeit hidden) frames of reference. Accordingly, practice in our 'adjudicative laboratories' aligned with the interactional theory to a large extent but not comprehensively.

IV. EMPLOYING THE THEORY

In concluding it is important to address the 'so what' question: what might the use of the interactional theory and frame for normative legitimacy be? One answer is that the use of the theory and its resulting frame have eminently practical applications. As this book has shown, the use of conceptual frames has a real effect. Policymakers use various frames of normative legitimacy to argue for the refinement of ECs legal nature, and the judiciary use different frames of normative legitimacy in a way that impacts the development of jurisprudence.

In relation to policymakers, the interactional theory will guide the creation or reform of ECs. It will help direct the constitutional make-up and particular functions of ECs. There is little point in creating new adjudicative bodies that cannot respond to the nature of the task they are set. As the Chief Justice of the Santiago Environment Court poignantly noted three years after the establishment of the new environment courts in Chile, '[r]egarding procedural aspects, the Court faces rules that are inconsistent with the flexibility and agility required by the adequate resolution of environmental conflicts'.[5]

In relation to the judiciary, the discussion in chapter two highlighted that despite ECs having particular forms and functions that facilitate creative problem-solving in environmental disputes, legal reasoning has at times been influenced by the wider frames of reference that decision-makers draw upon but the frames selected may differ, leading to inconsistencies. The interactional theory will inform decision-makers who may be faced with interstitial or vague legislative direction (pronounced features of environmental law, as chapter three demonstrated), ill-fitting doctrine, or who are empowered to create solutions to adjudicative challenges themselves. Having a discrete theory for environmental adjudication, if widely acknowledged and accepted, will help ensure discretionary decision-making is referable back to some intelligible and stable limit. And the use of a more detailed conceptual frame will promote greater consistency still. If the NZEnvC had drawn on the interactional theory, there might have been greater consistency in decision-making that falls under the rubric of 'access to justice'. Rather than grafting tests onto statutory text that closed down participation, the Court may have approached the interpretive exercise in a way that better shored up and made sense of its fundamental role.

The theory may also assist litigants in preparing and managing their case by helping them to craft legal arguments, guide the appropriate forms of evidence to be adduced, and understand any strengths and weaknesses in that evidence. For example, the discussion in chapter five addressing the methodologies

[5] R Asenjo, 'Environmental Justice in Chile: three years after the establishment of the Environmental Court of Santiago' (2017) 29 *Environmental Law & Management* 110, 114.

underpinning scientific opinions and economic tools, may help litigants to craft effective cross-examination that goes to the essence of any conflict.

However, aside from these practical uses, the theory also plays a more encompassing role. To date, the literature on environmental adjudication has been a theoretical and this book remedies that omission. The interactional theory can be used to explain and make sense of ECs, and support the empirical, socio-legal, descriptive and doctrinal scholarship in the field by laying down deep theoretical roots. The interactional theory and resulting frame for normative legitimacy have particular advantages over the other frames discussed in chapter three. In comparison with the administrative justice frame, the interactional theory sets parameters around ECs by referring them back to the immutable structural features of environmental problems. Using the interactional frame will result in (some of) the goals of generic instrumentalism, including greater adjudicative efficiency, but without privileging particular political ideologies. Maintaining independent judicial oversight over legal disputes that can impact rights adheres to particular conceptions of the separation of powers, but eschewing 'pure' versions will preserve ECs' ability to adjudicate over the environment effectively. The interactional theory allows us to tease out the legal nature of ECs rather than conflating it with a separation of the powers discourse or simply subsuming them within the messy administrative justice landscape. Fundamentally, developing a theory for environmental adjudication enables us to take ECs seriously, allowing us to draw the limits properly, while also acknowledging the significance of these important bodies in many nations' constitutional arrangements.

Finally, in standing back and thinking about the wider value of the theory, a core argument of this book is that *particular choices* concerning adjudicative forms, content and processes can provide a steadying and legitimising influence, especially in an area of law like environmental law that is notoriously messy and deemed incapable of fitting neatly within 'well-honed legal grooves'.[6] Accordingly, use of the theory will provide a stabilising influence, helping to anchor the wider environmental justice project.

V. FUTURE DIRECTIONS

In this book I have highlighted the present lack of theorising in environmental adjudication, demonstrated the real problems caused by this weakness, proposed a theory for specialist environmental adjudication, and held that theory out for critique. The remaining question is: where to from here? The purpose of this book was not to close down discussion by providing a definitive

[6] E Fisher, E Scotford and E Barritt, 'The Legally Disruptive Nature of Climate Change' (2016) 80 *MLR* 173, 174.

answer. Rather, it was to establish the need for theoretical underpinnings in environmental adjudication and prompt a serious debate about the approach to take. The theory proposed in this book is grounded in careful analysis but it is only a starting point – it should be critiqued and tested, particularly against the backdrop of other legal cultures, refined or rejected, and other theories developed. If the interactional theory bears up under the weight of scrutiny, this book has only begun the process of constructing the frame for normative legitimacy. Continuing to compile the internal criteria will help build a robust frame that provides an exemplar for environmental adjudication, a frame that will help to explain the complexity of environmental dispute-resolution, and show how ECs have in the past and might in the future respond to those complexities in a way that has legal integrity. Suggestions for possible future enquiries were made in chapter six and included exploring how ECs have responded to the polycentric nature of environmental problems; analysing ECs' interpretation of the principles and standards in different types of legal instruments; drawing on indigenous customary law; and scrutinising more closely the interaction of legal and non-legal expertise in the development of legal reasoning in environmental adjudication. Researchers will see many other possible avenues.

VI. CONCLUSION

Clearly, the complexity of environmental adjudication in and of itself justifies close study – amongst other things, it presents as a fascinating and significant social phenomenon, helping to craft the way we view ourselves and our place in the world[7] – but the need is becoming more pressing. At the time that I write this final chapter, one senses the battle lines over the environment are being drawn in starker terms than ever before. Certainly, the divide between those who see exploitation of the environment as a means to improving the human condition and those who see continuing environmental degradation as threatening life on earth appears distant and unbroachable. Those who value specialist environment courts, and the access to environmental justice that they promise, must buttress those institutions with robust theory. The aim of this book has been to start that process – to prompt serious debate about how we surmount present divides, foster a more reflective dialogue, and to propose a theory that allows us to imagine better ways to adjudicate over the environment.

[7] For a good illustration of this point, see the NZEnvC cases in ch 3 that gave a meaning to the statutory term 'landscape' that incorporated Māori lore rather than relying simply on aesthetics.

Index

access to justice, 18, 30, 160, 187, 188–90, 202
  case law, 190–93
  court fees, 75
  generic instrumentalist approach, 74–76
adaptive management, 18, 118, 166, 183–87, 201–2
  imposition on consents, 179
  risk management, 33, 171
adjudication as a concept, 13–14, 98–99
  constitutionalism, relationship with, 94–98
  futurity, impact on, 101–6
  interactive nature, 106–8
    debate between people, 106–9
    form and function, 106, 109–11
    harmonising purpose, 108
  polycentric nature of debate, 103–6
  public law adjudication, 105, 117–18
  traditional adjudication, 94–96, 117–18
  truth and discovery of truth, 99–101
adjudicative forms and practices, 12, 115, 158
  adjudicatory pluralism, 103–6
    commercial dispute resolution, 67–68
    legal history, 67–70
  evaluation, 96
  legitimacy, 101, 195, 198–99, 200
adjudicative integrity, 93–94, 111
  adjudicative responsiveness, relationship with, 124–25, 199–200
    consent requirement, 123–24
    development of rules, 123
    normative justifiability, 124
    swanimotes, 119–23
  coherence, 115, 119
  judicial integrity, 113–14
  normative justifiability, 111–12
  personal integrity, relationship with, 113–14
  responsiveness, 118–19
    legal history, 119–23
  self-validation of courts, 116–18, 119
  solidity, 115–16, 119
  stare decisis, 114–15
  swanimotes, 119–23
adjudicative responsiveness, 93–94
  adjudicative integrity, relationship with, 124–25, 199–200
    consent requirement, 123–24
    development of rules, 123
    normative justifiability, 124
    swanimotes, 119–23
  Environment Court of New Zealand, 158–63
  integrity and responsiveness, 199–200
  interactional theory for legitimacy:
    acknowledgement of challenges, 160–61
    contextual awareness, 161–62
    discretion and interpretation, 164–65
    need for specialisation, 162–63
  legal reasoning:
    discretion and interpretation, 164–65
  New South Wales Land and Environment Court, 158–63
administrative justice/adjudicative pluralism frame, 65–67, 198–99
  adjudicatory pluralism:
    commercial dispute resolution, 67–68
    legal history, 67–70
  legal nature, 72–73
  short-comings, 71, 199
    explicit constraints, 71–72
    implicit constraints, 72
air pollution, impact on humans, 141–42
appeals, 26–28
  English law, 187–88
  Environment Court of New Zealand, 39, 46–47, 128, 188
  locus standi, 187–88
  New South Wales Land and Environment Court, 51–53, 128, 188
  points of law, 38, 47, 71, 128

balance of probabilities test, 118, 138, 166, 174–76
balancing private rights and public wellbeing, 24–25, 29, 30–31, 38, 56, 69, 77, 162
  choice modelling, 148

community wellbeing, assessment of, 149
contingence valuation methodology, 148
economic rationalism, 146–48
bottom-up adjudication, 5, 17, 70, 104, 127, 200
burden of proof, 17–18, 33, 169–70, 171, 174, 179–80

choice modelling, 147, 148
collective action nature of disputes, 16, 29–30, 108, 186–87, 202
access to justice, 187, 188–90
case law, 190–95
locus standi issues, 187
appeal rights, 187–88
case law, 190–95
English law, 187–88
non-submitters,
third-party rights, 187–88
swanimotes example, 121–22
see also ethical pluralism
constitutional place of environmental adjudication, 4, 94–98
democratic legitimacy, 71
contingent valuation methodology, 148, 156
continuing mandamus, 18, 182
risk management, 33
costs orders, 18, 33, 189, 202

democratic legitimacy of environmental courts, 62, 71
discretionary powers of environmental courts, 8, 12, 29, 128, 203
administrative justice/adjudicative pluralism frame, 65, 70–71, 72
Environmental Court of New Zealand, 41–42, 48–49, 70–71, 74–75, 199, 202
generic instrumentalism frame, 74–75
New South Wales Land and Environment Court, 32, 55, 57, 70–71, 167, 191, 199, 202
disturbance of environment and ecosystems, *see* **humans as agents of change**

ecological, sustainable development test, 85–86
economic rationalism, 16, 145–47, 191
ecosystems, complexity of, 17–18, 131–33
English law, 67–68
adjudication, concept of, 95
appeal rights, 187–88
property-based approach to environmental issues, 147, 187

separation of powers doctrine, 77–78
swanimotes, 67, 119–20, 122–23
collective action nature of disputes, 121–22
development, 120
harmonious interaction and dispute resolution, 120–21
multifunctional nature, 121
Environment Court of New Zealand (NZEnvC), 8–12, 25–26
adjudicatory pluralism, 70
court v tribunal debate, 42–46
criticisms, 12–13, 46–51, 61
interactional theory for legitimacy:
acknowledgement of challenges, 160–61
contextual awareness, 161–62
need for specialisation, 162–63
legal nature, 37–42
legal validity, 62–63
merits review role, 163
normative legitimacy, 62–65
precautionary approach, 201–2
legislative interpretation, developing from, 172–73
risk assessment and management, 173–74
environmental courts:
democratic legitimacy, 71
discretionary powers:
administrative justice/adjudicative pluralism frame, 71
generic instrumentalism frame, 74–75
fact-finding, 6, 135–36
flexible approach, 34
importance of role, 197–98
independence and impartiality, 27–28, 77–78
legal nature, 26–27
contribution to environmental law, 28–29
impact of, 29–30
independence from government, 27–28
jurisdictional remit, 28
normative legitimacy, *see* normative legitimacy
scholarship on, 35–37
tensions and concerns, 59–60
Environment Court of New Zealand, 12–13, 46–51
New South Wales Land and Environment Court, 12–13, 54–59
see also Environment Court of New Zealand; New South Wales Land and Environment Court
environmental impact assessments, 7–8, 135–36

environmental impacts on humans:
air pollution, impact of, 141–42
odours, impact of, 139–41
physiological impacts, 139–42
psychological impacts, 139
environmental problem-solving, complexity of, 79–81, 205
challenges for adjudicators, 156–57
impact of, 81–83, 89–90
increased use of flexible standards, 82–83, 87–88, 89
indeterminacy of language, 88–89
law/politics divide, 83–87
polycentric decision-making, 142–43
environmental problems, features of:
diverse nature of environmental problems, 128–29, 142–43
interaction, change and uncertainty, 127–28, 129–30
see also interaction and change as inherent in environmental problems; uncertainty of
environmental problems
legal doctrine, development of, 146–47
environmental regulation, role in, 31–32, 34–35, 79–90
ethical pluralism, 16, 18, 150–52
categorisation of ideologies, 145–46
economic rationalists compared, 147–48
legal doctrine, development of, 146–47
legal reasoning, impact on, 143–44
value and evaluation:
choice modelling, 148
community wellbeing, assessment of, 149
contingence valuation methodology, 148
economic rationalism, 146–48
see also collective action nature of disputes
evaluating evidence:
balance of probabilities test, 174–76
contextual uncertainty, 179–80
Environment Court of New Zealand, 174–76, 177–80
New South Wales Land and Environment Court, 176–80
probability of likelihood, 177–78
quality and form of scientific information, 178–79
standard of proof, 174
evaluation, *see* **value and evaluation**
evidence, *see* **evaluating evidence**

fact-finding by environmental courts, 6, 15–16, 28–29, 69, 88–89, 100–1, 124–25, 135–36, 155–56, 159–60, 162
flexible approach of environmental courts, 11–12, 34, 37, 81–82, 87, 123, 139, 154, 156, 198, 203
administrative justice/adjudicative pluralism frame, 65–66, 68, 71
Environmental Court of New Zealand, 38–39, 40, 43, 158
New South Wales Land and Environment Court, 56, 158, 182
see also adaptive management
framing, 62–65
administrative justice/adjudicative pluralism frame, 65–73
see also administrative justice/ adjudicative pluralism frame
generic instrumentalism frame, 73–76
see also generic instrumentalism frame
separation of powers frame, 76–90
see also separation of powers

generic instrumentalism frame, 73–74, 198–99
criticisms, 74–76, 199
global environmental adjudication, 24–25, 194
green justice, 34–35

humans as agents of change, 133–35
assessing human impact, 135–36
scientific prediction of human behaviour, 136
limitations, 136–39
human domination over nature, 146–47

impartiality, *see* **independence and impartiality of environmental courts; separation of powers**
incoherence, *see* **legal coherence**
independence and impartiality of environmental courts, 27–28, 44, 76–77, 137
see also separation of powers
injunctions, 18, 34, 39, 52, 101–2, 180, 189, 202
integrity:
personal morality, as, 112–13
see also adjudicative integrity
interaction and change as inherent in environmental problems, 5–6, 129–31, 201
ecological complexity, 131–33
economic complexity, 142–44
ethical pluralism, 144–52
humans as agents of change, 133–39

impacts on humans, 139–42
socio-cultural complexity, 142–44
interactional theory for legitimacy, 4–7, 15–17, 158, 199–200
adaptive management, 183–87
adjudicative responsiveness:
discretion and interpretation, 164–65
caveats, 21–23
collective action nature of environmental problems, *see* collective action nature of environmental problems
core contextual foundations, *see* interaction and change as inherent in environmental problems; uncertainty of environmental problems
employing the theory, 203–4
Environment Court of New Zealand, 158–60
acknowledgement of challenges, 160–61
collective action nature of environmental problems, 187–95, 202
contextual awareness, 161–62
evaluating evidence, 174–76, 177–80
need for specialisation, 162–63
integrity and responsiveness, 199–200
New South Wales Land and Environment Court, 158–60
acknowledgement of challenges, 160–61
collective action nature of environmental problems, 187–95, 202
contextual awareness, 161–62
evaluating evidence, 176–80
need for specialisation, 162–63
testing the theory, 17–18
uncertainty challenge, 165–66
adaptive management, 183–87
Environment Court of New Zealand's response, 172–74
New South Wales Land and Environment Court's response, 166–72

judicial review, 41–42, 52, 55, 71, 181, 187, 194
justification for environmental adjudication, 4–5, 5, 12, 115, 124

law/policy divide:
content of statutes, 85–86
legal reasoning, 83–84
merging of law and fact, 86–87
flexible standards, impact of, 87–88, 89–90
legal coherence, 1, 20, 21, 23, 113–15, 116–17, 119
legal doctrine, development of, 146–47
legal history of adjudication/dispute resolution, 14–15
legal nature of environmental courts, 26–27
contribution to environmental law, 28–29
impact of, 29–30
independence from government, 27–28
jurisdictional remit, 28
legal reasoning:
adjudicative responsiveness:
discretion and interpretation, 164–65
Environment Court of New Zealand, 158
ethical pluralism, impact of, 143–44
interactional theory for legitimacy:
acknowledgement of challenges, 160–61
contextual awareness, 161–62
discretion and interpretation, 164–65
need for specialisation, 162–63
law/policy divide, 83–84
New South Wales Land and Environment Court, 158
legitimacy, *see* **normative legitimacy**
likelihood test, 176–77
***locus standi*,** 187
appeal rights, 187–88
case law, 190–93
English law, 187–88
Environment Court of New Zealand, 195
non-submitters,
third-party rights, 187–88

merits review powers, 102, 103, 180
Environmental Court of New Zealand, 41–42, 48, 128, 158, 163, 181
New South Wales Land and Environment Court, 52–53, 54, 56–57, 78, 85–86, 128, 143, 158, 167
methodology, 7–20
multi-dimension causes of environmental problems, 131

need for environmental adjudication, 2
New South Wales Land and Environment Court (NSWLEC), 8–12, 25–26
adjudicatory pluralism, 70
criticisms, 12–13, 54–59, 61
interactional theory for legitimacy:
acknowledgement of challenges, 160–61
contextual awareness, 161–62
need for specialisation, 162–63

legal nature, 51–54
legal validity, 62–63
normative legitimacy, 62–65
precautionary approach, 201–2
environmental knowledge, 169
factual uncertainty, 166–72
normative justifiability, 72, 92–93, 111–12
normative legitimacy, 198
administrative justice/adjudicative pluralism frame, *see* administrative justice/ adjudicative pluralism frame
generic instrumentalism frame, *see* generic instrumentalism frame
separation of powers frame, *see* separation of powers
theory, 8–10, 12, 14, 62–65

odours, impact on humans, 139–41

physiological impacts of the environment on humans, 139–42
polluter pays principle, 32, 59
precautionary principle, 32–33, 57–59, 118
New South Wales Land and Environment Court, 159–60, 166–72, 177–78, 179–80, 201–2
practice and procedure, impact on, 33–34
precedent, doctrine of, 98–99, 114–15
promotion of environmental governance, 30–31
psychological impacts of the environment on humans, 139
public interest, 33, 53, 56, 68, 167, 189–95, 202

real evidence test, 178
reasonable man test, 141
reasonableness, 55–56, 86–87
remedies, impact on, 33–34, 180–83
adaptive management, 183–87
continuing mandamus, 33
green justice, 34–35
mandatory environmental education, 34–35
restorative justice, 34–35
Resource Management Act 1991, 39–40, 42–43, 62
proposed reforms, 47–48
sustainable management, 85–86
responsiveness, *see* **adjudicative responsiveness**
restorative justice, 34–35
rise of environmental adjudication, 1–2, 24–25
risk management:
adaptive management processes, 33
writs of continuing mandamus, 33
see also adaptive management; continuing mandamus

scholarship on environmental courts, 35–37
scientific prediction of human behaviour, 136
limitations, 136
case law, 136–39
separation of powers, 4, 76–77, 198–99
complexity of environmental problem-solving, 83–87
criticisms, 78–79, 199
legal history, 77–78
specialist courts, 70–72
significance test, 87, 161
single-issue courts, 25
standard of proof, 163, 170, 174–77
standards and guidance frameworks:
flexible nature, 82–83, 87–88, 89
standing, *see* ***locus standi***
stare decisis, *see* **precedent, doctrine of**
sufficiency test, 153–54, 156
sustainable management, 39–41, 47, 50, 83–86, 165–66, 181, 194
swanimotes, 119–20, 122–23
collective action nature of disputes, 121–22
development, 120
harmonious interaction and dispute resolution, 120–21
multifunctional nature, 121

tensions and concerns about environmental courts, 59–60
Environment Court of New Zealand, 12–13, 46–51
New South Wales Land and Environment Court, 12–13, 54–59
third-party rights, 187–88
top-down adjudication, 5–7, 126
see also administrative justice/adjudicative pluralism frame; generic instrumentalism frame; separation of powers
truth and discovery of truth, 99–101, 153–55

uncertainty of environmental problems, 5–6, 152–53
knowledge/lack of, 152–53
practice, 165–66, 201
evaluating evidence, 174–80
precautionary approach, 166–74, 201–2
remedies, 180–87

precautionary approach:
- Environment Court of New Zealand, 172–74, 201–2
- New South Wales Land and Environment Court, 166–72, 201–2

sufficiency test, 153
truth and discovery of truth, 99–101, 153–55

value and evaluation:
- challenges for adjudicators, 156–57
- choice modelling, 148
- community wellbeing, assessment of, 149
- contingence valuation methodology, 148
- economic rationalism, 146–48
- evaluating evidence, *see* evaluating evidence

CPSIA information can be obtained
at www.ICGtesting.com
Printed in the USA
LVHW081513120521
687224LV00002B/53

9 781509 940066